Student Guide for

Physical Anthropology: The Evolving Human
Third Edition
for use with   Jurmain, Kilgore, Trevathan, and Ciochon's
Introduction to Physical Anthropology, 2011-2012 edition

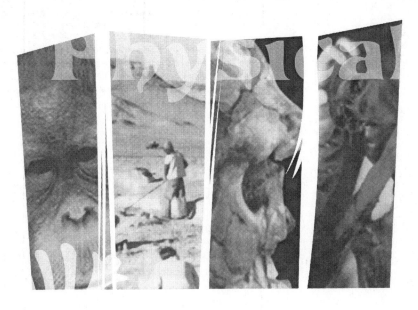

DIANE HARRISON
WENDY A. BIRKY
MARCUS YOUNG OWL
MAUREEN ZWEIG

Australia • Brazil • Canada • Mexico • Singapore • Spain • United Kingdom • United States

Coast Community College District

Ding-Jo H. Currie,
Chancellor, Coast Community College District

Loretta P. Adrian,
President, Coastline Community College

Dan C. Jones,
Executive Dean, Office of Instructional Systems
Development

Laurie R. Melby,
Director of Production

Lynn M. Dahnke,
Director, Marketing & Publisher Partnerships

Robert D. Nash,
Director, Instructional Design & Faculty Support

Judy Garvey,
Director, eMedia & Publishing

Wendy Sacket,
eMedia & Publishing Project Coordinator

Linda Wojciechowski,
Senior eMedia & Publishing Assistant

Thien Vu,
eMedia & Publishing Assistant

The course, *Physical Anthropology: The Evolving Human*, is produced by the Coast Community College District, in cooperation with Wadsworth Cengage Learning.

Library of Congress Control Number:
ISBN-13: 978-1-111-82901-8
ISBN-10: 1-111-82901-2

Distributed by:
Coast Learning Systems
Coastline Community College
11460 Warner Avenue
Fountain Valley, CA 92708
telephone: (800) 547-4748 fax: (714) 241-6286
e-mail: CoastLearning@coastline.edu
website: www.CoastLearning.org

Cengage Learning is a leading provider of customized learning solutions with office locations around the globe, including Singapore, the United Kingdom, Australia, Mexico, Brazil and Japan. Locate your local office at:
international.cengage.com/region

Cengage Learning products are represented in Canada by Nelson Education, Ltd.

For your course and learning solutions, visit **www.cengage.com**

Purchase any of our products at your local college store or at our preferred online store **www.cengagebrain.com**

Printed in the United States of America
1 2 3 4 5   16 15 14 13 12

Contents

Acknowledgments

Several of the individuals responsible for the creation of this course are listed on the copyright page of this book. In addition to these people, appreciation is expressed for the contributions of the following:

Members of the National Academic Advisory Committee

George Bagwell, M.A., Colorado Mountain College

Naomi H. Bishop, Ph.D., California State University, Northridge

Christina Brewer, M.A., Saddleback Community College, California

Benjamin Campbell, Ph.D., Harvard University

Gary Cummisk, Ph.D., Dickinson State University, North Dakota

Jeffrey David Ehrenreich, Ph.D., University of New Orleans

Barbra E. Erickson, Ph.D., California State University, Fullerton

Kathleen Godel-Gengenbach, Ph.D., Red Rocks Community College, Colorado

Carol Hayman, M.A., Austin Community College, Texas

Mikel Hogan, Ph.D., California State University, Fullerton

Robert Jurmain, Ph.D., San Jose State University

Diane P. Levine, M.A., Los Angeles Pierce College

Mark S. Lewine, Ed.D., M.A., Cuyahoga Community College, Ohio

Linda D. Light, M.A., California State University, Long Beach, and Santa Ana College

Barbara Mueller, Ph.D., Casper College, Wyoming

Jill Pfeiffer, M.A., Rio Hondo College, California

Monica Rothschild-Boros, Ph.D., Orange Coast College, California

Frank A. Salamone, Ph.D., Iona College, New York

Priscilla Schulte, Ph.D., University of Alaska Southeast

John J. Schultz, Ph.D., University of Central Florida

Michael Wesch, Ph.D., Kansas State University

Leanna Wolfe, Ph.D., Los Angeles Valley College

Marcus Young Owl, Ph.D., California State University, Long Beach

These scholars, teachers, and practitioners helped focus the approach and content of the video programs, student guide, and faculty manual to ensure accuracy, academic validity, accessibility, significance, and instructional integrity.

Lead Academic Advisors
Wendy A. Birky, Ph.D., California State University, Northridge
Marcus Young Owl, Ph.D., California State University, Long Beach

Many thanks go to Bob Nash for the instructional design of this course. Special thanks are extended to our lead academic advisors for their diligent review and scrutiny of content in the video lessons, for authoring the material for all of the Review Exercises in the Telecourse Student Guide and the Test Bank section of the Faculty Manual, and for reviewing the academic content of both these publications. Additional thanks are also extended to Diane Harrison, who authored this guide; to Maureen Zweig, for her invaluable assistance in editing; to Susan Wilcox, for her contributions to the lesson sidebars; and to Naomi Bishop, who revised and updated this third edition of the student guide.

Key Video Production Team
Marc A. Abdou, Shari Ast, John Bishop, Jason Daley, Weston Day, Cody Farley, Trip Gould, Steven D. Grossman, Marie Hulett, Dorothy McCollom, Laurie R. Melby, Salma Montez, Wendy Moulton-Tate, Bob Nash, Wendy A. Rakochy, Robin Rundle, Renee Tod, Martin Valles, Susan Wilcox, and the many other talented people who helped make the programs.

Additional thanks are extended to Lin Gaylord, John Chell, and the many other able and supportive individuals at Wadsworth/Cengage Learning.

How to Take
This Course

Introduction

To the Student

Welcome to **Physical Anthropology: The Evolving Human**. This course introduces the central concepts, concerns, and research methods of physical anthropology. **Physical Anthropology: The Evolving Human** provides students with an understanding of human evolution and diversity from a biological perspective. The course examines patterns of anatomical, behavioral, and genetic similarities and differences among living primates and humans, in addition to reconstructing the evidence for human evolution found in the fossil record. While new techniques and discoveries are continuing to alter our understanding of the human species and its place in the biological world, this course provides you with essential tools to appreciate the key theoretical and methodological issues involved in this subdiscipline of anthropology. Whether you are taking this course as part of your academic study or simply because you are interested in the subject, we believe that you will find this course both fascinating and useful.

Course Goals

The designers, academic advisors, and producers of this course have specified the following learning outcomes for students taking **Physical Anthropology: The Evolving Human**. After successfully completing the course assignments, you should be able to:

1. Define anthropology and describe its major fields, focusing on the core concepts, methods, and subdisciplines of physical anthropology.

2. Discuss the development of evolutionary theory, and explain the basic principles of biological evolution, natural selection, and heredity.

3. Describe the impact of molecular biology on our understanding of human evolution, and discuss how it may affect the future.

4. Discuss the place of humans in the natural world, as mammals and as primates, and describe the major characteristics that define the primate order.

5. Compare and contrast the morphology and behavior of human and nonhuman primates.

6. Discuss the general principles and methods of paleoanthropology and identify important hominin sites.

7. Discuss major theories relating to hominin evolution and the origin and dispersal of modern humans.

8. Describe human adaptations to environmental stresses, and discuss the concept of race in terms of human variation and adaptations.

9. Discuss the ways in which the human species has affected biodiversity and the physical environment.

Course Components

The Course Student Guide

The course student guide is an integral part of *Physical Anthropology: The Evolving Human*. Think of it as your "road map." This guide gives you a starting point for each lesson, as well as directions and exercises that will help you successfully navigate your way through each lesson. Reading this guide and completing the lesson exercises will provide you with information that you normally would receive in the classroom if you were taking this course on campus.

Each student guide lesson includes the following elements:

• Checklist

This is an outline of all activities to be completed for the lesson. You should refer to this checklist before starting each lesson and check off each item as you complete it so you are sure you have covered everything in that lesson.

• Preview

This section introduces the lesson topics, explains why they are important, and offers a quick review of previous lesson concepts that you'll need to remember.

• Learning Objectives

This is a list of what you will know and be able to do after you complete the lesson. After completing each lesson, you should be able to satisfy each of these learning objectives. (Note: Instructors often design test questions after learning objectives, so use them to help focus your study time.)

• Viewing Notes

This section provides a brief introduction to the lesson and offers important information that will help you understand the concepts illustrated in the video.

• Key Terms & Concepts

This is a list of the terms and concepts that are introduced in the lesson along with their definitions. You should be able to define each of the key terms and concepts for each lesson. You will also find definitions for key terms and concepts in the glossary that appears in the back of the course textbook, *Introduction to Physical Anthropology*.

• Summary

Review this section after you have read the textbook chapter and watched the lesson video. The Summary provides a final overview of the lesson by discussing key terms, offering examples, and making connections between concepts that will help you recall them at exam time.

- **Review Exercises**

This section includes a variety of study activities to help you learn and prepare for midterm and final examinations. These activities include matching and completion exercises, a multiple-choice self-test, and short-answer questions. These exercises are not typically graded by your instructor; they are designed as self-study tools to help you achieve the learning objectives in each lesson.

- **Answer Key**

Answers to the Review Exercises are conveniently located at the end of each lesson so that you can get immediate feedback. The Answer Key references pages in the textbook and segments in the video where you can learn more and also indicates which learning objectives the questions relate to. After completing an exercise, be sure to check the Answer Key to make sure you correctly understand the material.

- **Lesson Review**

This matrix at the end of each lesson identifies the textbook pages and student guide exercises that correspond to each learning objective. Use this matrix to focus your study time on those objectives you have yet to achieve.

The Textbook

The recommended textbook for this course is *Introduction to Physical Anthropology*, thirteen edition, written by Robert Jurmain, Lynn Kilgore, Wenda Trevathan, and Russell L. Ciochon (Wadsworth/ Cengage Learning, 2012).

Introduction to Physical Anthropology brings the study of physical anthropology to life for today's students. With a focus on human evolution and biology, each chapter of this textbook helps students master the basic principles of the subject and arrive at an understanding of the human species and its place in the biological world. The textbook's thorough coverage of cutting-edge advances in molecular biology, expanded coverage of population biology and human variation, and inclusion of the latest in new fossil finds provide an exceptional learning experience for students and present a comprehensive, well-balanced introduction to the field.

The Video Lessons

In addition to the student guide and textbook, this course includes sixteen half-hour video lessons. These video lessons feature leading practitioners, theoreticians, and academics in the fields of physical anthropology, cultural anthropology, archaeology, and related social and behavioral sciences. Each video lesson in the series integrates these expert interviews with supportive visuals as well as fieldwork and case studies that cover core learning objectives in a documentary style. Through compelling visual content, cutting-edge research, and clear discussions that move from description to interpretation, the video lessons work together to explore life's history and the place of human beings in the biological world.

How to Take a Distance Learning Course

If this is your first experience with distance learning, welcome. Distance learning courses are designed for busy people whose situations or schedules do not permit them to take a traditional on-campus course.

This student guide is designed to help you study effectively and learn the material presented in both the textbook and the video lessons. To complete a distance learning course successfully, you will need to schedule sufficient time to read the textbook, watch each video lesson, and study the materials in this guide.

This student guide is a complement to the textbook and the video lessons. It is not a substitute. By following the instructions in this guide, you should easily master the learning objectives for each lesson.

To complete this course successfully you will need to:

- Find and read the "syllabus" or "handbook" for this course provided by your instructor. This course syllabus will list and explain what you will be required to do to complete this course successfully. The syllabus describes assignments, explains the course grading scale, and offers a schedule for quizzes, exams, review sessions, and so on. If you have questions about what you are supposed to do in this course, look for the answer in your syllabus. If you are still unsure, contact your instructor.

- Purchase a copy of the course textbook.

- Read and study this student guide and the textbook.

- View each video lesson in its entirety. (The course syllabus or handbook should explain how you can view the lesson videos.)

- Review the Key Terms and Concepts presented in this guide and memorize their definitions.

- Focus your study time so you can achieve the Learning Objectives for each lesson.

- Complete the Review Exercises in this guide.

- Complete any additional assignments your instructor may require.

Even though you do not have scheduled classes to attend each week on campus, please keep in mind that this is a college-level course. It will require the same amount of work as a traditional, classroom version of this course and at the same level of difficulty. As a distance learner, however, it will be up to you alone to keep up with your deadlines. It's important that you schedule enough time to read, study, review, and reflect.

Do your best to keep up with the work. In a distance learning course, it's very difficult to catch up if you allow yourself to get behind schedule. We strongly recommend that you set aside specific times each week for reading, viewing the videos, completing assignments, and studying for quizzes and exams. You will be more likely to succeed if you make a formal study schedule and stick to it.

When you watch each video program, try to do so without any interruptions. If you are interrupted, you may miss an important point. If possible, view the videos in a recorded mode so you can stop the tape and take notes. Also, take some time immediately after watching the video to reflect on what you have just seen. This is an excellent time to discuss the lesson with a friend or family member. Your active thinking and involvement will promote your success.

Study Recommendations

Everyone has his or her own unique learning style. Some people learn best by studying alone the first thing in the morning, others by discussing ideas with a group of friends, still others by listening to experts and taking notes. While there is no best way to learn, psychologists and educators have identified several things you can do that will help you study and learn more effectively.

One of the advantages of distance learning is that you have many choices for how you study. You can tailor this course to fit your preferred learning style. Below are several study tips. These are proven methods that will improve your learning and retention. Please take the time to read through this list. By using one or more of these techniques, you can significantly improve your performance in this course.

Open your mind. One of the major obstacles to learning new information is that it often differs from what we already "know." To learn, you need to have an open mind. We are not suggesting that you simply believe everything you are told. In fact, we want you to think critically about everything you are told. However, try not to let old beliefs or opinions stop you from learning something new.

Reduce interference and interruptions. If possible, focus your study on one subject at a time. When you study more than one subject, you are increasing the likelihood of interference occurring. Too much information can overload your brain and make it difficult to store and recall what you want to learn. Also, do your best to avoid interruptions while you are studying. Find a quiet room with a good desk, chair, and adequate lighting. Of course, visiting with friends, listening to the radio, watching your kids, or any other distractions will also interfere with your ability to learn. Try to avoid these distractions so your mind can focus, and give yourself enough time to absorb the new information.

Don't cram. You probably already know that staying up all night cramming for an exam the following morning is not a good way to study. The opposite of cramming, is, in fact, one of the best ways to study. Spacing out your studying into smaller and more frequent study periods will improve retention. For example, instead of studying for six hours in one evening, you will learn more and retain more if you study one hour per night for six nights.

Reduce stress. In addition to being bad for your health, stress is bad for learning. Stress and anxiety interfere with learning. You will learn more and enjoy it more if you are relaxed when you study. One of the most effective ways of relaxing that does not interfere with learning is to exercise. A good brisk walk or run before you settle in to study is a good prescription for success. Ideally, you would study some, take a break, and then get some exercise while you think about what you have just learned. A little later, when you are relaxed, you can return and study some more.

Be a Smart Student. Most top students have one thing in common: excellent study habits. Students who excel have learned or were fortunate enough to have someone teach them how to study effectively. There is no magic formula for successful studying. However, there are a few universal guidelines.

- **Do** make a commitment to yourself to learn.
- **Don't** let other people interrupt you when you are studying.
- **Do** make a study schedule and stick to it.
- **Don't** study when you are doing something else, like listening to the radio.
- **Do** create a specific place to study.
- **Don't** study if you are tired, upset, or overly stressed.
- **Do** exercise and relax before you study.
- **Don't** study for extended periods of time without taking a break.
- **Do** give yourself ample time to study.
- **Don't** complain that you have to study.
- **Do** take a positive approach to learning.

Make the most of your assignments. You will master this material more effectively if you make a commitment to complete all of the assignments. The lessons will make more sense to you, and you will learn more, if you follow these instructions:

- Set aside a specific time to go read, study, and review each lesson.
- Before you read the textbook chapter for each lesson, read the Lesson Preview and Learning Objectives outlined in this guide.
- Complete all the assigned reading, both in the textbook and in this student guide, for the lesson you are studying.
- Watch the lesson video, more than once if necessary, to help you achieve the learning objectives.
- Review the Key Terms and Concepts in this guide. Check your understanding of all unfamiliar terms in the glossary.
- Complete the Review Exercises for each lesson.

Think about what you have learned. You are much more likely to remember new information if you use it. Remember that learning is not a passive activity. Learning is active. As soon as you learn something, try to repeat it to someone or discuss it with a friend. If you think about what you just learned, you will be much more likely to retain it. The reason we remember certain information has to do mostly with (1) how important that information is to us, and (2) whether or not we actively use the information. What do you do, however, when you need to learn some information that is not personally valuable or interesting to you? The best way to remember this type of information is to reinforce it—and the best reinforcer is actively using the information.

Get feedback on what you are studying. Feedback will help reinforce your learning. Also, feedback helps make sure you correctly understand the information. The Review Exercises in this guide are specifically designed to give you feedback and reinforce what you are learning. The more time and practice you devote to learning, the better you will be at recalling that information. When you take a Self-Test, make sure you immediately check your answers using the Answer Key. Don't wait to check your answers later. If you miss a question, review that part of the lesson to reinforce the correct understanding of the material. The review matrix at the end of each lesson in this guide will help guide your study.

A good gauge of how well you understand something is your ability to explain it to someone else. If you are unable to explain a term or concept to a friend, you probably need to study it further.

Contact your instructor. If you are having an especially difficult time with learning some information, contact your instructor. Your instructor is there to help you. Often a personal explanation will do wonders in helping you clear up a misunderstanding. Your instructor wants to hear from you and wants you to succeed. Don't hesitate to call, write, e-mail, or visit your instructor.

Study groups and partners. Some exercises are enhanced when done with a partner. However, some students do better studying alone. If study groups are helpful to you or you would like a partner to practice the exercises with, let your instructor know. Because study groups can sometimes turn into friendly chats, without much learning going on, you should use your group time wisely. Remember that study groups are not a substitute for individual effort.

Learn it well. One of the best methods for increasing retention is to "overlearn" the material. Just because you can answer a multiple-choice question or give a brief definition of a term doesn't mean you really understand the concept or that you'll be able to describe it in an essay or exam. Overlearning is simple. After you think you have learned a concept, spend an additional five or ten minutes actively reviewing it. Try to describe it to a friend or family member. Think up real-world examples of the concept. You will be amazed how much this will increase your long-term retention.

Enjoy learning. You do not need to suffer to learn. In fact, the opposite is true. You will learn more if you enjoy learning. If you have the attitude that "I hate to study" or "schoolwork is boring," you are doing yourself a disservice.

You will progress better and learn more if you adopt a positive attitude about learning and studying. Since you are choosing to learn, you might as well enjoy the adventure!

We are sure you will enjoy *Physical Anthropology: The Evolving Human*.

Lesson 1: The Anthropological Perspective

LESSON

1

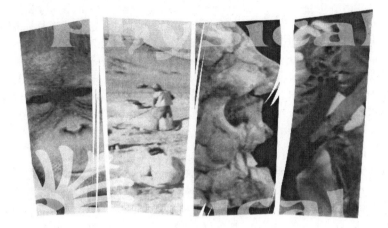

The Anthropological Perspective

Checklist

For the most effective study of this lesson, complete the following activities in this sequence.

Before Viewing the Video

- ❏ Read the Preview, Learning Objectives, and Viewing Notes below.

- ❏ Read Chapter 1, "Introduction to Physical Anthropology," pages 2–25, in *Introduction to Physical Anthropology*.

What to Watch

- ❏ After reading the textbook assignment, watch the video for Lesson 1, *The Anthropological Perspective*.

After Viewing the Video

- ❏ Briefly note your answers to the questions listed at the end of the Viewing Notes.

- ❏ Review the Summary below.

- ❏ Review all reading assignments for this lesson, including the Viewing Notes in this lesson.

- ❏ Write brief answers to the "Critical Thinking Questions" at the end of Chapter 1 in the textbook.

- ❏ Complete the Review Exercises below. Check your answers with the Answer Key and review when necessary.

- ❏ Use the Lesson Review matrix found at the end of this lesson to review and assess your knowledge of each Learning Objective.

Preview

One clichéd view of an anthropologist is that of a researcher in a remote jungle, studying the physical and material remains of a lost civilization. This somewhat stereotypical picture will always be an essential part of anthropology, but given the scope of the discipline as a whole, it is a limited part. Anthropology is the study of humankind, from its beginnings millions of years ago to the present day, which means every human on our planet is a focus of this wide-ranging discipline. There are numerous subspecialties under the anthropology "umbrella," because to truly understand the similarities and differences between and within human groups worldwide, to understand both the cultural and biological history of human beings, and to be able to speculate with a modicum of accuracy on the human past, present, and future, anthropologists must take as broad an approach as possible to the study of our species.

This course is on physical (or biological) anthropology, but Lesson 1 briefly introduces the other subspecialties as well. Anthropologist Eric Wolf described anthropology as "the most scientific of the humanities and the most humanistic of the sciences." Anthropologists apply the scientific method to all of their investigations, while they maintain the perspective that the goal of their research is to answer humanistic questions on how we became human, and what it means to be human. Physical anthropology's evolutionary perspective on human biology and behavior is essential to this analysis. Technology advances are greatly facilitating anthropological inquiry. For instance, the ability to sequence the entire human genome gives anthropologists deeper insights into the mechanisms that drive changes in human biology. New fossil finds and new technology to analyze them establishes the potential to better understand the processes and components of human evolution, variation, and adaptation, which are all aspects of our humanity that have puzzled and fascinated scientists for centuries. As you progress through this course, you will see how anthropology continues to be a work in progress.

Learning Objectives

After you complete this lesson, you should be able to:

1. Explain the concept of humans as biocultural beings and discuss the importance of the biocultural approach to the study of human evolution. (pp. 2–10)

2. Define anthropology and describe its four major subfields. (pp. 10–18)

3. Describe physical anthropology and the major fields of study it encompasses. (pp. 11–18)

4. Explain the scientific method and how it is used in physical anthropology. (pp. 20–23)

5. Discuss the unique approach of the anthropological perspective. (p. 24)

At this point, read Chapter 1, "Introduction to Physical Anthropology," pages 2–25.

Viewing Notes

The video opens with a somber memory of a recent event and a fascinating tale of discovery from the ancient past: the human remains recovered from the tragedy of September 11, 2001, and four-million-year-old fossil footprints found in East Africa. We know the animals who left the footprints behind weren't apes because it has been determined through careful anthropological analysis that they were bipedal. In other words, they walked habitually upright, on two legs. They were **hominins**, early relatives of *Homo sapiens*. We also know that the fragmented bits of bone, observed by Dr. Richard Gould, a forensic archaeologist, as he walked the areas close to Ground Zero, in New York City, shortly after September 11, 2001, belonged to modern *Homo sapiens*, who were caught unaware in one of the most unspeakably violent episodes this country has ever experienced. Dr. Gould and his colleagues use the knowledge of human skeletal anatomy acquired through the work of many physical anthropologists to reconstruct and identify victims. These two distinct examples serve to clearly illustrate the breadth of anthropology.

Note how the subdisciplines of anthropology offer an integrated look at the many facets of being human: Cultural anthropology is the study of all aspects of human behavior; archaeology is the study of the behavior of human in the past through an examination of material remains; linguistic anthropology is the study of human language, the most distinctive feature of the human species, and physical anthropology is the study of our biological origins, evolutionary development, and genetic diversity and adaptations through time. Physical anthropologists concern themselves with humans as biological organisms.

This video offers an example of **forensic anthropology**, the application of the knowledge of physical anthropology to a medical or legal context. Dr. Richard Gould, a forensic archaeologist, created Forensic Archaeology Recovery (FAR), a team consisting of anthropologists who volunteer their time to help with disaster recovery, victim identification, and recovery of personal belongings after catastrophic events. FAR combines the science of forensic anthropology with the techniques of analyses developed in archaeology. As one FAR anthropologist explains, disaster sites are essentially archaeological digs where experts need to recover data and interpret that data to reconstruct what happened.

Questions to Consider

※ What are the principle disciplines within the field of physical anthropology? How do they relate to one another?

※ Why is physical anthropology a scientific discipline?

※ What is osteology? How can it help answer questions in a forensics context?

※ How can the anthropological perspective be applied to our everyday lives?

Watch the video for Lesson 1, *The Anthropological Perspective.*

Segment 1: *The Subfields of Physical Anthropology*
Segment 2: *FAR and the Scientific Method*

Key Terms and Concepts

Page references are keyed to *Introduction to Physical Anthropology,* 13th edition.

1. **savanna:** A large flat grassland with scattered trees and shrubs. Savannas are found in many regions of the world with dry and warm-to-hot climates. Also spelled *savannah.* (p. 4; objective 1)

2. **hominins:** Colloquial term for members of the evolutionary group that includes modern humans and now extinct bipedal relatives. (p. 4; video lesson, introduction; objective 1)

3. **bipedally:** On two feet. Walking habitually on two legs. (p. 4; video lesson, introduction; objective 1)

4. **species:** A group of organisms that can interbreed to produce fertile offspring. Members of one species are reproductively isolated from members of all other species (i.e., they cannot mate with them to produce fertile offspring). (p. 4; video lesson, segment 1; objective 1)

5. **anthropology:** The field of inquiry that studies human culture and evolutionary aspects of human biology; includes cultural anthropology, archaeology, linguistics, and physical, or biological, anthropology. (p. 4; video lesson, introduction; objective 2)

6. **primates:** Members of the mammalian order Primates (pronounced "pry-may´-tees"), which includes prosimians, monkeys, apes, and humans. (p. 5; video lesson, segment 1; objective 1)

7. **evolution:** A change in the genetic structure of a population. The term is also frequently used to refer to the appearance of a new species. (p. 5; video lesson, introduction; objective 1)

8. **adaptation:** An anatomical, physiological, or behavioral response of organisms or populations to the environment. Adaptations result from evolutionary change (specifically, as a result of natural selection). (p. 5; video lesson, introduction; objective 1)

9. **genetic:** Having to do with the study of gene structure and action and the patterns of inheritance of traits from parent to offspring. Genetic mechanisms are the foundation for evolutionary change. (p. 5; objective 3)

10. **culture:** Behavioral aspects of human adaptation, including technology, traditions, language, religion, marriage patterns, and social roles. Culture is a set of *learned* behaviors that is transmitted from one generation to the next by nonbiological (i.e., nongenetic) means. (p. 5; objective 1)

11. **worldview:** General cultural orientation or perspective shared by members of a society. (p. 7; objective 1)

12. **behavior:** Anything organisms do that involves action in response to internal or external stimuli; the response of an individual, group or species to its environment. Such responses may or may not be deliberate, and they aren't necessarily the result of conscious decision making (which is absent in single-celled organisms, insects, and many other species). (p. 7; objective 1)

13. **biocultural evolution:** The mutual, interactive evolution of human biology and culture; the concept that biology makes culture possible and that developing culture further influences the direction of biological evolution; a basic concept in understanding the unique components of human evolution. (p. 7; objectives 1 & 3)

14. **applied anthropology:** The practical application of anthropological and archaeological theories and techniques. For example, many biological anthropologists work in the public health sector. (p. 10; objective 2)

15. **ethnographies:** Detailed descriptive studies of human societies. In cultural anthropology, an ethnography is traditionally the study of a non-Western society. (p. 10; objective 2)

16. **artifacts:** Objects or materials made or modified for use by hominins. The earliest artifacts are usually tools made of stone or, occasionally, bone. (p. 11; objective 2)

17. **paleoanthropology:** The interdisciplinary approach to the study of earlier hominids—their chronology, physical structure, archaeological remains, habitats, and so on. (p. 12; video lesson, segment 1; objective 3)

18. **primate paleontology:** The study of fossil primates, especially those that lived before the appearance of hominins. (p. 13; objective 3)

19. **anthropometry:** Measurement of human body parts. When osteologists measure skeletal elements, the term *osteometry* is often used. (p. 13; objective 3)

20. **DNA (deoxyribonucleic acid):** The double-stranded molecule that contains the genetic code. DNA is a main component of chromosomes. (p. 14; objective 3)

21. **osteology:** The study of skeletal material. Human osteology focuses on the interpretation of the skeletal remains from archaeological sites, skeletal anatomy, bone physiology, and growth and development. Some of the same techniques are used in paleoanthropology to study early hominids. (p. 15; video lesson, segment 1; objective 3)

22. **bioarchaeology:** The study of skeletal remains from archaeological sites. (p. 15; objective 3)

23. **paleopathology:** The branch of osteology that studies the evidence of disease and injury in human skeletal (or, occasionally, mummified) remains from archaeological sites. (p. 15; objective 3)

24. **forensic anthropology:** An applied anthropological approach dealing with legal matters. Forensic anthropologists work with coroners and others in identifying and analyzing human remains. (p. 15; video lesson, segment 1; objective 3)

25. **primatology:** The study of the biology and behavior of nonhuman primates (prosimians, monkeys, and apes). (p. 17; objective 3)

26. **science:** A body of knowledge gained through observation and experimentation; from the Latin *scientia*, meaning "knowledge." (p. 20; objective 4)

27. **hypotheses (*sing.*, hypothesis):** A provisional explanation of a phenomenon. Hypotheses require verification or falsification through testing. (p. 20; video lesson, segment 2; objective 4)

28. **empirical:** Relying on experiment or observation; from the Latin *empiricus,* meaning "experienced." (p. 20; objective 4)

29. **scientific method:** A research method whereby a problem is identified, a hypothesis (or hypothetical explanation) is stated, and that hypothesis is tested by collecting and analyzing data. If the hypothesis is verified, it becomes a theory. (p. 20; video lesson, segment 2; objective 4)

30. **data (*sing.*, datum):** Facts from which conclusions can be drawn; scientific information. (p. 21; video lesson, segment 2; objective 4)

31. **quantitatively:** Pertaining to measurements of quantity and including such properties as size, number, and capacity. When data are quantified, they are expressed numerically can be tested statistically. (p. 21; objective 4)

32. **theory:** A broad statement of scientific relationships or underlying principles that has been substantially verified through the testing of hypotheses. (p. 21; objective 4)

33. **scientific testing:** The precise repetition of an experiment or expansion of observed data to provide verification; the procedure by which hypotheses and theories are verified, modified, or discarded. (p. 21; objective 4)

34. **quadrupedal:** Using all four limbs to support the body during locomotion; the basic mammalian (and primate) form of locomotion. (p. 24; objective 5)

35. **ethnocentric:** Viewing other cultures from the inherently biased perspective of one's own culture. Ethnocentrism often results in other cultures being seen as inferior to one's own. (p. 24; objective 5)

Summary

Anthropology is the study of humankind. It examines every facet of human existence in geographic space and evolutionary time. Anthropology isn't the only social science that studies humans, but the "holistic" inclusion of all things human differentiates it from the many other disciplines that also study human beings.

The Jurmain textbook opens by taking us back 3.7 million years to a grassland savanna in Tanzania in East Africa. It is there that early hominid footprints were found at a site called Laetoli. After careful analysis, scientists have theorized that these footprints, which were fossilized in hardened volcanic ash, belong to individuals who were early **hominins**, the same taxonomic family to which modern humans belong.

Physical anthropologists study human beings as biological organisms shaped by evolutionary forces in order to determine where our species fits on the biological continuum. They want to understand where we came from, how we evolved, and why. Physical anthropology goes beyond the study of physiological systems and biological phenomena. On page 5, the textbook authors state, "When these topics are considered within the broader context of human evolution, another factor must be considered, and that factor is **culture**," the strategies by which humans adapt to the natural environment. Culture is what has ensured the survival of our species. Culture is learned, not genetically acquired. However, it is thought that human beings have a predisposition to assimilate culture and our functioning within it is "very much influenced by biological factors." (page 7 of the Jurmain textbook) This integral interaction of culture and biology in human development is called **biocultural evolution**.

Another reason why anthropology is considered "holistic" is that it integrates the findings of many disciplines: sociology, psychology, history, economics, and biology, to name but a few. As it is taught in the United States, anthropology comprises four main subfields, according to the Jurmain textbook: cultural (or social), linguistic, archaeology, and physical (or biological). Cultural anthropology is the study of all aspects of human behavior. Anthropologists have always been interested in traditional peoples, and in the **ethnographies** (the detailed, written descriptions of cross-cultural groups) that are produced by cultural anthropologists as a result of their fieldwork. These works enable comparative, cross-cultural studies of groups by aspiring anthropologists and other social scientists. Archaeology is the study of the lifeways of early cultures by anthropologists who recover and analyze the material remains of past societies. While archaeologists are concerned with culture, they differ from cultural anthropologists because their sources of information are not living people but artifacts, objects or materials made or modified by people of the past. Linguistic anthropology is the study of speech and language, including the origins of language and the relationship between language and culture.

Each area of anthropology can be divided into several subspecialized areas of interest. Physical (or biological) anthropology, as described on page 11 of the Jurmain textbook, "is the study of human biology within the framework of evolution and with an emphasis on the interaction between biology and culture." Physical anthropology is concerned with biological and behavioral characteristics of human beings, the nonhuman **primates** (apes, monkeys, and prosimians), and their ancestors. Two areas of interest among nineteenth century scholars fueled the development of physical anthropology. First, some were beginning to doubt the literal, biblical interpretation of creation. Charles Darwin's renowned work, *On the Origin of Species*, which was published in 1859, focused on the theory of human **evolution** by natural selection and fueled this interest even further. A second area of interest that propelled physical anthropology as a discipline was a desire to explain human variation, especially observable physical variations such as skin color. During the Age of Exploration in the late fifteenth and early sixteenth centuries, European explorers had encountered many groups of people who didn't look or act at all like Europeans. Unfortunately, some of this interest was motivated by racial bias. However, as you will learn, after decades of analyzing and verifying Darwin's monumental theory of evolution, physical anthropologists have concluded and now teach that skin color as a concept of "race" has no biological validity in humans. Rather, skin color is a biological **adaptation** to different environments as humans evolved in them. One reason anthropologists today are concerned with human variation is to learn why human traits adapt the way they do and how that fits in with the evolutionary process.

The Jurmain textbook points out that it would be impossible to study evolutionary processes without a knowledge of how traits are inherited. Therefore, **genetics**, the study of gene structure and action, is a crucial field for physical anthropologists to learn. Molecular anthropologists, or physical anthropologists who make genetics their main focus, use ever more sophisticated technologies to discover the evolutionary relationships between human populations and also between humans and nonhuman primates. **Primatology**, another subspecialty of physical anthropology, is the study of the biology and behavior of the nonhuman primates, the prosimians, monkeys, and apes. It is also the study of the underlying factors that relate to their social behavior, which helps us better understand many aspects of modern human behavior. As you will learn in later lessons, many species of nonhuman primates are endangered. Anthropologists who study them often act as advocates, recommending policies geared toward their protection.

Other subspecialties of physical anthropology include **paleoanthropology**, the study of human evolution through the fossil record; **osteology**, the study of skeletal structure and bone physiology, which is important in correctly analyzing fossil remains; and **forensic anthropology**, an area where physical anthropologists work with coroners and others in the identification and analysis of human remains. If you are a fan of the *CSI* television franchise, you are familiar with crime scene investigation. (Of course, that isn't to imply that the actors are necessarily depicting anthropologists or that crimes are solved with television's lightning speed.) Forensic anthropologists have been involved in many cases of legal and historical significance, including the terrorist attacks of September 11, 2001. Forensic anthropology is an example of **applied anthropology**, the practical application of anthropology to solve problems outside an academic setting. Applied anthropologists work in all areas of anthropology, but the majority are cultural anthropologists. These subfields demonstrate that to understand humans as fully as possible, they must be investigated in the broadest possible context.

Lesson 1 also reviews the **scientific method**, a term you undoubtedly have heard in previous science classes. This is a research method whereby a problem is identified and a **hypothesis** is formed and is then repeatedly tested. If the hypothesis continues to stand up against rigorous and repeated testing, it reaches the status of a theory. A **theory** is a broad statement of scientific relationships that has been repeatedly tested and that scientists have not been able to disprove. The Jurmain textbook makes the important note that in everyday conversation, the term *theory* is often erroneously defined as a hunch.

Anthropologists in all fields adhere to the principles of the scientific method. This is why anthropology is called a social science. The methodical way in which the Forensic Archaeology

Hominid or Hominin?

In 2001, paleoanthropologist Meave Leakey announced the discovery of a new species of human, *Kenyanthropus platyops*. The discovery was announced as a new hominid in *The New York Times* and as a new hominin by *National Geographic*. Who was right?

The confusion is indicative of the changes our system of taxonomy—or classification—have undergone in the past few decades.

Carl Linnaeus created the first system of classification in 1735, built around physical characteristics he lumped together based on their similarities. According to Linnaeus' classification, humans belong to:
- Kingdom Animalia,
- Phylum Chordata (because we have a backbone)
- Class Mammalia (because we have hair and are warm-blooded)
- Order Primates (due to a suite of characteristics)
- Superfamily Hominoidae, also known as hominoids (because we, among other things, don't have a tail)

Until recently, most taxonomists further divided the superfamily Hominoidea into:
- Hylobatidae (lesser apes)
- Pongidae (the great apes)
- Hominidae, or hominids (humans and their ancestors)

But Linnaeus created his system before scientists knew about evolution, and well before new technologies revealed the similarities and differences between species' protein sequences, including DNA. Many scientists have come to prefer a classification system that reflects evolution as revealed through biomolecular analysis.

Such analysis indicates that we have more in common with chimpanzees and gorillas than with orangutans, and so some adjustments in classification have been made. The new system also has additional layers between family and genus to reflect further divisions.

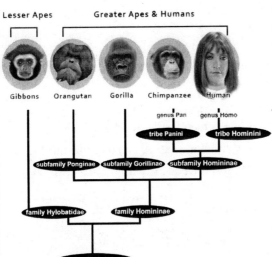

Lesser Apes   Greater Apes & Humans

Gibbons   Orangutan   Gorilla   Chimpanzee   Human

genus Pan   genus Homo

tribe Panini   tribe Hominini

subfamily Ponginae   subfamily Gorillinae   subfamily Homininae

family Hylobatidae   family Homininae

superfamily Hominoidea

As you can see from this chart, the hominins are now divided into two subfamilies:
- Ponginae (orangutans)
- Gorillinae (gorillas)
- Homininae (chimpanzees, humans, and their ancestors)

Homininae is divided into two "tribes":
- Panini (chimpanzees and bonobos)
- Hominini or hominins (humans and their ancestors)

As new discoveries are made, the charts continue to evolve and the labels with them. For now, humans and our ancestors are still hominids, just as before, but due to addition of new layers, we are also hominins. Both terms are correct, depending on the level to which we are referring. One way to think of it is that all hominins are hominids, but not all hominids are hominins!

Not all anthropologists have caught up with the new nomenclature, however. Don't be surprised if you see hominin and hominid used interchangeably in the text and videos in this course. Evolution in language, as in nature, doesn't happen overnight!

Recovery (FAR) team members, featured in the video for this lesson, collect their data to identify victims in a Rhode Island nightclub fire exemplifies how the scientific method is applied by anthropologists in the field.

The anthropological perspective allows for a broad examination of the human experience. How are humans different and similar to other animals, particularly nonhuman primates? What is the context of the biological and behavioral diversity among humans? What do the adaptations of humans over evolutionary time tell us about our biology and our culture? Such exploration can help us understand the limits and the potentials of human beings. By studying different groups of people, we learn what it means to be human. Through these efforts, we can rise above **ethnocentrism**, the habit of viewing other cultures as inferior to one's own, and instead we can achieve goals for peace on our planet by recognizing that all cultures are equal in their humanity.

Review Exercises

Matching I

Match each term with the appropriate definition or description.

1. __g__ adaptation
2. __j__ behavior
3. __k__ biocultural evolution
4. __c__ bipedally
5. __h__ culture
6. __f__ evolution

7. __b__ hominin
8. __e__ Primates
9. __d__ species
10. __a__ artifacts
11. __i__ worldview
12. __l__ quadrupedal

a. Objects or materials made or modified for use by hominins.

b. Colloquial term for members of the evolutionary group that includes modern humans and now extinct bipedal relatives.

c. Walking on two feet.

d. A group of organisms that can interbreed to produce fertile offspring.

e. The mammalian order to which prosimians, monkeys, apes, and humans belong.

f. A change in the genetic structure of a population; frequently used to refer to the appearance of a new species.

g. Functional response of organisms or populations to the environment.

h. A set of *learned* behaviors that is transmitted from one generation to the next by nonbiological (i.e., nongenetic) means.

i. General cultural orientation or perspective shared by members of a society.

j. Anything organisms do that involves action in response to internal or external stimuli.

k. The concept that biology makes culture possible and that developing culture further influences the direction of biological evolution.

l. Using all four limbs to support the body during locomotion.

Matching II

Match each term with the appropriate definition or description.

1. __a__ anthropology
2. __e__ anthropometry
3. __l__ applied anthropology
4. __g__ DNA
5. __b__ ethnographies
6. __k__ forensic anthropology
7. __f__ genetics

8. __i__ osteology
9. __c__ paleoanthropology
10. __j__ paleopathology
11. __d__ primate paleontology
12. __h__ primatology
13. __m__ bioarchaeology

a. Field of inquiry that studies human culture and evolutionary aspects of human biology.

b. Detailed descriptive studies of human societies.

c. The study of earlier hominids—their chronology, physical structure, archaeological remains, habitats, and so on.

d. The study of fossil primates.

e. Measurement of human body parts.

f. The study of gene structure and action and the patterns of inheritance of traits from parent to offspring.

g. The double-stranded molecule that contains the genetic code.

h. The study of the biology and behavior of nonhuman primates.

i. The study of skeletal material.

j. The study of the evidence of disease and injury in human skeletal remains.

k. An applied anthropological approach dealing with legal matters.

l. The practical application of anthropological and archaeological theories and techniques. For example, many biological anthropologists work in the public health sector.

m. The study of skeletal remains from archaeological sites.

Matching III

Match each term with the appropriate definition or description.

1. __e__ data
2. __c__ empirical
3. __i__ ethnocentric
4. __b__ hypothesis
5. __f__ quantitatively

6. __a__ science
7. __d__ scientific method
8. __h__ scientific testing
9. __g__ theory

a. A body of knowledge gained through observation and experimentation.

b. A provisional explanation of a phenomenon.

c. Relying on experiment or observation.

d. A research method whereby a problem is identified, a hypothesis (or provisional explanation) is stated, and that hypothesis is tested by collecting and analyzing data.

e. Facts from which conclusions can be drawn.

f. Pertaining to measurements of quantity, including size, number, and capacity.

g. A broad statement of scientific relationships or underlying principles that has been substantially verified.

h. The precise repetition of an experiment or expansion of observed data to provide verification.

i. Viewing other cultures from the inherently biased perspective of one's own culture.

Completion I

Fill each blank with the most appropriate term from the list below.

adaptation   hominins
behavior   primates
biocultural evolution   quadrupedal
bipedally   species
culture   savanna
evolution   worldview

1. Humans belong to a taxonomic tribe that is colloquially known as the **hominins** .

2. An **adaptation** is a functional response of an organism or population to the environment.

3. The **primates** is the mammalian order to which humans belong.

4. Animals that walk on two legs, such as humans and birds, are said to walk **bipedally**

5. A **savanna** is a large flat grassland with scattered trees and shrubs.

6. **culture** is a set of learned behaviors that is transmitted from one generation to the next by nonbiological means.

7. A **worldview** is a general cultural orientation or perspective shared by members of a society.

8. The interactive evolution of human biology and culture is called **biocultural evo.**

9. **evolution** is a change in the genetic structure of a population.

10. A group of organisms that can interbreed to produce fertile offspring are called a **species** .

11. **behavior** is anything an organism does that involves action in response to internal or external stimuli.

12. A **quadrupedal** ape uses all four limbs to support the body during locomotion.

Completion II

Fill each blank with the most appropriate term from the list below.

~~anthropology~~   ~~forensic anthropology~~
~~anthropometry~~   ~~genetics~~
~~applied anthropology~~   ~~osteology~~
~~artifacts~~   ~~paleoanthropology~~
~~bioarchaeology~~   ~~paleopathology~~
~~DNA~~   ~~primate paleontology~~
~~ethnographies~~   ~~primatology~~

1. The branch of osteology that studies evidence of disease and injury in human skeletal remains is *paleopathology*

2. *Primate paleont- ology* is the study of the biology and behavior of nonhuman primates.

3. The field of inquiry that studies human culture and evolutionary aspects of human biology is *anthropology*.

4. *Paleoanthro.* is the interdisciplinary approach to the study of earlier hominins.

5. The double-stranded molecule that contains the genetic code is *DNA*.

6. *ethnographies* are detailed descriptive studies of human societies.

7. The study of fossil primates is called *Primatology*.

8. *genetics* is the study of gene structure and action and the patterns of inheritance of traits.

9. Measurement of the human body is *anthropometry*

10. When biological anthropologists work in the public health sector, they are doing *applied anthropology*

11. Physical anthropologists who work with coroners are involved in *forensic anthro.*

12. *Osteology* is the study of skeletal material.

13. Objects made or modified for use by hominins are called *artifacts*.

14. The study of human remains from arcaeological sites is called *Bioarchaeology*

Completion III

Fill each blank with the most appropriate term from the list below.

~~data~~   ~~hypothesis~~   ~~scientific method~~
~~empirical~~   ~~quantitatively~~   ~~scientific testing~~
ethnocentric   ~~science~~   ~~theory~~

1. A *hypothesis* is a provisional explanation of a phenomenon.

2. When measurements are obtained for such things as size, number, and capacity, and we state how they were measured, which features were measured, and what the results were, we say they are expressed *quantitatively*

3. A broad statement of scientific relationships or underlying principles that has been at least partially verified is a _theory_ .

4. The _Scientific Method_ identifies a problem, states a hypothesis, and tests the hypothesis through the collection and analysis of data.

5. Facts from which conclusions can be drawn are called _data_ .

6. _Scientific testing_ is the precise repetition of an experiment or expansion of observed data to provide verification.

7. A person who views other cultures from the inherently biased perspective of his or her culture is called _ethnocentric_ .

8. A _empirical_ approach relies on experiment and/or observation.

9. _Science_ is a body of knowledge gained through observation and experimentation.

Self-Test

Select the best answer.

1. Walking on two legs, as humans and chickens do, is referred to as
   a. quadrupedalism.
   b. brachiation.
   c. bipedalism.
   d. cursorial.

2. Culture is
   a. learned.
   b. a biological trait of our species.
   c. the strategy by which most mammals adapt to their environments.
   d. inherited by a simple genetic transmission.

3. The biological characteristics of humans enabled culture to develop and culture, in turn, influenced human biological development. This is called
   a. microevolution.
   b. quantum evolution.
   c. convergent evolution.
   d. biocultural evolution.

4. Anthropologists who conduct excavations to recover artifacts and other aspects of material culture are
   a. archaeologists.
   b. cultural anthropologists.
   c. linguistic anthropologists.
   d. physical anthropologists.

5. The subdiscipline of anthropology that studies the various aspects of language is called

    a. primatology.

    (b) linguistic anthropology.

    c. ethnology.

    d. paleoanthropology.

6. An anthropologist who is studying the subsistence strategy of the Mbuti pygmies in Zaire belongs to the anthropological subfield of

    a. archaeology.

    (b) cultural anthropology.

    c. linguistic anthropology.

    d. physical anthropology.

7. The origins of physical anthropology arose from two areas of interest among nineteenth-century scientists. These areas concerned

    (a) origins of species and human variation.

    b. genetic determinants of behavior and osteology.

    c. human variation and osteology.

    d. human evolution and nonhuman primates.

8. Paleoanthropologists study

    a. diseases affecting modern Stone Age peoples.

    b. heredity.

    (c) human evolution.

    d. living primates.

9. The study of human evolution as revealed by the fossil record is

    (a) paleoanthropology.

    b. osteology.

    c. primatology.

    (d) paleopathology.

10. Researchers who study the fossil record of the primate order are called

    a. osteologists.

    b. forensic anthropologists.

    (c) primate paleontologists.

    d. geneticists.

11. Contemporary physical anthropologists, whose main interest is in modern human variation, approach their subject matter from the perspective of
    a. racial typologies.
    b. adaptive significance.
    c. behavioral genetics.
    d. constitutional typology.

12. Genetics is
    a. a requirement for physical anthropology to exist as an evolutionary science.
    b. the study of disease and trauma in human fossil remains.
    c. not important to the study of human variation.
    d. more important to cultural anthropologists than to physical anthropologists.

13. A researcher is studying the nutritional ecology of howler monkeys in Panama. Her area of expertise is
    a. osteology.
    b. forensic anthropology.
    c. primatology.
    d. genetics.

14. A physical anthropologist who studies bones exclusively is called a(n)
    a. adaptationist.
    b. anthropometrist.
    c. paleoanthropologist.
    d. osteologist.

15. Which of the following is a subfield of osteology that is concerned with disease and trauma in earlier populations?
    a. forensic anthropology
    b. paleopathology
    c. primate paleontology
    d. anthropometry

16. A family reports to the police that their dog has brought home a leg bone that appears to be human. The police also believe this bone is human. To find out vital information about the person this bone came from, the police will consult a(n)
    a. forensic anthropologist.
    b. primatologist.
    c. paleoanthropologist.
    d. evolutionary geneticist.

17. When anthropologists collect data on teeth, they state which teeth are measured, how they are measured, and the results of measurements. Such a study is said to be

    a. empirical.
    b. qualitative.
    c. quantitative.
    d. all of the above.

18. A hypothesis

    a. is a statement that has been proved.
    b. can be proved if it is well constructed.
    c. is the same thing as a theory.
    d. is a provisional statement regarding certain scientific facts.

19. Viewing other cultures from the inherently biased perspective of one's own culture is known as

    a. linguistics.
    b. ethnocentrism.
    c. ethnography.
    d. paleopathology.

20. To understand human beings, through time and space, we must broaden our views. The Jurmain textbook calls this

    a. the anthropological perspective.
    b. ethnocentrism.
    c. the peasant's perspective.
    d. profiling.

21. Monkeys who walk on four limbs are said to be

    a. bipedal.
    b. quadrupedal.
    c. manual.
    d. ambidextrous.

22. A bioarchaeologist studies

    a. measurement of human body parts.
    b. skeletal remains from archaeological sites.
    c. fossil primates.
    d. tools used by hominins.

23. Objects or materials made for use by hominins are called

    a. fossils.

    b. savannas.

    (c.) artifacts.

    d. paleoanthropology.

Short-Answer Questions

1. What is culture? How do physical anthropologists use this concept?

   Culture is learned ideas and believes. Physical Anthropologists applie the Concept of culture to their studies with another Concept called biocultural evo.

2. What is biocultural evolution?

   Is the concept that culture is not possible without Biology and/or biology is the cause of culture.

3. Briefly describe the four major subfields of anthropology.

   Physical: The Study of Human biology.
   linguistic: Human speech + language.
   Cultural: Human Believe + behavior.
   Archaeology: the Study of early humans.

4. List the subfields of physical anthropology presented in the Jurmain textbook.

   Paleoanthropology
   Forensic Anthro.

5. Why do anthropologists study nonhuman primates?

   Because of the beliefe that we ourselves come from the Primate family so learning how nonhuman Primates interact and behave shows a lot about our origins.

Application Questions

1. How do the three other subdisciplines of anthropology relate to physical anthropology?

   Well Physical Anthro. is the study of Human Biology, this lead to the Birth of the bioculture evo. Concept. This concept states that W/out Bio. Culture wouldn't exsist so understanding what makes up our Culture (his fee ect.)

2. Why is osteology important to physical anthropologist? What other major biomedical discipline is integral to osteology as well to other areas of physical anthropology?

   Shows a lot About the Bio.

   Osteology is the study of skeletal Material. This would naturally be important to Phy. Ant. because many remaines have lost their soft tissue. So Skeletal remains are left. Forensic Anthro. Connects to all other areas because it looks at everything that remains and Connects the pieces.

3. Explain what the scientific method is and how it is used?

   The Scientific Method is the Method used to create a theory, gather data, and create + test a hypotho. It is used to Prove Theories.

4. How do the colloquial and scientific definitions of "theory" differ?

5. What is meant by the "anthropological perspective"?

   Anthropological Prespective is the ability to have a broader view of the world. To step away from your natural way of thinking and see how things relate to others.

Answer Key
Matching I
1. g (video lesson, introduction; objective 1)
2. j (video lesson, introduction; objective 1)
3. k (objectives 1 & 3)
4. c (video lesson, introduction; objective 1)
5. h (objective 1)
6. f (video lesson, introduction; objective 1)
7. b (objective 1)
8. e (video lesson, introduction; objective 1)
9. d (video lesson, segment 1; objective 1)
10. a (video lesson, segment 1; objective 1)
11. i (objective 1)
12. l (objective 5)

Matching II
1. a (video lesson, introduction; objective 2)
2. e (objective 3)
3. l (objective 2)
4. g (objective 3)
5. b (objective 2)
6. k (video lesson, segment 1; objective 3)
7. f (objective 3)
8. i (video lesson, segment 1; objective 3)
9. c (video lesson, segment 1; objective 3)
10. j (objective 3)
11. d (objective 3)
12. h (video lesson, segment 1; objective 3)
13. n (objective 3)

Matching III
1. e (video lesson, segment 2; objective 4)
2. c (objective 4)
3. i (objective 5)
4. b (video lesson, segment 2; objective 4)

5. f (objective 4)

6. a (objective 4)

7. d (video lesson, segment 2; objective 4)

8. h (objective 4)

9. g (video lesson, segment 2; objective 4)

Completion I

1. hominins (video lesson, introduction; objective 1)

2. adaptation (video lesson, introduction; objective 1)

3. primates (video lesson, segment 1; objective 1)

4. bipedally (video lesson, introduction; objective 1)

5. Savanna (objective 1)

6. Culture (objective 1)

7. worldview (objective 1)

8. biocultural evolution (objectives 1 & 3)

9. Evolution (video lesson, introduction; objective 1)

10. species (video lesson, segment 1; objective 1)

11. Behavior (video lesson, introduction; objective 1)

12. quadrupedal (objective 5)

Completion II

1. paleopathology (objective 3)

2. Primatology (video lesson, segment 1; objective 3)

3. anthropology (video lesson, introduction; objective 2)

4. Paleoanthropology (video lesson, segment 1; objective 3)

5. DNA (objective 3)

6. Ethnographies (objective 2)

7. primate paleontology (objective 3)

8. Genetics (objective 3)

9. anthropometry (objective 3)

10. applied anthropology (objective 2)

11. forensic anthropology (video lesson, segment 1; objective 3)

12. Osteology (video lesson, segment 1; objective 3)

13. artifacts (objective 2)

14. bioarchaeology (objective 3)

Completion III

1. hypothesis (video lesson, segment 2; objective 4)
2. quantitatively (objective 4)
3. theory (video lesson, segment 2; objective 4)
4. scientific method (video lesson, segment 2; objective 4)
5. data (video lesson, segment 2; objective 4)
6. Scientific testing (objective 4)
7. ethnocentric (objective 5)
8. empirical (objective 4)
9. Science (objective 4)

Self-Test

1. c. is the correct answer. Evidence of bipedalism is found in all hominins that have been identified so far. (video lesson, introduction; objective 1)

2. a. is the correct answer. Culture is transmitted from one generation to another. (video lesson, introduction; objective 1)

3. d. is the correct answer. Biocultural evolution is a feedback system in which culture and biology interact with one another. (video lesson, introduction; objective 1)

4. a. is the correct answer. Archaeology is a subfield of anthropology. (video lesson, introduction; objective 2)

5. b. is the correct answer. Linguistics was developed within physical anthropology with the intent of studying migrations, relationships, and origins of different peoples. As late as the 1960s, physical anthropology textbooks had a chapter on linguistics. (video lesson, introduction; objective 2)

6. b. is the correct answer. Cultural anthropologists study all aspects of human behavior including subsistence strategies that peoples use to obtain calories. (objective 2)

7. a. is the correct answer. The original subject matter of physical anthropology was the origins of the races. Blumenbach (publishing in the eighteenth and nineteenth centuries) attempted to explain human physical differences as occurring as the descendants of Noah branch out from the ark that had landed in the Caucasus Mountains. The publication of Darwin's works would shift the focus from the origin of the races to the origin of the species. (objective 3)

8. c. is the correct answer. Paleoanthropologists may be either human paleontologists or archaeologists. (video lesson, segment 1; objective 3)

9. a. is the correct answer. Paleoanthropology studies human evolution as evidence by fossil and material culture remains. (video lesson, segment 1; objective 3)

10. c. is the correct answer. Primate paleontologists work in North America (Paleocene through Eocene), South America (Oligocene and later), Asia (Paleocene and later), Europe (Eocene through Miocene), and Africa (Paleocene through Pleistocene). (objective 3)

11.   b. is the correct answer. The modern approach to human variation places less emphasis on physical differences as a marker and more on how populations adapt to their environments. (objective 3)

12.   a. is the correct answer. Evolution requires a transmission of genes across generations. (objective 3)

13.   c. is the correct answer. Because the researcher is studying a monkey, a primate, she is a primatologist. (video lesson, segment 1; objective 3)

14.   d. is the correct answer. Osteology is the study of skeletal material and bone anatomy. (video lesson, segment 1; objective 3)

15.   b. is the correct answer. Paleopathologists look for signs of disease, trauma, even indication of occupations, in earlier populations and individuals. (objective 3)

16.   a. is the correct answer. In physical anthropology, forensic anthropologists generally work with physical remains of deceased individuals. However, the word *forensic* refers to the application of scientific knowledge to legal problems, and there are forensic anthropologists who are cultural and linguistic anthropologists. (video lesson, segment 1; objective 3)

17.   c. is the correct answer. When data are quantified, they are assigned a number enabling them to be tested statistically. Physical anthropology is highly quantitative, whereas cultural anthropology tends to be descriptive or qualitative. (objective 4)

18.   d. is the correct answer. Hypotheses can be shown to be false, but they cannot be proved (this would imply that they are true). Despite the fact that the word proved is used often in common language, even by scientists and especially in the legal system, we do not actually prove anything other than mathematical equations. (objective 4)

19.   b. is the correct answer. Ethnocentrism is an important concept that allows anthropologists to view another culture from a more objective view than would be otherwise. (objective 5)

20.   a. is the correct answer. The anthropological perspective is holistic and comparative. (objective 5)

21.   b is the correct answer. Quadrupedalism, or using all four limbs to support the body during locomotion, is the basic primate form of locomotion. (objective 5)

22.   b. is the correct answer. The term bioarchaeology has been applied over the past thirty years to the study of human skeletal remains from archaeological sites. (objective 3)

23.   c. is the correct answer. Artifacts are things made or modified for use by hominins and are usually made of stone. (objective 2)

Short-Answer Questions

Your answers should include the following:

1.   Culture is a broad term that encompasses a number of behavioral aspects of human adaptation. These include (but are not limited to) technology, traditions, language, religion, marriage patterns, and social roles. Essentially, culture is defined as all learned behaviors that are transmitted transgenerationally by nonbiological means. Physical

anthropologists use this concept to explain how culture gives humans an evolutionary potential beyond our biology. One example is the Inuit people, who are able to live in the Arctic Circle without having to evolve all of the physical traits necessary for existing in a cold and barren habitat. Instead they have adapted via cultural means. (objective 1)

2.   While the focus of physical anthropology is on human biology, culture is also considered in the evolution of our species. This approach is called biocultural evolution. It is the mutual interactive evolution of human biology and culture. This is a concept that biology makes culture possible (e.g., having a dexterous hand that enables us to use tools) and that developing culture further influences the direction of biological evolution (e.g., technological advances, such as in vitro fertilization, have an effect on human biological diversity). (objective 1)

3.   The four major subdisciplines of anthropology are cultural anthropology, archaeology, linguistic anthropology, and physical anthropology. As a subfield, cultural anthropology examines all aspects of human behavior. Cultural anthropologists study traditional societies and produced descriptions, called ethnographies, which emphasized behaviors such as religious practices, marriage patterns, use of symbols, and subsistence patterns. Ethnographies are then used in comparative studies to find commonalities among human groups. In recent years, techniques used to study traditional societies have been applied to subcultures found in modern societies. Some of the fields within cultural anthropology include medical anthropology and applied anthropology. Another major subfield of anthropology is archaeology, the study of material culture from past human groups. Archaeologists recover, analyze, and interpret these remains. Because these earlier people are no longer living, archaeologists cannot interview their subjects, but must get information from the artifacts and structures left behind. Together, prehistoric archaeology and physical anthropology form the core of a joint science called paleoanthropology. The third subfield of anthropology, linguistic anthropology, is the study of human speech and language, including the origins of language. Linguists use language to deduce relationships among human groups. Linguistics was once considered to be part of the fourth major subfield, physical anthropology. Physical anthropology, the topic of this course, is the study of human biology within the framework of evolutionary biology. In that respect, it is different from other human biology disciplines that usually have a medical or clinical approach. Physical anthropology emphasizes the interaction between biology and culture. (video lesson, introduction & segment 1; objective 2)

4.   The subdisciplines of physical anthropology presented in the Jurmain textbook are paleoanthropology, human variation, human genetics, primatology, osteology, and anatomy. Paleoanthropology is the study of human evolution, and the associated study of the primate fossil record is called primate paleontology. A second subfield of physical anthropology is human variation, the study of biological diversity among modern humans. Human genetics represents a third subfield and can be conducted at different levels, from molecular biology to population studies. Genetics is vital to the understanding of evolutionary processes because it provides the mechanisms for the inheritance of traits. Another subfield of physical anthropology, primatology, is the study of our closest genetic relatives, the other members of the order *Primates*.

The fifth subfield is osteology, the study of the skeleton, which has applications to the other subfields such as paleoanthropology, primate paleontology, and human variation. Osteology has two subdisciplines: paleopathology, the study of disease in ancient populations; and forensic anthropology, which often involves the identification of skeletal remains. Physical anthropologists who specialize in the field of anatomy are skilled in the study of the body's soft tissue, in addition to skeletal structure. Anatomy is the discipline from which physical anthropology developed, and many, if not most, physical anthropologists were in the anatomy departments of medical schools prior to the 1950s. (video lesson, segment 1; objective 3)

5. Anthropologists study nonhuman primates because they are our closest relatives. Therefore, we study their behavior to learn more about ourselves. Identifying the underlying factors related to social behavior, communication, infant care, and reproductive behavior, among others, helps us develop a better understanding of the natural forces that have shaped so many aspects of modern human behavior. (video lesson; segment 1; objective 3)

Application Questions

Your answers should include the following:

1. Anthropology is holistic and interdisciplinary. Physical anthropologists utilize the concepts and research results from the other three subfields: cultural anthropology, archaeology, and linguistic anthropology. Cultural anthropologists contribute studies on living humans, including hunters and gatherers who are one of the models used for the earlier humans studied by physical anthropologists. Archaeologists uncover and analyze material culture which elucidates the lives of earlier humans, even as far back as a million years ago. Linguistic anthropology might appear to be the subfield that has the least relevance to physical anthropology. Actually, it was originally part of physical anthropology. Physical anthropologists were interested in the relationships and migrations of modern peoples. Language families were one of the traits used to discern these relationships. A topic of interest to both linguistic and physical anthropologists is the origin of language. (objective 2)

2. Osteology, the study of the skeleton, is important to physical anthropology because when anthropology was first founded, physical differences between humans were measured on the skeleton. Also, fossil remains are almost entirely the physical remains of the skeleton. Therefore, paleoanthropologists need to have a thorough understanding of the skeleton. In addition, human adaptations, such as bipedalism, are often compared skeletally with nonhuman primates. Forensic anthropologists and paleopathologists also need to know skeletal anatomy. The discipline that ties all of these critical studies together is anatomy. It should be no surprise that prior to the 1950s most physical anthropologists were in anatomy departments. (video lesson, segment 1; objective 3)

3. The scientific method is a process by which scientific knowledge is obtained. The first step is to make an observation. This can be done by research in a library or by observing in a field or laboratory setting. Second, a testable hypothesis is formulated. The hypothesis must be falsifiable because only a falsifiable hypothesis can be tested. The third step is to set up and perform an experiment, either in the lab or in the field,

to test the hypothesis. Experimentation yields results that must be interpreted to form a conclusion about whether the original hypothesis has been supported or negated, or requires modification. If necessary, a modified hypothesis might then be formulated and tested. The cycle of this process may take years and might be carried forward by other researchers. When a hypothesis has been consistently supported after repeated testing, it becomes part of a body of theory, which is accepted scientific knowledge. (video lesson, segment 2; objective 4)

4.   The colloquial conception is that a theory is mere conjecture, and ranks below a law because it has not been "proven." Clearly the colloquial definition not only confuses theory with hypothesis, but it also illustrates a misunderstanding of the scientific method. In science, a hypothesis is never proven. It either fails or it is provisionally accepted after being tested by an experiment. If a hypothesis stands up to repeated testing, it may stand as a theory or be incorporated into a theory as an accepted part of the body of scientific knowledge. One example is evolutionary theory. Evolution itself is not a theory but a process observed in nature. There are a number of hypotheses that attempt to explain how this process works. Charles Darwin proposed one, that natural selection acts on existing variations, causing a species to change gradually over many generations. But Darwin was never able to formulate a testable hypothesis on how variations arise or how they are maintained in populations. He eventually resorted to ideas like blending inheritance and even pangenesis. Therefore, his explanations for the origin of variation have been rejected (but not the idea of existing variation). His idea on natural selection, on the other hand, has been repeatedly tested and consistently supported. As a result, natural selection has been incorporated into modern evolutionary theory, whereas Darwin's ideas on the origin of variation is a historical footnote. (objective 4)

5.   The anthropological perspective refers to a broadening of our viewpoint in both time and space. The goal is to understand the similarities and differences between humans and other animals, especially nonhuman primates. By broadening our perspective, the diversity of the human experience can be understood within the context of our biological and behavioral continuity with other species. By expanding our knowledge of cultures other than our own, we hope to avoid the pitfalls of ethnocentrism, a judgmental attitude toward other cultures based on the biases prevalent in our own culture. By studying the evolutionary changes leading to modern human anatomy and physiology, the differences and similarities between our forebears and us can be understood. (objective 5)

Notes:

Lesson Review

Lesson 1: The Anthropological Perspective

PLEASE NOTE: Use this matrix to guide your study and achieve the learning objectives of this lesson. It will also help you to view the video, which defines and demonstrates important concepts and principles as they relate to everyday life and actual case studies.

Learning Objective	Textbook	Student Guide	Video Lesson
1. Explain the concept of humans as biocultural beings and discuss the importance of the biocultural approach to the study of human evolution.	pp. 2–10	Key Terms: 1, 2, 3, 4, 6, 7, 8, 10, 11, 12, 13; Matching I: 1, 2, 3, 4, 5, 6, 7, 8, 9, 10, 11; Completion I: 1, 2, 3, 4, 5, 6, 7, 8, 9, 10, 11; Self-Test: 1, 2, 3; Short-Answer: 1, 2.	Introduction Segment 1: *The Subfields of Physical Anthropology*
2. Define anthropology and describe its four major subfields.	pp. 10–18	Key Terms: 5, 14, 15, 16; Matching II: 1, 3, 5; Completion II: 3, 6, 10, 13; Self-Test: 4, 5, 6, 23; Short-Answer: 3; Application: 1.	Introduction Segment 1: *The Subfields of Physical Anthropology*
3. Describe physical anthropology and the major fields of study it encompasses.	pp. 11–18	Key Terms: 9, 13, 17, 18, 19, 20, 21, 22, 23, 24, 25; Matching I: 3; Matching II: 2, 4, 6, 7, 8, 9, 10, 11, 12, 13; Completion I: 8; Completion II: 1, 2, 4, 5, 7, 8, 9, 11, 12, 14; Self-Test: 7, 8, 9, 10, 11, 12, 13, 14, 15, 16, 22; Short-Answer: 4, 5; Application: 2.	Segment 1: *The Subfields of Physical Anthropology*

Learning Objective	Textbook	Student Guide	Video Lesson
4. Explain the scientific method and how it is used in physical anthropology.	pp. 20–23	Key Terms: 26, 27, 28, 29, 30, 31, 32, 33; Matching III: 1, 2, 4, 5, 6, 7, 8, 9; Completion III: 1, 2, 3, 4, 5, 6, 8, 9; Self-Test: 17, 18; Application: 3, 4.	Segment 2: *FAR and the Scientific Method*
5. Discuss the unique approach of the anthropological perspective.	p. 24	Key Terms: 34, 35; Matching I: 12; Matching III: 3; Completion I: 12; Completion III: 7; Self-Test: 19, 20, 21; Application: 5.	

Lesson 2

Lesson 1: The Anthropological Perspective

 Lesson 2:   Development of Evolutionary Theory

Lesson 3: Biological Basis of Life

Lesson 4: Heredity & Evolution

Lesson 5: Macroevolution

Lesson 6, Part I : The Living Primates

Lesson 6, Part II : Overview of the Fossil Primates

Lesson 7: Primate Behavior

Lesson 8: Methods of Paleoanthropology

Lesson 9: The First Bipeds

Lesson 10: A New Hominin

Lesson 11: Premodern Humans

Lesson 12: Origin & Dispersal of Modern Humans

Lesson 13: Patterns of Variation

Lesson 14: Patterns of Adaptation

Lesson 15: Legacies of Human Evolutionary History

Lesson 16: Applied Anthropology

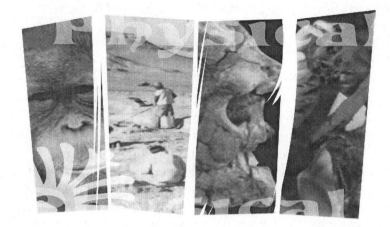

Development of Evolutionary Theory

Checklist

For the most effective study of this lesson, complete the following activities in this sequence.

Before Viewing the Video

❑ Read the Preview, Learning Objectives, and Viewing Notes below.

❑ Read Chapter 2, "The Development of Evolutionary Theory," pages 26–49, in *Introduction to Physical Anthropology*.

What to Watch

❑ After reading the textbook assignment, watch the video for Lesson 2, *Development of Evolutionary Theory*.

After Viewing the Video

❑ Briefly note your answers to the questions listed at the end of the Viewing Notes.

❑ Review the Summary below.

❑ Review all reading assignments for this lesson, including the Viewing Notes in this lesson.

❑ Write brief answers to the "Critical Thinking Questions" at the end of Chapter 2 in the textbook.

❑ Complete the Review Exercises below. Check your answers with the Answer Key and review when necessary.

❑ Use the Lesson Review matrix found at the end of this lesson to review and assess your knowledge of each Learning Objective.

Preview

In Lesson 1, you learned that physical anthropology is a scientific discipline that focuses on human biology and variation within the context of evolution, with an emphasis on the biological and behavioral characteristics of human beings and their ancestors. It is also referred to as biological anthropology. Most people view humanity as separate from the rest of the animal kingdom, because as far as we can determine, we are the only species to ponder our own existence. That reflection often involves considering not only why we are here, but how we got here. Lesson 2 examines, from a biological perspective, the latter point.

Because physical anthropology is concerned with all aspects of how humans came to be and how we adapt physiologically to the external environment, the details of the evolutionary process are crucial to the field. Most people have heard of Charles Darwin, but their knowledge of evolution is fuzzy at best. This lesson explains how the history of scientific thinking, particularly in the wake of the European Age of Exploration in the fifteenth century, gradually led to the development of the theory of evolution. It covers the important scientific contributions of scientists such as Carolus Linnaeus, Jean-Baptiste Lamarck, Georges Cuvier, Thomas Malthus, Charles Lyell, and others, and details how their work facilitated the eventual formulation of Charles Darwin's theory of evolution by natural selection. You will also learn why the concept of **natural selection**, the genetic change or changes in the frequencies of certain traits in populations because of differential reproductive success among individuals, is the key to Darwin's theory.

The theory of evolution can evoke controversy, most often because some see it as contrary to the traditional Judeo-Christian belief that all humankind was created in seven days by God, as it is written in the biblical book of Genesis. Even after Darwin had written down his views on natural selection by 1844, he remained reluctant to publish his ideas because evolutionary theory was viewed as a very serious threat to the strong religious convictions that held sway in society during that time. Furthermore, there continues to be stringent religious-based opposition to evolutionary theory in the United States today.

Concepts to Remember

✺ In Lesson 1, you learned that if a hypothesis cannot be falsified, it is accepted, over time, as a **theory**. There is a popular misconception that theories are nothing more than hunches or unfounded beliefs because this is how we use the term in everyday language. In scientific terms, a theory is something that has been repeatedly tested and scientists have not been able to disprove it. Evolutionary theory is a fundamental unifying force in biological science.

Learning Objectives

After you complete this lesson, you should be able to:

1. Describe accepted beliefs about the origin of life-forms and their relationships to one another prior to the development of evolutionary thought. (pp. 28–29)

2. Discuss major discoveries of the scientific revolution. (pp. 29–31)

3. State the major contributions of key figures in the history of evolutionary thought. (pp. 31–36)

4. Describe the discovery of the principles of natural selection by Darwin and Wallace. (pp. 36–41)

5. Explain the major tenets of natural selection. (pp. 41–42)

6. Give examples of natural selection in action. (pp. 42–45)

7. Describe some of the constraints on nineteenth-century evolutionary theory. (pp. 45–46)

8. Explain why evolutionary theory is controversial for some groups today. (pp. 46–49)

At this point, read Chapter 2, "The Development of Evolutionary Theory," pages 26–49.

Viewing Notes

A portion of Chapter 2 in the Jurmain textbook addresses the variation in beak shape and size that Darwin found among Galápagos finches during his expedition aboard the HMS *Beagle*. The video features this episode of the voyage as well. While his theory of evolution had not been fully formulated as yet, Darwin noted how the beaks of the finches took different shapes in their adaptation to different ecosystems, and this became a key observation of his journey. The video also points out how the work of earlier scientists came to provide some of the "building blocks" that supported the eventual formulation of Darwin's theory of evolution. For instance, a naturalist named Carolus Linnaeus created a system of **taxonomy** that showed the world was not a chaotic mix of creatures, but rather an organized system of species that could be grouped by their similarities. Darwin was intrigued by the work of Thomas Malthus, an economist who focused on the rapid growth of human populations relative to the slower growth of available resources. British geologist Charles Lyell disagreed with the conventional wisdom, based on religious belief, that the planet was 6,000 years old. His work in geology showed that canyons and valleys were shaped by natural forces that caused erosion of the earth and that this erosion occurred over perhaps millions of years. The current best estimate for the age of Earth, based on evidence from meteorites, is 4.6 billion years. Darwin had a notion that it would take a very long time for evolutionary change to occur in species. Lyell's ideas provided him with time, an element he needed in order to have a viable theory. It was Darwin's synthesis of all these ideas that helped him formulate the theory of evolution.

The video also highlights **natural selection** and some of the factors that make it work. One key factor is genetic variation, or genetic differences between individuals in the same population.

Variation, the experts say, is a key component if evolution is to occur, because the environment works on (selects for or against) traits, which results in a change of genetic frequencies of certain traits in a population. According to expert Jonathan Marks, the environment "might permit" certain genetic traits to proliferate. In the video, he gives the example of body build. In colder climates, short and stocky builds are more prevalent; conversely, in very hot climates, tall and skinny body builds proliferate.

Competition for resources is another factor involved in natural selection, and the video introduces the population of gray foxes living on Southern California's Channel Islands as an example of this competition. The foxes' small size is the result of a phenomenon called dwarfing, which is fairly common on islands, because of the limited space and limited food sources in island habitats. The story of how the foxes became smaller on the Channel Islands illustrates how critical the environment is in determining what is an advantageous trait and what is not. Food for the gray fox was limited on the Channel Islands, which exerted a very strong **selective pressure** on this species. Selective pressures are forces in the environment that influence reproductive success in individuals. Smaller foxes survived better than larger ones because they did not have to eat as much.

Questions to Consider

✿ Jean-Baptiste Lamarck suggested that giraffes' extraordinarily long necks were a result of them regularly stretching toward treetops for food, and that this constant effort created a physical difference for that giraffe. Although Lamarck's idea seemed plausible, it was incorrect. How would you explain a giraffe's long neck based on your understanding of the theory of evolution?

✿ What is the role of selective pressure in natural selection?

✿ The Jurmain textbook posed two questions some people ask concerning evolution. "If humans evolved from monkeys, then why do we still have monkeys?" and "If evolution happens, then why don't we ever see new species?" Now that you have read the textbook chapter and watched the video, how would you respond?

Watch the video for Lesson 2, *Development of Evolutionary Theory*.

Segment 1: *Natural Science Before Darwin*
Segment 2: *On the Beagle*

Segment 3: *Natural Selection*
Segment 4: *Natural Selection in Action*

Key Terms and Concepts

Page references are keyed to *Introduction to Physical Anthropology,* 13th edition.

1. **natural selection:** The most critical mechanism of evolutionary change, first described by Charles Darwin; refers to genetic change or changes in the frequencies of certain traits in populations due to differential reproductive success between individuals. (p. 26; video lesson, segment 3; objective 4)

2. **fixity of species:** The notion that species, once created, can never change; an idea diametrically opposed to theories of biological evolution. (p. 29; objective 1)

3. **reproductively isolated:** Pertaining to groups of organisms that, mainly because of genetic differences, are prevented from mating and producing offspring with members of other groups. For example, dogs cannot mate and produce offspring with cats. (p. 31; objective 3)

4. **binomial nomenclature:** (*binomial*, meaning "two names") In taxonomy, the convention established by Carolus Linnaeus whereby genus and species names are used to refer to species. For example, *Homo sapiens* refers to human beings. (p. 31; video lesson, segment 1; objective 3)

5. **taxonomy:** The branch of science concerned with the rules of classifying organisms on the basis of evolutionary relationships. (p. 31; video lesson, segment 1; objective 3)

6. **catastrophism:** The view that the earth's geological landscape is the result of violent cataclysmic events. Cuvier promoted this view, especially in opposition to Lamarck. (p. 32; objective 3)

7. **uniformitarianism:** The theory that the earth's features are the result of long-term processes that continue to operate in the present as they did in the past. Elaborated on by Lyell, this theory opposed catastrophism and contributed strongly to the concept of immense geological time. (p. 34; objective 3)

8. **fitness:** Pertaining to natural selection, a measure of relative reproductive success of individuals. Fitness can be measured by an individual's genetic contribution to the next generation compared to that of other individuals. The terms *genetic fitness*, *reproductive fitness*, and *differential reproductive success* are also used. (p. 41; objective 5)

9. **reproductive success:** The number of offspring an individual produces and rears to reproductive age; an individual's genetic contribution to the next generation. (p. 42; video lesson, segment 3; objective 5)

10. **selective pressures:** Forces in the environment that influence reproductive success in individuals. (p. 42; video lesson, segment 3; objective 5)

11. **fertility:** The ability to conceive and produce healthy offspring. (p. 44; objective 6)

12. **genome:** The entire genetic makeup of an individual or species. (p. 45; objective 7)

13. **biological continuity:** A biological continuum. When expressions of a phenomenon continuously grade into one another so that there are no discrete categories, they exist

on a continuum. Color is one such phenomenon, and life-forms are another. (p. 46; objective 3)

14. **Christian fundamentalists:** Adherents to a movement in American Protestantism that began in the early twentieth century. This group holds that the teachings of the Bible are infallible and are to be taken literally. (p. 47; objective 8)

Summary

The video and the textbook reading assignment for this lesson both show a progression of scientific ideas on the topic of biological change in organisms that ultimately supported Darwin as he worked to formulate his theory. In fact, British naturalist Alfred Russel Wallace was simultaneously writing on the same concepts as Darwin. During this time, the emergence of all of this scientific inquiry and growth indicated that thinkers were ready to accept a different explanation of life on Earth than that offered by religious factions in society.

The theory of evolution was mired in controversy from its inception and continues to this day. The Jurmain textbook provides a good overview of some of the recent debates that have been waged in the United States, and, as mentioned above in the Preview for this lesson, most of the fiercest opposition comes from powerful religious groups that still teach a literal interpretation of the story of Genesis—that God created Earth in six days. To these individuals, evolution is impossible within their belief system. During the sixteenth century, European intellectuals believed in the concept of the **fixity of species**, the notion that all life on Earth had been created by God exactly as it existed in the present and they never changed. Therefore, those who proposed that species evolved over time were considered heretics who opposed the teachings of Christianity.

The scientific revolution radically altered scientific thinking over the course of a 150-year time frame. Until the mid-1400s, Western science was firmly grounded on ancient Greek learning, with the Aristotelian tradition as its framework. A key element was Aristotle's cosmology, which placed Earth at the center of the universe with all objects in orbit around it. However, Christopher Columbus' voyages to the New World between 1492 and 1502, as well as the circumnavigation of Earth begun by Ferdinand Magellan in 1519 and completed in 1522 by his surviving crew, marked a turning point. Such discoveries raised general awareness of almost infinite biological diversity and ignited the idea that the earth was round rather than flat. Astronomer Nicolaus Copernicus argued for heliocentrism, the notion that the sun was at the center of the solar system. Interestingly, Copernicus was not the first scientist to propose this. Astronomers in India and the Islamic world were among those who had previously criticized the geocentric model, which proposed that the earth was the center of the universe. Galileo Galilei improved the telescope and discovered the four moons of Jupiter in 1610, and noted that these moons orbited Jupiter. That a planet could have smaller objects in orbit around it cast serious doubts on Aristotle's geocentric model, and the Catholic Church placed Galileo under house arrest for the last nine years of his life because he published findings that called the Aristotelian model, which was seen as accepted church doctrine, into question. Isaac Newton showed that the motion of objects on Earth and the motion of celestial bodies are governed by the same set of natural laws. Newton's work advanced the concepts of heliocentrism and the idea that rational investigation can reveal the inner workings of nature. The Catholic Church's opposition to evolutionary theory was based on its overarching view that the advances of the scientific revolution challenged its authority.

*H*ow quickly does evolution happen? We tend to think of evolution as taking place over eons and, indeed, much of it does.

However, experiments with a Caribbean species of lizard have shown that natural selection can work very quickly, over the course of months, not millennia.

Yes, experiments! While enough evidence has been gathered in support of evolution for scientists to consider it fact, the time frames involved with most evolutionary processes have largely eluded the experimental method. But researcher Jonathan B. Losos, who has spent many years investigating genetic changes in the tiny lizard, *Anolis sagrei*, has found a way to use the experimental method to study evolution.

Losos and his team identified 12 Caribbean cays—tiny islands, some no larger than a football field—with natural *Anolis sagrei* populations. On half of those islands, they introduced a predator, the curly-tailed lizard, *Leiocephalus carinatus*. The other six islands were a control group with no such introduction.

The team predicted that the predator would place a selective pressure on the lizards, one that would cause individuals with longer legs and faster running ability to better survive in the short term. And indeed they did. Six months after introducing the predators, the team found that half the lizards on the experimental islands were gone, but the remaining population had longer legs—probably because those with shorter legs were eaten.

However, it was the second six months that provided the strongest evidence for how quickly natural selection can work. Losos' team predicted that the remaining lizards would take to the trees and shrubs in order to survive, but because long legs are cumbersome on small twigs, natural selection would then favor shorter legs.

Again, the team's predictions were supported. Six months later, compared to the control islands, the average leg length of *Anolis sagrei* on the experimental islands was significantly shorter, more in line with arboreal species of the lizard on other islands.

Would future generations maintain the changes? A hurricane in 2004 wiped out the experiment, but earlier studies in which *Anolis sagrei* populations were introduced to islands with no preexisting populations indicated that such changes could become permanent in as little as 14 years.

Meanwhile, the new study indicates how quickly natural selection can work to change a species—and how scientific experimentation can be used to study evolutionary processes.

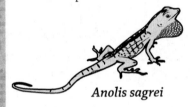

Anolis sagrei

Leiocephalus carinatus

The Jurmain textbook lists some of the many contributors to the development of evolutionary theory. The idea that evolution was a natural process was put forward by Charles Darwin's grandfather Erasmus Darwin, and was further developed by George-Louis Leclerc de Buffon, the French naturalist who recognized the relationship between the external environment and living forms. Jean-Baptiste Lamarck was the first to propose a mechanism for how evolution might occur. But, at that time, there was no knowledge of genetics, and the way inheritance worked was unclear. Lamarck's ideas were widely accepted, even by Charles Darwin. However, in time, the logical flaw in Lamarck's hypothesis became apparent and it was eventually superceded by Darwin and Wallace's theory of evolution by natural selection. That theory was lent support by the work of Charles Lyell, who refined the theory of **uniformitarianism**, the notion that the geological processes in the past are the same as they are now. This indicated that the earth was very old, and it gave a larger time span for evolution to occur in a generational sense. The ideas of Thomas Malthus on population growth and competition for scarce resources also contributed to the formation of the theory of evolution by natural selection.

As mentioned in the previous paragraph, Jean-Baptiste Lamarck was the first to try to explain a mechanism for the evolutionary process, however erroneously. Lamarck proposed that organic forms could be altered depending on the environmental circumstances in which they lived. Using the giraffe as an example, Lamarck posited that if a particular part of the body had to be used for a vital purpose, "fluids and forces" would modify that body part to meet the demand placed upon it. The giraffe's neck would get longer as it stretched to reach the food found in the upper branches of trees. Then this new trait, an elongated neck, in this case, would be passed on to offspring.

Darwin's evolutionary theory differs from Lamarck's in critical ways. Darwin's theory states that traits do not evolve during an individual's lifetime, but rather show up in offspring if the genetic information for them is contained within the eggs and sperm of the parents. The giraffe illustration on page 33 of the Jurmain textbook offers a good explanation of differences between the Lamarck view and the Darwin-Wallace view of natural selection. Individuals with traits better suited for survival in a particular environment are more likely to survive and reproduce offspring with those traits than individuals without them. Thus, there will be a higher frequency of those desirable traits for that environment in the next generation.

Darwin saw the process of natural selection as follows:

1. All species can reproduce at a faster rate than food supplies can increase.

2. All species have biological variation.

3. In each generation, there are more offspring produced than can survive. Because there are limited resources, there is competition between individuals.

4. Individuals that possess favorable traits (e.g., speed, protective color, and resistance to disease) for their environment will survive and reproduce better than individuals without those traits.

5. The environmental context determines whether or not a trait is beneficial for survival.

6. Traits are inherited and passed on to the next generation. Individuals with the favorable traits produce more offspring over time; hence, those traits become more common in the population.

7. Over long periods of geological time, successful variations accumulate in the population, so later generations may appear quite distinct from ancestral ones. (Think of the example of the moths from the video.) Thus, in time, a new species may appear.

8. Geographical isolation may lead to the formation of a new species because as groups of a species are separated from one another, each group adapts to its own environment and responds to different selective pressures. Eventually, they both look different and have enough genetic differences to be considered separate species. (Think of the finches in the Jurmain textbook and the foxes in the video.)

There are a few important points to remember about the mechanisms of evolution:

1. *A trait must be inherited (genetically based) if natural selection is to act on it.*

2. *Natural selection cannot occur without population variation in inherited characteristics.* If every Monarch butterfly had the exact same wing pattern, that is the only wing pattern that could be inherited and there would be no variation in the next generation.

3. *Fitness is a relative measure that changes as the environment changes.* **Fitness** is differential **reproductive success** based on a favorable response to the environment. The members of a species that have the traits most favorable to survival in a particular environment will be the most fit, meaning they will have the most reproductive success.

4. *Natural selection can only act on traits that affect reproduction.* That is, if a characteristic shows up later in life, natural selection has no opportunity to influence it because the traits in question have already been passed to offspring. Some studies suggest that heart disease, for example, is influenced by hereditary factors. However, the disease affects people later in life, after they have already had offspring. If there were deleterious traits present, they would have been passed to the offspring before they became noticeable in the parent.

When Darwin's *On the Origin of Species* was published more than 150 years ago, the debate concerning evolution had already begun. Many Christians were particularly offended because evolutionary theory seemed to contradict the special creation of man and woman as depicted in Genesis. Today, most Christians in the United States don't believe in the biblical depictions literally, but surveys show that many Americans are convinced that evolution does not occur. A study, which was published in *Science* in 2006 and was coauthored by Michigan State University, the National Center for Science Education, and Kobe University in Japan, found that, when it comes to public acceptance of evolution, the United States ranked thirty-third among the 34 countries surveyed (only Turkey ranked lower). This study found that in the United States, the number of adults who accepted evolution declined from 45 percent in a 1985 survey to 40 percent in the 2005 survey. Among the factors contributing to this rejection of evolutionary principles, the study's researchers identified Americans' poor understanding of biology, the introduction of evolution into political discussions, and a literal interpretation of the Bible by a small but vocal group of **Christian fundamentalists** in the United States.

Religion and science are two ways to explain natural phenomena. Religion is a faith-based belief system, while science is based in the scientific method of hypothesis testing. The conflict between these two ways of knowing has emerged primarily in the content of science curriculum in our public schools, where Christian fundamentalists seek to qualify and supplement the teaching of evolution with religious-based ideas. Beginning with the Scopes trial in 1925 and continuing into the twenty-first century with school boards in various parts of the United States, opposition to the teaching of evolution has played out primarily in the legal arena. And ultimately, evolution has prevailed. Creationism, or the belief that the universe was created by an omnipotent being, has been proposed as an alternative view to evolution, and there are even a few scientists engaged in the search for evidence to support this view and refute the existing evidence for evolution. The introduction of the concept of intelligent design in the mid-1980s was an attempt to avoid the clearly religious implications of creationism. Intelligent design theory is based on the idea that complex biological phenomena such as the eye could not have evolved through a process that depends on random variation and incremental change over time. Instead, there must be a "designer" involved. However, the U.S. District Court declared in 2005 that "ID (intelligent design) is not science and cannot be adjudged a valid, acceptable scientific theory. . . . [It] is grounded in theology, not science."

While debates continue, decades of experimental research in genetics and related fields have accumulated to support the validity of evolutionary theory. The dynamics of natural selection, outlined more than 150 years ago by Charles Darwin, provide an important foundation for understanding how life evolved on our planet. This historical background serves as a prologue for understanding how physical anthropologists study fossil remains as well as populations of living organisms to document how these organisms have changed over time to exhibit different characteristics and traits—concepts that will be explored further in the lessons that follow.

Review Exercises

Matching

Match each term with the appropriate definition or description.

1. __g__ biological continuity
2. __e__ catastrophism
3. __d__ fitness
4. __h__ fixity of species

5. __c__ natural selection
6. __b__ reproductive success
7. __f__ selective pressures
8. __a__ uniformitarianism

a. The theory that the earth's features are the result of long-term processes that operate in the present as they did in the past.

b. The number of offspring an individual produces and rears to reproductive age.

c. Genetic change or changes in the frequencies of certain traits in populations due to differential reproductive success between individuals.

d. A measure of an individual's genetic contribution to the next generation compared to that of other individuals.

e. The view that the earth's geological landscape is the result of violent cataclysmic events.

f. Forces in the environment that influence the reproductive success in individuals.

g. Condition that exists when expressions of a phenomenon continuously grade into one another so that there are no discrete categories.

h. The notion that species, once created, can never change.

Completion

Fill each blank with the most appropriate term from the list below.

binomial nomenclature
Christian fundamentalists
fertility
genome

New World
reproductively isolated
taxonomy

1. Groups of organisms that are prevented from mating and producing offspring with members of other groups are said to be __reproductively isolated__

2. __taxonomy__ is a branch of science that is concerned with the rules of classifying organisms. One of the basic conventions that are used in classification systems for naming of organisms is __binomial nomenclature__

3. The entire genetic makeup of an individual or species is called a __genome__.

4. __Christian Fund__ believe that the teachings of the Bible are infallible and are to be taken literally.

5. __Fertility__ is the ability to conceive and produce healthy offspring.

6. The discovery of the __New world__ and circumnavigation of the planet caused Europeans to reconsider some of their ideas about the earth.

Self-Test

Select the best answer.

1. The person who proposed a mechanism for the evolution that was widely accepted at the time it was proposed, but had a strong logical flaw was

   a. Jean-Baptiste Lamarck.
   b. Charles Darwin.
   c. Georges Cuvier.
   d. Charles Lyell.

2. Which of the following statements accurately describes the term *Homo sapiens?*

   a. It is a classification term based on binomial nomenclature.
   b. It represents the genus and species name of humans.
   c. It comes from a classification system developed by Thomas Malthus.
   d. a and b

3. The theory of evolution by natural selection for which Charles Darwin is famous was also independently proposed by

   a. Charles Lyell.
   b. Georges Cuvier.
   c. Alfred Russel Wallace.
   d. Thomas Malthus.

4. According to natural selection theory, which of the following statements is true?

   a. Individuals with the highest reproductive success have the greatest relative fitness.
   b. Individuals with the highest reproductive success have the most offspring that survive to reproductive age.
   c. a and b
   d. none of the above

5. The "scientific revolution" included

   a. the discoveries of Galileo.
   b. the invention of the microscope.
   c. the invention of the barometer.
   d. all of the above.

6. Darwin's theory of evolution by natural selection was proposed in the mid-nineteenth century. His knowledge was limited by constraints in the form of a lack of accurate knowledge in some areas. Constraints on nineteenth-century evolutionary theory included

    a. a universal belief in catastrophism.
    b. a lack of understanding of the exact source of variation.
    c. a widespread knowledge of genetics.
    d. none of the above.

7. Before the scientific revolution and Darwin's theory of evolution by natural selection, it was thought that

    a. life-forms changed on a regular basis.
    b. genetic recombination was very important.
    c. all organisms were created just as they exist in the present.
    d. the earth had existed for billions of years.

8. Which of the following is true about "intelligent design"?

    a. In many ways, it is just a new term for "creation science."
    b. Its proponents disagree with evolutionary scientists in that they claim that most biological functions and traits are too complicated to be explained by simple, undirected evolution, without the presence of a "creator."
    c. It is an approach that is religious and faith based, rather than being based on rigorous empirical testing.
    d. All of these statements are true.

9. During the scientific revolution, many traditional beliefs were challenged by new discoveries and knowledge. Which of the following beliefs were among those that were challenged?

    a. The sun and the other planets revolved around the earth.
    b. The earth was flat.
    c. Species were unchanging and had existed in their current form since they were created.
    d. All of the above beliefs were challenged.

10. Which of the following explains why "creation science" (or intelligent design) is **NOT** considered to be science?

    a. It is based on actual physical evidence.
    b. There are no testable hypotheses, which is necessary for scientific research.
    c. Its adherents have empirically proved their assertions.
    d. None of the above are true.

11. Which of the following must be present for natural selection to occur?

    a. uniformity in populations

    b. the absence of selective pressures

    (c.) variable inherited traits or characteristics

    d. none of these

12. The dominant color form for peppered moths changed from light to dark and back to light because

    a. predators consistently preferred light moths.

    (b.) industrial pollutants turned the tree trunks they rested on a dark color, making the light-colored moths more visible to predators. Later, industrial pollution was reduced and the tree trunks became light colored again and dark colored moths were more visible to predators.

    c. industrial pollutants turned the tree trunks they rested on a light color, making the light-colored moths more visible to predators. Later, industrial pollution was reduced and the tree trunks became dark colored again and dark colored moths were more visible to predators.

    d. genetic drift occurred.

Short-Answer Questions

1. What are the mechanisms of natural selection?

   Natural Selection States that Certain traits are more productive to survivale than others and those w/ those traits excel in their enviroments and pass those traits on. Where as Other Not so useful traits are weeded out. Survival of the Fittest.

2. Using Darwin's research in the Galápagos Islands as presented in the video lesson and the Jurmain textbook, give an example of a selective pressure and how it affects the evolutionary process. Darwin focused on the Finches he found on the Islands. He noticed that there were many different species of Finch that were similar to others, but all had variations w/ their beaks. They had adapted to better find food and have reporductive success.

3. How did the work of Thomas Malthus and Charles Lyell influence the development of Darwin's theory of evolution by natural selection? Malthus stated that the Human pop. reproduced to fast to maintain its food resources (Not fast enough). Lyell made the Hypothesis that the Earth had ongoing change due to Uniformitaianism. He applied these to Theories to Non-Human living organisms.

4. Although Lamarck's theory of acquired characteristics was close to being a good explanation of evolutionary change, it has a logical flaw. Why was it incorrect?

Lamarck's Theory was incorrect because evo. does not happen to an individual, but rather to a pop.

5. If all dog breeds are derived from a common ancestor, how did so many different shapes and sizes of dogs arise in such a short period of time?

Humans created + exerted Selective Pressures by breeding the animals for specific traits.

6. How did Copernicus and Galileo help to change ideas about the earth in relation to the sun and other planets during the scientific revolution. What were their contributions?

Application Questions

1. Explain the differences between the theory of natural selection and the theory of catastrophism in explaining the presence of the fossils of extinct animals, such as dinosaurs.

2. Charles Darwin did not completely understand how inherited traits were transmitted from one generation to another when he published his theory of evolution by natural selection. What ideas about inheritance were present in Darwin's time? How did Gregor Mendel's discoveries and the discovery of DNA as the material of inheritance provide a mechanism for this transmission?

3. What alternatives to evolution by natural selection have been proposed by creationists? Why don't most scientists consider these views to be scientific?

4. Outline how the Channel Islands fox could be considered an example of natural selection in action. How do they differ from other foxes? Why did they adapt in that way? What factors have contributed to the near extinction of the Channel Island fox population?

Answer Key
Matching
1. g (objective 3)
2. e (objective 3)
3. d (objective 5)
4. h (objective 1)
5. c (video lesson, segment 3; objective 4)
6. b (video lesson, segment 3; objective 5)
7. f (video lesson, segment 3; objective 5)
8. a (objective 3)

Completion
1. reproductively isolated (objective 3)
2. Taxonomy; binomial nomenclature (video lesson, segment 1; objective 3)
3. genome (objective 7)
4. Christian fundamentalists (objective 8)
5. Fertility (objective 6)
6. New World (objective 2)

Self-Test

1. a. is the correct answer. Jean-Baptiste Lamarck presented the "Theory of Acquired Characteristics," which proposed that characteristics acquired during an individual's lifetime could be passed to the next generation. This idea has a logical flaw in that many acquired characteristics are not directly heritable, such as losing an arm or working out a lot so that you have huge muscles. (objective 3)

2. d. is the correct answer. The term *Homo sapiens* is the genus and species name of humans that is based on a binomial nomenclature system. This system was developed by Carolus Linnaeus, not Thomas Malthus. (objective 3)

3. c. is the correct answer. Alfred Russel Wallace came up with a very similar idea around the same time. Both Alfred Russel Wallace and Charles Darwin shared credit for the idea, and they presented papers on the subject at the same time. (objective 4)

4. c. is the correct answer. Individuals with the greatest reproductive success tend to have more offspring that survive to reproductive age, and this gives them greater relative fitness. (objective 5)

5. d. is the correct answer. All of these inventions contributed to the "scientific revolution" discussed in the Jurmain textbook. (objective 2)

6. b. is the correct answer. At the time, scientists did not know anything about genetics and they did not know how variation was passed from one generation to the next. (objective 7)

7. c. is the correct answer. In the past, it was thought that all existing organisms were unchanging and existed exactly as they were created. People also thought that the earth had been created fairly recently, for some, as recently as 4004 B.C. We now know that the earth has existed for billions of years. (objective 1)

8. d. is the correct answer. All of the statements are true of "intelligent design." (objective 8)

9. d. is the correct answer. All of the stated concepts were widely believed before the scientific revolution, and many of the new discoveries during that time challenged those beliefs. (objective 2)

10. b. is the correct answer. Creation scientists generally do not conduct research that involves the empirical testing of hypotheses. This kind of testing is essential to scientific research. (objective 8)

11. c. is the correct answer. Variation in a population is important for natural selection to occur. If a population is uniform (i.e., all clone-like), all individuals will have the same response to selective pressures, and there will be no differential reproduction. (objective 5)

12. b. is the correct answer. Prior to the Industrial Revolution, most peppered moths were light colored, later the dark form became predominant due to industrial pollution turning the tree trunks they rested on a dark color. Once the pollution was reduced, the tree trunks returned to a light color and the light-colored moth form became predominant. (video lesson, segment 4; objective 6)

Short-Answer Questions

Your answers should include the following:

1. Individuals in a population vary in inherited characteristics. The environment exerts a selective force that favors some individuals over others. Because of this, some individuals will have higher reproductive success than others. This produces a change in the proportion of individuals in a population with certain genetic combinations. (video lesson, segment 3; objective 5)

2. Even though the various finches of the Galápagos Islands have a common ancestor, their beak sizes and shapes have evolved differently. Some have long, narrow beaks capable of extracting insects hidden under the bark of trees. In this case, the selective pressure was the ability to get at the insects living in tree bark. Finches with long, narrow beaks were best adapted to exploit this food source, and they left behind more offspring with that characteristic. Other Galápagos finches have short, thick beaks capable of breaking open large seeds. In this case, the selective pressure was the ability to break open large, tough seeds. Those that could do so gained more food from seeds found on the island, and they left more offspring with that characteristic. (video lesson, segment 3; objective 6)

3. Thomas Malthus proposed the idea that population sizes could increase exponentially if not checked by a limited resource of some kind. This then meant that there must be some competition for resources. This idea was important to Darwin's formation of a mechanism by which evolution could occur. Charles Lyell proposed that the world was much older than previously thought. He developed this hypothesis mainly by fleshing out the idea that the geological processes observed in the present are the same as those that have occurred in the past, thus some geological structure must be millions of years old. The theory of uniformitarianism contributed to Darwin's theory by providing a large time frame during which evolution could occur. (video lesson, segment 1; objective 3)

4. Lamarck tried to address the knowledge that traits are somehow transferred from one generation to the next, but he didn't know exactly how this happened. To explain this transfer, he proposed that that characteristics acquired during an individual's lifetime could be passed to the next generation. This idea has a logical flaw in that many acquired characteristics are not directly heritable. For example, if you lose an arm, you generally do not have one-armed offspring. Or, if you become very heavily muscled, your offspring will not be born with built-up muscles. (video lesson, segment 1; objective 3)

5. The large variety of dog breeds present today was achieved through artificial selection. Humans have bred dogs for certain characteristics, such as short legs. They chose the dogs with the shortest legs and bred them together. Then they chose the offspring with the shortest legs and crossbred them, repeating this process until they had a very short-legged dog breed. The same process can be applied to height, color, tail length, ear length, and other characteristics. (objective 6)

6. Copernicus proposed that the earth revolved around the sun along with the other planets. Galileo supported Copernicus using mathematics and logic to support his observations. (objective 2)

Application Questions

Your answers should include the following:

1. The theory of natural selection explains the presence of extinct forms, such as dinosaurs, in two ways. One is that the life-form became extinct because it could not adapt to ecological circumstances or because it was outcompeted by another type of organism. *Tyrannosaurus rex* is a good example of this theory. The other option is that a particular life-form did adapt to ecological changes, and its form has changed as it has adapted. The horse is a good example of this theory. We have fossil forms of horses that go back many millions of years, and the gradual changes that took place can be discerned from the fossil record. Catastrophism was proposed by Georges Cuvier as a way to explain the remains of extinct animals while preserving a creationist point of view. He proposed that extinct animals were no longer present on the earth because the entire species died out after some catastrophic ecological event, such as a flood or a fire. If this point of view is accepted, it is possible to believe that all organisms were created as they are now, without change over time, and that some were simply lost as a result of a large-scale ecological event. Some species have certainly died out during catastrophic events; a notable example is the demise of the dinosaurs 65 million years ago that probably resulted from a meteor crashing into the earth. Nevertheless, there is also a great deal of evidence for change in form over time. (objectives 3, 4, & 5)

2. During Darwin's time, it was thought that traits passed from one generation to the next through a blending process that involved both parents. Offspring were thought to express the traits of both parents. It was not known exactly how the blending worked. This lack of knowledge about the mechanism by which inheritance occurred was, by Darwin's own admission, the greatest weakness of his theory. Gregor Mendel's work contributed to the discovery of that mechanism by demonstrating that each individual has two particles for each heritable trait—one particle from each parent (see Chapter 4, pp. 82–83). Although Mendel presented his research during Darwin's lifetime, in the middle of the nineteenth century, the results of his research were not well known, and his findings were rediscovered in the early part of the twentieth century. Later, DNA was identified and the material of this particulate inheritance and the structure of DNA was worked out in 1953. Once scientists understood that genes, the segments of DNA that are coded for a specific protein, were the actual particles of inheritance, the mechanism for how inherited traits were passed from one generation to the next was complete. Darwin's theory was supported by this new information, and researchers have added to this knowledge at a rapidly increasing rate. (objective 7)

3. Creationists have proposed that living organisms, like ourselves, are too complex to be explained by simple evolution by natural selection without some kind of divine intervention or guidance. They have tried to create a "science" around this paradigm. However, religion and science take very different approaches to explaining natural phenomena. Scientific analyses are based on observable, measurable data. This data is generally generated through the empirical testing of hypotheses (see the discussion of the scientific method in Chapter 1 of the textbook). The theory of evolution by natural selection has been repeatedly supported through many scientific avenues, from paleobiology to genetics. Religion is based on a system of beliefs based on

faith rather than empirical testing. Faith does not depend on measurable data. These beliefs vary from religion to religion, and religious leaders have often had to change their positions in light of information discovered through scientific observation and testing. For example, Roman Catholic church doctrine maintained the infallibility of the geocentric model of the universe (the sun and the other planets revolved around the earth) for many years after it was clearly shown that the earth and the other planets revolved around the sun. Eventually the church had to change its position in the light of accumulated scientific knowledge that contradicted the belief in a geocentric universe. (objective 8)

4. Channel Island foxes are smaller than the grey foxes found on the Southern California mainland, from which they are descended. It is thought that a pregnant gray fox swam or drifted to Santa Rosa Island and began a new population. Subspecies are found on six of the eight Channel Islands (all but Anacapa and Santa Barbara). It is thought that these foxes became smaller than the mainland foxes through "island dwarfism." Because there are limited food resources available on most islands, it is an advantage to be smaller because less food is required for survival. Those foxes that had genetic traits that contributed to smaller body size were more likely to be adequately fed and to reproduce than foxes who did not have those traits. Over time, the population became smaller. This phenomenon is very common among island species. Island dwarfism may have occurred in some human populations, such as the recently discovered remains from the island of Flores in Southeast Asia near Java.

    The main bird of prey in the Channel Islands originally was the bald eagle. Because bald eagles concentrate on marine prey, they did not pose a great threat to the Channel Island fox population. After DDT and other pollutants wiped out the bald eagle populations in Southern California (although they have recently been returning), the remaining large birds of prey were golden eagles, which specialized in preying on land animals. Golden eagle predation, as well as other factors (including an outbreak of canine distemper), had a large negative effect, and Channel Island foxes came close to extinction in the 1990s. Humans have begun to intervene to save the Channel Island fox species from extinction, and the populations are starting to increase in size. (video lesson, segment 4; objective 6)

Lesson Review

Lesson 2: Development of Evolutionary Theory

PLEASE NOTE: Use this matrix to guide your study and achieve the learning objectives of this lesson. It will also help you to view the video, which defines and demonstrates important concepts and principles as they relate to everyday life and actual case studies.

Learning Objective	Textbook	Student Guide	Video Lesson
1. Describe accepted beliefs about the origin of life-forms and their relationships to one another prior to the development of evolutionary thought.	pp. 28–29	Key Terms: 2; Matching: 4; Self-Test: 7.	
2. Discuss major discoveries of the scientific revolution.	pp. 29–31	Completion: 6; Self-Test: 5, 9; Short-Answer: 6.	
3. State the major contributions of key figures in the history of evolutionary thought.	pp. 31–36	Key Terms: 3, 4, 5, 6, 7, 13; Matching: 1, 2, 8; Completion: 1, 2; Self-Test: 1, 2; Short-Answer: 3, 4; Application: 1.	Segment 1: *Natural Science Before Darwin*
4. Describe the discovery of the principles of natural selection by Darwin and Wallace.	pp. 36–41	Key Terms: 1; Matching: 5; Self-Test: 3; Application: 1.	Segment 3: *Natural Selection*
5. Explain the major tenets of natural selection.	pp. 41–42	Key Terms: 8, 9, 10; Matching: 3, 6, 7; Self-Test: 4, 11; Short-Answer: 1; Application: 1.	Segment 3: *Natural Selection*

Learning Objective	Textbook	Student Guide	Video Lesson
6. Give examples of natural selection in action.	pp. 42–45	Key Terms: 11; Completion: 5; Self-Test: 12; Short-Answer: 2, 5; Application: 4.	Segment 3: *Natural Selection* Segment 4: *Natural Selection in Action*
7. Describe some of the constraints on nineteenth-century evolutionary theory.	pp. 45–46	Key Terms: 12; Completion: 3; Self-Test: 6; Application: 2.	
8. Explain why evolutionary theory is controversial for some groups today.	pp. 46–49	Key Terms: 14; Completion: 4; Self-Test: 8, 10; Application: 3.	

LESSON 3

Lesson 1: The Anthropological Perspective

Lesson 2: Development of Evolutionary Theory

 Lesson 3:   Biological Basis of Life

Lesson 4: Heredity & Evolution

Lesson 5: Macroevolution

Lesson 6, Part I : The Living Primates

Lesson 6, Part II : Overview of the Fossil Primates

Lesson 7: Primate Behavior

Lesson 8: Methods of Paleoanthropology

Lesson 9: The First Bipeds

Lesson 10: A New Hominin

Lesson 11: Premodern Humans

Lesson 12: Origin & Dispersal of Modern Humans

Lesson 13: Patterns of Variation

Lesson 14: Patterns of Adaptation

Lesson 15: Legacies of Human Evolutionary History

Lesson 16: Applied Anthropology

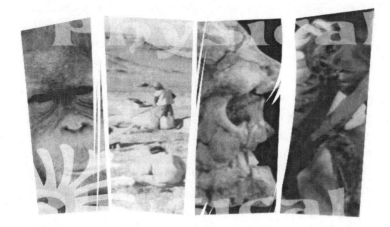

Biological Basis of Life

Checklist

For the most effective study of this lesson, complete the following activities in this sequence.

Before Viewing the Video

❑ Read the Preview, Learning Objectives, and Viewing Notes below.

❑ Read Chapter 3, "The Biological Basis of Life," pages 50–79, in *Introduction to Physical Anthropology*.

What to Watch

❑ After reading the textbook assignment, watch the video for Lesson 3, *Biological Basis of Life*.

After Viewing the Video

❑ Briefly note your answers to the questions listed at the end of the Viewing Notes.

❑ Review the Summary below.

❑ Review all reading assignments for this lesson, including the Viewing Notes in this lesson.

❑ Write brief answers to the "Critical Thinking Questions" at the end of Chapter 3 in the textbook.

❑ Complete the Review Exercises below. Check your answers with the Answer Key and review when necessary.

❑ Use the Lesson Review matrix found at the end of this lesson to review and assess your knowledge of each Learning Objective.

Preview

Perhaps you have read a newspaper article about a person released from prison because his DNA sample proved his innocence. Perhaps you watch *CSI* on television and have seen the forensic investigators take cheek swab samples from suspects to check their DNA. What does this have to do with anthropology, you might ask. As seen on various television shows and as commonly carried out for human health purposes, genetic testing is an application of genetics that is currently used in anthropological work.

Lesson 3 covers the basics of cell division, chromosomes, and the structure and function of DNA. To better understand human evolution and adaptation in a broad sense, it helps to know how life is organized at the cellular and molecular levels. The information presented in this lesson was almost entirely discovered after Charles Darwin and Alfred Russel Wallace presented their work on evolution through natural selection. By studying the fundamental units of life, the cell and DNA that is contained within the nucleus of the cell, you will more fully understand the biology of evolution.

Concepts to Remember

❋ Lesson 2 introduced the term **natural selection**, which refers to change or changes in the frequencies of certain genetic traits in populations due to differential reproductive success between individuals. As you study this lesson, consider genetics in relationship to natural selection.

Learning Objectives

After you complete this lesson, you should be able to:

1. Identify the basic molecular and structural components of cells, and recall the two basic types of cells. (pp. 52–53)

2. Describe the basic structure of DNA and its components. (pp. 53–54)

3. Describe the replication of DNA and the basic processes of protein synthesis. (pp. 54–59)

4. Distinguish between DNA and RNA, and define what is meant by the genetic code. (pp. 52–53, 57–59)

5. Explain what genes and chromosomes are. (pp. 59–69)

6. Contrast the processes and functions of mitosis with those of meiosis. (pp. 69–73)

7. Explain the evolutionary significance of meiosis. (pp. 73–74)

8. Describe examples of problems with meiosis. (pp. 74–75)

9. Discuss examples of recent discoveries in the study of genetics. (pp. 75–79)

At this point, read Chapter 3, "The Biological Basis of Life," pages 50–79.

Viewing Notes

The video offers a detailed explanation of DNA, with some specific examples of DNA discoveries that apply to anthropology, forensic medicine, and genetic research. **DNA**, or **deoxyribonucleic acid**, is the double stranded molecule found in every organism on Earth; it contains an organism's genetic code. Studying the DNA of Neandertal fossils offers clues to this extinct species of hominid. Although discussed more fully in later lessons, Neandertals are a distinct group within the genus *Homo*, inhabiting Europe and Southwest Asia from approximately 125,000 to 30,000 years ago. Our visual interpretation of Neandertals is the stereotypical "caveman" from films and television: individuals with extremely muscular bodies, large noses, no chins, sloping foreheads, and bony brow ridges over their eyes. Neandertal bone fragments are being examined at the Joint Genome Institute (JGI), and scientists there are attempting to extract nuclear DNA from the fragments in hopes that it can help determine the time period of the last common ancestor of humans and Neandertals. A **genome** is the entire genetic makeup of an individual or species. Acquiring the complete genome of Neandertal may never be achieved, particularly since the genetic samples to date are taken from fragments of bone and, some say, contamination of samples is a possibility. In spite of this, recent studies being released have indicated that scientists have been successful in analyzing some nuclear DNA from Neandertals. They are reported to have a FOXP2 gene that is virtually identical to that of humans. This gene is involved in the development of language and may indicate that Neandertals had similar language capabilities to humans.

The video then shifts to a crime laboratory in Phoenix, Arizona, where technicians analyze DNA found at crime scenes. Since DNA is contained in every cell nucleus, a crime scene offers almost endless opportunities to find DNA samples that have been left behind. Finding good samples of DNA can lead to identification of both victims and suspects. An entire sequence of DNA bases makes up what is called a gene. According to the Jurmain textbook, a **gene** is an entire sequence of DNA bases that specifies the order of amino acids in an entire protein, a portion of a protein, or any functional product. A gene may be made up of hundreds or thousands of DNA bases organized into coding and noncoding segments. The technicians at crime labs know that each sample of DNA is unique to a specific individual and that understanding the organization of genes is crucial in order to build a DNA profile of an individual. First of all, technicians must understand that genes have a locus, which is their position, or "address," on the chromosome, and that genes can have different variations, which are called alleles. **Alleles** are alternate forms of genes that occur at the same locus.

Genes are the key to the inheritance of both healthy and deleterious traits from parents during sexual reproduction. In the video, Rose-Lynn Fisher suffers from Gaucher (go-SHAY) disease. People with Gaucher disease are unable to produce an enzyme called beta-glucocerebrosidase. The most common symptoms are enlargement of the liver and spleen, anemia, reduced platelets (which help the blood to clot), bone pain, bone infarctions (cell death caused by loss of blood supply), and osteoporosis. Some people with the disease may display no symptoms, while others have severe skeletal problems or liver damage. Rose-Lynn's DNA code for this enzyme, which she inherited from her parents, had an alteration in the base sequence. As the narrator states in the video, Rose-Lynn's "genetic future was set in motion at the moment the egg cell from her mother and the sperm cell from her father came together." Egg and sperm cells are formed during **meiosis**, the cell division that leads to the development of new individuals. Each of Rose-Lynn's parents carried one defective allele and one normal one for the necessary enzyme production. Rose-Lynn inherited one faulty allele from her father and one from her mother, which gave her the disease. If she had inherited one faulty allele and one normal allele, she would have been a carrier of Gaucher disease (like her parents), but it would not have manifested in physical symptoms.

Questions to Consider

✳ How do crime lab researchers obtain and analyze DNA for use in criminal investigations?

✳ What role does cell division, especially meiosis, play in increasing genetic diversity?

✳ What evidence exists for Neandertals to be considered a different species from our own?

Watch the video for Lesson 3, *Biological Basis for Life*.

      Segment 1: *Genes & Alleles*
      Segment 2: *Cell Division & Mutation*

Key Terms and Concepts

Page references are keyed to *Introduction to Physical Anthropology*, 13th edition.

1. **proteins:** Three-dimensional molecules that serve a wide variety of functions through their ability to bind to other molecules. (p. 52; video lesson, introduction; objective 1)

2. **nucleus:** A structure (organelle) found in all eukaryotic cells. The nucleus contains chromosomes (nuclear DNA). (p. 52; objective 1)

3. **molecules:** Structures made up of two or more atoms. Molecules can combine with other molecules to form more complex structures. (p. 52; objective 1)

4. **DNA (deoxyribonucleic acid):** The double-stranded molecule that contains the genetic code. DNA is a main component of chromosomes. (p. 52; video lesson, introduction; objectives 2 & 4)

5. **RNA (ribonucleic acid):** A single-stranded molecule, similar in structure to DNA. Three forms of RNA are essential to protein synthesis. They are *messenger RNA (mRNA), transfer RNA (tRNA),* and ribosomal RNA (rRNA). (p. 53; objective 4)

6. **cytoplasm:** The semifluid, gel-like substance contained within the cell membrane. The nucleus and numerous structures involved with cell function are found within the cytoplasm. (p. 53; objective 1)

7. **protein synthesis:** The manufacture of proteins, the assembly of chains of amino acids into functional protein molecules. Protein synthesis is directed by DNA. (p. 53; objective 1)

8. **mitochondria (*sing.*, mitochondrion):** Structures contained within the cytoplasm of eukaryotic cells that convert energy, derived from nutrients, to a form that is used by the cell. (p. 53; objective 1)

9. **ribosomes:** Structures composed of a form of RNA called ribosomal RNA (rRNA) and protein. Ribosomes are found in a cell's cytoplasm and are essential to the manufacture of proteins. (p. 53; objective 1)

10. **mitochondrial DNA (mtDNA):** DNA found in the mitochondria; mtDNA is inherited only from the mother. (p. 53; objective 1)

11. **somatic cells:** Basically, all the cells in the body except those involved with reproduction. (p. 53; objective 1)

12. **gametes:** Reproductive cells (eggs and sperm in animals) developed from precursor cells in ovaries and testes. (p. 53; objective 1)

13. **zygote:** A cell formed by the union of an egg cell and a sperm cell. It contains the full complement of chromosomes (in humans, 46) and has the potential of developing into an entire organism. (p. 53; objective 1)

14. **nucleotides:** Basic units of the DNA molecule, composed of a sugar, a phosphate, and one of four DNA bases. (p. 53; video lesson, introduction; objective 2)

15. **replicate:** To duplicate. The DNA molecule is able to make copies of itself. (p. 54; objective 3)

16. **enzymes:** Specialized proteins that initiate and direct chemical reactions in the body. (p. 55; video lesson, introduction; objective 3)

17. **complementary:** In genetics, referring to the fact that DNA bases form pairs (called base pairs) in a precise manner. For example, adenine can bond only to thymine. These two bases are said to be *complementary* because one requires the other to form a complete DNA base pair. (p. 55; objective 3)

18. **hemoglobin:** A protein molecule that occurs in red blood cells and binds to oxygen molecules. (p. 56; video lesson, introduction; objective 3)

19. **hormones:** Substances (usually proteins) that are produced by specialized cells and that travel to other parts of the body, where they influence chemical reactions and regulate various cellular functions. (p. 56; objective 3)

20. **amino acids:** Small molecules that are the components of proteins. (p. 57; video lesson, introduction; objective 3)

21. **messenger RNA (mRNA):** A form of RNA that is assembled on a sequence of DNA bases. It carries the DNA code to the ribosome during protein synthesis. (p. 57; objectives 3 & 4)

22. **codon:** Triplets of messenger RNA bases that code for specific amino acids during protein synthesis. (p. 58; objectives 3 & 4)

23. **transfer RNA (tRNA):** The type of RNA that binds to specific amino acids and transports them to the ribosome during protein synthesis. (p. 58; objectives 3 & 4)

24. **mutation:** A change in DNA. The term can refer to changes in DNA bases (specifically called point mutations) as well as to changes in chromosome number and/or structure. (p. 58; objectives 3 & 4)

25. **gene:** A sequence of DNA bases that specify the order of amino acids in an entire protein, a portion of a protein, or any functional product (e.g., RNA). A gene may be made up of hundreds or thousands of DNA bases organized into coding and noncoding segments. (p. 59; video lesson, introduction; objective 5)

26. **genome:** The entire genetic makeup of an individual or species. In humans, it is estimated that each individual possesses approximately 3 billion DNA nucleotides. (p. 60; objective 9)

27. **noncoding DNA:** DNA that does not direct the production of proteins. However, such DNA segments may produce other important molecules, so the term *noncoding DNA* is not really accurate. (p. 60; objective 5)

28. **exons:** Segments of genes that are transcribed and are involved in protein synthesis. (The prefix *ex-* denotes that these segments are expressed). (p. 60; objective 5)

29. **introns:** Segments of genes that are initially transcribed and then deleted. Because they are not expressed, they are not involved in protein synthesis. (p. 60; objective 5)

30. **regulatory genes:** Genes that influence the activity of other genes. Regulatory genes direct embryonic development and are involved in physiological processes throughout life. They are extremely important to the evolutionary process. (p. 61; objective 5)

31. **homeobox genes:** An evolutionarily ancient family of regulatory genes that directs the development of the overall body plan and the segmentation of body tissues. (p. 61; objective 5)

32. **sickle-cell anemia:** A severe inherited hemoglobin disorder in which red blood cells collapse when deprived of oxygen. It results from inheriting two copies of a mutant allele. The type of mutation that produces the sickle-cell allele is a point mutation. (p. 64; objective 5)

33. **point mutation:** A change in one of the four DNA bases. (p. 66; video lesson, segment 2; objective 5)

34. **chromatin:** The loose, diffuse form of DNA seen when a cell isn't dividing. When it condenses, chromatin forms into chromosomes. (p. 66; objective 5)

35. **chromosomes:** Discrete structures composed of DNA and protein found only in the nuclei of cells. Chromosomes are visible under magnification only during certain phases of cell division. (p. 66; video lesson, introduction; objective 5)

36. **autosomes:** All chromosomes except the sex chromosomes. (p. 66; objective 6)

37. **sex chromosomes:** In mammals, the X and Y chromosomes. (p. 66; objective 6)

38. **locus (*pl.*, loci):** The position on a chromosome where a given gene occurs. The term is sometimes used interchangeably with *gene*. (p. 68; video lesson, segment 1; objective 6)

39. **alleles:** Alternate forms of a gene. Alleles occur at the same locus on paired chromosomes and thus govern the same trait. But because they are different, their action may result in different expressions of that trait. (p. 69; video lesson, segment 1; objective 5)

40. **karyotype:** The chromosomes of an individual, or what is typical for a species, viewed microscopically and displayed in a photograph. The chromosomes are arranged in pairs and according to size and position of the centromere. (p. 69; video lesson, segment 2; objective 5)

41. **mitosis:** Simple cell division; the process by which somatic cells divide to produce two identical daughter cells. (p. 69; video lesson, segment 2; objective 6)

42. **meiosis:** Cell division in specialized cells in ovaries and testes. Meiosis involves two divisions and results in four daughter cells, each containing only half the original number of chromosomes. These cells can develop into gametes. (p. 70; video lesson, segment 2; objective 6)

43. **recombination:** The exchange of genetic material between homologous chromosomes during meiosis; also sometimes called *crossing over*. (p. 73; video lesson, segment 2; objective 6)

44. **clones:** Organisms that are genetically identical to another organism. The term may also be used in referring to genetically identical DNA segments, molecules, or cells. (p. 73; objectives 6 & 7)

45. **random assortment:** The chance distribution of chromosomes to daughter cells during meiosis; along with recombination, the source of variation resulting from meiosis. (p. 73; objective 7)

46. **polymerase chain reaction (PCR):** A method of producing thousands of copies of a DNA sample. (p. 75; objective 9)

47. **Human Genome Project:** An international effort aimed at sequencing and mapping the entire human genome, completed in 2003. (p. 77; video lesson, introduction; objective 9)

Summary

As noted on page 5 of the Jurmain textbook, genetics is the study of "gene structure and action and the patterns of inheritance of traits from parent to offspring." Genetic mechanisms are the foundation of evolutionary change. While you may not have studied the science of this process, you have surely engaged in the everyday conversation about it. Consider a family reunion.

"You have your mother's eyes."
"You look exactly like cousin Fred."
"How on earth did you get so tall? Everyone in our family is short."

Lesson 2 explained that traits are passed from one generation to the next. This lesson offers a fundamental understanding of how that process takes place. It begins with cells, the basic unit of life in all living organisms. Bacteria consist of one cell; adult humans are made up of perhaps 1,000 billion cells. Yet the cells of all living organisms share many similarities as a result of their common evolutionary past.

There are two types of cells: somatic cells and gametes. **Somatic cells** are the cellular components of body tissue, such as muscle, bone, heart, and brain. **Gametes**, which are also called the sex cells, come in two types: egg cells, which are produced in a female's ovaries, and sperm cells, which are developed in a male's testes. When they join during sexual reproduction, they form a **zygote**, a cell that has the potential of developing into a new individual. In this way, gametes transmit genetic information from parent to offspring, determining which traits are passed along in a complex genetic code that is contained within our inherited DNA. In other words, this process can explain why you look like cousin Fred.

Cellular functions are directed by DNA. DNA is a long **molecule** that has the form of a double helix, resembling a ladder that has been twisted. **Nucleotides**, even smaller molecules, are the basic units of DNA. There are four components of nucleotides: sugar, phosphates, and one of four nitrogenous bases—adenine (A), guanine (G), thymine (T), and cytosine (C). One type of base can bond with only one other type, A with T and G with C. This exact formula is essential to a DNA molecule's ability to **replicate**, or make copies of itself, which is necessary for cell division. Growth and development of organisms and tissue repair after an injury take place because of the cell's ability to divide. Cells multiply by dividing in a way that ensures that each new cell receives a full set of genetic material, but for this to happen, DNA must first replicate. The most important property of DNA is that it can replicate itself.

DNA also directs **protein synthesis** within the cell. Growth, repair, and maintenance of all cells are dependent upon **proteins**. Some proteins are structural components of tissues; others bind directly to DNA to regulate genetic functions. Some proteins are **enzymes**, or material that initiates and enhances chemical reactions. One example is the digestive enzyme lactase, which breaks down lactose, or milk sugar, into simpler sugars. Enzymes and proteins are discussed further in Lesson 14. Proteins are composed of small molecules called **amino acids**. What makes one protein different from another is the number of amino acids in each one, as well as the *sequence* in which these amino acids are arranged. The Jurmain textbook states on page 57 that, "In part, DNA is a recipe for making a protein, since it's the sequence of DNA bases that ultimately determines the order of amino acids in a protein."

With some possible exceptions on the dating scene, no one would ever mistake a chimpanzee for a human being. And yet, genetically anyway, we are more similar than one might think. In fact, we are almost identical.

These are the results of a study that compared the human genome to that of a chimpanzee. Mapping of the human genome was completed in 2003 by the Human Genome Project, an international effort that included scientists from 18 countries. Shortly thereafter, the Chimpanzee Sequencing and Analysis Consortium completed its mapping of the chimpanzee genome.

The chimp genome was overlaid on the human genome to find points of comparison. The result: only 35 million base pairs out of 3 billion are different. That's 1.2%!

But that number is misleading. Besides the individual base pairs, there are a large number of duplicated sequences scattered around both human and chimpanzee genomes. Most of these duplications take place at sites that are prone to breakage, and those differ in the two species.

Taking the duplications into account increases the differences to 3.9%. So the DNA of humans and chimpanzees is 96.1% identical.

It is the differences, rather than the similarities, that are most interesting. The 3.9% represents sequences that have diverged over the past 6 million years since we shared a common ancestor.

Among those differences are areas of extreme variability—such as that found in the DNA coding for immune system function. This makes sense, since organisms that can readily adapt to new pathogens are more likely to survive.

Other differences show up in areas of extreme stability, "genetic deserts" as they've been called, that show little variation. One such stable area in the human genome that does not appear in the chimpanzee DNA is related to the production of speech.

On the other hand, the chimpanzee genome contains a gene that protects against Alzheimer's, one that has lost its function in humans. Further results may reveal genetic reasons why humans fall prey to some other illnesses, like HIV and malaria, to which chimps seem immune.

As exciting as these results are, they are just the beginning. We may have mapped the human genome and that of other species, but learning to read these maps may resolve some of humanity's most compelling mysteries: Where did we come from? What does it mean to be human? How can we increase our longevity? The answers are in our genes.

Here are some key characteristics of DNA code:

1. It appears in triplet form, since each amino acid is specified by a sequence of three base pairs.

2. It is continuous. There are no pauses separating one **codon**, or triplet of **messenger RNA** bases that refers to a specific amino acid during protein synthesis, from another. If a base is deleted, the entire frame would be moved, changing the message "downstream" for successive codons (messengers). A gross alteration is termed a frame-shift mutation.

3. It is redundant. Many amino acids are specified by more than one codon. This redundancy is useful because it serves as a safety net by helping to reduce the likelihood of severe consequences if there is a change, or mutation, in a DNA base. The Jurmain textbook uses the example of the amino acid alanine, which aids in the metabolism of glucose, a simple carbohydrate that the body uses for energy. Alanine helps keep blood sugar levels stable during exercise; it also strengthen the immune system by producing antibodies. Four different DNA triplets—CGA, CGG, CGT, and CGC—are the code for alanine. So, in the code CGA, if A mutates to G, the resulting triplet will still result in alanine.

4. Its code is universal, in that the same basic DNA structure is found in all life-forms.

A **gene** is a sequence of DNA that specifies the order of amino acids in an entire protein or a portion of a protein. Very simply, it tells the proteins what to do. A gene may be composed of only a few hundred bases, or it may be thousands of bases long. Some proteins result from the action of only one gene, and others are produced by two or more. Some genes regulate others, producing enzymes and other proteins that can turn other segments of DNA on or off. Gene regulation also means that some genes are expressed only at certain times during the organism's life cycle. For example, in humans, certain genes on the Y chromosome only function during the development of the embryo, and they are what "tells" the embryo to become male. Gene action is an incredibly complex phenomenon that scientists still do not fully understand.

As mentioned earlier, sometimes redundancy protects the DNA sequence so that a **mutation**, when a gene changes, is not harmful to an organism. But that is not always the case. The Jurmain textbook explains that **sickle-cell anemia** is a severe **hemoglobin** disorder that results when an individual inherits two copies of the allele that causes the disorder. In the video, Rose-Lynn's Gaucher disease is the result of a genetic mutation received from both parents. As a result, Rose-Lynn's DNA code for the amino acid sequence that would produce beta-glucocerebrosidase had a change in its base sequence, meaning that she could not produce the particular enzyme. Both parents must carry the mutation for the child to have the disease. If the parents are carriers of this genetic disorder, there is a one in four chance that an offspring will have Gaucher disease, a one in two chance a child won't have the disease but will be a carrier herself, and a one in four chance that a child will neither be a carrier nor have the disease. As you learned in Lesson 2, a new mutation can only have evolutionary significance if it is passed on to offspring through the gametes. Natural selection can play a strong role in determining how a mutation affects a population. So mutations that are beneficial to a species will ultimately end up becoming more frequent in the population and will be passed on to offspring more often, because mature organisms displaying this characteristic will have a better chance at survival and reproduction.

One kind of cell division is called **mitosis**, the simple cell division of the somatic cells that occurs during growth and tissue repair and replacement. During mitosis, the cell divides one time to produce two daughter cells that are genetically identical to each other and to the original cell. Each new daughter cell inherits an exact copy of all 46 chromosomes. Mitosis is different from meiosis in a crucial way. Meiosis requires a second division to reduce the number of chromosomes present in each gamete by one half.

Both the egg cell and the sperm cell result from **meiosis**, a process that occurs only in sex cells and is characterized by two divisions resulting in four daughter cells. Before meiosis occurs, the gametes contain the full complement of chromosomes (46 in humans), but after the first division, called "reduction division," the number of chromosomes in the two resulting daughter cells is 23, or half the original amount. This reduction of chromosome number is a critical feature of meiosis because the resulting gamete, with its 23 chromosomes, may eventually unite with another gamete that also has 23 chromosomes (see page 70 of Jurmain), which results in a **zygote** that contains the full complement of DNA, or 46 chromosomes. **Chromosomes** are discrete structures composed of DNA and protein and are found only in the nuclei of cells. They are visible under magnification only during certain phases of cell division. There are two basic types of chromosomes: autosomes and sex chromosomes. **Autosomes** carry genetic information that governs all physical characteristics in the body, except sex determination. The **sex chromosomes** are called X and Y and determine maleness and femaleness. Interestingly, the Jurmain textbook points out that among mammals, all genetically normal females have two X chromosomes (XX) and they are female only because that don't have a Y chromosome. (In other words, female is the default setting for mammals.) All genetically normal males have one X and one Y chromosome (XY). In other classes of animals, such as birds or insects, primary sex determination is governed by various other chromosomal mechanisms.

Meiosis occurs in all sexually reproducing organisms and is important in the evolutionary progression of a species. This **random assortment**, or chance distribution of chromosomes to daughter cells during meiosis, results in great genetic diversity. As you learned from the peppered moth example in Lesson 2, there must be variation in a population for natural selection to occur. The most common color of these moths before the nineteenth century was a mottled gray color, providing good camouflage as they rested on lichen-covered trees. The dark moths were fewer in number because they stood out against the lighter color of the trees and were thus eaten by birds more frequently. As a result, they reproduced less frequently. When increased air pollution killed the lichen and turned the trees a darker color, the lighter-colored moths decreased substantially and the darker moths became more prevalent. Importantly, the genes for the darker color were always in the gene pool of the moth population, which added the diversity upon which natural selection acted. If that variation did not exist, chances are the peppered moth species would not have survived.

Since the discovery of DNA structure in the 1950's, the field of genetics has progressed at a rapid pace. For instance, in 1986, a technique called **polymerase chain reaction (PCR)** was developed that enables scientists to make copies of small samples of DNA for subsequent analysis. This technique is a hugely significant innovation because, in the past, the samples collected at crime scenes often contained such small surviving quantities of fragmented DNA that adequate analysis was not possible.

A controversial aspect of genetic engineering is **cloning**, the creation of an organism that is genetically identical to another organism, through the process of nuclear transfer. This process is complicated and entails several stages, each of which must work perfectly for a cloned organism to be successfully produced. Again, there is rancorous debate surrounding this procedure. A number of mammals have been successfully cloned, but, as of the publication of this student guide, all attempts to clone nonhuman primates have failed, and how successful cloning will be in the future has yet to be determined. The Jurmain textbook reports that long-term studies have not yet shown whether cloned animals live a normal lifespan. Studies on mice suggest that they do not.

Genetic discoveries and technologies advance daily. As a result, human beings are called on to adjust to a continuous stream of new innovations in such areas as human cloning, genetically modified foods, biological weapons, the development of reproductive technologies, stem cell breakthroughs, and new medical treatments based on genetic knowledge. In order to understand genetics and evolution, the main topics of this physical anthropology course, understanding cell function is essential. Lesson 3 provides the basics necessary to more fully comprehend the lessons to come at the same time that it offers important beginning information on the molecular basis of all life, how this varies from species to species, and ultimately, how human beings fit into the biological continuum that is life on this planet.

Review Exercises

Matching

Match each term with the appropriate definition or description.

1. __c__ autosomes
2. __g__ cytoplasm
3. __d__ DNA
4. __a__ exon
5. __h__ intron
6. __b__ meiosis

7. __f__ messenger RNA
8. __k__ mitochondria
9. __e__ mitosis
10. __l__ nucleus
11. __i__ sex chromosomes
12. __f__ transfer RNA

a. Segments of genes that are transcribed and are involved in protein synthesis.

b. Cell division in specialized cells in ovaries and testes; these cells can develop into gametes.

c. All chromosomes except the sex chromosomes.

d. Deoxyribonucleic acid, the double-stranded molecule that contains the genetic code and is a main component of chromosomes.

e. Simple cell division; the process by which somatic cells divide to produce two identical daughter cells.

f. A form of RNA that is assembled on a sequence of DNA bases; it carries the DNA code to the ribosome during protein synthesis.

g. The portion of the cell contained within the cell membrane, excluding the nucleus.

h. Segments of genes that are initially transcribed and then deleted; therefore, they are not expressed (they aren't involved in protein synthesis).

i. In mammals, the X and Y chromosomes.

j. The type of RNA that binds to specific amino acids and transports them to the ribosomes during protein synthesis.

k. Structures contained within the cytoplasm of eukaryotic cells that convert energy, derived from nutrients, into a form that is used by the cell.

l. A structure (organelle) found in all eukaryotic cells. The nucleus contains chromosomes (nuclear DNA).

Completion

Fill each blank with the most appropriate term from the list below.

amino acids
DNA (deoxyribonucleic acid)
gametes
gene
nucleotide

point mutation
polymerase chain reaction (PCR)
random assortment
RNA (ribonucleic acid)
somatic cells

1. The two main types of cells are _Somatic cells_ and _gametes_.
2. A _nucleotide_ is made up of a sugar molecule, a phosphate unit, and a nitrogenous base.
3. During the process of protein synthesis, strings of _amino acids_ are linked together at the ribosome.
4. _RNA_ differs from _DNA_ in that it contains a different kind of sugar molecule and it can have a single stranded form.
5. A sequence of DNA that specifies the sequence of amino acids in an entire protein is called a _gene_ ✗.
6. Meiosis increases genetic variation through the _random assortment_ of chromosomes during the process of producing gametes.
7. A change in one of the four DNA bases is called a _point mutation_
8. DNA fingerprints help scientists identify crime suspects using _polymerase chain reaction. (PCR)_ technology.

Self-Test

Select the best answer.

1. Scientists have discovered traces of cells that date back to about
   a. 37 million years ago.
   b. 370 million years ago.
   c. 3.7 billion years ago.
   d. 370 million years ago.

2. Mitochondria are organelles that have which of the following characteristics?
   a. They produce energy that is used by cells.
   b. They have their own distinct DNA.
   c. They have a folded membrane within their oval-shaped bodies.
   d. All of the above are true.

3. Within a DNA molecule, which of the following base pairs bond with one another?
   a. adenine and guanine
   b. thymine and adenine
   c. cytosine and thymine
   d. none of the above

4. During DNA replication, new DNA strands are formed in which of the following ways?

    a. A new strand is formed as enzymes break the bonds between base pairs and new nucleotides are attracted to the open bases. In this way, half of the DNA molecule consists of the old strand and the other half is newly formed.

    b. A new DNA molecule is formed by observing the old molecule and putting together new base pairs in that order. In this way, the old molecule is intact and an entirely new copy is made.

    c. Using the old DNA molecule as a model, two entirely new DNA molecules are constructed and the old one is destroyed and discarded.

    d. All of these; new DNA molecules may be formed by any of these methods.

5. Messenger RNA performs which of the following functions during protein synthesis?

    a. It carries information for making proteins from the cytoplasm to the nucleus.

    b. An mRNA molecule forms on a DNA template strand, detaches, and goes to a ribosome where it is read.

    c. It carries amino acids to the ribosome where they are joined to form a protein.

    d. It induces the strands in a DNA molecule to separate and permanently replaces the former strand with new nucleotides.

6. Homeobox (HOX) genes are important regulatory genes in which of the following ways?

    a. They are evolutionarily ancient and highly conserved.

    b. They play an important role in the development of the body plan.

    c. They interact with other genes during the development process.

    d. All of these statements are true.

7. DNA is a biological molecule that

    a. is a universal code that translates into the form of all living organisms.

    b. is not necessary for most organisms to survive.

    c. is not found in bacteria.

    d. specifies amino acids in groups of four base pairs.

8. Sickle-cell anemia is

    a. a condition that results from an enzyme deficiency.

    b. caused by a diet deficient in iron.

    c. caused by a point mutation in the beta chain of the hemoglobin molecule.

    d. none of the above.

9. In terms of chromosome number, humans have

    a. more chromosomes than any other organism.

    b. fewer chromosomes than frogs.

    c. fewer chromosomes than chimpanzees and gorillas.

    d. more chromosomes than chimpanzees and gorillas.

10. Cell division in somatic cells that results in two identical daughter cells is called mitosis. Mitosis occurs

    a. during growth and development.
    b. to repair injured tissues.
    c. to replace older cells with new ones.
    d. as a result of all of the above.

11. In humans, at the completion of the meiotic process, each resulting cell contains

    a. 48 chromosomes.
    b. 23 chromosomes.
    c. 46 chromosomes.
    d. 24 chromosomes.

12. The process of recombination during meiosis

    a. consists of members of homologous chromosome pairs exchanging bits of genetic material.
    b. contributes to an increase in genetic variation in the resulting gametes.
    c. has no effect on the genetic content of the gametes that are produced.
    d. involves a and b.

13. "Down syndrome" is a condition associated with having three copies of chromosome 21. Which of the following statement is **FALSE**?

    a. This condition arises because of nondisjunction during meiosis.
    b. This condition occurs because of random assortment during meiosis.
    c. This condition occurs more often in children born to older women.
    d. This condition is associated with various developmental and health problems.

14. The polymerase chain reaction (PCR)

    a. is used in DNA fingerprinting.
    b. is a technique where scientists can make many copies of a DNA sample.
    c. has many applications in forensic science and evolutionary biology.
    d. involves all of the above.

15. Recombinant DNA technology involves transferring the genes from the cells of one species into those of another. This technology has been used to produce insulin for human consumption using which of the following organisms?

    a. bacterial cells
    b. yeast cells
    c. plant cells
    d. none of the above

Short-Answer Questions

1. What are the characteristics of the DNA code?

   DNA is a double-stranded molecule that contains the genetic code and makes up all living organisms.

2. What is the difference between chromatin and chromosomes?

   Chromosomes are made from chromatin during cell division they group together and become visable (w/ Microscope), Chromatin is what happens when cell division is not present.

3. List four of the chromosomal abnormalities that are associated with nondisjunction in the sex chromosomes. Describe the effects of each one.

   (female) XXX - Posible inability to reproduce + Mental impa.
   (male) XYY - Maybe more hight.
   (female) XO - inability to give birth + Physical disformity.
   (male) XXY - More Femine, Slight Mental impair.

4. List and define five structural components of cells and their functions within the cell.

   DNA: Contains genetic code.

   Nucleus: Contains Chromosomes

   Cytoplasm: Semi-fluid gel like substence contains Chromo.

   Ribosomes: a form of RNA Contained in Cyto.

5. DNA crime labs use cells left behind by crime suspects to extract DNA that they then use in making a DNA fingerprint of the suspect. Name three sources of those cells that were mentioned in the video for this lesson.

   From the handle of a gun, tag in Shirt, Sneeze Residue + Blood or body Fluid.

Application Questions

1. What is a mutation? How do mutations contribute to the evolutionary process and natural selection? To the presence of certain diseases such as Gaucher disease? What is another disease that is genetically based? A mutation is a change in the DNA strand. W/out mutation all humans would be carbon copies w/ one another. Sickel cell anemia is a disease that is genetically based.

2. Compare and contrast the processes of mitosis and meiosis. How does meiosis contribution to an increase in genetic variation? Why doesn't mitosis contribute to genetic variation in this way? Mitosis is simple cell divison, they break apart to become 2 daughter cells. Meiosis is a cell division that produces a sex chromo. these are givin to the off spring and it Means that the off spring won't get the excate same DNA as the parents. Mitosis creates Nothing New.

3. How do crime labs use DNA to build a DNA profile of a crime suspect? To identify the (PCR) remains of an unknown individual? Please outline some of the steps and procedures involved. DNA tells the police weather the suspect is male or female. Their health and can trace them back to the family. It places the suspect at the scene of the crime. and overall helps them solve the crime

Answer Key
Matching
1. c (objective 6)
2. g (objective 1)
3. d (video lesson, introduction; objectives 2 & 4)
4. a (objective 5)
5. h (objective 5)
6. b (video lesson, segment 2; objective 6)
7. f (objectives 3 & 4)
8. k (objective 1)
9. e (video lesson, segment 2; objective 6)
10. l (objective 1)
11. i (objective 6)
12. j (objectives 3 & 4)

Completion
1. somatic cells; gametes (objective 1)
2. nucleotide (video lesson, introduction; objective 2)
3. amino acids (video lesson, introduction; objective 3)
4. RNA; DNA (objective 4)
5. gene (video lesson, introduction; objective 5)
6. random assortment (objective 7)
7. point mutation (objective 5)
8. polymerase chain reaction (PCR) (objective 9)

Self-Test
1. c. is the correct answer. Single-celled organisms appeared at least 3.7 billion years ago. (objective 1)
2. d. is the correct answer. Mitochondria have all of these characteristics; they contain their own DNA, have folded membranes, and produce energy that is used by cells. (objective 1)
3. b. is the correct answer. Thymine and adenine bond with one another. (objective 2)
4. a. is the correct answer. New DNA molecules are formed when the molecule is separated into complementary strands and new nucleotides come in and attach to the open bases. (objective 2)

5. b. is the correct answer. An mRNA strand forms on a DNA template, detaches, and carries that information to the ribosome where proteins are assembled. (objectives 3 & 4)

6. d. is the correct answer. Homeobox (HOX) genes are very ancient and highly conserved; they are important in the development process and in interacting with other genes. (objective 5)

7. a. is the correct answer. DNA represents a universal code that translates in the form of all organisms, from bacteria to humans, by using a triplet code to specify amino acids. (objective 4)

8. c. is the correct answer. Sickle-cell anemia is caused by a genetic point mutation in the beta chain of a hemoglobin molecule. Hemoglobin is a large protein found in red blood cells, it is not an enzyme, and since it is a genetic disease, diet does not have an effect on its expression. (objective 5)

9. c. is the correct answer. Humans have 46 chromosomes. Chimpanzees and gorillas have 48 chromosomes, and frogs have 26 chromosomes. There are many organisms with more chromosomes than humans and many with fewer chromosomes. (objective 5)

10. d. is the correct answer. Mitosis occurs during growth and development to repair tissues and to replace older cells. (video lesson, segment 2; objective 6)

11. b. is the correct answer. At the completion of meiosis, each cell (gamete) contains 23 chromosomes. (video lesson, segment 2; objective 6)

12. d. is the correct answer. Recombination results in the exchange of bits of genetic material between homologous chromosomes. This results in an increase in the genetic variation of the resulting gametes. At the end of the meiotic process, no two gametes are identical. (video lesson, segment 2; objective 7)

13. b. is the correct answer. The random assortment process is not related to Down syndrome. It is caused by nondisjunction during meiosis. (objective 8)

14. d. is the correct answer. PCR is a technique where many copies of DNA are made from a sample. This "amplified" DNA is used in DNA fingerprinting, forensic analyses, medicine, and evolutionary biology. (objective 9)

15. a. is the correct answer. Insulin is routinely produced by using recombinant DNA technology with bacterial cells. (objective 9)

Short-Answer Questions

Your answers should include the following:

1. The DNA code is universal among all living organisms. The base pairs are the same, and they bond in the same way. Amino acids are specified in triplet form, by a sequence of three base pairs. The code is continuous in that there are no spaces between triplets in the code. The code is also redundant in that many amino acids are specified by more than one codon. (video lesson, introduction; objective 2)

2. Chromatin is the loose uncoiled form of DNA. It is in this form when it is directing cellular functions. When the cell is ready to divide, it becomes tightly coiled around proteins into structures called chromosomes. (objective 5)

3. An XXX female is usually normal but may have a higher chance of sterility or mental impairment. An XYY male is usually normal but tends to be taller on average. An XO female has Turner syndrome, which results in sterility and some physical abnormalities. An XYY male has Klinefelter syndrome, which results in reduced fertility, some feminization of the body, and mental impairment in some cases. (objective 8)

4. The structural components that are listed in the Jurmain textbook include the nucleus, organelles, DNA, RNA, cytoplasm, mitochondria, and ribosomes. The nucleus is where the DNA is contained. There are many organelles in cells that perform many different functions. The DNA contains the genetic code. RNA serves many functions in the cell and it is particularly important in protein synthesis. The cytoplasm is a semifluid substance inside the cell membrane in which the organelles and other cell structures are embedded. Mitochondria produce energy within a cell, and ribosomes provide a site where protein synthesis occurs. (objective 1)

5. Cells from a suspect can be found on the handle of a gun, on the tag of a shirt, in an areas where the suspect sneezes, as well as in blood or other bodily fluids left behind by the suspect. (video lesson, segment 2; objective 9)

Application Questions

Your answers should include the following:

1. Mutations are changes in DNA structure and they can be in the form of point mutations, where one nitrogenous base is substituted for another, or changes in chromosome number or structure. Mutations are thought to be the source of all biological variation. Natural selection acts on these variants and can shape the evolutionary process. Gaucher disease results from a point mutation inherited from both parents that produces an enzyme deficiency. Basically, the mutation causes the enzyme to not function properly. This causes imbalances in the body and a build-up of toxic substances that the body cannot get rid of without the enzyme. Gaucher disease is usually treated by giving the patient the appropriate enzyme to compensate for the deficiency. Conditions such as sickle-cell disease, cystic fibrosis, muscular dystrophy, phenylketoneuria, hemophilia, and many others also result from point mutations. (video lesson, segment 2; objective 5)

2. Mitotic cell division results in the production of two identical daughter cells. It functions in the growth and development of an organism, the repair of injured tissue, and the replacement of older cell with newer cells. The meiotic division process results in four daughter cells that are not identical and that have half the number of chromosomes of somatic cells. These cells are called gametes. During sexual reproduction, a gamete from one individual combines with that of another to produce a new individual with a unique combination of genes. Meiosis contributes to genetic variation through recombination and through the random assortment of the members of homologous chromosome pairs during cell division. Since the main function of mitosis is to maintain a specific individual, producing genetic variants within one individual

would not be advantageous. In this situation, it makes sense that mitosis does not produce variants. (video lesson, segment 2; objectives 6 & 7)

3. DNA found at a crime scene is analyzed in the lab. PCR is often used to amplify a small amount of DNA to create larger samples. A DNA fingerprint is made from these samples. This DNA fingerprint is then matched up with DNA fingerprints made from DNA taken from the victim and the suspect(s). This allows investigators to place suspects at the scene of a crime. To identify the remains of an unknown individual, investigators will analyze the DNA of close family members of a missing person. If the remains are found in an areas where a missing person was last known to be, it allows the investigators to focus their analysis on the family of a specific individual. Certain markers in the DNA fingerprints of family members are matched to the DNA fingerprint of the unidentified remains. If there is a close match, then the unidentified remains can be assigned to a specific individual. This technique was used extensively in identifying the fragmented remains of the victims of the September 11 tragedy. (video lesson, segment 2; objective 9)

Lesson Review

Lesson 3: Biological Basis of Life

PLEASE NOTE: Use this matrix to guide your study and achieve the learning objectives of this lesson. It will also help you to view the video, which defines and demonstrates important concepts and principles as they relate to everyday life and actual case studies.

Learning Objective	Textbook	Student Guide	Video Lesson
1. Identify the basic molecular and structural components of cells, and recall the two basic types of cells.	pp. 52–53	Key Terms: 1, 2, 3, 6, 7, 8, 9, 10, 11, 12, 13; Matching: 2, 8, 10; Completion: 1; Self-Test: 1, 2; Short-Answer: 4.	Introduction
2. Describe the basic structure of DNA and its components.	pp. 53–54	Key Terms: 4, 14; Matching: 3; Completion: 2; Self-Test: 3, 4; Short-Answer: 1.	Introduction
3. Describe the replication of DNA and the basic processes of protein synthesis.	pp. 54–59	Key Terms: 15, 16, 17, 18, 19, 20, 21, 22, 23, 24; Matching: 7, 12; Completion: 3; Self-Test: 5.	Introduction
4. Distinguish between DNA and RNA, and define what is meant by the genetic code.	pp. 52–53, 57–59	Key Terms: 4, 5, 21, 22, 23, 24; Matching: 3, 7, 12; Completion: 4; Self-Test: 5, 7.	Introduction
5. Explain what genes and chromosomes are.	pp. 59–69	Key Terms: 25, 27, 28, 29, 30, 31, 32, 33, 34, 35, 39, 40; Matching: 4, 5; Completion: 5, 7; Self-Test: 6, 8, 9; Short-Answer: 2; Application: 1.	Introduction Segment 1: *Genes & Alleles* Segment 2: *Cell Division & Mutation*

Learning Objective	Textbook	Student Guide	Video Lesson
6. Contrast the processes and functions of mitosis with those of meiosis.	pp. 69–73	Key Terms: 36, 37, 38, 41, 42, 43, 44; Matching: 1, 6, 9, 11; Self-Test: 10, 11; Application: 2.	Segment 1: *Genes & Alleles* Segment 2: *Cell Division & Mutation*
7. Explain the evolutionary significance of meiosis.	pp. 73–74	Key Terms: 44, 45; Completion: 6; Self-Test: 12; Application: 2.	Segment 2: *Cell Division & Mutation*
8. Describe examples of problems with meiosis.	pp. 74–75	Self-Test: 13; Short-Answer: 3.	
9. Discuss examples of recent discoveries in the study of genetics.	pp. 75–79	Key Terms: 26, 46, 47; Completion: 8; Self-Test: 14, 15; Short-Answer: 5; Application: 3.	Introduction Segment 2: *Cell Division & Mutation*

LESSON 4

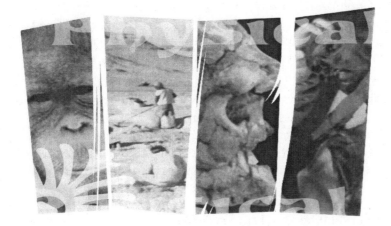

4

Heredity & Evolution

Checklist

For the most effective study of this lesson, complete the following activities in this sequence.

Before Viewing the Video

❏ Read the Preview, Learning Objectives, and Viewing Notes below.

❏ Read Chapter 4, "Heredity and Evolution," pages 80–109, in *Introduction to Physical Anthropology*.

What to Watch

❏ After reading the textbook assignment, watch the video for Lesson 4, *Heredity & Evolution*.

After Viewing the Video

❏ Briefly note your answers to the questions listed at the end of the Viewing Notes.

❏ Review the Summary below.

❏ Review all reading assignments for this lesson, including the Viewing Notes in this lesson.

❏ Write brief answers to the "Critical Thinking Questions" at the end of Chapter 4 in the textbook.

❏ Complete the Review Exercises below. Check your answers with the Answer Key and review when necessary.

❏ Use the Lesson Review matrix found at the end of this lesson to review and assess your knowledge of each Learning Objective.

Preview

If you took biology in high school, you very likely spent some time in class seeing whether you and your classmates could curl your tongues lengthwise into a tube shape. You can either do it or you can't. Are you trying right now? In any event, the goal of your biology class was to teach you that the ability to curl your tongue, or your blood type, or eye color, or being born with a cleft chin, or hitchhiker thumb, or attached or unattached earlobes are all examples of genetically inherited traits that are passed to you from your parents one way or another.

The study of genetics has grown exponentially during the past fifty years. The foundation of our current knowledge concerning heredity was set forth by an Austrian monk named Gregor Mendel 150 years ago. In Lesson 3, we discussed the structure and function of cells and the DNA they contain, as well as the roles they play in heredity. Lesson 4 examines the various ways traits are inherited from generation to generation, and the principles covered here form much of the basis of modern genetics, which has direct relevance to the evolutionary process.

Concepts to Remember

※ Lessons 1 and 2 defined **evolution** as a change in the genetic structure of a population, often in reference to the appearance of a new species. **Natural selection** refers to genetic changes in the frequencies of certain traits in populations as a result of differential reproductive success between individuals and is crucial to Darwin's theory. Lesson 4 further explores the details of evolution by natural selection by looking at how this process influences inheritance.

※ Lesson 3 introduced the two basic types of chromosomes: autosomes and sex chromosomes. **Autosomes** carry genetic information that governs all physical characteristics except sex determination. In mammals, the **sex chromosomes** are the X and Y chromosomes.

Learning Objectives

After completing this lesson, you should be able to:

1. Describe the work of Gregor Mendel that led to the principles of segregation and independent assortment. (pp. 82–83, 85–86)

2. Describe the concepts of dominant, recessive, and codominant alleles, genotype and phenotype, and heterozygous and homozygous genotypes. (pp. 83–88)

3. Discuss Mendelian inheritance in humans, including autosomal and sex-linked traits and genetic disorders. (pp. 86–93)

4. Provide examples of polygenic inheritance, and how it differs from Mendelian inheritance. (pp. 93–98)

5. Describe the modern synthesis of evolution, and define evolution from a microevolutionary perspective. (pp. 98–99)

6. Identify and describe the factors that produce and redistribute variation, including mutation, gene flow, genetic drift, recombination, and natural selection. (pp. 100–105)

7. Use the malaria and sickle-cell trait distribution to discuss the action of natural selection on variation. (pp. 106–108)

At this point, read Chapter 4, "Heredity and Evolution," pages 80–109.

Viewing Notes

Gregor Mendel's influence on our understanding of inherited characteristics is apparent in the California sweet pea nurseries seen in the video for Lesson 4. Commercial growers plan the height, color, and fragrance of the plants they sell to consumers. All living things are categorized by their observable characteristics or **phenotype**, the physical expression of genetic instructions. **Mendelian traits** are coded at a single locus and involve dominant or recessive genes, and growers can crossbreed plants for desired characteristics. Humans have Mendelian traits, too. A cleft chin, for instance, is the result of a single dominant gene at one locus. Most traits are **polygenic**, influenced by genes at two or more loci. Skin color and height are two polygenic traits.

Some diseases and medical disorders have a genetic basis for transmission. Tay-Sachs disease is common among Ashkenazi Jews, whose ancestry can be traced to the Jews of Central and Eastern Europe, and the disease causes degeneration of the nervous system beginning when a child is about six months old. The affected individual rarely lives beyond his or her third birthday. Huntington disease is another well-documented, fatal genetic disorder, determined at a single locus, that affects the individual in mid-life. Genetics can be instrumental in preventing some types of disease transmissions. The work of Dr. Donald Mosier, a physician at the Scripps Research Institute in La Jolla, California, is shown in the video. Mosier explains that researchers have identified people who seemed to be immune to HIV/AIDS, even though they engaged in high-risk sexual behavior. As it turns out, these people possess a "deletion mutation," or an allele that has lost a section of DNA. People who are **homozygous**, who possess two copies of the deletion allele, are immune to the AIDS virus. These individuals lack a certain protein on the surface of the T4, a type of white blood cell that HIV invades. The HIV virus generally uses this protein to latch onto and to gain entry into the cell. For individuals who lack this protein, the HIV virus cannot get into the cell and it cannot reproduce. As a result, the infection never takes hold. Recall from Lesson 2 that natural selection would act on this mutation, selecting for those who have it. These individuals, because of their immunity, have a better chance of survival and of reproducing offspring who would then live long enough to reproduce—the measure of reproductive fitness.

The video also illustrates how anthropology looks at genetics to find out how the Chumash Indians in Santa Barbara, California, have managed to survive in that area for the last 5,000 years. Researchers believe that over time, the Chumash have exchanged genes with the general population, a process known as **gene flow**. The Jurmain textbook discusses mitochondrial inheritance in regard to the Chumash as well. This is another genetic aspect generating increasing interest among scientists as they work to trace components of inheritance among populations. Mitochondria contain several copies of mtDNA, which is distinct from nuclear DNA. It is important to stress that both sexes inherit all of their mtDNA through their mothers and, since mtDNA is inherited from only one parent, meiosis and recombination don't occur. Rather, all the variation found in mtDNA is a result of mutation. This mtDNA has been used to trace ancestral relationships among humans and to study genetic variability between individuals and populations. The video points out that the Chumash from the Channel Islands off the coast of California belong to a distinctive genetic type, an mtDNA type that is not found anywhere else in California. The researchers believe these Chumash are distinct because of genetic drift. **Genetic drift** occurs when the genetic makeup of a small population changes simply because they have been isolated from the general population. Additionally, comparing DNA samples of living tribe members with a sample from a human skeleton found in Alaska that is 10,300 years old has helped anthropologists hypothesize this tribe's migration.

Questions to Consider

✺ How do alleles that have the "deletion mutation" in regard to HIV/AIDS compare with the Hb^S allele in regard to malaria?

✺ How do gene flow and genetic drift figure in the investigation of the Chumash Indians' heritage?

Watch the video for Lesson 4, *Heredity & Evolution*.

Segment 1: *Non-Mendelian Inheritance*
Segment 2: *Microevolution at Work*
Segment 3: *Gene Flow & Genetic Drift*

Key Terms and Concepts

Page references are keyed to *Introduction to Physical Anthropology,* 13th edition.

1. **selective breeding:** A practice whereby animal or plant breeders choose which individual animals or plants will be allowed to mate based on the traits (such as coat color or body size) they hope to produce in offspring. Animals or plants that don't have the desirable traits aren't allowed to breed. (p. 82; objective 1)

2. **hybrids:** Offspring of parents that differ from each other with regard to certain traits or certain aspects of genetic makeup; heterozygotes. (p. 82; objective 1)

3. **principle of segregation:** Genes (alleles) occur in pairs because chromosomes occur in pairs. During gamete formation, the members of each pair of alleles separate so that each gamete contains one member of each pair. (p. 83; video lesson, introduction; objective 1)

4. **recessive:** Describing a trait that isn't expressed in heterozygotes; also refers to the allele that governs the trait. For a recessive allele to be expressed, an individual must have two copies of it (i.e., the person must be homozygous). (p. 83; video lesson, introduction; objective 2)

5. **dominant:** In genetics, describing a trait governed by an allele that's expressed in the presence of another allele (i.e., in heterozygotes). Dominant alleles prevent the expression of recessive alleles in heterozygotes. (This is the definition of *complete dominance.*) (p. 83; video lesson, introduction; objective 2)

6. **homozygous:** Having the same allele at the same locus on both members of a pair of chromosomes. (p. 84; video lesson, introduction; objective 2)

7. **heterozygous:** Having different alleles at the same locus on members of a pair of chromosomes. (p. 84; video lesson, introduction; objective 2)

8. **genotype:** The genetic makeup of an individual. Genotype can refer to an organism's entire genetic makeup or to the alleles at a particular locus. (p. 85; video lesson, introduction; objective 2)

9. **phenotypes:** The observable or detectable physical characteristics of an organism; the detectable expressions of genotypes, frequently influenced by environmental factors. (p. 85; video lesson, introduction; objective 2)

10. **principle of independent assortment:** The distribution of one pair of alleles into gametes does not influence the distribution of another pair. The genes controlling different traits are inherited independently of one another. (p. 85; objective 1)

11. **random assortment:** The chance distribution of chromosomes to daughter cells during meiosis; along with recombination, a source of genetic variation (but not new alleles) from meiosis. (p. 85; objective 1)

12. **Mendelian traits:** Characteristics that are influenced by alleles at only one genetic locus. Examples include many blood types, such as ABO. Many genetic disorders, such as sickle-cell anemia and Tay-Sachs disease, are also Mendelian traits. (p. 87; video lesson, introduction; objective 3)

13. **antigens:** Large molecules found on the surface of cells. Several different loci govern various antigens on red and white blood cells. (Foreign antigens provoke an immune response.) (p. 88; objective 3)

14. **codominance:** The expression of two alleles in heterozygotes. In this situation, neither allele is dominant or recessive so they both influence the phenotype. (p. 88; objective 3)

15. **pedigree chart:** A diagram showing family relationships; it is used to trace the hereditary pattern of particular genetic (usually Mendelian) traits. (p. 89; objective 3)

16. **polygenic:** Refering to traits that are influenced by genes at two or more loci. Examples include stature, skin color, eye color, and hair color. Many (but not all) polygenic traits are also influenced by environmental factors such as nutrition. (p. 94; video lesson, segment 1; objective 4)

17. **pigment:** In reference to polygenic inheritance, molecules that influence the color of skin, hair, and eyes. (p. 94; objective 4)

18. **pleiotropy:** The capacity of a single gene to influence several phenotypic expressions. (p. 97; objective 4)

19. **variation:** In genetics, inherited differences among individuals; the basis of all evolutionary change. (p. 98; objective 5)

20. **allele frequency:** In a population, the percentage of all the alleles at a locus accounted for by one specific allele. (p. 98; video lesson, segment 2; objective 5)

21. **population:** Within a species, a community of individuals where mates are usually found. (p. 98; video lesson, segment 2; objective 5)

22. **gene pool:** All of the genes shared by the reproductive members of a population. (p. 98; objective 5)

23. **microevolution:** Small changes occurring within species, such as a change in allele frequencies. (p. 99; video lesson, segment 2; objective 5)

24. **macroevolution:** Changes produced only after many generations, such as the appearance of a new species. (p. 99; objective 6)

25. **tandem repeats:** Short, adjacent segments of DNA within a gene that are repeated several times. (p. 100; objective 6)

26. **gene flow:** Exchange of genes between populations. (p. 101; video lesson, segment 3; objective 6)

27. **genetic drift:** Evolutionary changes, or changes in allele frequencies that are produced by random factors in small populations. Genetic drift is a result of small population size. (p. 103; objective 6)

28. **founder effect:** A type of genetic drift in which allele frequencies are altered in small populations that are taken from, or are remnants of, larger populations. (p. 103; objective 6)

29. **sickle-cell trait:** Heterozygous condition where a person has one Hb^A allele and one Hb^B allele. Thus they have some normal hemoglobin. (p. 107: objective 7)

Summary

Although people have been trying to understand inherited characteristics for thousands of years, it wasn't until the last two centuries that the mechanics of inheritance were truly identified.

Gregor Mendel's experiments with garden peas established important patterns of inheritance that apply to all biological organisms, including humans. Mendel's first principle of inheritance is the **principle of segregation**. This means that the genes (alleles) for a trait separate when gametes are formed and that only one allele from each pair passes into each gamete. At fertilization, the allele pairs reform so the zygote has a full complement of chromosomes (genes). An illustration of Mendel's experiment with a pea's height is illustrated on page 84 of the Jurmain textbook. A tall plant (TT) crossed with a short plant (tt) produces a first generation, F_1, of all tall plants (Tt). The F_1 plants are all **heterozygous** tall because they each have different alleles at the specific locus for height. Tall (T) is **dominant** over short (t), meaning that tallness is expressed in all the offspring. The **recessive** allele (t) is present in the F_1 generation, but it is masked by the dominant allele and is not expressed in the offspring. The next generation, F_2, is produced when the F_1 generation is allowed to self-fertilize. The offspring consists of tall (TT or Tt) and short (tt) plants, because each parent has one dominant allele (T) and one recessive allele (t) for height that can be passed along to F_2 offspring. An effective way of determining the possible **genotypes** and **phenotypes** and their proportions in the F_2 generation is by the use of a Punnett square, found in Figure 4-5 on page 85 of the Jurmain textbook. When F_1 plants cross (Tt × Tt), the possible outcomes for the F_2 plants are TT, Tt, tT, and tt. In other words, three-fourths of the F_2 generation are tall and one-fourth are short.

Mendel also learned through his experiments that traits do not have to be inherited together. The **principle of independent assortment** states that different pairs of alleles are passed to offspring independently of each other. That is, Mendel realized that plant height has no bearing on its color. We know now that this occurs because the genes for independently assorted traits are located on different chromosomes.

Some of the information regarding dominant and recessive traits has been found to be oversimplified. As mentioned earlier, tongue curling has often been used to demonstrate a dominant gene's influence on a trait. In reality, this example is a poor one because this trait is influenced by many different genetic factors. It is not a true Mendelian trait. According to page 86 of the Jurmain textbook, "*Mendelian traits*, also called *discrete traits* or *traits of simple inheritance*, are controlled by alleles at only one genetic locus." Most Mendelian traits do not have phenotypic expressions, are biochemical in nature, and many genetic disorders result from harmful alleles that are inherited in Mendelian fashion. Table 4–1 on page 87 of the Jurmain textbook provides a list of Mendelian traits that result from both dominant and recessive alleles. For example, Tay-Sachs disease results from a Mendelian recessive allele (ts) on chromosome 15. It is a fatal condition that is seen in individuals who are homozygous for this allele, since they cannot produce an enzyme called hexosaminidase A and invariably die early in childhood. Another example of Mendelian traits in humans in the ABO system of blood groups. Dominance and recessiveness, as well as **codominance**, are clearly illustrated by this system. Codominance is seen when a person has two different alleles but, instead of one masking the other, the products of both are evident in the phenotype. When both A and B alleles are present, both A and B antigens can be detected in the individual's red blood cells.

The Jurmain textbook points out that as genetic technologies advance and change, they may guide new theories on dominance and recessiveness. However, at this time, there are important reasons to establish patterns of inheritance or whether a trait is Mendelian or not. A **pedigree chart**, which is a diagram showing family relationships in order to trace the hereditary pattern of particular genetic traits, is a way to establish these patterns. Diagrams on pages 89–93 of the Jurmain textbook illustrate how pedigree charts work. By finding out whether the locus is located on either an autosome or sex chromosome and whether it is dominant or recessive, researchers have identified six different modes of Mendelian inheritance in humans: autosomal dominant, autosomal recessive, X-linked recessive, X-linked dominant, Y-linked recessive, and mitochondrial.

Autosomal Dominant Traits: These traits are controlled by loci on autosomes. The dominant allele means that anyone who inherits just one copy will express the trait. Each person who is affected by an autosomal dominant trait also has at least one parent with the same trait.

Autosomal Recessive Traits: These traits are also influenced by loci on autosomes but show a different pattern of inheritance. An affected offspring can be produced by two phenotypically normal parents, or two parents who are both affected. The Jurmain textbook uses the example of albinism on pages 91–93. Unaffected parents who produce an albino child must both be carriers. Their genotype is Aa. The affected child is homozygous (aa) for the recessive allele that causes the abnormality. The possible outcomes for two carrier parents (Aa × AA) include AA, Aa, Aa, and aa. This is a typical phenotypical ratio of 3:1, so there is a 25 percent chance that the parents will have an affected child. (See the Punnett square in Figure 4–13 on page 92 of the Jurmain textbook.)

Sex-Linked Traits: These traits are controlled by genes located on the X and Y chromosomes. Most are influenced by genes on the X chromosomes, since most of the coding sequences on the Y chromosome are involved in determining maleness and testes function, according to the Jurmain textbook. Females have two X chromosomes, so the only way an X-linked recessive allele can be phenotypically expressed is when she is homozygous for it, which means that she has two recessive alleles. A heterozygous female is unaffected unless the alleles are dominant. Males have one Y and one X chromosome, so any allele located on their X chromosome, even a recessive one, will be expressed because they have no other allele present to counterbalance it. With only one X chromosome, males can't be homozygous or heterozygous for X-linked loci. Instead, they are referred to as hemizygous.

Mendel's pea plants were either tall or short because the phenotypic expression for height does not overlap. Instead, they fall into clearly defined categories. This condition is describe as *discrete*, or *discontinuous*. However, many traits have a wide range of phenotypic expression that forms a graded series and are called **polygenic**, or continuous traits. Human height is an example of a continuous trait. The three charts that comprise Figure 4–15 on page 94 of the Jurmain textbook illustrate the difference between continuous and discontinuous traits. Mendelian traits are governed by only one genetic locus. Polygenic characteristics are influenced by alleles at two or more loci. The video states that there are an estimated 100 genes involved in pigmentation of eyes, skin, and hair. The Jurmain textbook also adds that melanin production, crucial in the influence of skin color, is influenced by between three and six genetic loci, with each locus having at least two alleles, neither one dominant. So, there are a number of ways in which these alleles can combine to produce different levels of pigmentation. For example, if a person inherits 11 alleles that code for maximum pigmentation and only 1 allele

Who does your DNA belong to? You? All of humanity as part of the human genome? The company who processes it to make it available for study?

The question is at the heart of the difficulties faced by *The Genographic Project*, which seeks to establish patterns of human migration by analyzing DNA samples from over 700 different ethnic groups around the world.

Consider the case of John Moore, who was treated for leukemia in 1980. After he regained his health, he discovered that cells taken from his body had been cultivated and sold at a profit for medical purposes. He filed suit against the company marketing his cell line, and lost. That's right. The California Supreme Court ruled that he had no right to the cells once they were removed from his body.

He is not the only one to feel wronged. In the Amazon, the *Karitiana* people are demanding that their DNA, derived from blood samples taken by researchers in the 1970s and 1990s, be returned to them. The samples are being sold for research, not commercial purposes. Even so, because they did not understand this possible usage, the *Karitiana* feel violated at worst, or at least entitled to some of the revenues.

With the human genome mapped and genetic technology capable of manipulating DNA to create new living organisms, the question of who owns "life" is an ethical dilemma that is especially disturbing to indigenous peoples. Corporations have received patents not only for genetically modified varieties of fruits and vegetables, but also for botanical substances used by indigenous peoples for thousands of years, such as the neem tree in India. Small wonder that local groups are concerned that similar "biopiracy" might occur with samples of their blood.

All of this is wreaking havoc with efforts like *The Genographic Project*. While the intended research is mainly anthropological, some groups are wary of giving the blood samples needed to establish where humans came from, how we evolved, and how we spread across the planet.

For some peoples, religious beliefs make unthinkable the taking and processing of genetic material. To them, the genome has its own spirit, attached to the land. For other groups, a history of colonialism and its impact on their culture makes them distrustful of all things Western.

So until the question of who owns DNA is settled to everyone's satisfaction, it may be some time before the promise of using genetic research to trace human history can be fulfilled.

for reduced pigmentation, his or her skin color will be very dark. Conversely, a person who inherits more alleles for reduced pigmentation will have lighter skin color. This is an example of the additive effect—each allele that codes for melanin production makes a contribution to increase or decrease melanization. Polygenic traits account for most of the easily observable phenotypic variation seen in humans and have served as a basis for racial classification.

Phenotypes are not solely determined by the genotype. Environmental conditions can influence phenotypes as well. Nutrition, altitude, temperatures, and exposure to toxic waste and airborne pollutants all can affect phenotypes. Mendelian traits are less likely to be influenced by environmental factors. For example, the ABO blood trait is determined at fertilization and remains fixed throughout an individual's life.

This lesson discusses the genetic definition of evolution—a change in the frequency of alleles from one generation to another. In Lesson 2, Darwin's theory of evolution focused on the gradual unfolding of new varieties of life from previous forms over long periods of time. But such changes occur only with the accumulation of many small genetic changes occurring over the generations. Genetic **variation** must first be produced through genetic mutation and then distributed before such variation can be acted on by natural selection.

Mutation is the only source of completely new genetic material. If a gene is altered, a mutation has occurred. Interestingly, alleles or variation of genes are the result of mutations. Even the substitution of just one single DNA base for another, called a point mutation, can cause an allele to change. Point mutations must occur in sex cells if they are to have any evolutionary significance, because then they are passed to future generations. Mutation rates for any given trait are quite low; but when mutation is coupled with natural selection, evolutionary changes can occur more rapidly.

Gene flow is the exchange of genes between populations. Migration between populations has occurred throughout hominid history, and gene flow takes place when and if migrants interbreed. Even when people move temporarily and mate in their new locations, leaving a genetic contribution, gene flow has taken place. Good examples of this occur when, during times of war, temporarily placed soldiers mate with females in the local population. The offspring of such unions represent gene flow. Interestingly, some anthropologists have proposed that gene flow helps explain why speciation is rare among hominids throughout time, but there is no real consensus on this subject.

Genetic drift is changes in allele frequencies produced by random factors, and it is directly tied to small population size. Genetic drift occurs in small populations that are not exposed to gene flow. When there are relatively few new offspring each generation because of small population size, some individuals may contribute disproportionately to the future generations, or some alleles can be lost because they are less common than other ones and simply by chance do not get passed to the next generation. Other more common alleles might not get lost, but will experience frequency change for the same reasons. Drift has been a factor in producing evolutionary changes in certain circumstances, but since it is random, the effects have been nondirectional.

Natural selection provides directional change in **allele frequency** relative to specific environmental factors. A good example of natural selection in humans involves hemoglobin S, an altered form of hemoglobin that results from a point mutation in the gene that produces the hemoglobin beta chain. If a child inherits the Hb^S allele, which is more common in populations that inhabit tropical areas of Africa, the Middle East, and parts of Asia, from both parents, he or she will suffer from sickle-cell anemia and die young. However, those born with only one Hb^S allele are carriers of the **sickle-cell trait** but do not suffer the disease. These carriers have a greater resistance to malaria in tropical regions, where malaria is prevalent, and they can experience higher reproductive success than those with normal hemoglobin. This is true because people with normal hemoglobin in tropical areas can be severely afflicted by malaria. Therefore, natural selection favors the frequency of Hb^S in populations of malarial regions.

Note that mutation, gene flow, and genetic drift can produce some evolutionary changes by themselves, but they are **microevolutionary**, producing small changes within the species over the short term. For **macroevolutionary** changes, those produced after many generations that can result in entire new taxonomic groups, natural selection is necessary. Since mutation is necessary for genetic variation to occur, genetic drift, gene flow, and natural selection cannot work without mutation. All four factors, sometimes referred to as the "four forces of evolution," interact to produce variation and to distribute genes within and between populations over time.

Review Exercises

Matching

Match each term with the appropriate definition or description.

1. __e__ founder effect
2. __g__ gene flow
3. __b__ gene pool
4. __h__ genetic drift
5. __d__ genotype

6. __i__ heterozygous
7. __c__ homozygous
8. __j__ phenotype
9. __e__ pleiotropy A
10. __a__ polygenic F

8696

a. The capacity of a single gene to influence several phenotypic expressions.

b. All of the genes shared by the reproductive members of a population.

c. Having the same allele at the same locus on both members of a pair of chromosomes.

d. The genetic makeup of an individual.

e. Occurs when allele frequencies are altered in small populations that are taken from, or are remnants of, larger populations.

f. Traits that are influenced by genes at two or more loci.

g. Exchange of genes between populations.

h. Changes in gene frequencies produced by random factors.

i. Having different alleles at the same locus on members of a pair of chromosomes.

j. The observable or detectable physical characteristics of an organism.

Completion

Fill each blank with the most appropriate term from the list below.

allele frequency	principle of independent assortment
codominance	principle of segregation
hybrids	recessive
Mendelian traits	sickle-cell trait
pedigree chart	tandem repeats
pigment	

85%

1. A _pedigree chart_ is used to trace the hereditary pattern of particular genetic (usually Mendelian) traits.

2. The percentage of all the alleles at a locus accounted for by one specific allele is the _allele frequency_

3. Hair or eye color is influenced by _pigment_ molecules.

4. _Codominance_ occurs when two alleles at a particular locus are expressed in a heterozygote.

5. The _Principle of Seg._ states that the members of each pair of alleles separate during gamete formation so that each gamete contains one member of each pair.

6. The ___Princ. of inde. assort.___ states that the distribution of one pair of alleles into gametes does not influence the distribution of another pair.

7. When an allele is expressed in the homozygote but not the heterozygote it is ___recessive___.

8. A ___Mandlin trait___ is a chemical change in a single base of a DNA sequence.

9. ___hybrids___ are the offspring of individuals that differ with regard to certain traits or certain aspects of genetic makeup.

10. Short, adjacent segments of DNA within a gene that are repeated several times are called ___tandame repeates___.

11. A person with one Hb^A allele and one Hb^B allele is said to have ___Sickel-cell trait___.

Self-Test

Select the best answer.

1. In Mendel's experiments, the ratio of tall to short plants in the F_2 generation was
   a. 15 to 1.
   b. 3 to 1.
   c. one-half tall, one-half short.
   d. 4 to 1.

2. In Mendelian terms, a hybrid is
   a. an alien species.
   b. a mutant type.
   c. a heterozygote
   d. none of the above.

3. Which of the following statements describes an individual that is homozygous recessive for a particular gene?
   a. The individual has the same allele at both loci for that gene.
   b. The individual shows the recessive phenotype.
   c. The individual shows the recessive genotype.
   d. All of the above statements are true.

4. In a heterozygous individual who has one dominant allele and one recessive allele for a particular trait, which one is likely to be expressed in the phenotype?
   a. the recessive allele
   b. the dominant allele
   c. both alleles
   d. none of these

5. Two people (**both** heterozygotes) have a cleft chin. The cleft chin phenotype is caused by a dominant allele (C). The lack of a cleft chin is caused by the recessive allele (c). What proportion of their children would be expected to have a cleft chin?
   a. three-fourths
   b. one-half
   c. all
   d. one-quarter

   3/14

6. Which of the following traits are more often expressed in male than in females?
   a. hemophilia
   b. Tay-Sachs syndrome
   c. PKU
   d. All of these are sex-linked traits.

7. Polygenic traits
   a. result in a continuous distribution of phenotypes.
   b. account for most of the readily observable phenotypic variation in humans.
   c. may be influenced by the environment.
   d. involve all of the above.

8. Polygenic inheritance differs from Mendelian inheritance in that polygenic traits are
   a. influenced by alleles at more than one genetic locus.
   b. discrete.
   c. rare in humans.
   d. a and c.

9. Microevolution is defined as
   a. long-term evolutionary changes over many generations.
   b. short-term evolutionary effects such as changes in allele frequency from one generation to the next.
   c. an exchange of genes between populations.
   d. none of the above.

10. The CCR5 mutation
   a. produced an allele that increased in frequency over many generations.
   b. gives us a good example of how evolution by natural selection works.
   c. is likely to increase in frequency because it is beneficial as it protects against HIV infection.
   d. involves all of the above.

11. Which of the following statements describes genetic drift?
    a. It is most common in large populations.
    b. It is a random factor in evolution.
    c. It was found in Chumash Indians living in the Channel Islands.
    d. both b and c

12. Which of the following statements is **FALSE**?
    a. Founder effect is a type of genetic drift.
    b. Point mutations are always harmful.
    c. Gene flow occurs when migrants interbreed.
    d. Recombination occurs during the sexual reproduction process.

13. People who are heterozygous for sickle-cell trait have which of the following genotypes?
    a. $Hb^S Hb^S$
    b. $Hb^A Hb^A$
    c. $Hb^A Hb^S$
    d. none of the above

14. Even though the Hb^S allele is harmful when a person has two Hb^S alleles, it has increased in frequency in some regions where malaria is common. Scientists have proposed that this increase in allele frequency occurred because
    a. people who are homozygous for the Hb^A allele are more susceptible to malaria infection.
    b. people who are heterozygous, with one Hb^S allele, are more resistant to malaria.
    c. people who are homozygous for the Hb^S allele have low reproductive success.
    d. all of the above are true.

Short-Answer Questions

1. What is a Mendelian trait? List at least three Mendelian traits found in humans.

   A mendelian trait is a chra. influenced by alleles at

2. How do homozygous individuals differ from heterozygous individuals?

   Homozygous indi. have 2 allels that are the Same/where as Heterozygous Have different on a loci alleles at the same loci on a 2 chrom.

3. How does a sex-linked trait differ from other traits? Why are sex-linked traits expressed more often in males than females?

4. What is a polygenic trait? List three examples of polygenic traits in humans.

A Polygenic traits is are traits that are influenced by genes at 2 or more loci These include Hair, Stature, Skin Plus eye color.

5. Why is our current definition of evolution called a "modern synthesis"?

Because it combines the ideas and theories of Natural selection and Mutation together.

6. How does natural selection act on mutations to cause them to become more common in a population?

Natural selection will influence the Mutations. If a Mutation isn't to some Benefit it's Not kept or if it does help in someway it is expressed whereas more.

7. How are the distribution of malaria and sickle-cell trait related to one another?

People with HB^s are more resistant malaria so even though Hb^s is Harmful it usually gets passed down more frequently because thouse w/out it are more succtible to Malaria.

Application Questions

1. Explain the dominance system in the ABO blood group. Which alleles are dominant, recessive, or codominant to one another?

A and B are Codominant if both A and B are Present both will be expressed. O is a recessive alle if A or B is Present with o it will most likely be an A or B Blood type.

2. Compare and contrast the terms "polygenic" and "pleiotropy," and give an example of each in humans. How does each affect the phenotype of an individual?

Polygenic is are traits influenced by genes at 2 or more loci. Where as pleiotrophy is the ability for a single gene to control 7ral Phenotypic traits.

3. Briefly explain how the research on the genetics of the Chumash Indians, outlined in segment 3 of the video, relates to genetic drift and gene flow.

The chumash Indian Population is a small group so their Genes started from One group and of the founders.

4. Explain how the CCR5 mutation spread in Northern European populations. What was its proposed function 5,000 to 7,000 years ago? How does it help to protect people today?

Answer Key
Matching
1. e (objective 6)
2. g (video lesson, segment 3; objective 6)
3. b (objective 5)
4. h (video lesson, segment 3; objective 6)
5. d (video lesson, introduction; objective 2)
6. i (video lesson, introduction; objective 2)
7. c (video lesson, introduction; objective 2)
8. j (video lesson, introduction; objective 2)
9. a (objective 4)
10. f (video lesson, segment 1; objective 4)

Completion
1. pedigree chart (objective 3)
2. allele frequency (video lesson, segment 2; objective 5)
3. pigment (objective 4)
4. Codominance (objective 3)
5. principle of segregation (video lesson, introduction; objective 1)
6. principle of independent assortment (objective 1)
7. recessive (video lesson, introduction; objective 2)
8. tandem repeats (objective 6)
9. Hybrids (objective 1)
10. Mendelian traits (video lesson, introduction; objective 3)
11. sickle-cell trait (objective 7)

Self-Test

1. b. is the correct answer. A cross between heterozygotes, such as those in Mendel's F_2 generation, yields an average 3:1 ratio of individuals with the dominant phenotype vs. those with the recessive phenotype. (objective 1)

2. c. is the correct answer. A hybrid is defined as an individual that differs with regard to certain traits or certain aspects of genetic makeup, in other words, a heterozygote. (objective 1)

3. d. is the correct answer. An individual that is homozygous recessive for a particular trait will show the recessive phenotype. (video lesson, introduction; objective 2)

4. b. is the correct answer. The dominant allele masks the recessive allele and the dominant phenotype is expressed. (video lesson, introduction; objective 2)

5. a. is the correct answer. The dominant allele for cleft chin is expressed in both heterozygotes and those who are homozygous dominant. Only homozygous recessive individuals will lack a cleft chin. In a cross between two heterozygotes this will occur in a 3:1 ratio. (objective 3)

6. a. is the correct answer. Hemophilia is a sex-linked trait because the gene locus is on the X chromosome. The genes for Tay-Sachs syndrome and PKU are found on autosomal chromosomes. (objective 3)

7. d. is the correct answer. Polygenic traits do result in a continuous distribution of phenotypes that are influenced by the environment. Many aspects of the human phenotype, such as skin color, height, hair color, and eye color, are polygenic traits. (video lesson, segment 1; objective 4)

8. a. is the correct answer. Polygenic traits are influenced by more than gene locus. Mendelian traits involved only one gene locus. Both types of traits are very common in humans. (objective 4)

9. b. is the correct answer. Microevolution involves short-term changes in allele frequency from one generation to the next. When changes accumulate over many generations that often lead to speciation, it is called macroevolution. (video lesson, segment 2; objective 5)

10. d. is the correct answer. The CCR5 mutation provides a natural protection from HIV infection because it keeps the HIV virus from being able to enter cells. This mutation is found in certain populations and must have spread through natural selection over many generations in those populations in response to another pathogen. (video lesson, segment 3; objectives 5 & 6)

11. d. is the correct answer. Genetic drift involves random changes in allele frequency, or the random loss of alleles in a population. Genetic drift has been noted among Chumash Indians living in the Channel Islands. (video lesson, segment 3; objective 6)

12. b. is the correct answer. Point mutations are the main sources of all genetic variation and they may be harmful, beneficial, or neutral. (objective 6)

13. c. is the correct answer. Heterozygous individuals have two different alleles at a particular gene locus. Individuals who are heterozygous for sickle-cell trait will have the $Hb^A\,Hb^S$ genotype. (objective 7)

(14) d. is the correct answer. People without the *Hb^S* allele are more likely do become ill or die from malaria. People with two *Hb^S* alleles are likely to become ill or die from sickle-cell anemia. But people who have one of each allele are more resistant to malaria. This causes selection for the heterozygote and it has caused the *Hb^S* allele to be maintained and sometimes increase in allele frequency in populations where malaria exerts a strong selection pressure. (objective 7)

Short-Answer Questions

Your answers should include the following:

1. A Mendelian trait is a characteristic that is influenced by alleles at only one genetic locus. Table 4-1 on page 87 of the Jurmain textbook lists a number of Mendelian traits found in humans. (video lesson, introduction; objective 1)

2. Homozygous individuals have the same allele at the same gene locus on both members of a pair of chromosomes. Heterozygous individuals have different alleles at the same gene locus on both members of a pair of chromosomes. (video lesson, introduction; objective 2)

3. Sex-linked traits are those whose gene locus is on the sex chromosomes, mainly the X chromosome since it contains many more genes than the Y chromosome. Other traits have gene loci on the autosomal chromosomes. Sex-linked traits are expressed more often in males than females because females have two X chromosomes while males have only one. A harmful recessive allele on one X chromosome may be masked by a normal allele in a female while it will be expressed in a male. (objective 3)

4. Polygenic traits are those that are influenced by more than one gene. Height, hair color, eye color, and skin color are just a few of the polygenic traits found in humans. (video lesson, segment 1; objective 4)

5. The current definition of evolution is a combination of how evolution was defined by Charles Darwin and our current knowledge about genetics. Charles Darwin saw evolution as a change where new life forms developed from older forms. We now know that those changes in life forms arise from the accumulation of small genetic changes over time. So evolution in now defined as a change in the frequency of alleles from one generation to the next. (objective 5)

6. Natural selection theory contends that a mutation that is advantageous to the reproductive success of an individual is more likely to be passed on to the next generation. If selective pressures remain the same, with regard to that mutation, then those offspring are likely to have better reproductive success as well. Over time, the mutation will increase in frequency in the population, causing a shift in that population. (objective 6)

7. The sickle-cell trait allele, *Hb^S*, tends to occur at higher frequency where malaria is present. (objective 7)

Application Questions

Your answers should include the following:

1. In the ABO blood system, the A and B alleles are codominant to one another. That means that both alleles are expressed if they are present. The expression of these alleles is in the form of an antigen that is on the surface of their red blood cells. So if a person has a B allele, they have a B antigen on their red blood cells and they have type B blood. If an A allele is present, there is an A antigen present and they have type A blood. If a person has both an A and a B allele, both antigens are present and they have type AB blood. However, both the A and B allele are dominant to the O allele. So if a person had the genotype BO, they have type B blood. An AO genotype would yield type A blood. For a person to have type O blood, they must have two O alleles. (objective 3)

2. A polygenic trait is one that is influenced by many different gene loci. Pleiotropy occurs when a single gene locus influences more than one phenotypic expression. Skin color is a good example of a polygenic trait. Many different genes influence the production of melanin and the other pigments in the skin, and the resulting baseline skin color of a person is the result of the interaction between these genes. An example of a gene with pleiotropic effects is the one that causes phenylketoneuria (PKU). People with this condition lack the enzyme that breaks down the amino acid phenylalanine. This condition has many different effects on the phenotype. It causes a diminished ability to produce melanin, so affected people tend to have light skin, hair, and eyes. It also causes mental deficiencies and other problems in the central nervous system. (video lesson, segment 1; objective 4)

3. The mitochondrial DNA analyses conducted by researchers shows that the Chumash Indians of the Channel Islands experienced genetic drift, which is the random loss of alleles in a population. The genetic analysis of 10,300-year-old human remains from Southern Alaska show similarities to Chumash populations. These genetic markers have also been found in other populations of Pacific Coast peoples as far away as Chile. In this way, they are able to demonstrate gene flow in the migration of these people from Alaska to Chile along the Pacific Coast. Gene flow is also apparent in that many present-day Chumash people have interbred with local populations and the genetic admixture present in these populations has been noted by researchers. (video lesson, segment 3; objective 6)

4. The CCR5 mutation arose approximately 5,000 to 7,000 years ago. It has the effect of making it difficult or impossible for certain pathogens to enter the cells that they infect. Scientists hypothesize that it probably increased in allele frequency in Northern Europe in response to a pathogen. Those with the CCR5 mutation were better able to resist the pathogen. This may have increased their reproductive success, and the CCR5 mutation was passed to the next generation and so on. Today, the CCR5 mutation protects against a relatively new pathogen, the HIV virus. This new pathogen challenge is likely to increase the allele frequency of CCR5 once again. (video lesson, segment 2; objective 6)

Lesson Review

Lesson 4: Heredity & Evolution

PLEASE NOTE: Use this matrix to guide your study and achieve the learning objectives of this lesson. It will also help you to view the video, which defines and demonstrates important concepts and principles as they relate to everyday life and actual case studies.

Learning Objective	Textbook	Student Guide	Video Lesson
1. Describe the work of Gregor Mendel that led to the principles of segregation and independent assortment.	pp. 82–83, 85–86	Key Terms: 1, 2, 3, 10, 11; Completion: 5, 6, 9; Self-Test: 1, 2; Short-Answer: 1.	Introduction
2. Describe the concepts of dominant, recessive, and codominant alleles, genotype and phenotype, and heterozygous and homozygous genotypes.	pp. 83–88	Key Terms: 4, 5, 6, 7, 8, 9; Matching: 5, 6, 7, 8; Completion: 7; Self-Test: 3, 4; Short-Answer: 2.	Introduction
3. Discuss Mendelian inheritance in humans, including autosomal and sex-linked traits and genetic disorders.	pp. 86–93	Key Terms: 12, 13, 14, 15; Completion: 1, 4, 10; Self-Test: 5, 6; Short-Answer: 3; Application: 1.	Introduction
4. Provide examples of polygenic inheritance, and how it differs from Mendelian inheritance.	pp. 93–98	Key Terms: 16, 17, 18; Matching: 9, 10; Completion: 3; Self-Test: 7, 8; Short-Answer: 4; Application: 2.	Segment 1: *Non-Mendelian Inheritance*
5. Describe the modern synthesis of evolution, and define evolution from a microevolutionary perspective.	pp. 98–99	Key Terms: 19, 20, 21, 22, 23; Matching: 3; Completion: 2; Self-Test: 9, 10; Short-Answer: 5.	Segment 2: *Microevolution at Work* Segment 3: *Gene Flow & Genetic Drift*

Learning Objective	Textbook	Student Guide	Video Lesson
6. Identify and describe the factors that produce and redistribute variation, including mutation, gene flow, genetic drift, recombination, and natural selection.	pp. 100–105	Key Terms: 24, 25, 26, 27, 28; Matching: 1, 2, 4; Completion: 8; Self-Test: 10, 11, 12; Short-Answer: 6; Application: 3, 4.	Segment 2: *Microevolution at Work* Segment 3: *Gene Flow & Genetic Drift*
7. Use the malaria and sickle-cell trait distribution to discuss the action of natural selection on variation.	pp. 103–106	Key Terms: 29; Completion: 11; Self-Test: 13, 14; Short-Answer: 7.	

LESSON 5

Macroevolution

Checklist

For the most effective study of this lesson, complete the following activities in this sequence.

Before Viewing the Video

❑ Read the Preview, Learning Objectives, and Viewing Notes below.

❑ Read Chapter 5, "Macroevolution: Processes of Vertebrate and Mammalian Evolution," pages 110–141, in *Introduction to Physical Anthropology*.

What to Watch

❑ After reading the textbook assignment, watch the video for Lesson 5, *Macroevolution*.

After Viewing the Video

❑ Briefly note your answers to the questions listed at the end of the Viewing Notes.

❑ Review the Summary below.

❑ Review all reading assignments for this lesson, including the Viewing Notes in this lesson.

❑ Write brief answers to the "Critical Thinking Questions" at the end of Chapter 5 in the textbook.

❑ Complete the Review Exercises below. Check your answers with the Answer Key and review when necessary.

❑ Use the Lesson Review matrix found at the end of this lesson to review and assess your knowledge of each Learning Objective.

Preview

Lesson 1 discussed the anthropological perspective, and how it broadens our viewpoint on the enormous diversity of all life through time and space. There are millions and millions of species on Earth, and biologists have constructed methods of organizing them that creates an orderly way to study, learn, and teach the diversity that continues to evolve on our planet.

Lesson 5 investigates the evolution of vertebrates and mammals and the biological principles used to classify them. When we understand the general aspects of the evolution of vertebrate and mammals, we can better understand the biological context in which humans (*Homo sapiens*) fit. A paleontologist featured in the video points out that the discovery of fossils is an important part of documenting this evolution, even though fossil records are far from complete. "There's still a huge gap in our understanding of the history of life, so new discoveries can change everything in terms of how we view relationships."

Lesson 4 explained that *microevolution* refers to small changes within species, such as a change in allele frequencies within populations. Lesson 5 is concerned with **macroevolution**, large-scale evolutionary processes, or changes produced after many generations. Natural selection plays a major role in such changes. Learning macroevolutionary processes requires learning geological history, the principles of classification, and modes of evolutionary change. The definition of species is expanded in this lesson, and some theories of how **speciation**, the process by which a new species evolves, occurs are explained.

Concepts to Remember

* Lesson 2 introduced the term **taxonomy**, the branch of science concerned with the rules of classifying organisms on the basis of evolutionary relationships. Carolus Linnaeus, an eighteenth-century naturalist, established the four-level system of classification that became the basis for taxonomy. One of Linnaeus' innovations was to include humans in his classification of animals.

* A goal of classification is to make meaningful biological statements about the variation that is present. Lesson 3 looked at the molecular basis for life. **Recombination** is the exchange of genetic material between homologous chromosomes during meiosis (cell division in ovaries and testes.) This can account for individual variation in a population. Scientists must use care in evaluating such variation in classifying organisms.

Learning Objectives

After you complete this lesson, you should be able to:

1. Compare and contrast two concepts of taxonomy known as *evolutionary systematics* and *cladistics*. (pp. 112–119)

2. Define the concept of an ecological niche, and offer an example. (p. 121)

3. Define the three main species concepts identified by evolutionary biologists and describe the current debate surrounding these concepts. (pp. 119–122)

4. Describe the various processes of speciation and how they differ. (pp. 121–124)

5. Discuss the difficulties of identifying species in the fossil record. (pp. 124–126)

6. Explain the concept of geologic time and the action of continental drift over long periods of geologic time. (pp. 128–132)

7. Describe the major characteristics of placental and nonplacental mammals as adaptations. (pp. 132–134)

8. Define macroevolution and discuss the processes of macroevolution. (pp. 134–136)

9. Explain the difference between gradualism and punctuated equilibrium, two modes of the evolutionary process. (pp. 136–138)

At this point, read Chapter 5, "Macroevolution: Processes of Vertebrate and Mammalian Evolution," pages 110–141.

Viewing Notes

While *microevolution*, small changes in a species, results in variations within a population, **macroevolution** is when these variations and mutations lead to a new species. The study of the evolutionary history of the plesiadapiforms is used in the video as an illustration of the methods used to classify species and their paths of divergence over an immense expanse of time.

In the ten million years following the extinction of the dinosaurs, the dominant primate-like mammal was a group called the plesiadapiforms, who were about the size of a small mouse. Plesiadapiforms were identified from teeth and fragmentary jaws, but such fossil evidence was not strong enough to categorically assert they were primates, although this was the general belief. Dr. Jonathan Bloch, a paleoanthropologist who is featured in the video for this lesson, believes that plesiadapiforms may be the early ancestors of primates. Bloch and his team have discovered well-preserved skeletons of plesiadapiforms in the Big Horn Basin in Wyoming, and these more complete fossils allow the scientists to examine finger bones, toes, joints, and legs. In the video, Bloch says that "what we believe we are looking at with plesiadapiforms during the Paleocene is literally the first 10 million years of primate evolution, which hadn't been taken into account before." The Paleocene is a reference to the geological time scale which breaks down very large time spans into eras, and within eras, separate periods. Periods are divided into epochs. During most of the Mesozoic era, from 225 to 136 million years ago (mya), dinosaurs were the dominant animals. The Jurmain textbook comments that the earliest mammals are known from fossil traces fairly early in the Mesozoic, but the rapid expansion of mammals did not occur until the next era, the Cenozoic. The Paleocene—the epoch Bloch mentions—is the earliest one of the Cenozoic.

Scientists look at fossils and attempt to relate their characteristics to living organisms. This is a first step in classification, and one the research team in Wyoming used when presented with plesiadapiform skeletons. Common physical features may be the result of a shared ancestry, or they may be similar because they serve the same function but in fact evolved separately. Homologies are structures that are shared by species based on having a common ancestor. Analogies are structures that are similar because they fulfill the same function, not because the species are related to each other. A great number of the characteristics of plesidapiforms are characteristic of living primates. For instance, Jonathan Bloch believes that the nail on the big toe of the *Carpolestes* plesiadapiform is an homologous feature, inherited from a common ancestor of living primates.

The video and the Jurmain textbook explore two systems of classification. The traditional approach is evolutionary systematics, which traces a species' ancestors and descendents in time by analyzing shared physical, or **homologous**, characteristics. You most likely are familiar with the concept of a family tree. The phylogenetic tree is an evolutionary one with branches that diagram the evolutionary connections between organisms. The second system scientists use to classify species is called **cladistics**, an approach to classification that tries to make rigorous evolutionary interpretations based solely on analysis of certain types of derived homologous characteristics. **Derived characteristics** are those that have been modified through time from the original **ancestral characteristic**. In the case of the plesiadapiforms, Bloch's early fossil finds suggest that the hands of these animals had limited grasping ability, similar to a squirrel. On the basis of such evidence, some authorities who do not consider the plesiadapiforms to be primates have left open the possibility that these species may have been early ancestors of the primates. While Bloch's analysis has drawn some criticism from other scholars, the possibility exists that, during a period of 10 million years after dinosaurs became extinct, the evolving plesiadapiforms took on some of the characteristics of modern primates, such as grasping hands and feet, nails instead of claws, relatively large brains, and an ability to leap among trees. This evolution was part of an **adaptive radiation**, which occurs when organisms rapidly fill ecological niches made available by environmental changes or the extinction of other types of organisms, such as the dinosaurs.

When the genetic structure of a group shifts, a new species can emerge. Members of a species are able to reproduce with one another, but not with organisms outside their species. Speciation can occur in a number of ways, but in general, scientists look at ways in which reproductive boundaries are created between organisms; some are geographical, others ecological.

There are mammal fossils found in China that date to the Triassic period of the early Mesozoic era which are quite primitive, but scientists find it difficult to determine how these fossils relate to living mammals. Wyoming's Big Horn Basin is an area of the United States that provides one of the best records of the evolution of terrestrial mammals. The sediment produced by the uplift of the Rocky Mountains was carried down the rivers and provided the perfect medium for preserving mammal bones. The discoveries in Big Horn Basin may be the first occurrence of what is referred to as the modern orders of mammals.

Questions to Consider

✱ How have biologists dealt scientifically with organizing and classifying the diversity of organisms, living and extinct, that have existed on Earth?

✱ What are evolutionary systematics and cladistics?

✱ What is meant by speciation and what are some of the theories that have been developed to explain how species originate?

Watch the video for Lesson 5, *Macroevolution*.

Segment 1: *Principles of Classification*
Segment 2: *Speciation & Evolutionary Forces*
Segment 3: *Vertebrate & Mammalian Evolutionary History*

Key Terms and Concepts

Page references are keyed to *Introduction to Physical Anthropology,* 13th edition.

1. **classification:** In biology, the ordering of organisms into categories, such as orders, families, and genera, to show evolutionary relationships. (p. 112; video lesson, segment 1; objective 1)

2. **Chordata:** The phylum of the animal kingdom that includes vertebrates. (p. 112; objective 1)

3. **vertebrates:** Animals with segmented, bony spinal columns; includes fishes, amphibians, reptiles (including birds), and mammals. (p. 112; video lesson, segment 3; objective 1)

4. **homologies:** Similarities between organisms based on descent from a common ancestor. (p. 114; video lesson, segment 1; objective 1)

5. **analogies:** Similarities between organisms based strictly on common function, with no assumed common evolutionary descent. (p. 114; video lesson, segment 1; objective 1)

6. **homoplasy:** (*homo* meaning "same," and *plasy*, meaning "growth") The separate evolutionary development of similar characteristics in different groups of organisms. (p. 114; objective 1)

7. **evolutionary systematics:** A traditional approach to classification (and evolutionary interpretation) in which presumed ancestors and descendants are traced in time by analysis of homologous characters. (p. 115; video lesson, segment 1; objective 1)

8. **cladistics:** An approach to classification that attempts to make rigorous evolutionary interpretations based solely on analysis of certain types of homologous characters (those considered to be derived characters). (p. 115; video lesson, segment 1; objective 1)

9. **ancestral (primitive):** Referring to characters inherited by a group of organisms from a remote ancestor and thus not diagnostic of groups (lineages) that diverged after the character first appeared. (p. 115; video lesson, segment 1; objective 1)

10. **clade:** A group of organisms sharing a common ancestor. The group includes the common ancestor and all descendants. (p. 115; objective 1)

11. **monophyletic:** Referring to an evolutionary group (clade) composed of descendants all sharing a common ancestor. (p. 115; objective 1)

12. **polyphyletic:** Referring to an evolutionary group composed of descendants with more than one common ancestor (and thus not a true clade). (p. 115; objective 1)

13. **derived (modified):** Referring to characters that are modified from the ancestral condition and thus diagnostic of particular evolutionary lineages. (p. 116; video lesson, segment 1; objective 1)

14. **theropods:** Small- to medium-sized ground-living dinosaurs, dated to approximately 14 million years ago (mya) and thought to be related to birds. (p. 117; objective 1)

15. **shared derived:** Relating to specific character traits shared in common between two life-forms and considered the most useful for making evolutionary interpretations. (p. 118; objective 1)

16. **phylogenetic tree:** A chart showing evolutionary relationships as determined by evolutionary systematics. It contains a time component and implies ancestor-descendant relationships. (p. 118; video lesson, segment 1; objective 1)

17. **cladogram:** A chart showing evolutionary relationships as determined by cladistic analysis. It is based solely on interpretation of shared derived characters. It contains no time component and does not imply ancestor-descendant relationships. (p. 118; objective 1)

18. **biological species concept:** A depiction of species as groups of individuals capable of fertile interbreeding but reproductively isolated from other such groups. (p. 119; video lesson, segment 2; objective 3)

19. **speciation:** The process by which a new species evolves from an earlier species. Speciation is the most basic process in macroevolution. (p. 120; video lesson, segment 2; objectives 4 & 8)

20. **recognition species concept:** A depiction of species in which the key aspect is the ability of individuals to identify members of their own species for purposes of mating (and to avoid mating with members of other species). In theory, this type of selective mating is a component of a species concept emphasizing mating and is therefore compatible with the biological species concept. (p. 120; objective 3)

21. **ecological species concept:** The concept that a species is a group of organisms exploiting a single niche. This view emphasizes the role of natural selection in separating species from one another. (p. 121; video lesson, segment 2; objective 3)

22. **ecological niche:** The position of a species within its physical and biological environments, together making up the *ecosystem*. A speciesí ecological niche is defined by such components as diet, terrain, vegetation, type of predators, relationships with other species, and activity patterns, and each niche is unique to a given species. Together, ecological niches make up an ecosystem. (p. 121; video lesson, segment 2; objective 2)

23. **phylogenetic species concept:** Splitting many populations into separate species based on an identifiable parental pattern of ancestry. (p. 121; objective 3)

24. **allopatric:** Living in different areas. The allopathic pattern is important in the divergence of closely related species from each other and from their shared ancestral species because it leads to reproductive isolation. (p. 122; objective 4)

25. **sexual dimorphism:** Differences in physical characteristics between males and females of the same species. For example, humans are slightly sexually dimorphic for body size, with males being taller, on average, than females of the same population. Sexual dimorphism is very pronounced in many species, such as gorillas. (p. 125; objective 5)

26. **intraspecific:** Within species; refers to variation seen within the same species. (p. 125; objective 5)

27. **interspecific:** Between species; refers to variation beyond that seen within the same species to include additional aspects seen between two different species. (p. 125; objective 5)

28. **paleospecies:** Species defined from fossil evidence, often covering a long time span. (p. 125; objective 5)

29. **genus (*pl.*, genera):** A group of closely related species. (p. 126; objective 5)

30. **fossils:** Traces or remnants of organisms found in geological beds on the earth's surface. (p. 126; objective 5)

31. **mineralization:** The process in which parts of animals (or some plants) become transformed into stone-like structures. Mineralization usually occurs very slowly as water carrying minerals, such as silica or iron, seeps into the tiny spaces within a

bone. In some cases, the original minerals within the bone or tooth can be completely replaced, molecule by molecule, with other minerals. (p. 127; objective 5)

32.   **taphonomy:** The study of how bones and other materials come to be buried in the earth and preserved as fossils. (p. 128; objective 5)

33.   **geological time scale:** The organization of earth history into eras, periods, and epochs; commonly used by geologists and paleoanthropologists. (p. 128; video lesson, segment 3; objective 6)

34.   **continental drift:** The movement of continents on sliding plates of the earth's surface. As a result, the positions of large landmasses have shifted drastically during the earth's history. (p. 129; video lesson, segment 3; objective 6)

35.   **epochs:** Categories of the geological time scale; subdivisions of periods. In the Cenozoic, epochs include the Paleocene, Eocene, Oligocene, Miocene, and Pliocene (from the Tertiary) and the Pleistocene and Holocene (from the Quaternary). (p. 132; objective 6)

36.   **neocortex:** The more recently evolved portions of the cortex of the brain that are involved with higher mental functions and composed of areas that integrate incoming information from different sensory organs. (p. 132; objective 7)

37.   **placental:** A type (subclass) of mammal. During the Cenozoic, placentals became the most widespread and numerous mammals and today are represented by upward of 20 orders, including the primates. (p. 133; objective 7)

38.   **heterodont:** Having different kinds of teeth; characteristic of mammals, whose teeth consist of incisors, canines, premolars, and molars. (p. 133; objective 7)

39.   **endothermic:** (*endo,* meaning "within" or "internal") Able to maintain internal body temperature by producing energy through metabolic processes within cells; characteristic of mammals, birds, and perhaps some dinosaurs. (p. 134; objective 7)

40.   **macroevolution:** Changes produced only after many generations, such as the appearance of a new species. (video lesson, segment 1; objective 8)

41.   **adaptive radiation:** The relatively rapid expansion and diversification of life-forms into new ecological niches. (p. 135; video lesson, segment 3; objective 8)

42.   **punctuated equilibrium:** The concept that evolutionary change proceeds through long periods of stasis punctuated by rapid periods of change. (p. 136; objective 9)

Summary

There are millions and millions of species living today, so to approach such enormous diversity biologists simplify the task by using a system of **classification** that organizes species into categories to indicate evolutionary relationships. The classification chart on page 113 of the

Jurmain textbook is a good reference that shows how animals are classified. Lesson 5 delves more fully into the evolution of vertebrates and mammals. Note on the chart that **vertebrates,** animals with segmented, bony spinal columns, are subdivided into six groups: bony fishes, cartilaginous fishes, amphibians, reptiles, birds, and mammals.

Recall from Lesson 2 that *taxonomy* is the field that specializes in establishing the rules of classification. A starting point in placing an organism into a category is to compare physical similarities. This was the basis of the first system devised by Linnaeus in the eighteenth century. But for such similarities to be useful, they must reflect evolutionary descent. **Homologies** are similarities between organisms based on descent from a common ancestor. The bones of the forelimbs of all terrestrial, air-breathing vertebrates (tetrapods) are so similar in number and form that the obvious explanation for the striking resemblance is that all four kinds of air-breathing vertebrates derived their forelimb structure from a common ancestor. However, the Jurmain textbook points out that while homologies are reliable indicators of evolutionary relationships, more study is needed before placing an animal into a particular category. Birds and butterflies have wings, but butterflies are insects and differ in many other ways from birds. Birds and butterflies developed wings independently in response to similar functional demands and they share a very remote ancestry. Thus, they are called **analogies** because there is a similarity of a trait based on function, not on a common evolutionary descent. Similar analogies might be drawn between the fin of a carp (a freshwater fish) and the fin of a dolphin (an aquatic mammal), which have similar functions but belong to very different organisms. **Homoplasy** is the process that leads to the development of analogies; it is the separate evolutionary development of similar characteristics in different groups of organisms.

Evolutionary biologists use two major approaches to interpret evolutionary history and create classifications. **Evolutionary systematics** is the more traditional approach in which presumed ancestors and descendants are traced in time by analysis of homologous characters. **Cladistics** is a newer strategy, interpreting evolutionary history based solely on analysis of certain types of derived, homologous characteristics. Both methods share the same goal of tracing evolutionary relationships based on homologies, but the difference is that cladistics is more strictly focused on defining the kinds of homologies that yield the most useful information. The Jurmain textbook explains that while some similarities are useful in showing that large evolutionary groups are all related from a distant ancestor, they don't help biologists distinguish the groups from one another. Such **ancestral** (primitive) characters do not provide enough evidence about relationships within the group. Cladistics looks at the similar characteristics among species that provide evidence of relationship within a group. These characteristics are referred to as **derived** or **modified**. In other words, characteristics that are modified from the ancestral condition become diagnostic of particular evolutionary lineages. Scientists scrutinize characteristics carefully to determine which traits are ancestral and which are derived.

The diagrams on pages 117–118 of the Jurmain textbook illustrate another difference in these two methods. Evolutionary systematics shows the hypothesized relationships using a phylogenetic tree. A **phylogenetic tree** incorporates the element of time, indicating how and when a new species arose. A **cladogram** isn't concerned with time; all the organisms are indicated along one dimension. A phylogenetic tree is, in a way, similar to a family tree, in that it attempts to show the ancestor-descendant relationships. The cladogram doesn't imply any ancestor-descendant relationship and ignores *when* a "branch" might have occurred. When an organism does not share a common characteristic with the rest of the group, it is branched off into its own **clade**, lineages that share a common ancestor. The Jurmain textbook points out how the classification of birds has changed in more recent years. According to the diagrams, recent fossil finds show that birds, rather than being a distinct group from reptiles, are descendants of dinosaurs. The phylogenetic tree shows that descent. But in the cladogram, birds *are* dinosaurs because of their common ancestor. The cladogram isn't interested in the ancestor-descendant relationship, just the evolutionary relationship. Despite the difference in these methods, most physical anthropologists use aspects of both to interpret a more complete picture of evolutionary history.

As this lesson has explained so far, biologists can investigate evolutionary relationships by comparing species. The common definition of species, from Lesson 1, is a group of organisms that can interbreed to produce fertile offspring. Members of one species are reproductively isolated from members of all other species, meaning they are unable to mate with them and produce fertile offspring. This explanation is the **biological species concept**, the one favored by most zoologists. The biological species concept involves some form of isolation. *Geographical isolation* means there is a physical boundary that separates populations and limits gene exchange between the groups. As long as the gene flow is limited, the populations grow more genetically different over time. If the groups are small, genetic drift will also cause allele frequencies to change in the populations. If the groups live in different habitats, additional genetic differences would be incorporated through natural selection because different traits would be favored in each population. Individuals with those traits in each population would be more successful than others in passing their genes along.

Behavioral isolation can also interfere with breeding. As groups are geographically separated, each may adopt different methods of courtship and mating. **Recognition species concept** means that individuals have distinct ways to recognize other members of their species and avoid mating with those they do not recognize. For example, when groups are isolated for a long time, phenotypic differences begin to establish themselves; coloration patterns of face or the size, location, coloration, or even the smell of the female genital swelling might vary from group to group.

Ecological species concept defines species as a group of organisms exploiting a single niche. This concept focuses on the importance of natural selection and emphasizes that speciation results from influences of different habitats. As the Jurmain textbook states on page 121, "For each population, the ecological niche will vary slightly, and different phenotypes will be more advantageous in each. For example, one population might be more arboreal, and another more terrestrial; but there would not be an intermediate population equally successful on the ground and in the trees."

Speciation is hypothesized to have occurred in three different ways: **allopatric** speciation, parapatric speciation, or sympatric speciation. The first, allopatric, is the most widely accepted among scientists and requires complete reproductive isolation within a population, leading to species separated from its ancestral population. Only partial reproductive isolation is necessary in parapatric speciation. That means that populations could overlap. However, in this situation, a hybrid zone would form in an area between two partially separated populations. In sympatric speciation, a population diverges into multiple species without geographical separation. But biologists question whether this is a viable theory. One last type of speciation may also play a part in the evolution of certain species. In *instantaneous speciation*, chromosome

*S*ince man is a primate, the early primates were our ancestors. But who were we before primates appeared on the scene? The answer to that question is an evolving one—pun entirely intended!

Because humans are mammals, our evolutionary history before the appearance of primates follows mammalian evolution. Most of the fossils of living mammals begin to appear around 65 million years ago, which coincides with the mass extinction of the dinosaurs. But recent discoveries indicate that mammals evolved far earlier than previously thought. Fossils of mammal-like reptiles have been found dating back to the *Permian* period more than 250 million years ago, with the first "true" mammals appearing in the fossil record during the *Triassic* period, around 30 million years later.

Another question upon which light has been recently shed is the question of when marsupials (pouched mammals) and eutherians (placental mammals, like us) split. In the last decade, DNA analysis from living mammals has indicated that the split occurred sometime between 130 and 190 million years ago. These dates are supported by another exciting find: an almost complete skeleton of a mammal, given the name *Eomaia scansoria*, from deposits in China dated at 125 million years ago. This amazing specimen, described in 2002, is touted as the first eutherian.

Some discoveries have led to controversy; for instance, the question about whether primates evolved from plesiadapiformes, a widespread mammalian group of North America, or whether we are just relatives. In the video, Jonathan Bloch suggests that the genus *Carpolestes* was actually an early primate. This is based on a fossil he has found of a grasping paw with a nail—an adaptation that would support the arboreal hypothesis that early primates selected for traits that made it possible to live in trees.

But others, notably Matt Cartmill and Richard Kay from Duke University, challenge *Carpolestes* as the ancestor of today's primates. According to the visual predation hypothesis, we should expect the earliest primates to have modifications that would lead to stereoscopic vision. *Carpolestes* lacks a postorbital bar, a key primate characteristic, which suggests that this animal did not have primate-like vision. There is also controversy regarding its number of teeth and whether *Carpolestes* was too specialized to lead to the primates of the Eocene.

However, as more fossils come to light and new technologies develop, the story of where we came from continues to unfold. It is an exciting time for primate evolutionary biology. Stay tuned!

mutations produce immediate reproductive barriers. While common in plants, such a rapid chromosomal rearrangement in animals would not produce live offspring.

The identification of species in living organisms can be verified through observations of reproductive behavior—do they or do they not interbreed? This observation, however, is not possible when working with fossils. Scientists define fossil species by comparing the variation seen in fossil populations with the variation in known living species. There are two types of variation: **intraspecific** (within species), which is variation that can reflect age and sex differences among members of the same species, and **interspecific** (between species), which is variation among individuals that suggests they belong to reproductively isolated groups, or different species. Comparisons to living species and their reproductive behavior can determine which variation rings most true.

Identifying a genus from fossil records presents challenges as well. A **genus** is a group of closely related species, and that means that for one genus, there must be at least two species. Grouping species together into genera results in quite a bit of subjectivity. One test for contemporary animals is to check for the results of mating between two species—rare in nature but common in captivity. Two normally separate species who can interbreed and produce live, but not necessarily fertile, offspring can probably be placed in the same genus. Horses and donkeys are in the same genus, and when crossed, they produce a live but sterile offspring, the mule. Note that a mule is not a species, but a hybrid.

Since breeding experiments cannot be performed on extinct animals, other factors come into play. Members of the same genus share the same broad adaptive zone, meaning they share a basic ecological lifestyle. Teeth are usually the most plentiful **fossils**, and they provide excellent general ecological inferences. Cladistic analysis, which uses derived characters, helps determine genus as well.

Biologists are not only challenged in classification by the number of organisms present, but also by the vast amount of time involved. Geologists devised a **geological time scale** to organize that time. The earth's history is organized into eras and periods, which can further be broken down into epochs. Refer to the chart on page 129 of the Jurmain textbook for this time scale. The first vertebrate fossils are from the Paleozoic era, some 500 million years ago, when several varieties of mammal-like reptiles were diversifying. Geographical events influenced their evolutionary history from that point.

Continental drift, the movement of continents on sliding plates of the earth's surface, had profound effects on animals. Groups of land animals were isolated from each other by large water boundaries, and the distribution of reptiles and mammals was affected as well. During the next era, the Mesozoic, reptiles were the dominant land vertebrates, exploiting both aerial and marine habitats. The most famous of these reptiles were the dinosaurs.

As dinosaurs and other Mesozoic forms became extinct, ecological niches opened up for more animal diversity. The Cenozoic is known as the Age of Mammals because all the major lineages of modern mammals appear during this time. The success of mammals is, in part, the result of their ability to learn and their flexible behaviors. Mammals were selected for larger brains than are typically found in reptiles, allowing them to process more information. For a larger and complex brain to develop, mammals required more intense periods of growth which can occur *in utero* as well as after birth. Internal fertilization and development occurs among other animals, too, but with few exceptions, mammals give birth to live young, which makes them viviparous. Mammals differ in their length of gestation, with humans having very extended gestational periods.

Mammals and reptiles also differ in many other ways. Living reptiles have teeth that are all the same shape, while the teeth in mammals have a variety of shapes and are used to process a variety of food types. A third adaptive complex that aided in the success of mammals is that they can maintain a constant internal body temperature, referred to as **endothermy**, which allows them more flexibility with regard to climate extremes. Reptiles must acquire the energy to maintain body temperature from external sources; for instance, you have most likely seen a lizard lying on a rock sunning itself.

According to the Jurmain textbook, there are three major subgroups of living mammals: the egg-laying mammals, or monotremes; the pouched mammals, or marsupials; and the **placental** mammals. Development *in utero* is extremely important for brain development. Therefore, because monotremes are egg-laying mammals, it is understandable that they are considered "extremely primitive." Marsupial young are born extremely immature and must complete their development in an external pouch. They do not experience the benefit of a long gestational period inside the mother's body, connected to a nourishment source, as is common among placental mammals. Placental mammals have developed specialized tissue, known as the placenta, that provides for fetal nourishment over a longer gestational period that gives time for complex neural structures to form. Note, too, that the "bond of milk" between mother and offspring allows for increased physiological development and gives the offspring more exposure to learning stimuli. As the Jurmain textbook points out, a bigger brain more capable of learning isn't useful unless the organism has the opportunity to learn.

Macroevolutionary mechanisms operate more on the whole species and take much longer than the microevolutionary processes discussed in Lesson 4. While a group of organisms may have ample opportunity to reproduce, their actual numbers are regulated by the available resources of food, shelter, and space. If populations increase and resources decrease, some members of the population may seek new environments, which in turn may produce diverse species. This expansion and diversification of life-forms into new ecological niches is called adaptive radiation. The rapid expansion of placental mammals at the beginning of the Cenozoic era is a good example of this process. Another aspect of evolution closely related to adaptive radiation is the change from generalized characteristics (those adapted for many functions) to specialized characteristics (those limited to a more narrow set of functions).

The traditional view of evolution has emphasized that change occurs gradually in evolving lineages. This notion is referred to as phyletic gradualism. As noted on page 136 of the Jurmain textbook, phyletic gradualism would ideally produce the complete fossil record of evolving groups, if it could be recovered, showing "finely graded transitional differences between each ancestor and its descendant." Since the 1970s, an alternative process called **punctuated equilibrium** has gained prominent support. This is a process whereby species exist unchanged, or in equilibrium, for thousands of generations. Then this equilibrium is "punctuated" by rapid periods of change as the result of ecological, geological, or other catastrophic events in nature that can cause abrupt change. Punctuated equilibrium is an idea that views evolution as an uneven, gradual process, explaining the absence of "missing links." Advocates of this theory are not disputing evolutionary change, but rather the tempo and manner of such change. They hypothesize that an additional evolutionary mechanism—a punctuated event—is required to push the process along. The best evidence for punctuated equilibrium is found among fossil records of marine invertebrates.

Review Exercises

Matching I

Match each term with the appropriate definition or description.

1. _e_ analogies
2. _i_ ancestral
3. _b_ Chordata
4. _j_ clade
5. _h_ cladistics
6. _o_ cladogram
7. _a_ classification
8. _k_ derived
9. _g_ evolutionary systematics

10. _d_ homologies
11. _f_ homoplasy
12. _p_ monophyletic
13. _n_ phylogenetic tree
14. _q_ polyphyletic
15. _m_ shared derived
16. _l_ theropods
17. _c_ vertebrates

a. The ordering of organisms into categories.

b. The animal phylum to which the vertebrates belong.

c. Animals with segmented, bony spinal columns.

d. Similarities based on descent from a common ancestor.

e. Similarities based on function rather than ancestry.

f. Evolutionary development of similar characteristics by unrelated groups of organisms.

g. Traditional approach to classification in which presumed ancestors and descendants are traced by analysis of homologous characters through time, some of which may be primitive.

h. An approach to classification in which interpretations are based solely on analysis of derived characters.

i. Characters that are inherited from a remote ancestor, but may not be diagnostic of a lineage after the character first appeared.

j. A group of organisms sharing a common ancestor.

k. Characters modified from the ancestral condition and diagnostic of a particular lineage.

l. Small- to medium-sized ground-living dinosaurs, dated to approximately 150 million years ago and thought to be related to birds.

m. Relating to specific character traits shared in common between two life-forms and considered to be the most useful for making evolutionary interpretations.

n. A chart showing evolutionary relationships as determined by evolutionary systematics. It contains a time component and implies ancestor-descendant relationships.

o. A chart showing evolutionary relationships as determined by cladistic analysis. Its based solely on interpretation of shared derived characters. It contains no time component and does *not* imply ancestor-descendant relationships.

p. Referring to an evolutionary group (clade) composed of descendants all sharing a common ancestor.

q. Referring to an evolutionary group composed of descendants with more than one common ancestor.

Matching II

Match each term with the appropriate definition or description.

1. __F__ allopatric

2. __a__ biological species concept

3. __L__ ecological niche

4. __d__ ecological species concept

5. __k__ genus

6. __i__ interspecific

7. __h__ intraspecific

8. __j__ paleospecies

9. __e__ phylogenetic species concept

10. __c__ recognition species concept

11. __g__ sexual dimorphism

12. __b__ speciation

a. A group of individuals who are capable of fertile interbreeding, but are reproductively isolated from other such groups.

b. The most basic process in macroevolution.

c. A species concept that is defined by individuals recognizing others like themselves for mating purposes.

d. A group of organisms that exploit a single niche.

e. The splitting of populations into species based on an identifiable parental pattern of ancestry.

f. Living in different areas.

g. Physical differences between the sexes.

h. Within the same species.

i. Between species.

j. Species defined from fossil evidence.

k. A group of closely related species.

l. The role species play within their physical and biological environments.

Matching III

Match each term with the appropriate definition or description.

1. __g__ adaptive radiation
2. __b__ continental drift
3. __f__ endothermic
4. __d__ epoch
5. __i__ fossil
6. __a__ geological time scale
7. __e__ heterodont
8. __k__ mineralization
9. __c__ placental
10. __h__ punctuated equilibriumt
11. __j__ taphonomy

a. The organization of earth history.

b. Movement of continents on sliding plates.

c. The most widespread and numerous type of mammal during the Cenozoic.

d. A subdivision of a geological period.

e. Possession of different types of teeth that have specialized functions.

f. The ability to produce internal body heat through metabolic processes.

g. The relatively rapid expansion and diversification of life-forms into new ecological niches.

h. An evolutionary concept that change proceeds through long periods of stasis punctuated by rapid periods of change.

i. Remnants of organisms found in geological beds on the earth's surface.

j. The study of how bones and other materials come to be buried in the earth.

k. The transformation of plants or animals into stone-like structures.

Completion I

Fill each blank with the most appropriate term from the list below.

analogies   evolutionary systematics
ancestral   homologies
Chordata   homoplasy
clade   monophyletic
cladistics   phylogenetic tree
cladogram   polyphyletic
classification   shared derived
derived   theropods
ecological niche   vertebrates

1. A _analogies_ is the development of similar characteristics in different organisms that are not closely related.

2. Vertebrates are a subphylum of the animal phylum _Chordata_.

3. Similarities based on descent from a common ancestor are called _Homologies_.

4. _Vertebrates_ are chordate animals with segmented, bony spinal columns.

5. _Classification_ is the ordering of organisms into categories called taxa.

6. Similarities based on function are called _Homoplasy_.

7. A character that is inherited from a remote ancestor, but may not be diagnostic of a lineage after the character first appear is an _ancestral_ trait.

8. Characters that are modified from the ancestral condition and are diagnostic of a particular lineage are called _Derived_.

9. _Shared derived_ traits are characteristics shared in common between two life-forms.

10. A _Phylogenetic tree_ is a chart that shows evolutionary relationships.

11. A _Clade_ is a group of organisms sharing a common ancestor.

12. _evolu. Systematics_ is the traditional approach to classification and evolutionary interpretation in which lineages are traced in time by analysis of homologous characters.

13. A chart showing evolutionary relationships based on cladistic analysis is called a _cladogram_.

14. The classificatory system in which interpretations are based only on derived traits is called _Cladistics_.

15. _theropods_ were small to medium-sized ground-living dinosaurs that may be related to birds.

16. An evolutionary grouping that shares a single common ancestor is said to be a _Monophyletic_ group.

17. A _Polyphyletic_ grouping has more than one ancestor and therefore cannot be a clade.

18. An _eco. Niche_ is the position of a species within its physical and biological environments.

Completion II

Fill each blank with the most appropriate term from the list below.

adaptive radiation
allopatric
biological species concept
continental drift
ecological species concept
endothermic
epochs
genus
geological time scale
heterodont
interspecific
intraspecific
neocortex
paleospecies
phylogenetic species concept
placentals
punctuated equilibrium
recognition species concept
sexual dimorphism
speciation
taphonomy

1. _intra specific_ refers to studies within a species.

2. A _genus_ is a group of closely related species.

3. A species defined from fossil evidence is a _paleospecies_.

4. The _recognition species_ is defined by individuals recognizing others like themselves for mating.

5. The splitting of populations into species based on an identifiable parental pattern defines the _Phylogenetic species_

6. The _ecological species_ is defined as a group of organisms that exploit a single niche.

7. _Speciation_ is the process by which new species evolve from earlier species.

8. _interspecific_ refers to studies between species.

9. Species that lived in different geographic areas are _allopatric_.

10. A depiction of species as groups of individuals capable of fertile interbreeding but reproductively isolated from other such groups defines the _Biological species_.

11. _Sexual dimorph._ refers to physical differences between the sexes.

12. _Placentals_ are a subclass of mammals that are characterized by a nutritive connection between the mother and the developing offspring and by live births.

13. The concept that evolutionary change proceeds through long periods of stasis punctuated by rapid periods of change is called _Punctuated equilibrium_

14. An ___*adaptive rad.*___ is the relatively rapid expansion and diversification of life-forms into new ecological niches.

15. The movement of continents on sliding plates is called ___*Contenital drift*___.

16. ___*endothermic*___ refers to the production of internal body heat through metabolic processes.

17. The ___*geological time scale*___ organizes earth history into eras, periods, and epochs.

18. The Paleocene, Eocene, Oligocene, Miocene, and Pliocene are ___*epochs*___ of the Cenozoic.

19. ___*Heterodont*___ teeth are different types of teeth specialized for particular functions.

20. The ___*Neocortex*___ is the part of the brain involved with higher mental functions.

21. The study of how stream action affects the burial of fossil bones is called ___*taphonomy*___.

Self-Test

Select the best answer.

1. Taxonomic classification
   - a. reflects evolutionary relationships.
   - b. is based on acquired characteristics.
   - c. reflects current geographic distribution of species.
   - d. is applied only to nonhuman species.

2. Humans are
   - a. animals.
   - b. chordates.
   - c. mammals.
   - d. all of the above.

3. Animals possessing a dorsal hollow nerve cord and pharyngeal gill slits at some stage of their development are called
   - a. insects.
   - b. invertebrates.
   - c. chordates.
   - d. metazoans.

4. The primary basis for classifying organisms is similarities

   (a) that reflect evolutionary descent.
   b. in physiology.
   c. in ecological niches.
   d. in ancestral traits.

5. Bats have wings that allow them to fly. So do insects. Similarities, such as wings in different animals, that have a common function

   a. do not indicate a common ancestry.
   b. develop through homoplasy.
   c. are called analogies.
   (d.) involve all of the above.

6. Humans and other apes have certain characteristics in common, such as a broad sternum, a Y-5 cusp pattern on the molars, and the lack of a tail. These traits are all

   a. analogies.
   b. primitive traits.
   (c.) shared derived traits.
   d. general traits.

7. The approach to classification that analyzes derived characters only is

   (a.) cladistics.
   b. phenetics.
   c. evolutionary systematics.
   d. typology.

8. When assessing evolutionary relationships, one approach is to interpret patterns of ancestral and derived characters. This approach is termed

   a. cladistics.
   b. phenetics.
   (c.) evolutionary systematics.
   d. typology.

9. Structural similarities shared by a wide array of very distantly related species inherited from a common ancestor are called

   a. derived traits.
   b. ancestral traits.
   c. primitive traits.
   (d.) both b and c.

10. A lineage that shares a common ancestor, also called a clade, is said to be

    a. monophyletic.
    b. derived.
    c. polyphyletic.
    d. interspecific.

11. Which of the following describes a diagram that shows relationships based on shared derived traits?

    a. a cladogram
    b. a phylogenetic tree
    c. numerical states
    d. both b and c

12. The most commonly used species concept is the

    a. biological species concept.
    b. recognition species concept.
    c. ecological species concept.
    d. phylogenetic species concept.

13. The recognition species concept emphasizes

    a. reproductive isolation.
    b. natural selection separating species from one another.
    c. the ability of individuals to recognize one another for mating.
    d. metrical similarity.

14. Diet, terrain, vegetation, type of predators, relationship with other species, and activity patterns help to define an animal's

    a. phylogeny.
    b. evolutionary lineage.
    c. ecological niche.
    d. physiology.

15. Which of the following describes the position of a species within their physical and biological environments?

    a. ecological niche
    b. ontogeny
    c. phylogeny
    d. both b and c

16. The ecological species concept emphasizes
    a. reproductive isolation.
    b. natural selection separating species from one another.
    c. the ability of individuals to recognize one another for mating.
    d. metrical similarity.

17. The formation of a species that is geographically separated from its ancestral population is called
    a. sympatric speciation.
    b. allopatric speciation.
    c. parapatric speciation.
    d. instantaneous speciation.

18. Which of the following are factors that must be considered when interpreting fossil species?
    a. individual variation
    b. age differences
    c. sexual dimorphism
    d. all of the above

19. Closely related species are grouped together in a
    a. paleospecies.
    b. subspecies.
    c. genus.
    d. family.

20. Fossil genera can best be defined by
    a. a broad adaptive zone.
    b. ancient DNA.
    c. ancestral traits.
    d. primitive traits.

21. How has continental drift isolated breeding populations?
    a. by water barriers
    b. by geographical barriers such as mountains
    c. by increasing the opportunities for gene flow
    d. Both a and b are ways that continental drift has isolated organisms.

22. Continental drift is explained by

    a. parallel evolution.

    b. the Big Bang.

    c. Pangea.

    (d.) plate tectonics.

23. In the early Mesozoic, Pangea broke into two large continents, Gondwana and Laurasia. Laurasia consisted of the present-day continents of

    a. South America and Africa.

    b. South America, Africa, and Australia.

    c. North America and Europe.

    d. North America, Europe, and Asia.

24. Scientists organize time by

    a. the pentatonic scale.

    b. taxonomy.

    c. the geological time scale.

    d. all of the above.

25. Compared to reptiles, mammals

    a. have similarly shaped teeth.

    (b.) have larger brains.

    c. are all egg layers.

    d. obtain their body heat from the environment through behavior.

26. The fossil material that is available for most vertebrates, including primates, are

    a. pelves.

    b. humerus and other arm bones.

    (c.) teeth.

    d. femurs, which are the largest bones in any vertebrate.

27. After birth, a young mammal has a period of neural development coupled with learning. Some refer to this period of close association between the young mammal and its mother as the

    a. rehearsal period.

    (b.) placental connection.

    c. biosocial perspective.

    (d.) "bond of milk."

28. The opening up of ecological niches that accompanied the extinction of the dinosaurs provided opportunities for rapid mammalian diversification. This is a good example of
    a. parallel evolution.
    b. adaptive radiation.
    c. phyletic gradualism.
    d. convergent evolution.

29. The fossil record of many marine invertebrates shows long periods where there is very little change in species. Then a new species appears without any transitional species. These observations best support the idea of
    a. convergent evolution.
    b. punctuated equilibrium.
    c. phyletic gradualism.
    d. small microevolutionary changes lead to transspecific evolution.

30. The primate fossil record does **NOT** seem to support
    a. slow gradual change from ancestor to descendant.
    b. punctuated equilibrium.
    c. phyletic gradualism.
    d. small microevolutionary changes that lead to transspecific evolution.

31. The process of transforming a living tooth into a stone-like fossil tooth is called
    a. mineralization.
    b. adaptation.
    c. adaptive radiation.
    d. punctuated equilibrium.

32. The study of how bones and tools came to be buried in the earth is called
    a. ecology.
    b. mineralization.
    c. evolutionary systematics.
    d. taphonomy.

33. The rapid evolutionary success of the mammmals can be attributed in part to their larger brains, and in particular, the outer covering of the cerebrum called the
    a. placenta.
    b. neocortex.
    c. cortex.
    d. clade.

Short-Answer Questions

1. Discuss the two main approaches to classification.

   Evolutionary Systematics: More traditional and does based on ancestor-decent relationships.

   Cladistics: Based soley on Homologous traits, derived Character.

2. Describe analogous and homologous traits. Please provide an example for each.

   Homologous: Traits derived from a Common ancestor.

   Analogous: Based on Function alone

3. Discuss the difference between ancestral and derived traits.

4. Explain what allopatric speciation is.

   Where closely related species live in different Areas and Creates divergance + Reproductive isolation.

5. What is continental drift?

   The Movement of major landmasses (continent on sliding Plates on the earths serface

Application Questions

1. Compare and contrast the biological, recognition, and ecological species concepts.

   Eco: Species exploits Single Niche
   Recog: Ability to identify their own species for mating.
   Bio: Capable of Fertil Interbreeding but reproductive Isolated.

2. Explain why it is difficult to recognize a fossil species.

3. Describe the traits that distinguish placental mammals from reptiles.

4. Define adaptive radiation and provide a major example.

Adaptive Radiation is the rapid expansion + diversification of life forms in ecological niches. For instence the extention of dino. left large eco. Niches for other smaller animals to inhabit.

5. Compare phyletic gradualism with punctuated equilibrium.

Phyletic= life form are constently going through small Microevolution.
Punctuated = long times w/ no change.

Answer Key

Matching I

1. e (video lesson, segment 1; objective 1)
2. i (video lesson, segment 1; objective 1)
3. b (objective 1)
4. j (objective 1)
5. h (video lesson, segment 1; objective 1)
6. o (objective 1)
7. a (video lesson, segment 1; objective 1)
8. k (video lesson, segment 1; objective 1)
9. g (video lesson, segment 1; objective 1)
10. d (video lesson, segment 1; objective 1)
11. f (objective 1)
12. p (objective 1)
13. n (video lesson, segment 1; objective 1)
14. q (objective 1)
15. m (objective 1)
16. l (objective 1)
17. c (video lesson, segment 3; objective 1)

Matching II

1. f (objective 4)
2. a (video lesson, segment 2; objective 3)
3. l (video lesson, segment 2; objective 2)
4. d (video lesson, segment 2; objective 3)
5. k (objective 5)
6. i (objective 5)
7. h (objective 5)
8. j (objective 5)
9. e (objective 3)
10. c (objective 3)
11. g (objective 5)
12. b (video lesson, segment 2; objectives 4 & 8)

Matching III

1. g (video lesson, segment 3; objective 8)
2. b (video lesson, segment 3; objective 6)
3. f (objective 7)
4. d (objective 6)
5. i (objective 5)
6. a (video lesson, segment 3; objective 6)
7. e (objective 7)
8. k (objective 5)
9. c (objective 7)
10. h (objective 9)
11. j (objective 5)

Completion I

1. homoplasy (objective 1)
2. Chordata (objective 1)
3. homologies (video lesson, segment 1; objective 1)
4. Vertebrates (video lesson, segment 3; objective 1)
5. Classification (video lesson, segment 1; objective 1)
6. analogies (video lesson, segment 1; objective 1)
7. ancestral (video lesson, segment 1; objective 1)

8. derived (video lesson, segment 1; objective 1)

9. Shared derived (objective 1)

10. phylogenetic tree (video lesson, segment 1; objective 1)

11. clade (objective 1)

12. Evolutionary systematics (video lesson, segment 1; objective 1)

13. cladogram (objective 1)

14. cladistics (video lesson, segment 1; objective 1)

15. Theropods (objective 1)

16. monophyletic (objective 1)

17. polyphyletic (objective 1)

18. ecological niche (video lesson, segment 2; objective 2)

Completion II

1. Intraspecific (objective 5)

2. genus (objective 5)

3. paleospecies (objective 5)

4. recognition species concept (objective 3)

5. phylogenetic species concept (objective 3)

6. ecological species concept (video lesson, segment 2; objective 3)

7. Speciation (video lesson, segment 2; objectives 4 & 8)

8. Interspecific (objective 5)

9. allopatric (objective 4)

10. biological species concept (video lesson, segment 2; objective 3)

11. Sexual dimorphism (objective 5)

12. Placentals (objective 7)

13. punctuated equilibrium (objective 9)

14. adaptive radiation (video lesson, segment 3; objective 8)

15. continental drift (video lesson, segment 3; objective 6)

16. Endothermic (objective 7)

17. geological time scale (video lesson, segment 3; objective 6)

18. epochs (objective 6)

19. Heterodont (objective 7)

20. neocortex (objective 7)

21. taphonomy (objective 5)

Self-Test

1. a. is the correct answer. Whether it is evolutionary systematics or cladistics, the two approaches discussed in the Jurmain textbook, a classificatory approach should reflect evolutionary relationships. (video lesson, segments 1 & 2; objective 1)

2. d. is the correct answer. Humans are animals and belong to the Phylum Chordata. A subphylum of the chordates are the vertebrates, to which the mammals are a class. Humans are, of course, mammals also. (objective 1)

3. c. is the correct answer. In addition, unique chordate characteristics include a notochord and a muscular postanal tail. (objective 1)

4. a. is the correct answer. Such similarities are called homologies. (video lesson, segment 1; objective 1)

5. d. is the correct answer. Wings in bats and insects have different origins. They are analogies, or structures that serve a similar function, and they develop through a process called homoplasy. Insects and vertebrates have not shared a common ancestor for at least 550 million years ago at the latest, and probably longer than that. Thus, all of these answers are correct. (video lesson, segment 1; objective 1)

6. c. is the correct answer. The broad sternum, Y-5 cusp pattern, and lack of a tail are traits that arose in the hominoid lineage after divergence from a catarrhine ancestor. They are unique to the hominoids within the Anthropoidea. (video lesson, segment 1; objective 1)

7. a. is the correct answer. It is emphasized in cladistics that several traits that appear to be unique to a lineage need to be analyzed to prevent/avoid errors due to homoplasy. (video lesson, segment 1; objective 1)

8. c. is the correct answer. Evolutionary systematics utilizes primitive traits as well as derived traits. Critics of this approach say that primitive traits tell us little about relationships. (video lesson, segment 1; objective 1)

9. d. is the correct answer. Examples of primitive traits in primates include the five-digit paw and the clavicle (also known as the collarbone). (video lesson, segment 1; objective 1)

10. a. is the correct answer. A clade is a group of organisms made up of a common ancestor and all descendants of that common ancestor. Thus, it is monophyletic, or a single evolutionary lineage. (objective 1)

11. a. is the correct answer. A cladogram depicts relationships in branches. (objective 1)

12. a. is the correct answer. The biological species concept was formulated by evolutionary biologist Ernst Mayr in 1942. (video lesson, segment 2; objective 3)

13. c. is the correct answer. This approach puts some organisms that are currently separate in the same species, such as the red wolf and the coyote who produce hybrids. (objective 3)

14. c. is the correct answer. The niche is the organism's role in the environment. (video lesson, segment 2; objective 2)

15. a. is the correct answer. Each niche is unique to a species. (video lesson, segment 2; objective 2)

16. b. is the correct answer. This concept views a species as a group of individuals exploiting a single ecological niche. (video lesson, segment 2; objective 3)

17. b. is the correct answer. Allopatric speciation is also known as geographic speciation and is another concept developed by Ernst Mayr. (objective 4)

18. d. is the correct answer. Paleontologists work with limited materials from extinct species They are dealing with a small sample in both time and space. Therefore, there is a great deal of variation. We must look at living species to get an idea of the variation we should expect. Three factors that provide most of the variation are age differences, sexual dimorphism, and variation found among individuals. (objective 5)

19. c. is the correct answer. These species achieve genus rank because they are incapable of breeding and producing viable fertile offspring. For example, a mare and a jackass, both in the genus *Equus*, can produce a hybrid (the mule) but it is sterile. (objective 5)

20. a. is the correct answer. There is no clear definition of what a genus is for living species, but ecological adaptation has been offered. In the case of fossil mammals, especially if teeth have been recovered, a broad adaptive zone is one of the best pieces of evidence for how this animal lived. (objective 5)

21. d. is the correct answer. Plate tectonics have moved continents and created mountain ranges. As this occurred, populations of organisms became separated from one another. (video lesson, segment 3; objective 6)

22. d. is the correct answer. The continents are on plates that move and collide with one another. (video lesson, segment 2; objective 6)

23. d. is the correct answer. Laurasia was the northern continent. (objective 6)

24. c. is the correct answer. Geological time is organized into eras, periods, and epochs. (video lesson, segment 3; objective 6)

25. b. is the correct answer. The cerebral cortex, in particular, has increased in size on the mammalian brain. (objective 7)

26. c. is the correct answer. Teeth are the hardest substance in the body of a mammal and the structures that are most likely to be preserved. (objective 7)

27. d. is the correct answer. This bond is a period of great learning for a young mammal and some of the things it learns are what foods are safe or unsafe to eat, what animals are predators, and, in social species, who is likely to be an ally or a competitor. (objective 7)

28. b. is the correct answer. The mammalian adaptive radiation of the Paleocene was a ecological release, meaning that many niches had been vacated by the extinction of the dinosaurs. (video lesson, segment 3; objective 8)

29. b. is the correct answer. Punctuated equilibrium theory predicts that a long period of stasis will be followed by a punctuated event. (objective 9)

30. b. is the correct answer. Primates, and especially humans, do not appear to fit the expectations of punctuated equilibrium. (objective 9)

31. a. is the correct answer. In mineralization, water-born minerals seep into the spaces within the bone or tooth, or can actually replace the bone's original minerals with different ones. (objective 5)

32. d. is the correct answer. Taphonomy, or the study of how bones and other materials come to be buried in the earth and preserved as fossils, can provide clues to ancient environments and how they affect the process of fossilization. (objective 5)

33. b. is the correct answer. The neocortex is the outer covering of the cerebrum of the brain which is enlarged in mammals. The neocortex is associated with higher mental functions, including the integration of incoming information from different sensory organs. (objective 7)

Short-Answer Questions

Your answers should include the following:

1. Evolutionary systematics and cladistics are the two main approaches to classification. Evolutionary systematics uses homologies, which may be both ancestral and derived characters, to trace descent through time. Cladistics uses only derived traits in analysis of relatedness and does not consider time. (video lesson, segment 1; objective 1)

2. Analogous traits among different organisms are structures that have arisen for a particular function, but there is no common evolutionary descent of the trait. One example is the wings of a butterfly *versus* the wings of a bat. These two organisms have not had a common ancestor since at least 550 million years ago. Bats are vertebrates, whereas butterflies are insects. Both have evolved wings independent of one another. Homologies are similarities between organisms based on common descent. These structures may not even have the same function. For example, the hands of a human are homologous to the wings of a bat and to the pectoral fin of a whale. These appendages have different functions but the bones that make up all of these structures have common ancestral origins. (video lesson, segment 1; objective 1)

3. Ancestral (also called primitive) traits are characters inherited by a group of organisms from a distant common ancestor. Having five digits is an ancestral trait in primates that was present in the common ancestor for all mammals. A derived (also referred to as specialized or modified) trait is a character that has developed from the ancestral condition and is particular to an evolutionary lineage. Most of the structures involved with bipedalism in humans, such as the highly modified foot, are derived traits and are unique to the hominin lineage. (video lesson, segment 1; objective 1)

4. Allopatric (sometimes called geographic) speciation is a process by which a population speciates. The population is located in the same area, but it becomes divided in some way that causes reproductive isolation. This could be, for example, a river forming in the middle of the range of a species that will not cross water (this is believed to have occurred with the bonobos and chimpanzees). Allopatric speciation is widely accepted as the most common process for speciation within a population. (objective 4)

5. Continental drift is the changing position of the continents on the face of the earth. Continental drift occurs because the continents rest on gigantic tectonic plates that move and collide with one another. Such massive geological movement can induce

earthquakes, volcanic activity, and mountain building. One of the results of continental drift is that the position of the continents that which we are familiar with today has changed over time. This change has profound ramifications for the evolution of organisms that become isolated in the process. (video lesson, segment 3; objective 6)

Application Questions

Your answers should include the following:

1. The biological species concept is the most commonly used concept for species definition. This concept defines a species as a group of individuals that are capable of fertile interbreeding and are reproductively isolated from other such groups. Most vertebrate zoologists prefer this concept. The recognition species concept considers a species to be a group of individuals capable of recognizing one another for mating purposes. In theory, this type of selective mating is a component of a species concept emphasizing mating and is compatible with the biological species concept. The ecological species concept defines a species as a group of organisms exploiting a single niche. They are molded into a species by natural selection that separates them from other species (who occupy other niches). (video lesson, segment 2; objective 3)

2. Explanations such as the biological species concept do not apply well to fossil species. Because the biological species concept depends on knowing whether two individuals are capable of fertile interbreeding, it cannot be applied to fossils. Fossils exhibit variation but is the variation significant? This has to be inferred from living species in which variation may be due to individual, age, and sex differences. To decide whether fossil specimens belong in different species we need to look at the variation we observe in contemporary species. However, this is still a difficult task. As a result, any paleospecies will show more variation than is found in extant species. Add to this a temporal component and assigning fossils to species becomes even more uncertain. Because this undertaking is so daunting, other methods have been tried instead of using standard Linnaean taxonomy. These include using clusters of derived traits to define species. Nevertheless, this can be ambiguous also. As a result, two main philosophical approaches have developed. "Splitters" are those taxonomists who split fossil material into a number of species. "Lumpers" are those scientists who tend to condense the material into a smaller number of species. (video lesson, segment 2; objective 5)

3. Several characteristics of mammals relate to learning and general flexibility. Mammals have larger brains than are generally found in reptiles. Specifically, the neocortex has expanded and covered the deeper primitive brain. This outer layer controls higher brain functions. Some mammals (usually after a lineage has reached a particular body size) have convoluted brains. Associated with a more complex brain is a longer, more intense period of growth. Eutherian mammals are characterized by a nutritive connection between the mother and the developing offspring called the placenta. After birth, they require a period of learning in which there is a close bond with the mother.

   Mammals have heterodont dentition. These are specialized teeth with particular functions, such as slicing by incisors and grinding by cheek teeth (premolars and molars). This dentition enables mammals to mechanically breakdown difficult morsels, such as bones and fibrous leaves, which no living reptile can handle. Mammals are also endothermic (they metabolically produce heat) and homeothermic (i.e., they can maintain a stable body temperature) instead of being ectothermic like reptiles, which obtain much of their heat from the environment. (video lesson, segment 3; objective 7)

4. An adaptive radiation is the rapid expansion and diversification of organisms into new ecological niches. This has occurred countless times over the history of the earth. Adaptive radiation depends on two factors: the adaptive potential of a taxon and the availability of niches. When reptiles became fully terrestrial they were able to take advantage of open niches away from water and this class underwent an adaptive radiation. Similarly, when the large reptiles underwent a mass extinction at the end of the Mesozoic, mammals underwent an adaptive radiation as they occupied the niches vacated by the reptiles. (video lesson, segment 3; objective 8)

5. The traditional view of evolution is that change occurs gradually over a long period of time. Charles Darwin first proposed this model of evolution. Such slow evolution would produce a series of intermediate species, "missing links," if they could be found. Unfortunately, according to this perspective, the fossil record is incomplete. This view is called phyletic gradualism. Another perspective was presented in the 1970s. It is called punctuated equilibrium. In this model, there are no "missing links." The gaps are real, not artifacts of an imperfect fossil record. In punctuated equilibrium, there is a long period when no change occurs. This is called stasis. Stasis is only interrupted occasionally by sudden bursts, punctuated events, in which there is rapid evolution resulting in new species. Punctuated equilibrium does not produce intermediate species. (objective 9)

Notes:

Lesson Review

Lesson 5: Macroevolution

PLEASE NOTE: Use this matrix to guide your study and achieve the learning objectives of this lesson. It will also help you to view the video, which defines and demonstrates important concepts and principles as they relate to everyday life and actual case studies.

Learning Objective	Textbook	Student Guide	Video Lesson
1. Compare and contrast two concepts of taxonomy known as *evolutionary systematics* and *cladistics*.	pp. 112–119	Key Terms: 1, 2, 3, 4, 5, 6, 7, 8, 9, 10, 11, 12, 13, 14, 15, 16, 17; Matching I: 1, 2, 3, 4, 5, 6, 7, 8, 9, 10, 11, 12, 13, 14, 15, 16, 17; Completion I: 1, 2, 3, 4, 5, 6, 7, 8, 9, 10, 11, 12, 13, 14, 15, 16, 17; Self-Test: 1, 2, 3, 4, 5, 6, 7, 8, 9, 10, 11; Short-Answer: 1, 2, 3.	Segment 1: *Principles of Classification* Segment 2: *Speciation & Evolutionary Forces* Segment 3: *Vertebrate & Mammalian Evolutionary History*
2. Define the concept of an ecological niche, and offer an example.	p. 121	Key Terms: 22; Matching II: 3; Completion I: 18; Self-Test: 14, 15.	Segment 2: *Speciation & Evolutionary Forces*
3. Define the three main species concepts identified by evolutionary biologists and describe the current debate surrounding these concepts.	pp. 119–122	Key Terms: 18, 20, 21, 23; Matching II: 2, 4, 9, 10; Completion II: 4, 5, 6, 10; Self-Test: 12, 13, 16; Application: 1.	Segment 2: *Speciation & Evolutionary Forces*
4. Describe the various processes of speciation and how they differ.	pp. 121–124	Key Terms: 19, 24; Matching II: 1, 12; Completion II: 7, 9; Self-Test: 17; Short-Answer: 4.	Segment 2: *Speciation & Evolutionary Forces*

Learning Objective	Textbook	Student Guide	Video Lesson
5. Discuss the difficulties of identifying species in the fossil record.	pp. 124–126	Key Terms: 25, 26, 27, 28, 29, 30, 31, 32; Matching II: 5, 6, 7, 8, 11; Matching III: 5, 8, 11; Completion II: 1, 2, 3, 8, 11, 21; Self-Test: 18, 19, 20, 31, 32; Application: 2.	Segment 2: *Speciation & Evolutionary Forces*
6. Explain the concept of geologic time and the action of continental drift over long periods of geologic time.	pp. 128–132	Key Terms: 33, 34, 35; Matching III: 2, 4, 6; Completion II: 15, 17, 18; Self-Test: 21, 22, 23, 24; Short-Answer: 5.	Segment 2: *Speciation & Evolutionary Forces* Segment 3: *Vertebrate & Mammalian Evolutionary History*
7. Describe the major characteristics of placental and nonplacental mammals as adaptations.	pp. 132–134	Key Terms: 36, 37, 38, 39; Matching III: 3, 7, 9; Completion II: 12, 16, 19, 20; Self-Test: 25, 26, 27, 33; Application: 3.	Segment 3: *Vertebrate & Mammalian Evolutionary History*
8. Define macroevolution and discuss the processes of macroevolution.	pp. 134–136	Key Terms: 19, 40, 41; Matching II: 12; Matching III: 1; Completion II: 7, 14; Self-Test: 28; Application: 4.	Segment 1: *Principles of Classification* Segment 2: *Speciation & Evolutionary Forces* Segment 3: *Vertebrate & Mammalian Evolutionary History*
9. Explain the difference between gradualism and punctuated equilibrium, two modes of the evolutionary process.	pp. 136–138	Key Terms: 42; Matching III: 10; Completion II: 13; Self-Test: 29, 30; Application: 5.	

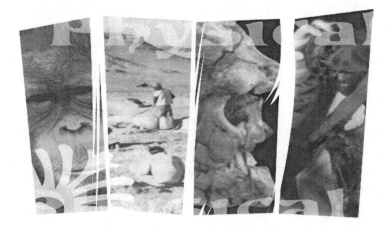

Part I: The Living Primates

Checklist

For the most effective study of this lesson, complete the following activities in this sequence.

Before Viewing the Video

❑ Read the Preview, Learning Objectives, and Viewing Notes below.

❑ Read Chapter 6, "Survey of the Living Primates," pages 142–181, in *Introduction to Physical Anthropology*.

What to Watch

❑ After reading the textbook assignment, watch the video for Lesson 6, *The Living Primates*.

After Viewing the Video

❑ Briefly note your answers to the questions listed at the end of the Viewing Notes.

❑ Review the Summary below.

❑ Review all reading assignments for this lesson, including the Viewing Notes in this lesson.

❑ Write brief answers to the "Critical Thinking Questions" at the end of Chapter 6 in the textbook.

❑ Complete the Review Exercises below. Check your answers with the Answer Key and review when necessary.

❑ Use the Lesson Review matrix found at the end of this lesson to review and assess your knowledge of each Learning Objective.

Preview

Lesson 2 explored the development of evolutionary theory and began to illuminate some common misconceptions concerning human evolution. For example, humans didn't evolve directly from monkeys. Rather, the earliest human ancestor evolved from a species that lived 5 to 8 million years ago. The lineage that our human ancestors evolved from separated from monkey-like ancestors some 20 million years ago, and it also gave rise to the lineage now represented by apes. Over time, monkeys, apes, and humans evolved into the respective species that we see today. Lesson 6 describes the physical characteristics that define the order Primates, gives a brief overview of the major groups of living primates, and describes some methods anthropologists use to compare genetic data on living primate species.

Human and nonhuman primates have retained a number of ancestral characteristics, which is why scientists can group them all into one category. Primatologists look to our closest relatives, the living nonhuman primates, to better understand not only human origins, but current human behavior as well. Comparing anatomy and behavior of nonhuman primates to humans helps explain the significance of physiological and behavioral systems as adaptive responses to various selective pressures during the evolutionary process. Therefore, studying nonhuman primates offers us an incredible opportunity to discover our own evolutionary history.

Physical anthropologists are also extremely sensitive to the social issues that surround these species today. Most of these researchers feel that the lack of knowledge within the general public about nonhuman primates contributes to abuse of these primate species when they are most endangered. This concern fuels the desire, within the anthropological community to educate the public.

Perhaps if more humans understood the connection between *Homo sapiens* and monkeys and apes, we would be more fervent in our attempts to stop, or at least slow down, the human behaviors that are leading to their extinction, a tragedy that would affect us all.

Concepts to Remember

※ Lesson 5 defined the term **classification** as the ordering of organisms into categories, such as orders, families, and genera, to show evolutionary relationships. Classification is a way scientists have of simplifying the diversity they find in nature. Organisms are classified first on the basis of physical similarities. However, for similarities to be useful in classification, they must reflect evolutionary descent.

※ Lesson 5 also explained the idea of generalized and specialized characteristics. A trait that is adapted for many functions is said to be generalized, while a trait that is limited to a few functions is referred to as specialized.

Learning Objectives

After you complete this lesson, you should be able to:

1. Describe the primates in terms of their ancestral mammalian traits as well as derived traits unique to primates. (pp. 144–147)

2. Discuss the evolutionary trends that define the order Primates, emphasizing habitat, dentition/diet, locomotion, and brain size in relation to complex social behavior. (pp. 144–154)

3. Discuss primate locomotor patterns and their morphological correlations. (pp. 153–154)

4. Outline the taxonomic classification of primates, emphasizing the major taxa (suborder, superfamily, family, genus, and species). (pp. 154–156)

5. List the distinguishing features of prosimians and monkeys. (pp. 156–166)

6. List the members of the superfamily Hominoidea (including *Homo sapiens*), and describe their morphological traits and social structures. (pp. 166–174)

7. Discuss the conditions that imperil many primate species as well as what is being done to reverse these trends. (pp. 174–180)

At this point, read Chapter 6, "Survey of the Living Primates," pages 142–181.

Viewing Notes

The video opens with a visual montage of primates—a ring-tailed lemur, a baboon, and a gorilla. As you watch the lemur on the screen, you may wonder how it is possible that you are, however remotely, related to it. After all, a lemur has a tail, some are only 5 inches long, and they eat bugs. However, as you now know from Lesson 5, organisms are classified according to a specific set of criteria, and the lemur, baboon, and gorilla are all primates, just as humans are. Primates, both human and nonhuman, all share some identifying characteristics—a grasping hand and foot, nails instead of claws, eyes that sit on the front of the face with overlapping visual fields, an increased dependence on vision, a generalized dentition, a larger brain for their body size, and young who mature slowly.

Nevertheless, while primates share some characteristics, the variations in characteristics allows them to be subdivided into smaller groups. The primates are divided into two large categories: **prosimians** and **anthropoids**. Prosimians include lemurs and lorises. Tarsiers, while traditionally considered prosimians because they share some physical similarities with them, straddle both categories because they also share anthropoid features. The Jurmain textbook addresses this by putting them along with the anthropoids into the subfamily Strepsirhini. Anthropoids include monkeys, apes, and humans. On pages 154–156, the Jurmain textbook describes some recent molecular studies that are helping us to refine taxonomic categories within the order Primates.Lesson 5 introduced the term *adaptive radiation*, meaning the relatively rapid expansion and diversification of life-forms into new ecological niches. The prosimian radiation occurred between 33 and 55 million years ago and a wide variety of prosimian forms emerged at that time. The prosimians living today are the closest examples we have of those earliest primates. They depend more on their sense of smell than do monkeys and apes and have a moist nose and a long muzzle that contains anatomical structures that guide scent into the brain. Their eyes are set more to the side of the face, which reduces stereoscopic vision. However, it is theorized that since many prosimians are active at night, their sense of smell is more important to their survival than vision. In the video, anthropologist Wendy Birky mentions that many prosimians possess one or more claws used for grooming, called the "grooming claw," and many have a "dental comb," formed by forward-projecting lower incisors and canines. The dental comb is used for both grooming and feeding.

The video segments of the primates in action offer an opportunity to compare and contrast them with each other. For instance, sections concerning the commonalities and differences between chimpanzees and bonobos expand on the information in the Jurmain textbook. These two apes may look like the same species, but their social structures and behavior are quite different.

Questions to Consider

✻ What are some of the differences between chimpanzees and bonobos regarding their behaviors and social structures?

✻ What are the particular characteristics necessary for an animal to be placed into the Order Primates?

✻ What is meant by "adaptive niche"?

✻ What are some examples of differences between Old World monkeys and New World monkeys?

✻ What is meant by the term "brachiation"? According to the video, what species of nonhuman primates are "master brachiators"?

Watch the video for Lesson 6, *The Living Primates.*

Segment 1: *Prosimians*
Segment 2: *Anthropoids*
Segment 3: *New World Monkeys*
Segment 4: *Old World Monkeys*
Segment 5: *Apes*

Key Terms and Concepts

Page references are keyed to *Introduction to Physical Anthropology,* 13th edition.

1. **prosimians:** Members of a suborder of Primates, the Prosimii (pronounced "pro-sim´-ee-eye"). Traditionally, the suborder includes lemurs, lorises, and tarsiers. (video lesson, introduction; objective 1)

2. **primates:** Members of the order of mammals Primates (pronounced "pry-may-tees"), which includes lemurs, lorises, tarsiers, monkeys, apes, and humans. (p. 144; video lesson, introduction; objective 1)

3. **anthropoids:** Members of the primate infraorder *Anthropoidea* (pronounced "ann-throw-poid´-ee-uh"), which includes monkeys, apes, and humans (p. 144; video lesson, introduction; objective 1)

4. **morphology:** The form (shape, size) of anatomical structures; can also refer to the entire organism. (p. 145; video lesson, introduction; objective 2)

5. **omnivorous:** Having a diet consisting of many food types, such as plant materials, meat, and insects). (p. 146; video lesson, segment 4; objective 2)

6. **diurnal:** Active during the day. (p. 146; video lesson, segment 1; objective 2)

7. **olfaction:** The sense of smell. (p. 146; objective 2)

8. **nocturnal:** Active during the night. (p. 146; video lesson, segment 1; objective 2)

9. **stereoscopic vision:** The condition whereby visual images are, to varying degrees, superimposed. This provides for depth perception, or viewing the external environment in three dimensions. Stereoscopic vision is partly a function of structures in the brain. (p. 146; video lesson, introduction; objective 2)

10. **binocular vision:** Vision characterized by overlapping visual fields provided by forward-facing eyes. Binocular vision is essential to depth perception. (p. 146; objective 2)

11. **hemispheres:** The two halves of the cerebrum that are connected by a dense mass of fibers. (The cerebrum is the large, rounded, outer portion of the brain.) (p. 146; objective 2)

12. **neocortex:** The more recently evolved portions of the cortex of the brain that are involved with higher mental functions and composed of areas that integrate incoming information from different sensory organs. (p. 147; objective 2)

13. **sensory modalities:** Different forms of sensation (e.g., touch, pain, pressure, heat, cold, vision, taste, hearing, and smell). (p. 147; objective 2)

14. **arboreal:** Tree-living; adapted to life in the trees. (p. 147; video lesson, introduction; objective 2)

15. **adaptive niche:** An organism's entire way of life; where it lives, what it eats, how it gets food, how it avoids predators, and so on. (p. 147; video lesson, introduction; objective 2)

16. **dental formula:** Numerical device that indicates the number of each type of tooth in each side of the upper and lower jaws. (p. 152; objective 2)

17. **cusps:** The bumps on the chewing surface of premolar and molars. (p. 152; objective 2)

18. **quadrupedal:** Using all four limbs to support the body during locomotion; the basic mammalian (and primate) form of locomotion. (p. 152; video lesson, segment 2; objective 3)

19. **brachiation:** Arm swinging, a form of locomotion used by some primates. Brachiation involves hanging from a branch and moving by alternately swinging from one arm to the other. (p. 152; video lesson, segment 5; objective 3)

20. **lumbar:** Pertaining to the lower back. The lumbar area is longer in monkeys than it is in humans and apes. (p. 154; objective 3)

21. **Strepsirhini:** (strep´-sir-in-ee) The primate suborder that includes lemurs and lorises. (Colloquial form: strepsirhine.) (p. 154; objective 4)

22. **Haplorhini:** (hap´-lo-rin-ee) The primate suborder that includes tarsiers, monkeys, apes, and humans. (Colloquial form: haplorhine.) (p. 154; objective 4)

23. **rhinarium:** (rine-air´-ee-um) The moist, hairless pad at the end of the nose seen in most mammalian species. The rhinarium enhances an animal's ability to smell. (p. 157; objective 5)

24. **New World monkeys:** Phrase used to distinguish those monkey species that are geographically distributed in the Western hemisphere (primarily southern Mexico and Central and South America) with a separate evolutionary history from species found in Africa and Asia (pp. 160–163; video lesson, segment 2; objective 5)

25. **Old World monkeys:** Phrase used to distinguish those monkey species that are geographically distributed in sub-Saharan Africa, southern Asia, and Japan with a separate evolutionary history from species found in southern Mexico and Central and South America. (pp. 163–165; video lesson, segment 2; objective 5)

26. **Cercopithecidae:** (serk-oh-pith´-eh-see-dee) The taxonomic family that includes all Old World monkeys. (p. 163; objective 4)

27. **cercopithecines:** (serk-oh-pith´-eh-seens) Common name for members of the subfamily of Old World monkeys that includes baboons, macaques, and guenons. (p. 163; video lesson, segment 4; objective 4)

28. **colobines:** (kole´-uh-beans) Common name for members of the subfamily of Old World monkeys that includes the African colobus monkeys and Asian langurs. (p. 163; video lesson, segment 4; objective 4)

29. **ischial callosities:** Patches of tough, hard skin on the buttocks of Old World monkeys and chimpanzees. (p. 164; objective 5)

30. **sexual dimorphism:** Differences in physical characteristics between males and females of the same species. For example, humans are slightly sexually dimorphic for body size, with males being taller, on average, than females of the same population. Sexual dimorphism is very pronounced in many species, such as gorillas. (p. 165; video lesson, segment 4; objective 5)

31. **Hominoidea:** The formal designation for the superfamily of anthropoids that includes apes and humans. (pp. 155, 166; video lesson, segment 5; objectives 4 & 6)

32. **hominoids:** Members of the primate superfamily (Hominoidea) that includes apes and humans. (p. 166; objectives 4 & 6)

33. **territorial:** Pertaining to the protection of all or part of the area occupied by an animal or group of animals. Territorial behaviors range from scent marking to outright attacks on intruders. (p. 167; objective 6)

34. **frugivorous:** (fru-give´-or-us) Having a diet composed primarily of fruit. (p. 168; objective 2)

35. **natal group:** The group in which animals are born and raised. (*Natal* pertains to birth.) (p. 169; objective 6)

36. **intelligence:** Mental capacity; ability to learn, reason, or comprehend and interpret information, facts, relationships, and meanings; the capacity to solve problems, whether through the application of previously acquired knowledge or through insight. (p. 174; objective 6)

Summary

To identify the components that have shaped the evolution of *Homo sapiens*, a good starting point is a comparison between humans and our closest living relatives, the nonhuman primates—prosimians, monkeys, and apes.

All **primates** share a number of characteristics with other placental mammals, including body hair, a fairly long gestation period followed by live birth, mammary glands, different kinds of teeth, the ability to maintain a constant internal body temperature, increased brain size, and the capacity for learning and behavioral flexibility. On the other hand, there are characteristics that set primates apart from other mammals. This isn't a simple task. Primates have remained *generalized*, meaning they have retained ancestral traits that some other mammalian species have lost over time. Other mammalian species have become *specialized* as a result of particular selective pressures on them. In Figure 6-1 on page 145 of the Jurmain textbook, the first photo shows how a horse's hoof illustrates this type of adaptation. Primates, however, cannot be defined by one or even two traits that they share in common. Anthropologists therefore identify a group of characteristics that considered together characterize the entire order. All primates share a number of characteristics with other placental mammals, including mammary glands and body hair. They also have a fairly long gestation period followed by live birth, different kinds of teeth, the ability to maintain a constant internal body temperature, increased brain size, and the capacity for learning and behavioral flexibility. (A more detailed explanation of these attributes can be found in the Jurmain textbook on pages 144–147.)

Limbs and Locomotion: A tendency towards erect posture; flexible limb structure permitting the different ways primates move; ability to grasp objects

Diet and Teeth: Lack of dietary specialization; generalized dentition, indicating a wide variety of food sources

Senses and the brain: Reliance on visual sense and less dependence on the sense of smell reflected in changes in the skull, eyes, and brain; color vision; **stereoscopic vision** (ability to perceive objects in three dimensions)

Maturation, learning, and behavior: Delayed maturation and longer life span; greater dependence on learned behavior, in part because of more intense parental attention, more efficient rearing; social group living with adult males in the group; **diurnal** activity patterns

Primate anatomical traits evolved as adaptations to environmental circumstances, such as climate, diet, and predation risks. One explanation for primate adaptations is the **arboreal** *hypothesis*, which proposes that the challenges of tree living resulted in selection for primate characteristics such as grasping hands and feet, **binocular** and stereoscopic **vision**, and increased cognitive processing ability. The *visual predation hypothesis* contradicts the arboreal hypothesis, suggesting that primates evolved as a result of the pressure to forage fruit and hunt insects on the ground and lower tree canopy. This hypothesis points out that forward-facing eyes are characteristic not only of primates, but also of predators such as cats and owls. Also, other arboreal creatures, like squirrels, have not evolved the same set of characteristics as have primates. A third hypothesis for the selective factors favoring primate characteristics points to the rise of *angiosperms* (flowering plants), which offered new dietary choices and increased the need for fine visual and tactile discrimination to partake of nectar, seeds, fruits and other plant by-products. The emergence of flowering plants roughly coincides with the emergence of the earliest primates. Keep in mind that these hypotheses are not mutually exclusive. Primate characteristics might have begun in nonarboreal settings, but at some point the primates did inhabit the trees. However the basic primate traits began to evolve, they are well suited to life in the trees. Grasping hands and feet are beneficial for movement through the trees.

The majority of primates are arboreal, even though some **Old World monkeys**, such as baboons in Africa or macaques in India and Southeast Asia, have adapted to life on the ground in areas where forests are sparse. Still, all primates spend some time in trees. Almost all nonhuman primates are found in tropical or semitropical settings. Most eat a variety of fruits, nuts, seeds, leaves, and insects; a few eat small mammals. Their overall lack of dietary specialization correlates to their generalized dentition, since primates are able to exploit many food sources.

There is a good reason why the playground apparatus is called the "monkey bars." Primates can move in a variety of ways because of a generalized limb structure and hip and shoulder **morphology** (the form of anatomical structure). Almost all primates are **quadrupedal**, meaning they use all four limbs to support the body during locomotion. Some prosimians and tarsiers move by *vertical clinging and leaping*. They cling vertically to a trunk or a branch and then leap to the next trunk. As described in the video by anthropologist Naomi Bishop, they leap from trunk to trunk to trunk instead of running along branches. Tarsiers, weighing about a half pound and measuring just four inches long, are capable of leaping up to seven feet. **Brachiation**, or arm swinging, is the main form of locomotion in apes, especially gibbons. Humans have also retained a brachiator anatomy, particularly in the shoulder girdle. Some **New World monkeys** are *semibrachiators,* meaning they move by a combination of arm swinging and leaping.

The order *Primates* includes all primates. But at the next taxonomic level down, the *suborder*, primates are divided into two large categories: Prosimii (lemurs, lorises, and usually, tarsiers) and Anthropoidea (monkeys, apes, and humans). The suborder is narrower than the order. At the suborder level, the prosimians are grouped together, distinct from all the other primates, implying they are more closely related to each other than to **anthropoids**. Similarly, all anthropoid species are more closely related to each other than to the prosimians. **Strepsirhini** (lemurs and lorises) and **Haplorhini** (tarsiers, monkeys, apes, and humans). The suborder is narrower than the order. At the suborder level, lemurs and lorises are grouped together, distinct from other primates, implying they are more closely related to each other than to any other primates. Currently, biomolecular evidence is helping scientists refine classifications and identify the biological relationships between species. For instance, scientists compared 97 human genes to the genes of chimpanzees, gorillas, and orangutans and determined that humans and chimpanzees have between 98.4 and 99.4 identical genes. Based on the rate of genetic change, they then calculated that the last common ancestor between humans and chimpanzees existed between 5 and 6 million years ago, when the lineage then diverged. This time frame is very recent in evolutionary terms and helps to explain the close biological and genetic similarities between chimpanzees and ourselves.

Classifying tarsiers is a bit problematic. Tarsiers are highly specialized and display several unique physical characteristics. Traditionally, they have been placed in the prosimian subgroup because of some of the traits they share with lemurs and lorises. But biochemically, they are more closely related to anthropoids. The term **prosimian** is commonly used to distinguish the more primitive lemurs and lorises and tarsiers from the anthropoids, and is used this way in the video. However, acknowledging the debate concerning the taxonomic status of tarsiers, the Jurmain textbook classifies tarsiers as members of the suborder Haplorhini along with the anthropoids (monkeys, apes, and humans).

The following is a brief explanation of the classification of primates. For further details, refer to pages 154–174 in the Jurmain textbook.

Lemurs and Lorises

These are the most primitive of the primates, meaning that anatomically, they are more similar to earlier mammalian ancestors than are the other primates. They depend on a more pronounced sense of smell (**olfaction**), and they mark territories with a scent in a way other primates do not. Recall the video segment in which a male lemur marked the tree by rubbing the scent glands on his wrists onto the bark of a tree. Prosimian eyes are more laterally placed than anthropoids, and they have shorter gestation and maturation periods. Lemurs and lorises have a grooming claw on the second toe. The claw points up, making it ideal for self scratching. Both lemurs and lorises show the same general adaptive level. They have good grasping and climbing skills and developed vision, although not completely stereoscopic. Lemurs are found only on the island of Madagascar and adjacent islands off the east coast of Africa. Lorises are found in tropical forest and woodland habitats of India, Sri Lanka, Southeast Asia, and Africa.

Tarsiers

The five recognized tarsier species all inhabit island areas in Southeast Asia. They are **nocturnal** insectivores that leap onto their prey. Their most striking physical characteristics are their enormous eyes, which are adapted for night vision; each is the size of a tarsier brain. The eyes are immobile within their sockets, so to compensate for this, tarsiers are able to rotate their heads 180 degrees in the same manner as owls.

Traits of Anthropoids

There are many differences between the various anthropoids (monkeys, apes, and humans), but there are certain traits which they share and which distinguish them as a group from lemurs and lorises:

1. Larger average body size
2. Larger brain
3. Reduced reliance on the sense of smell
4. Increased reliance on vision
5. Greater degree of color vision
6. Back of eye socket formed by a bony plate
7. Different pattern of blood supply to brain
8. Fusion of two sides of the mandible at the midline to form one bone
9. Less specialized dentition
10. Different female reproductive anatomy
11. Longer gestation and maturation periods
12. Increased parental care
13. More mutual grooming

Monkeys

Approximately 85 percent of all primates are monkeys and they are divided into two groups separated by geographical area and several million years of separate evolutionary history. *New World monkeys* consist of approximately 70 species and vary in size from 12 ounces for the marmoset to 20 pounds for the howler monkey. They are found in a wide range of arboreal habitats in southern Mexico and central and South America. All except the owl monkey are diurnal. Most are quadrupedal, although some are semibrachiators. Some species of New World monkeys, marmosets and tamarins, live in social groups composed of a mated pair, or in a polyandrous mating situation composed of a female and two males and their offspring. Among these species, males are highly involved in infant care. Other species are found in mixed-sex groups of all age categories, and some form monogamous pairs and live with their subadult offspring.

Old World monkeys are found throughout sub-Saharan Africa and southern Asia, ranging from tropical jungles to semiarid desert conditions. Although most Old World monkeys are found in tropical zones, they also range as far north and east as Japan, and a few species live in temperate zones, such as Nepal, that can get fairly cold. Most monkeys are quadrupedal and primarily arboreal, although some, such as baboons, have adapted to life on the ground. They spend much of their time sleeping, feeding, and grooming while sitting with their upper bodies held erect. They exhibit various forms of locomotion, from arboreal quadrupedalism to terrestrial quadrupedalism to semibrachiation. **Sexual dimorphism** (marked differences in body size or shape between sexes) is typical of some terrestrial species. Different forms of social organization exist among the different species of Old World monkeys. Some live in small groups with only a few adult males while others are found in large social groups. Monogamous pairing is not common.

As primatologists learn more and more about our closest evolutionary relatives, the way in which we care for those in captivity has also evolved. Take the saga of Bill the chimp.

Bill was captured in Africa as an infant in 1946. By age six, still a youngster, he was fighting mock boxing matches in the circus, where he was a favorite performer. When adolescence arrived, Bill, like most male chimps, became aggressive and tried to dominate his trainers. Soon he was deemed unmanageable and was sold to a zoo.

Although the zoo was delighted to have him, they—like most zoos at the time—put their new chimp in a cage in the belief that food, water, and shelter were all a captive primate needed. It was a far cry from the freedom of his life in the circus, and even farther from that of chimps in the wild.

As the years went by, and research into primates revealed more about their cognitive abilities and social needs, the zoo bought another chimp, Ziggy, to be a companion for Bill. However, the two did not take to each other and soon became enemies. When Ziggy died in 1996, Bill did not seem the least bit upset.

Finally, in 2007, the zoo embarked upon a renovation that would create an environment more like Bill's African home. But a week after construction started, Bill became seriously ill and was euthanized. He was 61 years old. This highly intelligent, quite social creature had spent 49 years in a cage.

While the zoo's awareness of chimps' needs unfolded too late for Bill, others are reaping the benefits of primatologists' attention to their species. *The National Chimpanzee Sanctuary*, known as "Chimp Haven," is a 200-acre environment located near Shreveport, Lousiana, that was designed to mimic chimpanzees' African habitat, providing lifetime care for otherwise unwanted chimps who are retired from medical research, the entertainment industry, and service as personal pets.

Unlike Bill's austere cage, Chimp Haven was built to stimulate behaviors that would be natural to chimps in the wild: large social groups, "fission-fusion" social organization, environmental manipulation, and nesting and foraging behavior. The environment is a continuum that meets the needs of different personalities and personal histories, from indoor bedrooms, to outdoor play areas, to larger forested expanses of up to five acres with towering trees and 20-foot climbing structures.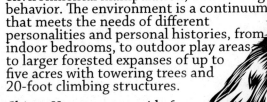

Chimp Haven can provide for up to 200 chimps, who are placed in social settings depending upon their individual needs. Established chimps help newer arrivals adjust to the more natural environment and to relearn their native behaviors.

Hominoids (Apes and Humans)

Hominoids are the other large grouping of anthropoids and include apes and humans.
Hominoidea is the formal designation for the superfamily that includes gibbons and siamangs,
orangutans, gorilla, bonobos, chimpanzees, and humans. Apes and humans differ from monkeys
in numerous ways:

1. Larger body size (except for gibbons and siamangs)
2. Absence of a tail
3. Shortened trunk
4. Differences in the shoulder joint (adapted for suspensory locomotion)
5. More complex behavior
6. More complex brain and cognitive abilities
7. Increased period of infant development and dependency

Gibbons and Siamangs

These animals are found in the southeastern tropical areas of Asia. The smallest of the apes,
gibbons and siamangs have extremely long arms, curved fingers, and powerful shoulder
muscles that are ideal for brachiation. Such anatomical adaptations may be related to their
behavior of feeding while hanging beneath branches. They primarily eat fruit plus a variety of
leaves, flowers, and insects. The basic social unit is an adult male and female with dependent
offspring. Although they may appear monogamous, adults do mate with others outside the
group. Male gibbons and siamangs are very much involved in rearing their young.

Orangutans

Found in heavily forested areas on the Indonesian islands of Borneo and Sumatra, orangutans
are threatened by extinction because of poaching and the continuing loss of habitat. They are
almost completely arboreal, although they sometimes travel quadrupedally on the ground. They
are large apes with pronounced sexual dimorphism. They are solitary, although adult females
are usually accompanied by a few dependent offspring.

Gorillas

There are traditionally three subspecies recognized: the western lowland gorilla is found in
eastern central Africa; the eastern lowland gorilla inhabits the eastern border of the Democratic
Republic of the Congo (DRC; formerly known as Zaire); and mountain gorillas are found in
the mountainous areas of central Africa in Rwanda, the DRC, and Uganda. The largest of all
living primates, gorillas exhibit marked sexual dimorphism. Because of their size, they are
primarily terrestrial and use a semiquadrupedal manner of locomotion. Gorillas are almost
exclusively vegetarian. The social structure of the mountain gorillas is a group of one or two
large *silverback* males, some adult females, and their offspring. The term *silverback* refers to
the saddle of white hair across the back of a full adult male. Typically, both females and males
leave their **natal group** (the group in which animals are born and raised) as young adults;
females join other groups, and males often live alone for awhile and eventually form their
own group. Westland lowland gorillas seem to have a similar social structure, but with smaller
groups. Contrary to popular belief and storytelling, gorillas are not ferocious but actually shy
and gentle, although certainly aggressive when threatened.

Chimpanzees

Chimpanzees are found in equatorial Africa. Chimpanzees are anatomically similar to gorillas, although much smaller, but the ecological adaptations between the two differ in that chimpanzees spend more time in the trees. They use quadrupedal knuckle walking like gorillas, but because of their smaller size, they also may swing from tree to tree. While gorillas are shy and quiet, chimpanzees are active, easily excitable, and noisy. They live in large, fluid communities with a group of bonded males at the center, especially in East Africa. In some West African groups, females appear to be more central to the community. Individuals of a chimpanzee community are rarely all together at the same time. For instance, adult females forage alone or with their offspring. Individuals form lifelong attachments with friends and relatives, and if they stay in their natal group, the bond between mothers and infants can remain strong until one of them dies. Among chimpanzees, males generally remain in their natal group, while females leave to join another group.

Bonobos

Bonobos only inhabit an area south of the Zaire River in the Democratic Republic of the Congo. Bonobos physically resemble chimpanzees, but they are more arboreal and less excitable and aggressive. They, too, live a large, fluid community, but in bonobos, the community is centered on female-male bonding. This is different from chimpanzees and most other nonhuman primates. This bonding may be related to bonobo sexuality, which is also different from that of other primates. Copulation is frequent and occurs throughout a female's estrous cycle, so sex isn't linked solely to reproduction. Physical violence is uncommon within these communities.

Humans

Humans are the only living representatives of the habitually bipedal hominids. Our primate heritage is evident in our anatomy, genetic makeup, and many behaviors. Our teeth very much resemble ape teeth, except our canines are small; we are dependent on vision with decreased reliance on our sense of smell; and we have flexible limbs and grasping hands. We, too, are generally **omnivorous**.

During the last 800,000 years, however, our species has been characterized by dramatic increases in brain size and other neurological changes. We also are completely dependent on culture. Lesson 1 explained that culture is learned, passed from one generation to the next independently of biological factors. Many other primates rely on learned behavior, but in humans, the predisposition for culture is perhaps the most critical component of human evolutionary history.

Two other traits, habitual bipedal locomotion and spoken language, are unique to humans. Later lessons in this course explain how our bodies are anatomically suited for walking on two legs. Human evolution has also modified certain neurological and anatomical structures in the brain and throat to allow us to speak. Apes cannot form words, but they are able to communicate through the use of symbols. Lesson 7 examines these evolutionary changes in greater detail.

Endangered Primates

According to the Jurmain textbook, more than half of all nonhuman primate species are in danger of extinction. Habitat destruction, hunting, and live capture for export or local trade are the human behaviors that are responsible for this circumstance. Many primate species are threatened by habitat destruction regardless of where they live, and they are also hunted for display in zoos, for medical research, for the exotic pet trade, and for food in some areas. Steps are being taken to ensure the survival of some species. Several private international efforts are aimed at stemming the loss of habitats and stopping the "bushmeat" trade in efforts to prevent further nonhuman primate species from disappearing.

Review Exercises

Matching

Match each term with the appropriate definition or description.

1. _C_ arboreal
2. _j_ binocular vision
3. _a_ diurnal
4. _b_ frugivorous
5. _h_ morphology

6. _e_ neocortex
7. _i_ omnivorous
8. _f_ quadrupedal
9. _d_ stereoscopic vision
10. _g_ territorial

a. Active during the day.

b. Having a diet composed primarily of fruit.

c. Tree-living; adapted to life in the trees.

d. The condition whereby visual images are, to varying degrees, superimposed on one another, that is in part a function of structures in the brain.

e. The more recently evolved portions of the cortex of the brain that are involved with higher mental functions.

f. Using all four limbs to support the body during locomotion.

g. Pertaining to the protection of all or part of the area occupied by an animal or group of animals.

h. The form of anatomical structures or an entire organism.

i. Having a diet consisting of many food types.

j. Vision characterized by overlapping visual fields provided by forward-facing eyes.

Completion

Fill each blank with the most appropriate term from the list below.

bonobo	ischial callosities
brachiation	mammal
cercopithecines	New World monkeys
chimpanzee	rhinarium
gorilla	tarsier
hominoids	vertical clinging and leaping

1. A type of primate whose characteristics are intermediate between prosimians and anthropoids is _tarsier_.

2. The largest living primate is the _gorilla_.

3. _Chimpanzee_ and _bonobo_ are thought of as our closest living relatives.

4. A _rhinarium_ is found only in prosimians.

5. _New world Monkeys_ found in the Western hemisphere (primarily southern Mexico and Central and South America), have a separate evolutionary history from the baboons and macaques of Africa.

6. Primates are a type of _mammal_.

7. _vir. cling. + leap_ is a type of locomotion found mainly in some lemurs, while _brachiation_ is found mainly in apes.

8. Baboons, macaques, and guenons are _Cercopithecines_ a subfamily of Old World monkeys.

9. Together, apes and humans are called _hominoids_.

10. _ischial callosities_ are patches of tough skin found on the buttocks of Old World monkeys and chimpanzees.

Self-Test

Select the best answer.

1. Which of the following are **NOT** apes?

    a. chimpanzees

    b. lemurs

    c. bonobos

    d. gibbons

2. Which of the following are New World monkeys?

    a. tarsiers

    b. lemurs

    c. marmosets

    d. gibbons

3. Which of the following is the most pressing cause of decline in primate populations?

    a. the overpopulation of nonhuman primate groups

    b. the trapping of live primates for biomedical research

    c. habitat loss

    d. the trapping of live primates for the pet trade

4. The 2.1.2.3 dental formula is found in which types of primates?

   a. most prosimians

   b. New World Anthropoids

   c. Old World Anthropoids

   d. only lemurs

5. Quadrupedal locomotion is

   a. a locomotion type where all four limbs support the body.

   b. a common form of locomotion in many primates.

   c. found only in some types of lemurs.

   d. both a and b.

6. Identifying single traits that define primates is **NOT** easy because they

   a. are very specialized.

   b. retain many primitive traits.

   c. share little in common with other kinds of animals.

   d. do b and c.

7. Some traits used to describe primates include

   a. a large brain relative to body size.

   b. tactile pads on the digits.

   c. an opposable thumb.

   d. all of the above.

8. The suite of characteristics shared by primates is thought to be the result of adaptation to

   a. a desert climate.

   b. an arboreal environment.

   c. ground living.

   d. none of the above.

9. Vertical clinging and leaping is characteristic of which types of primates?

   a. some prosimians

   b. hominoids

   c. tarsiers

   d. a and c

10. Primates are divided into the following two suborders:

    a. Platyrrhini and Catarrhini.

    b. Cercopithecines and Colobines.

    c. Haplorhini and Strepsirhini.

    d. Hylobatidae and Pongidae.

11. Prosimians (lemurs and lorises) differ from monkeys in that

    a. some prosimians have a dental comb.

    b. prosimians have a rhinarium.

    c. prosimians have a postorbital bar and lack an enclosed bony orbit.

    d. all of the above statements are true.

12. New World monkeys differ from Old World monkeys in which of the following ways?

    a. Most New World monkeys have a 2.1.2.3 dental formula.

    b. New World monkeys have downward-facing nostrils.

    c. Some New World monkeys have prehensile tails.

    d. All of the above statements are true.

13. Humans differ from other living primates in that

    a. they are bipedal.

    b. they have a 2.1.2.3 dental formula.

    c. they are very dependent upon culture.

    d. a and c are true.

14. Hominoid distinguishing features include

    a. the absence of a tail.

    b. a relatively larger brain to body size ratio.

    c. arms that are longer than legs (in most species).

    d. all of the above.

15. Which of the following are steps that are being taken to ensure the survival of some primate species?

    a. National parks and reserves are being set aside.

    b. The bushmeat trade is being promoted in many countries.

    c. The body parts of a wider variety of species is being promoted for use in medicines.

    d. all of the above

Short-Answer Questions

1. List three primate species in danger of extinction, their location, and their estimated population size.

2. What are the three types of primate locomotion? Connect each locomotor type with the body proportions typical for that form of locomotion.

Quadrupel loco: arms + legs OF = length
vertical cling + leapeing: legs longer than arms.
Brachiation: arms longer than legs

3. List three primate features that are thought to be primitive traits.

5 digits, Flexiable limb Structure, No dietary Specilization.

4. List three differences between chimpanzee and bonobo behavior and social structure.

Bonobos are Smaller in Structure and have a Calmer in temperment. Also Chimpanzee's have a more male dominated Society.

5. Why is primate classification currently in a state of transition?

Because we now have more ways to discover traits that Primates have in their genetics.

Application Questions

1. What are the three main threats to nonhuman primate populations? How has human population growth contributed to the this problem?

As Human Pop. Grow they require more land and resources to Support their needs. They also hunt and trap Nonhuman Primates.

2. How is the adaptive niche of a primate reflected in the characteristics of a species or taxa? Please use at least three examples from the video and the Jurmain textbook.

Their developement Places them in an aboreal niche with Forward Facing eyes, grasping hands + feet + the ability to Survive on plants. lorises and the aye-aye Have grasp

3. Explain the taxonomic dilemma of the tarsier. Why is there disagreement about whether to place it with prosimians or anthropoids?

They lack fingers + large eyes

a rhinarium that is Found in all Prosimians, but they do Share Characteristics with both anthropoids + Prosimians.

Answer Key
Matching
1. c (video lesson, introduction; objective 2)
2. j (objective 2)
3. a (video lesson, segment 1; objective 2)
4. b (objective 2)
5. h (video lesson, introduction; objective 2)
6. e (objective 2)
7. i (video lesson, segment 4; objective 2)
8. f (video lesson, segment 2; objective 3)
9. d (video lesson, introduction; objective 2)
10. g (objective 6)

Completion
1. tarsier (objective 5)
2. gorilla (objective 6)
3. Chimpanzee; bonobo (objective 4)
4. rhinarium (objective 5)
5. New World monkeys (video lesson, segment 4; objective 5)
6. mammal (objective 1)
7. Vertical clinging and leaping; brachiation (objective 3)
8. cercopithecines (video lesson, segment 5; objective 4)
9. hominoids (video lesson, segment 5; objectives 4 & 6)
10. ischial callosities (objective 5)

Self-Test
1. b. is the correct answer. Lemurs are prosimians; they are not apes. (objective 4)
2. c. is the correct answer. Marmosets and tamarins are in the family Callitrichidae, which is included in the New World monkeys. (objective 4)
3. c. is the correct answer. Habitat loss is the single greatest threat to primate populations resulting from human overpopulation. (objective 7)
4. c. is the correct answer. The 2.1.2.3 dental formula is characteristic of Old World monkeys and hominoids, including humans. New World monkeys have a 2.1.3.3 or 2.1.3.2 dental formula, while prosimians' dental patterns are highly variable. (objective 2)

5.　d. is the correct answer. Quadrupedal locomotion involves using all four limbs for support of the body. It is the most common form of locomotion for most primates and almost all monkeys use this form of locomotion. (video lesson, segment 2; objective 3)

6.　b. is the correct answer. The primate order is difficult to define because primates have retained many primitive traits. They are not particularly specialized and share many traits in common with other animals. It is an overall suite of traits that distinguishes the primates from other mammal groups. (objective 1)

7.　d. is the correct answer. All of these traits are used to describe the order Primates. (objective 1)

8.　b. is the correct answer. It is thought that primates evolved in an arboreal environment. This idea is supported by the nature of their adaptations and the ancient environments in which primate fossils have been found. (video lesson, segment 1; objective 2)

9.　d. is the correct answer. Vertical clinging and leaping is only found in some lemurs and in tarsiers. (video lesson, segment 2; objective 3)

10.　c. is the correct answer. The two primate suborders are Haplorhini and Strepsirhini. (objective 4)

11.　d. is the correct answer. All of these characteristics are found in lemurs and lorises but not in anthropoids. (objective 5)

12.　c. is the correct answer. Prehensile tails are only found in some New World monkeys. The 2.1.2.3 dental formula and downward-facing nostrils are found in Old World anthropoids. (video lesson, segment 3; objective 5)

13.　d. is the correct answer. Bipedality and an extreme dependence on culture are traits only found in humans. Humans share having an enclosed bony orbit with other anthropoids. (objective 6)

14.　d. is the correct answer. All of these are distinguishing features of Hominoids. (objective 6)

15.　a. is the correct answer. The establishment of national parks has helped some endangered primate species as well as other threatened and endangered plants and animals. The bushmeat trade and the use of primate parts in medicines is highly discouraged by conservation organizations and others interested in primate conservation. (objective 7)

Short-Answer Questions

Your answers should include the following:

1.　For a list of a few of the many primates in danger of extinction, please use Table 6-1 on page 175 of the Jurmain textbook. (objective 7)

2.　Quadrupedal locomotion: arms and legs of equal or nearly equal length.

Vertical clinging and leaping: legs longer than arms.

Brachiation: arms longer than legs. (video lesson, segments 1, 2, & 5; objective 3)

3. On pages 144 through 147 of the Jurmain textbook, you will find a list of many primate traits. Some indicate in parentheses that they are derived, others are listed as ancestral. Some ancestral traits include: the retention of five digits, a lack of dietary specialization, a generalized dentition, and a flexible, generalized limb structure. (objective 1)

4. Bonobos are slightly smaller, more arboreal, less aggressive, and less excitable than chimpanzees. They also have a female-dominated society, while chimpanzee society is very male dominated. In addition, bonobos tend to use sexual contact to diffuse tension in a group in a way that chimpanzees do not. (video lesson, segment 5; objective 6)

5. The classification system of primates, and many other organisms is in transition because of the advent of many new biochemical techniques for looking at phylogeny, in particular the recent rapid expansion of our knowledge of genetics. (objective 4)

Application Questions

Your answers should include the following:

1. There are three main threats to nonhuman primate populations, habitat destruction, human predation, and live capture for trade. As human populations grow they require more land for human use—for shelters, farming, lumber for paper, and so on. People also need food and many nonhuman primates are considered to be good to eat, or their parts are used in medicine. More people means more demand for these goods. The same principle applies to live trade. The more people there are, the more demand there will be for live primates as pets, or research subjects. (objective 7)

2. Primates, in general, are adapted for an arboreal niche. They have grasping hands and feet, forward-facing eyes with stereoscopic and binocular vision, and good color vision. Colobines and howler monkeys eat mainly leaves and they have evolved specialized guts that help them to digest leaves. Nocturnal primates, like the lorises, tend to have very large eyes. The aye-aye has a specialized digit for finding and extracting grubs from hollow spaces in trees. Many more examples can be found in the Jurmain textbook and the video. (video lesson, introduction; objective 2)

3. Tarsiers are very interesting taxonomically because they share characteristics of both prosimians and anthropoids. Experts disagree over which group they are most closely related to. Tarsiers lack a rhinarium, a trait found in all prosimians. But genetic analyses show that they are more similar to the prosimians. Tarsiers are a very ancient taxa and they probably evolved into a new lineage around the time that prosimians and anthropoids were becoming separate groups. (video lesson, segment 1; objectives 4 & 5)

Lesson Review

Lesson 6, Part I: The Living Primates

PLEASE NOTE: Use this matrix to guide your study and achieve the learning objectives of this lesson. It will also help you to view the video, which defines and demonstrates important concepts and principles as they relate to everyday life and actual case studies.

Learning Objective	Textbook	Student Guide	Video Lesson
1. Describe the primates in terms of their ancestral mammalian traits as well as derived traits unique to primates.	pp. 144–147	Key Terms: 1, 2, 3; Completion: 6; Self-Test: 6, 7; Short-Answer: 3.	Introduction
2. Discuss the evolutionary trends that define the order Primates, emphasizing habitat, dentition/diet, locomotion, and brain size in relation to complex social behavior.	pp. 144–154	Key Terms: 4, 5, 6, 7, 8, 9, 10, 11, 12, 13, 14, 15, 16, 17, 34; Matching: 1, 2, 3, 4, 5, 6, 7, 9; Self-Test: 4, 8; Application: 2.	Introduction; Segment 1: *Prosimians;* Segment 4: *Old World Monkeys*
3. Discuss primate locomotor patterns and their morphological correlations.	pp. 153–154	Key Terms: 18, 19, 20; Matching: 8; Completion: 7; Self-Test: 5, 9; Short-Answer: 2.	Segment 1: *Prosimians;* Segment 2: *Anthropoids;* Segment 5: *Apes*
4. Outline the taxonomic classification of primates, emphasizing the major taxa (suborder, superfamily, family, genus, and species).	pp. 154–156	Key Terms: 21, 22, 26, 27, 28, 31, 32; Completion: 3, 8, 9; Self-Test: 1, 2, 10; Short-Answer: 5; Application: 3.	Segment 1: *Prosimians;* Segment 4: *Old World Monkeys;* Segment 5: *Apes*

156 PHYSICAL ANTHROPOLOGY: THE EVOLVING HUMAN

© 2012 Cengage Learning. All Rights Reserved. May not be scanned, copied or duplicated, or posted to a publicly accessible website, in whole or in part.

Learning Objective	Textbook	Student Guide	Video Lesson
5. List the distinguishing features of prosimians and monkeys.	pp. 156–166	Key Terms: 23, 24, 25, 29, 30; Completion: 1, 4, 5, 10; Self-Test: 11, 12; Application: 3.	Segment 1: *Prosimians*; Segment 2: *Anthropoids*; Segment 3: *New World Monkeys*; Segment 4: *Old World Monkeys*
6. List the members of the superfamily Hominoidea (including *Homo sapiens*), and describe their morphological traits and social structures.	pp. 166–174	Key Terms: 31, 32, 33, 35, 36; Matching: 10; Completion: 2, 9; Self-Test: 13, 14; Short-Answer: 4.	Segment 4: *Old World Monkeys*; Segment 5: *Apes*
7. Discuss the conditions that imperil many primate species as well as what is being done to reverse these trends.	pp. 174–180	Self-Test: 3, 15; Short-Answer: 1; Application: 1.	

LESSON 6, PART II

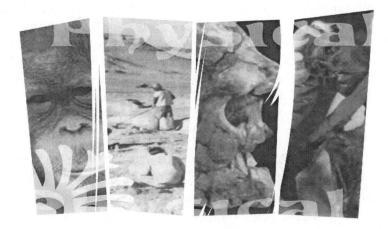

LESSON

6

Part II: Overview of the Fossil Primates

Checklist

For the most effective study of this lesson, complete the following activities in this sequence.

- ❑ Read the Preview and Learning Objectives below.

- ❑ Read Chapter 9, "Overview of the Fossil Primates," pages 238–281, in *Introduction to Physical Anthropology*.

- ❑ There is no video for Lesson 6, Part II.

- ❑ Review the Summary below.

- ❑ Review all reading assignments for this lesson.

- ❑ Write brief answers to the "Critical Thinking Questions" at the end of Chapter 9 in the textbook.

- ❑ Complete the Review Exercises below. Check your answers with the Answer Key and review when necessary.

- ❑ Use the Lesson Review matrix found at the end of this lesson to review and assess your knowledge of each Learning Objective.

Preview

Lesson 6, Part I, offered an overview of the major groups of living primates and explained how two species as seemingly diverse as a human and a ring-tailed lemur could be identified as primates. Lesson 6, Part II, shifts attention to the fossil remains of the oldest primates. Consider it a way of extending our family tree, bridging the gap between these early primates and ourselves. Chapter 9 of the Jurmain textbook begins in the Paleocene epoch, tracing the development of mammals that resemble humans more and more over time and concludes in the Miocene with the appearance of the first apes. Note that many fossil groups examined in this lesson are extinct and are not related to our own hominid ancestors. The abundance of primate lineages, however, points to their successful radiations at the time and help us see the progression of human evolution.

Concepts to Remember

❀ Lesson 5 introduced the term **homoplasy**, the separate evolutionary development of similar characteristics in different groups of organisms, and also discussed **shared derived** *characteristics*, which are specific character traits shared in common between two life-forms and considered the most useful for making evolutionary interpretations. Such terminology once again comes into play in this lesson as scientists examine traits of the primate fossils they have discovered.

❀ In Lesson 6, Part I, you encountered an outline of primate characteristics on pages 144–147 in the Jurmain textbook. Much of the outline explained aspects of primate **morphology**, the shape and size of anatomical structures, as well as behavioral adaptations. A quick review of this outline will assist in your reading for this lesson as scientists use the fossil evidence to sort out what belongs in which primate lineage.

Learning Objectives

After you complete this lesson, you should be able to:

1. Define the member species of the superorder Euarchonta, explain when they developed, and discuss why they are important in primate evolution. (pp. 240–244)

2. Identify where and when the plesiadapiforms are found and discuss their place in primate evolution. (pp. 244–246)

3. Identify which epoch and where the earliest undoubted primates appeared and discuss what type of modern primates the earliest primates most resemble. (pp. 246–265)

4. Discuss the debate surrounding anthropoid origins, and compare and contrast prosimian and anthropoid characteristics. (pp. 255–256)

5. Describe the types of primates found at the Fayum during the Oligocene. (pp. 256–260)

6. Discuss the current ideas for the origins of New World monkeys and how they arrived in the Americas. (pp. 260–262)

7. Contrast the characteristics of New World and Old World monkeys. (p. 259)

8. Discuss the lineage of the cercopithecoids. (pp. 262–265)

9. Describe early Miocene apes and where they are found. (pp. 265–269)

10. Compare and contrast ape and Old World monkey characteristics. (p. 264)

11. Discuss the hominoid radiation of the mid-Miocene and the geographical regions in which it took place; review the evolution of the extant hominoids. (pp. 269–276)

At this point, read Chapter 9, "Overview of the Fossil Primates," pages 238–281.

Key Terms and Concepts

Page references are keyed to *Introduction to Physical Anthropology*, 13th edition.

1. **strepsirhines:** (strep-sir′-rines) Members of the primate suborder Strepsirhini, which includes lemurs and lorises. (p. 240; objective 4)

2. **haplorhines:** (hap-lore′-ines) Members of the primate suborder Haplorhini, which includes tarsiers, monkeys, apes, and humans. (p. 240; objective 4)

3. **orthograde:** Referring to an upright body position. This term relates to the position of the head and torso during sitting, climbing, and similar activities, and doesn't necessarily mean that an animal is bipedal. (p. 240; objective 3)

4. **Euarchonta:** The superorder designated for the sister (closely related) orders of tree shrews, flying lemurs, and primates. (p. 240; objective 1)

5. **superorder:** A taxonomic group ranking above an order and below a class or subclass. (p. 240; objective 1)

6. **sister groups:** Two new clades that result from the splitting of a single common lineage. (p. 240; objective 8)

7. **last common ancestor (LCA):** The final evolutionary link between two related groups. (p. 241; objective 1)

8. **crown group:** All of the taxa that come after a major speciation event. Crown groups are easier to identify than stem groups because the members possess the clade's shared derived traits. (p. 241; objective 1)

9. **stem group:** All of the taxa in a clade before a major speciation event. Stem groups are often difficult to recognize in the fossil record, since they don't often have the shared derived traits found in the crown group. (p. 241; objective 1)

10. **semiorder:** The taxonomic category above suborder and below order. (p. 244; objective 2)

11. **euprimates:** "True primates." This term was coined by Elwyn Simons in 1972. (p. 244; objective 3)

12. **postcranial:** Referring to all or part of the skeleton not including the skull. The term originates from the fact that in quadrapeds, the body is posterior to the head; the term literally means "behind the head." (p. 245; objective 2)

13. **subfossil:** Bone not old enough to have become completely mineralized as a fossil. (p. 251; objective 3)

14. **bilophodont:** Refers to molars that have four cusps, oriented in two parallel rows, resembling ridges or "lophs." This trait is characteristic of Old World monkeys. (p. 252; objective 7)

15. **paleoprimatologists:** Anthropologists specializing in the study of the nonhuman primate fossil record. (p. 252; objective 3)

16. **catarrhine:** Member of Catarrhini, a parvorder of Primates, one of the three major divisions of the suborder Haplorhini. It contains the Old World monkeys and the apes. (p. 256; objective 5)

17. **platyrrhines:** Members of Platyrrhini, a parvorder of Primates, one of the three major divisions of the suborder Haplorhini. It contains only the New World monkeys. (p. 257; objective 5)

18. **island-hopping:** To travel from one island to the next. (p. 262; objective 6)

19. **Y-5 molar:** Molar that has five cusps with grooves running between them, forming a Y shape. This is characteristic of hominoids. (p. 267; objectives 9 & 10)

20. **zygomatics:** Cheekbones. (p. 270; objective 11)

21. **terrestrial:** Living and locomoting primarily on the ground. (p. 274; objective 11)

Summary

Researchers are still searching for the exact origins of the earliest primates. Although that information may never be known, fossil discoveries often offer scientists new data to fill in missing pieces of the puzzle. As you have learned in previous lessons, the extinction of the dinosaur was followed by a great expansion of mammal lineages of which primates were one.

During the last period of the Mesozoic, primates began to diverge from closely related mammalian lineages. Some scientists classify these related mammalian lineages as **Euarchonta**, the **superorder** of tree shrews, flying lemurs, plesiadapiforms, and primates.

Primate evolution occurred during the Cenozoic, a time period divided into seven epochs. Particular phrases of primate evolution occurred during each epoch, but keep in mind that it is not possible to assign a definitive time line for each phase. For instance, new evidence has resulted in some scientists hypothesizing that the initial radiation of primate-like animals occurred as early as 90 million years ago rather than the traditional view of 65 million years ago. The difficulty in pinpointing these dates stems from the problems of identifying the **last common ancestor (LCA)** between primates and their Archontan relatives. The LCA is the final evolutionary link between two related groups.

The Paleocene (65 million years ago)

The video for Lesson 5 introduced the plesiadapiforms, an animal the size of a rodent and the dominant primate-like mammal during the Paleocene epoch some 65 million years ago. Recall that well-preserved skeletons of plesiadapiforms were discovered in the Big Horn Basin in Wyoming. Much of what we know of these animals is gleaned from fossils discovered in the American West. Anthropologist Jonathan Bloch, who led a team that discovered the skeletons, notes in the video that "the main controversy surrounding our work has been whether or not plesiadapiforms are actually primates." While that classification is debated, scientists do generally view plesiadapiforms as members of an extinct group that is either related to Primates or is the actual precursor to our order.

Six families are commonly recognized within the plesiadapiform group; the Jurmain textbook concentrates on the three most pertinent to the discussion of primate origins. The first family includes the oldest-recognized archaic primate, Purgatorius, a rat-sized mammal found in the

Amerian Northwest at the beginning of the Paleocene, about 65 million years ago. The second family, the plesiadapids, were chipmunk- to marmot-sized mammals. This family probably originated in North America, but later colonized Europe via a land bridge across Greenland before becoming extinct. The third family, the carpolestids, were common in North America but not as successful as the plesiadapids. They were smaller, mouse- to rat-sized mammals. A nearly complete skeleton was discovered in Wyoming, and the **postcranial** anatomy reveals the carpolestids were highly adapted to an arboreal environment (particularly because they had nails instead of claws), although they showed no adaptation for leaping. This combination of primitive and primate-like traits has caused many to reexamine the plesiadapiforms' place in primate evolutionary history. On page 244, the Jurmain textbook concludes that "they are now gaining acceptance as a **semiorder** within Primates that is separate from the later euprimates (Silcox, 2007)."

The Eocene (55.8 to 33 million years ago)

The plesiadapiforms eventually became extinct during the Eocene epoch, replaced by the **euprimates**, or "true primates." Their recognizable derived primate traits such as forward-facing eyes, greater encephalization, a postorbital bar, nails instead of claws, and an opposable big toe indicate an adaptation to environmental conditions much changed from the Paleocene Epoch: a warmer climate with year-round rainfall and lush forests. North America and Europe, and later North America and Asia, were connected at certain times during the Eocene epoch, resulting in shared species on each continent. The earliest euprimates seem to appear on Asia first, with a westward migration through Europe, and eventually to North America.

There are two main branches of euprimates, grouped into different superfamilies (Adapoidea and Omomyoidea). The adapoids include more than 35 genera; they are the most primitive of any primate group, as recognized by their dental anatomy. A dental formula is a numerical shorthand for the number and kind of tooth found in one side of either the upper or lower jaw, and the primitive teeth of the adapoids offer a baseline from which later, more derived varieties of dental specializations could evolve.

The adapoids are divided into five families, based mostly on geographic locales. The notharctids of North America, the adapids of Europe, and the amphipithecids of Asia are the most prominent. *Cantius*, the earliest notharctid, resided primarily in North America. It was a small, diurnal creature, foraging during the day and most likely able to leap quadrupedally through trees. Its dental formula suggests it was a fruit eater. The family of adapids appeared and disappeared quite quickly in Europe near the end of the Eocene. The best known of the group is the *Adapis*, a slow, arboreal quadruped, foraging for leaves during the daytime hours. The third group, the amphipithecids from Myanmar (Burma) and Thailand, has features difficult to interpret. Rather than being anthropoid antecedents, the amphipithecids may actually be an example of convergent evolution, their anthropoid-like traits actually homoplasies.

The adapoids were lemur-like, but this resemblance is due to modern lemurs retaining some primitive traits. There is no clear evolutionary relationship between the Eocene adapoids and later lemurs, galagos, and lorises.

The tarsier-like omomyoids are more taxonomically diverse than the adapoids and appear to be more closely related to the tarsier. Some scientists believe that the earlier members of this group represent the stock for all later New World monkeys, Old World monkeys, apes, and humans.

Recent fossil finds in Egypt and China from the middle Eocene and fragments found in Thailand from the late Eocene show that modern tarsiers have retained essentially the same body plan that they had in the Eocene. Toward the end of this epoch, the tropical environment changed to drier, more seasonal climates, opening many niches for the highly adaptable primates to exploit.

As indicated in the Jurmain textbook, the origins of the anthropoids (the suborder of the Order Primates that includes monkeys, apes, and humans) during the Eocene is uncertain. Recent molecular evidence indicates that anthropoid primates most likely emerged separately from either the adapoids or omomyoids. Current evidence, from fossils, molecular data, and biogeography, all point to an African origin for anthropoids.

Most of the early anthropoid fossils have been discovered in the Fayum Depression in Egypt. One recent find, the most complete remains of an early African anthropoid, is dated to 37 million years ago and is identified as part of the extinct superfamily Parapithecoidea, significant as the root stock from which the later anthropoids evolved.

The Oligocene (33 to 23 million years ago)

During the Eocene and Oligocene epochs, the El-Fayuom (or Fayum) was a swampy forest where primates lived in large numbers. Now, this arid spot in the Sahara desert about 40 miles southwest of Cairo offers abundant fossil specimens, which in turn tell us much about the early primates of the Oligocene epoch. They are generally placed into three families: the oligopithecids, parapithecids, and propliopithecids.

The oligopithecids are known from fossil finds of the Fayum from the late Eocene epoch. Later discoveries from the early Oligocene are estimated to have weighed approximately three pounds, with body size and dental proportions similar to those seen in some contemporary small New World monkeys (marmosets and tamarins). These general comparisons support the idea of Fayum primate radiation at the base of the New World anthropoid evolutionary clade.

The genus *Apidium*, in the parapithecid family, provide the most abundant fossil finds from the Fayum. *Apidium* was the size of a squirrel, but its dental formula indicates it most likely appeared before the Old and New World anthropoids diverged. It could be an early ancestor of New World anthropoids (platyrrhines).

The third family, the propliopithecids, includes the genus *Aegyptopithecus*, proposed as an ancestor of both later Old World monkeys and hominoids. About 13 to 18 pounds, with a dental formula shared by Old World anthropoids, the *Aegyptopithecus*' skull resembles a modern monkey skull, while the brain size and morphology appear to have been somewhere between that of prosimians and anthropoids.

The first primates found in the New World (fossils found in Bolivia) date to around 27 million years ago, about 10 million years after fossil evidence for the first anthropoids appears in the Fayum of Egypt. They probably evolved from ancestors similar to those seen within the Fayum primate radiation. Based on the fossil records, it is probable that the very first anthropoids arrived in the New World during the late Eocene to early Oligocene (37 to 32 million years ago). Recent molecular data indicate that the **platyrrhine** (New World anthropoid) and **catarrhine** (Old World anthropoid) lineages diverged approximately 35 million years ago.

How platyrrhines made a transatlantic migration and arrived in the New World has resulted in several fascinating, competing theories. The North American migration theory argues that the

North American tarsier-like omomyoids journeyed down to South America, but a problem with this theory is that during the Eocene, North and South America were separated by a huge body of water, with currents flowing south to north. The Antarctic migration theory believes that early platyrrhines could have migrated to South America by first crossing the water from Africa to South Antarctica and then by crossing a land bridge that linked Antarctica to South America. The distance from Africa to Antarctica at that time, however, was 1,600 miles. Also, no primate fossils have been found in Antarctica, but given the digging conditions, that is not definitive proof that none exist there.

The most likely scenario of transatlantic travel is the Atlantic "rafting" theory. No, early primates did not build rafts and set course to destinations unknown. Rather, naturally formed mats of vegetation which broke away from the mainland could have carried primates across the ocean. A great drop in the sea level occurred during the middle Oligocene, meaning that mid-Atlantic islands existed, allowing early platyrrhines to **island-hop** from Africa to South America. (For more information on rafting, refer to the "Closer Look" section on page 263 of the Jurmain textbook).

The Miocene (23 to 5.3 million years ago)

The diversification of anthropoids during the Miocene epoch resulted in the groups we recognize today. Fossil evidence points to further diversification of later catarrhines (the Old World monkeys and the hominoids). Old World monkeys are called cercopithecoids and fall into two families, an extinct one called victoriapithecids and the second group consisting of the living cercopithecids.

The extinct victoriapithecidae represent the earliest members of the lineage leading to present-day Old World monkeys. They were found throughout northern and eastern Africa as early as 19 million years ago and may represent the last common ancestors of all living Old World monkeys. But another scenario holds they represent an extinct **sister group**, meaning two lineages that diverged from a particular common ancestor.

By 12 million years ago, the victoriapithecids were replaced by the Old World monkeys still here today, including the baboons, macaques, and colobines. The earliest colobine fossil was found in Africa and dates to approximately 9 million years ago; the colobines quickly radiated into Europe and Asia. Fossil macaques are geographically widespread, but most appear very similar to each other and to their present-day counterparts, indicating that primitive macaque morphology has been retained for more than five million years.

Geographical changes during the Miocene significantly affected the climate, causing the early part of this epoch to be much warmer and wetter than the previous Oligocene. Rain forests and dense woodlands became the dominant environments of Africa. The first ape-like primates evolved in this period. Scientists have used molecular evidence to suggest that the monkey and ape lineage diverged approximately 23 million year ago. Recall how dental formula can offer important evidence to a species' evolution. Early apelike fossils share many anatomical characteristics with monkey; in the superfamily Proconsuloidea (an early apelike family), the only apelike feature is the presence of the **Y-molar** pattern. This describes molars that have five cusps with grooves running between them, forming a Y shape. Monkeys typically have four bilophodant cusps. (Refer to page 261 of the Jurmain textbook for a visual comparison of both molar patterns.) Proconsuloids are called dental apes since their teeth are apelike but their postcranial skeletons resemble that of monkeys. These dental apes varied in size and locomotor patterns; almost all of the fossil records are from East Africa, although a few have been found in other parts of the continent.

Members of the superfamily Pliopithecoidea also date to the early Miocene of Africa. They are the most primitive of the catarrhines. Evidence indicates they were an early, small-bodied offshoot of the ape family tree, highly successful with an adaptive radiation during this time period.

Near the end of the early Miocene about 19 million years ago, the Arabian plate moved to its current location, forming a land bridge between Africa and Eurasia. Scientists believe that the African pliopithecoids were among the first animals to make this transcontinental trip. But since fossil remains had only been found in Eurasia, this idea that the pliopithecoids had African roots was only assumed. In Uganda, a recently discovered pliopithecoid, *Lomorupithecus*, dated at 20 million years ago, provides proof that pliopithecoids had their roots in Africa.

Pliopithecus is the best-known pliopithecoid from Europe. Its mandible features and sagittal crest (a ridge of bone that runs down the middle of the cranium) suggest its diet consisted of relatively tough foods, most likely leaves, and might have used suspensory locomotion (arm hanging) similar to that of some large platyrrhines. Later, during the Pliocene, all forms of pliopithecoids became extinct.

Approximately 16 million years ago during the middle Miocene, the first true apes appeared. *Kenyapithecus* is the best known of the early African hominoids. It was a large-bodied **terrestrial** quadruped, perhaps the first to adapt to life on the ground. Similar to the pliopithecoids, the hominoids also began to migrate out of Africa, rapidly colonizing the Old World with two highly successful adaptive radiations in Europe and in Asia. Europe was most likely the first stop, at about 16 million years ago. *Dryopithecus* was a common species then, with fossil finds in southern France and northern Spain. *Dryopithecus* resembles modern hominoids in many cranial and postcranial features. Other fossil remains suggest it was a highly arboreal species, rarely descending from the trees. In Asia, *Sivapithecus*, and its descendant *Gigantopithecus*, are representative hominoids. The *Sivapithecus* facial characteristics strongly resemble that of the modern orangutan, although it body is much different. The *Gigantopithecus* (or "Giganto") most likely weighed more than 900 pounds and was possibly ten feet tall when standing erect. Because of its size and ape-like qualities, scientists infer it was probably a ground-dwelling, fist-walking animal that became extinct approximately 200 thousand years ago.

There is little evidence linking fossil hominoids to the nonhuman hominoids living in Africa today—gorillas, chimpanzees, and bonobos. Curiously, hominoids disappear from the African fossil record around 13 million years ago and reappear during the late Miocene around 9.5 million years ago, causing some scientists to speculate that the hominoids left Africa and, later, Eurasian hominoids migrated back. The ancestor of the living African great apes is uncertain, but *Ouranopithecus* is one candidate. This large-bodied hominoid from Greece has facial similarities to African apes, meaning if it is an ape ancestor, then it is a human ancestor as well. The next lesson explores more fully the ancestors of the African apes—and of modern humans.

Review Exercises

Matching I

Match each term with the appropriate definition or description.

1. ____ adapoid
2. ____ bilophodonty
3. ____ Euarchonta
4. ____ euprimate
5. ____ haplorhine
6. ____ last common ancestor (LCA)
7. ____ omomyoid
8. ____ orthograde
9. ____ plesiadapiforms
10. ____ strepsirhine
11. ____ *Teilhardina*

a. Molars that have four cusps, oriented in two parallel rows, that resemble ridges or "lophs."

b. An Eocene primate genus found on three continents.

c. The superorder designated for the sister orders of tree shrews, flying lemurs, plesiadapiforms, and primates.

d. A tarsier-like prosimian of the Eocene.

e. A primate of modern aspect that first appears in the Eocene.

f. The final evolutionary link between two related groups.

g. A superfamily of lemur-like prosimians of the Eocene.

h. An extinct group that is either closely related to primates or is the actual precursor to the group.

i. An upright body position during sitting, climbing, and other activities.

j. Members of the primate suborder that includes lemurs and lorises.

k. Members of the primate suborder that includes monkeys, apes, and humans.

Matching II

Match each term with the appropriate definition or description.

1. ____ *Apidium*
2. ____ *Branisella*
3. ____ dental ape
4. ____ Fayum
5. ____ island-hop
6. ____ *Proconsul*
7. ____ sister group
8. ____ stem group
9. ____ *Victoriapithecus*
10. ____ Y-5 molar

a. An early ape that postcranially resembles a monkey, but dentally is hominoid.

b. A small fruit-eating monkey that lived in Bolivia about 27 million years ago.

c. To travel from one island to the next.

d. The first Old World monkey.

e. Molars that have five cusps with grooves running between them, forming a Y shape.

f. A genus of dental apes from the Miocene of Africa; its taxonomic placement is uncertain.

g. All of the taxa within a clade before a major speciation event.

h. Two lineages that diverged from a particular common ancestor.

i. An important paleontological site located in Egypt and spanning the late Eocene through the Oligocene (37 to 26 million years ago).

j. A fossil primate genus from the Fayum that has three premolars. It may be ancestral, or related to whatever was ancestral, to the New World monkeys.

Matching III

Match each hominoid name with the appropriate definition or description.

1. ____ *Dryopithecus*   4. ____ *Lufengpithecus*

2. ____ *Gigantopithecus*   5. ____ *Ouranopithecus*

3. ____ *Kenyapithecus*   6. ____ *Sivapithecus*

a. A fossil hominoid recovered from Greece that shares facial traits with the living African apes.

b. The largest primate that ever lived.

c. A possible relic species that may have survived until 5 million years ago in China.

d. A Miocene hominoid that may have been the first to adapt to life on the ground and shows evidence of a form of knuckle-walking.

e. Miocene hominoid whose face resembles the face of living orangutans.

f. An European hominoid whose teeth indicate a diet of fruit and leaves and whose postcrania suggest an arboreal life.

Completion

Fill each blank with the most appropriate term from the list below.

Africa	*Nakalipithecus*
dental apes	omomyoids
euprimates	orangutan
gibbon	*Ouranopithecus*
Gigantopithecus	Primate
Kenyapithecus	sister group
last common ancestor	35 million years ago
mammalian	

1. Primates were part of the general _____ radiation that took place at the end of the Cretaceous, when many ecological niches opened with the extinction of the dinosaurs.

2. The _____ is a hypothetical species that existed before two or more lineages diverged.

3. The plesiadapiformes are _____-like mammals that are either the ancestors of the order Primates or related to whatever gave rise to the primates.

4. The plesiadapiformes were gradually replaced by _____, primates of modern aspect.

5. The tarsier-like_____ are diverse and some researchers believe that they may have provided the stock for all the later anthropoids, not just the living tarsiers.

6. Current fossil, molecular, and biogeographic evidence suggests that _____ was the site of origin for the anthropoids.

7. Recent molecular data indicates that the platyrrhine-catarrhine lineages diverged approximately between 53 and _____.

8. The victoriapithecids may be the last common ancestor for the cercopithecines and colobines, or they may represent an extinct _____.

9. The proconsuloids share many anatomical traits with monkeys, but they possess a Y-5 molar. Thus, they are referred to as_____.

10. Among the earliest true apes, probably the best known is _____ a large-bodied terrestrial quadruped from Africa.

11. A possible ancestor of the Africa apes, found in Greece, is _____.

12. Although the body is distinctly different, the face of *Sivapithecus* strongly resembles the face of the living _____.

13. The largest ape that ever lived, _____ may have coexisted in China and Vietnam with *Homo erectus*.

14. Biomolecular evidence suggests that the _____ –great ape divergence occurred somewhere between 15 and 18 million years ago.

15. *Chororapithecus* and _____ are two recently described genera that suggest an African origin rather than an Asian origin for the living African apes.

Self-Test

Select the best answer.

1. The Euarchonta include all of the following **EXCEPT**
   a. tree shrews.
   b. bats.
   c. flying lemurs.
   d. primates.

2. Primate-like mammals of the Paleocene were the
   a. adapids.
   b. omomyids.
   c. plesiadapiforms.
   d. euprimates.

3. A primate trait found in *Carpolestes* is
   a. nails instead of claws.
   b. cat body size.
   c. forward-facing eyes.
   d. none of the above.

4. The time of the greatest prosimian radiation was during the
   a. Paleocene.
   b. Eocene.
   c. Oligocene.
   d. Miocene.

5. The Adapidae were
   a. lemur-like.
   b. tarsier-like.
   c. anthropoid-like.
   d. hominoid-like.

6. The most primitive primates of any known primate group are the
   a. carpolestids.
   b. plesiadapids.
   c. adapoids.
   d. omomyoids.

7. The amphipithecids were once touted as potential anthropoid ancestors. What is the current consensus?
   a. They are not actually primates.
   b. They are an example of convergent evolution.
   c. Their anthropoid traits are homoplasies.
   d. Both b and c are correct.

8. The tarsier-like primates of the Eocene are the
   a. carpolestids.
   b. plesiadapids.
   c. adapoids.
   d. omomyoids.

9. Recent molecular evidence suggests that anthropoids are descended from

    a. adapoids.
    b. omomyoids.
    c. a separate lineage that separated from prosimians around 77 million years ago.
    d. the amphipithecids.

10. What group is considered by most researchers to be the root stock from which the later New World anthropoids evolved?

    a. plesiadapiforms
    b. propliopithecids
    c. parapithecoids
    d. omomyoids

11. Which of the following is a prosimian characteristic?

    a. dental comb
    b. grooming claw
    c. unfused mandible
    d. all of the above

12. Which of the following is **NOT** an anthropoid characteristic?

    a. closure of the back of the orbit (eye socket)
    b. unfused frontal bone
    c. nails on all digits
    d. fused mandible

13. The primary paleontological site for Oligocene primates is

    a. the Fayum Depression in Egypt.
    b. Rooney Ranch in Colorado.
    c. Bir el Ater in Algeria.
    d. Pondaung in Myanmar (formerly Burma).

14. The most abundant Oligocene fossil primate genus recovered from the Fayum site is

    a. *Aegyptopithecus.*
    b. *Apidium.*
    c. *Catopithecus.*
    d. *Branisella.*

15. *Saadanius* has replaced *Aegyptopithecus* as the ancestor of both Old World Monkeys and hominoids because
    a. its limb bones indicate it is a brachiator.
    b. it comes from Asia.
    c. it is older than *Aegyptopithecus*.
    d. it shares a feature with the crown catarrhines (monkeys, apes, and humans) that it doesn't share with the propliopithecids (e.g., *Aegyptopithecus*).

16. Which of the following hypotheses of New World monkey evolution involves crossing a land bridge?
    a. North American migration
    b. Antarctic migration
    c. Atlantic "island-hopping."
    d. North American "walk."

17. The most likely scenario for the arrival of platyrrhines in South America is
    a. North American migration.
    b. Antarctic migration.
    c. Atlantic "island-hopping."
    d. North American "walk."

18. Which of the following is **NOT** a New World Monkey characteristic?
    a. sideways facing nostrils
    b. dental formula of 2.1.3.3
    c. ischial callosities
    d. grasping tail

19. Which of the following is an extinct group of Old World monkeys?
    a. colobines
    b. cercopithecines
    c. victoriapithecids
    d. All of these are extinct.

20. Which of the following statements is correct?
    a. Modern macaques are remarkably similar to fossil forms that lived 5 million years ago.
    b. The largest monkey that ever lived was a fossil *Theropithecus*.
    c. It appears that the genera *Macaca* and *Papio* separated around 20 million years ago.
    d. *Papio* outcompeted *Theropithecus* in the Ethiopian highlands.

21. Which of the following appears to be the earliest member of the Old World monkeys?

    a. *Victoriapithecus*
    b. *Theropithecus brumpti*
    c. African colobine
    d. Asian colobine

22. The only apelike feature in the Proconsuloidea is the presence of

    a. short arms.
    b. Y-5 molars.
    c. bilophodont molars.
    d. a long tail.

23. Early Miocene apes are commonly referred to as

    a. leaf-eating apes.
    b. forest apes.
    c. small-bodied apes.
    d. dental apes.

24. The event that resulted in an exchange of animals between Africa and Eurasia was

    a. a land bridge formed when the Arabia moved into its current location.
    b. extensive mountain building along the Great African Rift.
    c. the replacement of forests by desert.
    d. an ice age.

25. Where was *Dryopithecus* found?

    a. Africa
    b. Europe
    c. Western Asia
    d. South Asia

26. Which of the following is suggested as an ancestor of the African apes?

    a. *Kenyapithecus*
    b. *Dryopithecus*
    c. *Ouranopithecus*
    d. *Sivapithecus*

27. The Miocene ape that bears a remarkable resemblance to the living orangutan in the face, but **NOT** in the postcranium, is
    a. *Kenyapithecus.*
    b. *Dryopithecus.*
    c. *Ouranopithecus.*
    d. *Sivapithecus.*

28. Which of the following is a descendant of *Sivapithecus*?
    a. *Kenyapithecus*
    b. *Dryopithecus*
    c. *Ouranopithecus*
    d. *Gigantopithecus*

29. The largest primate that ever lived is
    a. *Gigantopithecus.*
    b. *Dryopithecus.*
    c. *Sivapithecus.*
    d. the living gorilla.

30. Which of the following is **NOT** as closely related as the other three?
    a. orangutan
    b. gorilla
    c. chimpanzee
    d. gibbon

Short-Answer Questions

1. Discuss the conditions that led to the eventual rise of the Euarchonta.

2. What is the place of the plesiadapiforms in primate evolution?

3. Discuss the appearance of the euprimates, where they appeared, and the living primates that they most resemble.

4. Review the debate surrounding anthropoid origins.

5. Compare Old World monkeys with New World monkeys. When do the earliest representatives of these groups first appear?

6. Provide a description of the hominoid radiation of the Miocene and the end results.

Application Questions

1. Why is it difficult to distinguish the earliest members of the primate order from other placental mammals? If you found a nearly complete skeleton of an early Paleocene mammal, what structural traits might lead you to determine that it was a primate?

2. Compare and contrast the adapoids and omomyoids with living members of the primate order. Why do we call them lemur- or tarsier-like and not lemurs and tarsiers?

3. What are some of the ways in which monkeys are thought to have colonized the New World? How likely do you find each of the explanations and why?

4. Where is the Fayum Depression, and why is it significant in primate evolution? Are there any other sites where so many fossil primates have been found? Why or why not?

5. What is meant by "dental apes" compared to true hominoids? If you were given a jaw to study of a supposed dental ape, what particular features would you look for first?

6. Compare *Gigantopithecus* in Asia with the modern gorilla in Africa. How do their dietary niches differ?

Answer Key

Matching I

1. g (objective 3)
2. a (objective 7)
3. c (objective 1)
4. e (objective 3)
5. k (objective 4)
6. f (objective 2)
7. d (objective 3)
8. i (objective 1)
9. h (objective 2)
10. j (objective 4)
11. b (objective 3)

Matching II

1. j (objective 5)
2. b (objective 6)
3. a (objectives 9 & 10)
4. i (objective 5)
5. c (objective 6)
6. f (objective 9)
7. h (objective 8)
8. g (objective 1)
9. d (objective 8)
10. e (objectives 9 & 10)

Matching III

1. f (objective 11)
2. b (objective 11)
3. d (objective 11)
4. c (objective 11)
5. a (objective 11)
6. e (objective 11)

Completion

1. mammalian (objective 1)
2. last common ancestor (objective 1)
3. primate (objective 2)
4. euprimates (objective 3)
5. omomyoid (objective 3)
6. Africa (objective 4)
7. 35 million years ago (objective 6)
8. sister group (objective 8)
9. dental apes (objectives 9 & 10)
10. *Kenyapithecus* (objective 11)
11. *Ouranopithecus* (objective 11)
12. orangutan (objective 11)
13. *Gigantopithecus* (objective 11)
14. gibbon (objective 11)
15. *Nakalipithecus* (objective 11)

Self-Test

1. b. is the correct answer. Since the time of Linnaeus, bats were considered to be closely related to primates, presumably sharing a common ancestor in the Paleocene. Recent molecular analysis shows that the bats are not related at all to the other euarchontans. (objective 1)

2. c. is the correct answer. The adapids and omomyids are euprimates, and they do not appear until the Eocene. The plesiadapiforms are the primate-like mammals of the Paleocene. (objective 2)

3. a. is the correct answer. Nails are present on the digits of the primate-like mammal *Carpolestes*. This is the only example of nails on a mammal outside of the true primates. (objective 2)

4. b. is the correct answer. The Paleocene witnessed a spectacular mammalian radiation, but it was in the Eocene that the great prosimian radiation occurred. (objective 3)

5. a. is the correct answer. The adapids were lemur-like in appearance. (objective 3)

6. c. is the correct answer. The carpolestids and plesiadapids are primate-like mammals of the Paleocene, but they are not primates themselves. The adapoids are the earliest euprimates. (objective 3)

7. d. is the correct answer. Rather than being anthropoid antecedents, the amphipithecids may actually be an example of convergent evolution and their anthropoid-like traits homoplasies. (objective 3)

8. d. is the correct answer. The omomyoids are the tarsier-like primates of the Eocene. (objective 3)

9. c. is the correct answer. Until recently, there were considered to be two primate groups that existed in the Eocene, the adapoids and omomyoids. Molecular evidence now suggests that a poorly known group of primates represents a third lineage that led to the anthropoids of the Oligocene. (objective 4)

10. c. is the correct answer. The dental morphology of the parapithecoids suggests that this superfamily is the root stock from which the entire New World anthropoid evolutionary group evolved. (objective 4)

11. d. is the correct answer. A dental comb, grooming claw, and an unfused mandible are all characteristics of prosimians. (objective 4)

12. b. is the correct answer. Anthropoids have an enclosed orbit, nails on all digits and a fused mandible, but they do not possess an unfused frontal bone. (objective 4)

13. a. is the correct answer. The vast majority of Oligocene primate fossils were recovered from the Fayum Depression. (objective 5)

14. b. is the correct answer. The squirrel-size *Apidium* is the most common fossil primate recovered at the Fayum site. (objective 5)

15. d. is the correct answer. The propliopithecids such as *Aegyptopithecus* do not have the tubelike middle ear that *Saadanius* shares with the crown catarrhines. This suggests that *Saadanius* is an advanced stem catarrhine. (objective 5)

16. b. is the correct answer. The Antarctic migration hypothesis posits that primates rafted from Africa onto Antarctica. During this period of the Oligocene, there was a land bridge between Antarctica and South America that primates could have then used to walk onto South America. (objective 6)

17. c. is the correct answer. All of these answers have been proposed at one time or another, but current consensus is that island-hopping across the Atlantic Ocean from Africa via rafting is the most likely explanation. At that time, South America and Africa were much closer to each other than they are today, paleocurrent directions would have favored this, and low sea levels may have exposed mid-Atlantic islands. (objective 6)

18. c. is the correct answer. New World monkeys characteristics include sideways facing nostrils, a dental formula of 2.1.3.3, and grasping tails. They do not have ischial callosities. (objective 7)

19. c. is the correct answer. The victoriapithecids became extinct around 12 million years ago. They may have given rise to all the Old World monkeys living today, or they may have been a sister group that left no descendants. (objective 7)

20. d. is the correct answer. *Theropithecus* thrives in the Ethiopian highlands today, specializing on grass. This genus was once more widespread but it is believed it was outcompeted by *Papio*. (objective 8)

21. a. is the correct answer. *Victoriapithecus* appears around 19 million years ago and, as portrayed in Figure 9-19 on page 264 of the Jurmain textbook, it predates the split that led to the Cercopithecidae and its two subfamilies of the colobines and cercopithecines. The extinct *Theropithecus brumpti* was a member of the Cercopithecinae. (objective 8)

22. b. is the correct answer. Y-5 molars refer to a condition in which there are five cusps separated by a Y-shaped fissure. This is a derived trait found only in hominoids, but the

only uniquely ape trait found in the proconsuloids; see also question 23. (objectives 9 & 10)

23. d. is the correct answer. The proconsuloids are the best known of these early Miocene apes and their Y-5 molar (see question 22 above) is the major, usually the only, hominoid trait found in these species. Hence, they are called "dental apes." (objective 9)

24. a. is the correct answer. The Arabian plate connected Africa to Western Asia, ending Africa's existence as an isolated island continent. The land bridge allowed apes and other African animals to migrate out of Africa and allowed mammals (particularly the hoof stock that is characteristic of modern Africa) to migrate into Africa. (objective 11)

25. b. is the correct answer. Europe is an unlikely place to find primates today, but it appears to have been the first stop on the migrations out of Africa once it was attached to Asia. *Dryopithecus* was found in both France and Spain. (objective 11)

26. c. is the correct answer. *Ouranopithecus* is the best candidate as the ancestor of the African apes. The fossil record of Africa at this time is remarkably sparse, so there is no suitable candidate there. (objective 11)

27. d. is the correct answer. *Sivapithecus* and the orangutan are striking in appearance of the face. However, postcranially, the two apes are very different. (objective 11)

28. d. is the correct answer. *Sivapithecus* is believed to be the ancestor of two apes. *Gigantopithecus* is one of these, the living orang is the other. (objective 11)

29. a. is the correct answer. The modern gorilla is the largest living primate at around 400 pounds. However, *Gigantopithecus* was possibly 10 feet tall and weighed more than 1,000 pounds, making it the largest primate ever. (objective 11)

30. d. is the correct answer. Biomolecular evidence suggests that gibbons, a hylobatid, diverged from the great apes some 15 to 18 million years ago. (objective 11)

Short-Answer Questions

Your answers should include the following:

1. At the end of the Cretaceous, a mass extinction occurred that led to the extinction of the ruling reptiles, such as the dinosaurs. The demise of the dinosaurs left many niches vacant. With little or no competition for those niches, mammals underwent an adaptive radiation with different groups of mammals diversifying in a way that allowed them to occupy the niches left vacant by the dinosaurs. The Euarchonta is a superorder of three living closely related (sister) lineages that are believed to be descended from a common ancestor. In the process of diversification, the primates, colugos (flying lemurs), and tree shrews became adapted for different niches. (objective 1)

2. The plesiadapiforms are archaic primates that appeared between 65 and 52 million years ago in the Paleocene. These earliest primates are currently considered a semiorder within the Primates, separate from the later euprimates. *Purgatorius*, a member of the earliest family of plesiadapiforms, is characterized by a nail on the big toe, just like the earliest strepsirhines from the later Eocene epoch. In the video for Lesson 5 (Macroevolution), paleontologist Johnathon Bloch says this is a homologous structure

shared through common ancestry. Members of the plesiadapid family *Carpolestes* have opposable grasping big toes with nails and are highly adapted to life in the trees, although they lack adaptations for leaping like later euprimates. (objective 4)

3. The euprimates first appear in the Eocene of North America and Europe. Among the living primates, they most resemble prosimians, the adapoids being lemur-like and the omomyoids being tarsier-like. (objective 3)

4. The origins of the anthropoids are uncertain. Both of the well-known Eocene primate groups—the lemur-like adapoids and the tarsier-like omomyoids—have been proposed as anthropoid stock, but Jurmain cites recent molecular evidence suggesting that neither of these groups gave rise to the anthropoids. Instead, there is a third, poorly known, primate group that is separate from the other primates as far back as 77 million years ago. Evidence continues to support an African origin for the anthropoids. (objective 4)

5. New World monkeys possess nostrils that face sideways, whereas Old World monkeys have downward facing nostrils. The entrance to the ear in New World monkeys has a ring like hole, whereas in Old World monkeys there is a long auditory tube. The dental formula of the two groups is different; for New World monkeys, it is 2.1.3.3, while the dental formula for Old World monkeys is 2.1.2.3 (the same as in apes). New World monkeys have a grasping tail that helps them in negotiating branches in trees; Old World monkeys have the ends of the ischium (of the pelvis) visible with the bone covered by calluses of skin (i.e., they have ischial callosities). As their names imply, the two groups have different geographic distributions. New World monkeys are found in the New World from Mexico to Argentina. Old World monkeys are found in Africa, southern Asia, and Japan. Current consensus is that both groups share a common ancestor, such as *Apidium*, from Oligocene Africa. The earliest New World monkey is from the late Oligocene of Bolivia, around 27 million years ago. Good candidates for the earliest Old World monkey are present at the Fayum site by the mid-Oligocene, represented by *Aegyptopithecus*. (objective 7)

6. Dental apes appear in Africa in the early Miocene. Their most ape-like feature is the Y-5 pattern on their molars. Other features, such as quadrupedal locomotion, are not particularly ape-like and the dental apes may have even predated the hominoid/cercopithecoid split. The first true apes appear in the middle Miocene (around 16 million years ago) of Africa, *Kenyapithecus* being a representative of this group. Soon thereafter, the anthropoids colonize other parts of the Old World. *Dryopithecus* is a common species found in the forests of Europe. *Sivapithecus*, and its descendant *Gigantopithecus*, are representative hominoids found in South Asia and the Far East. *Sivapithecus* may be the ancestor of the living orangutan. The ancestor of the living African great apes is uncertain, but recent finds from Kenya (*Chororapithecus* and *Nakalipithecus*) with dates that precede *Ouranopithecus* from Greece are suggesting an African origin for the living African apes. (objectives 9, 10, & 11)

Application Questions

Your answers should include the following:

1. The earliest primates had only recently diverged from other placental mammals and, as a result, share many primitive traits with their closest relatives. Thus, the earliest primate is still somewhat general. Structural traits that we would look for in a primate ancestor are of two types. First, they must not have lost features that appear in later undoubted primates; e.g., a fossil mammal with the dental formula of 2.1.2.3 could not have descendants that are primates because the earliest euprimates of the Eocene have a dental formula of 2.1.4.3 (see page 246 of the Jurmain textbook). The other traits that would be important are primate traits: nails on the digits, evidence of grasping paws, and forward-facing eyes. We would not expect to find all of these traits together. However, we need to be cautious because even seemingly primate traits can be homoplasies. (objectives 1 & 2)

2. The adapoids were the more primitive euprimates of the Eocene. They have a generalized dental formula of 2.1.4.3 that serves as a base for later primates to have evolved from. One species possesses what some authorities think may be an incipient dental comb, a trait of modern lemurs. The body plan is similar to modern lemurs leading to some workers to say that lemurs, galagos, and lorises retain many primitive anatomical features. The omomyoids, on the other hand, are more derived. The dental formula is reduced (1.1.3.3), similar to the living tarsier, and this reduction in dentition is accompanied by a flatter snout. It also has larger orbits, a trend that reaches its culmination in the tarsier. While both the adapoids and omomyoids exhibit features that resemble the living lemurs and tarsiers, there is no direct line of descent that can be recovered from the fossil record. In life, these animals may have been very different. (objective 3)

3. The explanation for how New World monkeys came to be on South America has a long history. An earlier explanation was that they walked to South America from North America. Recall that there were prosimians in North America during the Eocene. This explanation had to be modified in light of continental drift—North and South America were not connected by Central America until well past the time of the earliest New World monkey.

   A newer explanation is that Eocene primates from North America rafted or island-hopped (were carried on natural mats of vegetation or land that has broken away from a larger piece of land). The problem is that there is no good candidate for a New World monkey ancestor to be found among the North American prosimians.

   Another explanation that has been proposed is that primates rafted from Africa to Antarctica. At this time, Antarctica was connected to South America and the primates could have migrated via a land bridge. This hypothesis has two problems: (1) the distance required to raft is twice the distance from Africa to South America, and (2) there have never been any primate fossils found on Antarctica. The hypothesis most favored by primate evolutionary biologists is that primates rafted from Africa to South America. During the Oligocene, there were many islands in the South Atlantic because of reduced sea levels and primates could have landed on islands and several generations later some of their descendants might have been on a raft that went farther west to another island. Thus, they "island-hopped" over a number of generations. Africa also has the best fossil candidates, such as *Apidium*, for a New World monkey ancestor. (objective 6)

4. The Fayum Depression is a paleontological site about 40 miles southwest of Cairo, Egypt. During the Oligocene, the Fayum site was a tropical forest that bordered the sea. It is significant in primate evolution because anthropoid evolution is well documented with three major groups of anthropoid primates (there are also prosimians that have been recovered here). Preservation of the Oligocene Fayum community was excellent, accounting for the large number of fossils recovered here. In fact, it is one of the very few Oligocene sites that has yielded primate fossils, and the others have yielded very few fossils. (objective 5)

5. Fossils have been recovered from the early Miocene, attributed to the superfamily Proconsuloidea, that have very few traits that would identify them as apes. One feature that does, however, are the molars. They have the distinctive Y-5 pattern, five cusps surrounding a Y-shaped fissure. Monkeys, on the other hand, have bilophodont molars, four cusps oriented in two parallel rows (see Figure 9-22 on page 267 of the Jurmain textbook). Other features of the proconsuloids and pliopithecoids, another dental ape, give the impression of a monkey. They are quadrupedal and retain a long torso like monkeys rather than the short torso characteristic of apes. Some researchers do not include these anthropoids among the hominoids. However, if you only had a mandible you would probably note that the molars fit the apes and classify it as such. (objective 9)

6. *Gigantopithecus* was the largest primate that has ever lived. It was twice the size of the largest living primate, another ape, the gorilla. Nevertheless, the gorilla is a large primate and the adult males tend to be confined to the ground. Although we have no postcrania of *Gigantopithecus*, we can infer from its large size that it must also have been confined to life on the ground. The dentition of *Gigantopithecus* and gorillas is different. Gorillas possess large canines and thin enamel on their molars. *Gigantopithecus* had a reduced canine and thickly enameled molars. This suggests very different diets for the two species. *Gigantopithecus* must have consumed tough fibrous food morsels that would have worn down the chewing surfaces of their molars. Gorillas are also vegetarians, but their food consists of less abrasive morsels, including fruit. (objective 11)

Lesson Review

Lesson 6, Part II: Overview of the Fossil Primates

PLEASE NOTE: Use this matrix to guide your study and achieve the learning objectives of this lesson. It will also help you to view the video, which defines and demonstrates important concepts and principles as they relate to everyday life and actual case studies.

Learning Objective	Textbook	Student Guide	Video Lesson
1. Define the member species of the superorder Euarchonta, explain when they developed, and discuss why they are important in primate evolution.	pp. 240–244	Key Terms: 4, 5, 7, 8, 9; Matching I: 3, 8; Matching II: 8; Completion: 1, 2; Self-Test: 1; Short-Answer: 1; Application: 1.	
2. Identify where and when the plesiadapiforms are found and discuss their place in primate evolution.	pp. 244–246	Key Terms: 10, 12; Matching I: 6, 9; Completion: 3; Self-Test: 2, 3; Short-Answer: 2; Application: 1.	
3. Identify which epoch and where the earliest undoubted primates appeared and discuss what type of modern primates the earliest primates most resemble.	pp. 246–265	Key Terms: 3, 11, 13, 15; Matching I: 1, 4, 7, 11; Completion: 4, 5; Self-Test: 4, 5, 6, 7, 8; Short-Answer: 3; Application: 2.	
4. Discuss the debate surrounding anthropoid origins, and compare and contrast prosimian and anthropoid characteristics.	pp. 255–256	Key Terms: 1, 2; Matching I: 5, 10; Completion: 6; Self-Test: 9, 10, 11, 12; Short-Answer: 4.	
5. Describe the types of primates found at the Fayum during the Oligocene.	pp. 256–260	Key Terms: 16, 17; Matching II: 1, 4; Self-Test: 13, 14; Application: 4.	

Learning Objective	Textbook	Student Guide	Video Lesson
6. Discuss the current ideas for the origins of New World monkeys and how they arrived in the Americas.	pp. 260–262	Key Terms: 18; Matching II: 2, 5; Completion: 7; Self-Test: 16, 17; Application: 3.	
7. Contrast the characteristics of New World and Old World monkeys.	p. 259	Key Terms: 14; Matching I: 2; Self-Test: 18, 19; Short-Answer: 5.	
8. Discuss the lineage of the cercopithecoids.	pp. 262–265	Key Terms: 6; Matching II: 7, 9; Completion: 8; Self-Test: 20, 21.	
9. Describe early Miocene apes and where they are found.	pp. 265–269	Key Terms: 19; Matching II: 3, 6, 10; Completion: 9; Self-Test: 22, 23; Short-Answer: 6; Application: 5.	
10. Compare and contrast ape and Old World monkey characteristics.	p. 264	Key Terms: 19; Matching II: 3, 10; Completion: 9; Self-Test: 22; Short-Answer: 6.	
11. Discuss the hominoid radiation of the mid-Miocene and the geographical regions in which it took place; review the evolution of the extant hominoids.	pp. 269–276	Key Terms: 20, 21; Matching III: 1, 2, 3, 4, 5, 6; Completion: 10, 11, 12, 13, 14, 15; Self-Test: 24, 25, 26, 27, 28, 29, 30; Short-Answer: 6; Application: 6.	

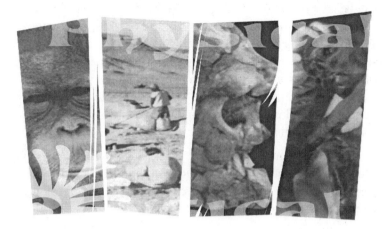

Primate Behavior

Checklist

For the most effective study of this lesson, complete the following activities in this sequence.

Before Viewing the Video

- ❑ Read the Preview, Learning Objectives, and Viewing Notes below.

- ❑ Read Chapter 7, "Primate Behavior," pages 182–209, and Chapter 8, "Primate Models for the Evolution of Human Behavior," pages 210–237, in *Introduction to Physical Anthropology*.

What to Watch

- ❑ After reading the textbook assignment, watch the video for Lesson 7, *Primate Behavior*.

After Viewing the Video

- ❑ Briefly note your answers to the questions listed at the end of the Viewing Notes.

- ❑ Review the Summary below.

- ❑ Review all reading assignments for this lesson, including the Viewing Notes in this lesson.

- ❑ Write brief answers to the "Critical Thinking Questions" at the end of Chapters 7 and 8 in the textbook.

- ❑ Complete the Review Exercises below. Check your answers with the Answer Key and review when necessary.

- ❑ Use the Lesson Review matrix found at the end of this lesson to review and assess your knowledge of each Learning Objective.

Preview

Do you remember the last time that you watched a nature documentary featuring primates or visited a large zoo or wild animal reserve that had an area dedicated to monkeys and great apes? Think about the types of primate behaviors that you have observed firsthand. These behaviors may have included how those primates moved, how their eyes focused on objects, how they gripped objects and picked them up with their hands, how they behaved with others of their species, including vocalizations, playful interaction, grooming, and disagreements. These are the actions that reveal the similarities and differences between humans and our primate cousins. Lesson 7, which covers material from Chapters 7 and 8 of the Jurmain textbook, includes the social behavior of nonhuman primates, our closest relatives, and what humans can learn about their own evolutionary development by studying this behavior.

Physical anthropologists study nonhuman primates in an effort to explain what it means to be human. Lesson 7 examines the current anthropological knowledge of the social and individual behaviors of nonhuman primates and the interactions between environmental and physiological variables that make up the "underlying principles" of behavioral evolution.

Concepts to Remember

※ Lesson 2 explained **natural selection**, the mechanism of evolutionary change that refers to genetic change or changes in the frequencies of certain traits in populations due to differential reproductive success between individuals. Note that while natural selection plays out on entire species, each individual is concerned with his or her own reproductive success, which influences the social behavior of primates.

※ Lesson 6 explained how primate anatomical traits evolved as adaptations to many different environments, resulting in the species' **adaptive niche**. Primate behavior is also adapted to environmental conditions. Some primates have evolved specialized locomotor patterns and diets through natural selection and other evolutionary processes. While natural selection does play a role in primate social behavior, primates can also adjust their behavior to environmental circumstances without specific genes directing a particular behavior—just like humans. Many researchers study primates to learn about the roots of human behaviors and how they might have evolved or resulted from environmental adaptations.

Learning Objectives

After you complete this lesson, you should be able to:

1. Summarize the history of primate field studies, and list some of the scientists who initiated pioneering research. (pp. 184–185)

2. Define primate behavioral ecology, and discuss how it is the current theoretical perspective in primate behavioral studies. (pp. 185–186)

3. Describe the types of food primates eat and how species vary with regard to dietary preferences. (pp. 186–192)

4. Define the types of primate social interactions and communication methods, including grooming, dominance, and affiliative and aggressive behaviors. (pp. 192–200)

5. Differentiate between male and female reproductive strategies and their influence on sex-specific behaviors. (pp. 201–205)

6. Discuss the importance of the mother-infant bond in contributing to the normal social and psychological development of primate infants. (pp. 205–208)

7. Define language and describe the evolution of language and the results of ape language experiments. (pp. 217–224)

8. List the criteria for cultural acts in nonhuman species, and discuss whether chimpanzees meet these criteria. (pp. 224–231)

9. Contrast between group aggression and altruism/cooperation among chimpanzees. (pp. 231–236)

10. From an anatomical and behavioral perspective, discuss how humans fit into the "biological continuum." (pp. 236–237)

At this point, read Chapter 7, "Primate Behavior," pages 182–209, and Chapter 8, "Primate Models for the Evolution of Human Behavior," pages 210–237.

Viewing Notes

Much of this course, thus far, has focused on the process of evolution and how biological change occurs. However, it is not just human biology that has evolved. Human behavior has evolved as well through selective pressures in the environment. Studying free-ranging nonhuman primates is a good way for researchers to learn about human evolution, because it shows the present evolutionary pressures that could have been at work in the past. The Jurmain textbook points out on page 185 that because most primates live in social groups, extensive research is devoted to primate social behavior, and primatologists test hypotheses relating to how behaviors have evolved.

The video explains behavioral ecology as a study of the interaction between animals and their environment, focusing on how behavior enables and promotes reproductive success. As expected, primates in different climates develop different behaviors for adaptation and survival. Field studies of primates in the wild give us insight into how body size, diet, predation, and resource availability affect the behavior and social structure of these animals today and may have shaped their evolution in the past. For example, Himalayan langurs have thicker coats, larger bodies, longer birth intervals, and are less active in the winter months than their counterparts at lower altitudes. Observing how an essentially tropical primate survives in a harsh climate can help us understand the difficulties our human ancestors had to overcome in order to move out of the tropics and into Europe and Northern Asia. It is notable that early humans are not found living year round in northern latitudes until the control and use of fire.

Reproductive strategies are the behavioral patterns used by nonhuman primates that contribute to individual reproductive success. Males and females have similar goals in terms of maximizing the number of offspring they produce, but their behavior differs in achieving these goals. A social group that includes one adult male and several adult females should satisfy the reproductive needs of both sexes, yet not all primate groups take this form. The video shows other configurations of social groups and highlights the importance of the mother-child bond.

As noted in the video, anthropologists study nonhuman primates because they are our closest living relatives and they can serve as models for understanding how human behavior might have evolved, including that human hallmark, culture. When a behavior is learned, anthropologists speak of it as culturally based, and primatologists historically have looked at tool use and manufacture to find the potential for cultural behavior in nonhuman primates. With each new discovery of innovative behaviors among nonhuman primates, our understanding of how this relates to human culture grows.

Questions to Consider

* According to Jurmain, why do most nonhuman primates live in groups?

* What are some of the factors that influence social structures in nonhuman primate groups?

* What are dominance hierarchies and what important functions to they serve?

* What is sexual selection and how does it contribute to sexual dimorphism?

Watch the video for Lesson 7, *Primate Behavior.*

  Segment 1: *Reproductive Strategies*
  Segment 2: *Life in a Social Group*
  Segment 3: *Primate Cultural Behavior*

Key Terms and Concepts

Page references are keyed to *Introduction to Physical Anthropology,* 13th edition.

1. **behavior:** Anything organisms do that involves action in response to internal or external stimuli; the response of an individual, group, or species, to its environment. Such responses may or may not be deliberate, and they aren't necessarily the results of conscious decision-making (which is absent in one-celled organisms, insects, and many other species). (p. 184; objective 2)

2. **social structure:** The composition, size, and sex ratio of a group of animals. Social structure is the result of natural selection in a specific habitat, and it influences individual interactions and social relationships. In many species, social structure varies, depending on different environmental factors. Thus, in primates, social structure should be viewed as flexible, not fixed. (p. 185; video lesson, introduction; objective 2)

3. **behavioral ecology:** The study of the evolution of behavior, emphasizing the role of ecological factors as agents of natural selection. Behaviors and behavioral patterns are favored by natural selection because they increase the reproductive fitness of individuals (i.e., they are adaptive) in specific environmental contexts. (p. 185; objective 2)

4. **metabolism:** The chemical processes within cells that break down nutrients and release energy for the body to use. (When nutrients are broken down into their component parts, such as amino acids, energy is released and made available for the cell to use.) (p. 187; objective 3)

5. **matrilines:** Groupings of females who are all descendants of one female (a female, her daughters, granddaughters, and their offspring). Matrilines also include dependent male offspring. Among macaques, some matrilines are dominant to others, so that members of dominant matrilines have greater access to resources than do members of subordinate ones. (p. 188; objective 4)

6. **philopatric:** Remaining in one's natal group or home range as an adult. In most species, members of one sex disperse from their natal group as young adults, and members of the philopatric sex remain. In the majority of nonhuman primate species, the philopatric sex is female. (p. 190; objective 4)

7. **life history traits:** Characteristics and developmental stages that influence rates of reproduction. Examples include longevity, age at sexual maturity, and length of time between births, etc. (p. 190; objective 4)

8. **strategies:** Behaviors or behavioral complexes that have been favored by natural selection because they're advantageous to the animals that perform them. Examples include actions that enhance an animal's ability to obtain food, rear infants, or increase one's social status. Ultimately, strategies influence reproductive success. (p. 190; objective 4)

9. **sympatric:** Living in the same area; pertaining to two or more species whose habitats partly or largely overlap. (p. 190; objective 4)

10. **home range:** The total area exploited by an animal or social group; usually given for one year or for the entire lifetime of an animal. (p. 192; objective 4)

11. **reproductive strategies:** The complex of behavioral patterns that contributes to individual reproductive success. The behaviors need not be deliberate, and they often vary considerably between males and females. (p. 192; video lesson, segment 1; objective 5)

12. **conspecifics:** Member of the same species. (p. 194; objectives 4 & 7)

13. **dominance hierarchies:** Systems of social organization wherein individuals within a group are ranked relative to one another. Higher-ranking individuals have greater access to preferred food items and mating partners than do lower-ranking individuals. Dominance hierarchies are sometimes referred to as pecking orders. (p. 194; video lesson, segment 2; objective 4)

14. **communication:** Any act that conveys information, in the form of a message, to another individual. Frequently, the result of communication is a change in the recipient's behavior. Communication may not be deliberate, but may instead be the result of involuntary processes or a secondary consequence of an intentional action. (p. 196; video lesson, segment 2; objective 4)

15. **autonomic:** Pertaining to physiological responses not under voluntary control. An example in chimpanzees would be the erection of body hair during excitement. Blushing is a human example. Both convey information regarding emotional states, but neither behavior is deliberate, and communication is not intended. (p. 196; objective 4)

16. **grooming:** Picking through fur to remove dirt, parasites, and other materials that may be present. Social grooming is common among primates and reinforces social relationships. (p. 196; video lesson, segment 2; objective 4)

17. **displays:** Sequences of repetitious behaviors that serve to communicate emotional states. Nonhuman primate displays are most frequently associated with reproductive or agonistic behavior. (p. 197; objective 4)

18. **ritualized behaviors:** Behaviors removed from their original context and sometimes exaggerated to convey information. (p. 198; objective 4)

19. **affiliative:** Pertaining to amicable associations between individuals. Affiliative behaviors, such as grooming, reinforce social bonds and promote group cohesion. (p. 198; video lesson, segment 2; objective 4)

20. **intragroup:** (*intra*, meaning "within") Within the group, as opposed to between groups (intergroup). (p. 198; objective 4)

21. **K-selected:** Pertaining to K-selection, an adaptive strategy whereby individuals produce relatively few offspring, in whom they invest increased parental care. Although only a few infants are born, chances of survival are increased for each individual because of parental investments in time and energy. Examples of nonprimate K-selected species are birds and canids (e.g., wolves, coyotes, and dogs). (p. 202; objective 5)

22. **r-selected:** Pertaining to r-selection, an adaptive strategy that emphasizes relatively large numbers of offspring and reduced parental care (compared to K-selected species). K-selection and r-selection are relative terms (e.g., mice are r-selected compared to primates, but K-selected compared to most fish). (p. 202; objective 5)

23. **sexual selection:** A type of natural selection that operates on only one sex within a species. Sexual selection results from competition for mates, and it can lead to sexual dimorphism regarding one or more traits. (p. 202; video lesson, segment 1; objective 5)

24. **polyandry:** A mating system characterized by an association between a female and more than one male (usually two or three), with whom she mates. Among nonhuman primates, the pattern is seen only in marmosets and tamarins. (p. 205; objective 5)

25. **alloparenting:** A common behavior in many primate species whereby individuals other than the parent(s) hold, carry, and in general interact with infants. (p. 208; objective 6)

26. **encephalization:** The proportional size of the brain relative to some other measure, usually an estimate of overall body size, such as weight. More precisely, the term refers to increases in brain size beyond that which would be expected given the body size of a particular species. (p. 213; objective 10)

27. **allometry:** Also called scaling; the differential proportion among various anatomical structures (e.g., the size of the brain in proportion to overall body size changes during the development of an individual). Scaling effects must also be considered when comparing species. (p. 214; objective 10)

28. **cortex:** Layer. In the brain, the cortex is the layer that covers the cerebral hemispheres, which in turn cover more primitive or older structures related to bodily functions and the sense of smell. The cortex is composed of nerve cells called neurons, which communicate with each other and send and receive messages to and from all parts of the body. (p. 214; objective 10)

29. **neocortex:** The more recently evolved portions of the cortex of the brain that are involved with higher mental functions and composed of areas that integrate incoming information from different sensory organs. (p. 214; objective 10)

30. **lateralized:** Localized to one side of the brain. Lateralization is the functional specialization of the hemispheres of the brain for specific activities. (p. 221; objective 7)

31. **motor cortex:** The areas of the brain's cortex involved with movement. The motor cortex is located just behind the frontal lobe and is composed of cells that send information to muscle cells throughout the body. (p. 221; objective 7)

32. **anvils:** Surfaces on which an object such as a palm nut, root, or seed is placed before being struck with another object such as a stone. (p. 228; objective 8)

33. **anthropocentric:** Viewing nonhuman organisms in terms of human experience and capabilities; emphasizing the importance of humans over everything else. (p. 231; objective 8)

34. **core area:** The portion of a home range containing the highest concentration and most reliable supplies of food and water. The core area is frequently the area that will be most aggressively defended. (p. 231; objective 9)

35. **territory:** The portions of an individual's or group's home range actively defended against intrusion, particularly by conspecifics. (p. 231; objective 9)

36. **prosocial behaviors:** Actions that benefit another individual even when there is no reward to the performer. Prosocial behaviors include sharing, assisting, and comforting and in humans are motivated in part by empathy and compassion. (p. 233; objective 9)

37. **altruism:** Behavior that benefits another individual but at some potential risk or cost to oneself. (p. 234; objective 9)

38. **empathy:** The ability to identify with the feelings and emotions of others. (p. 234; objective 9)

39. **free-ranging:** Pertaining to noncaptive animals living in their natural habitat. Ideally, the behavior of wild study groups would be free of human influence. (video lesson, introduction; objective 2)

Summary

Lesson 6, Part I, offered a survey of the living primates, with special attention to their physical characteristics and social structure. Lesson 7 examines nonhuman primate behavior so we may learn more about our own behavioral evolution.

The video offered depictions of **behavioral ecology**, which is the study of **free-ranging** primates with a special focus on the relationship between individual and social behaviors, the natural environment, and various physiological traits of the species in question. Behavioral ecology assumes that all of these components evolved together. This approach is based on the premise that behaviors evolve through the operation of natural selection. That is, if behaviors are influenced by genes, then behaviors are subject to natural selection in the same way physical characteristics are. As noted on page 185 of the Jurmain textbook, it is important to "remember that, within a specific environmental context, natural selection favors traits that provide a reproductive advantage to the individuals who have them…. Behavior constitutes a phenotype, and individuals whose behavioral phenotypes increase reproductive fitness will pass on their genes at a faster rate than others." This does not mean that genes code for specific behaviors. Studying complex behavior from an evolutionary perspective does not imply that scientists expect to find a "one gene, one behavior" relationship. In complex organisms, such as mammals and birds, behaviors are increasingly attributed to learning rather than genetic influence. This, according to the Jurmain textbook, is especially true of primates. On page 186, the textbook authors explain that **behavior** "must be viewed as the product of complex interactions between genetic and environmental factors." One important reason why researchers study primate behavior is so that they can identify some of these factors and begin to understand how they interact. It is important to note that primate behavior is very flexible, depending on environmental conditions. While the capacity for flexibility may be genetically influenced, the actual behaviors are rarely the direct result of genetic programming.

Studying the social behavior of nonhuman primates requires looking at all the behaviors that occur in social groupings, even eating and mating. To understand the function of any one behavioral element, scientists try to determine how that behavior is influenced by other interrelated factors. For example, what a primate eats is related to nutritional requirements that are themselves related to body size and basal metabolic rate (BMR).

Body Size: Primate body size is diverse, ranging from some lemurs at 2.5 ounces to gorillas at 260 pounds. As a general rule, larger animals require fewer calories per unit of weight because they have a smaller ratio of surface area to mass than smaller animals have. Since body heat is lost at the surface, larger animals can retain heat more efficiently, so they require less energy overall.

Basal metabolic rate (BMR): The BMR of primates concerns **metabolism**, which is the chemical processes within cells that breakdown nutrients and release energy for the body to use. BMR (metabolism) is connected to body size, so in general, smaller animals have a higher BMR than larger ones. This means that smaller animals need an energy-rich diet high in protein (insects), fats (nuts and seeds), and carbohydrates (fruits and seeds). Some larger primates have a lower BMR, so their nutritional needs don't necessarily require such high-energy foods.

Diet: The Jurmain textbook points out that nutritional requirements of animals are related to the previous two factors, and all three have evolved together. When primatologists study the relationship between diet and behavior, they look at the benefits of energy-rich foods and the costs, or energy expended, in getting it.

Distribution of resources: The problem of finding food influences primate social groupings and foraging techniques. For instance, fruits and nuts in trees are best harvested by smaller groups of animals since these foods are less abundant than leaves. Primates that rely on seasonally available food must be able to find different sources at different times, so this type of feeding also favors small groups able to move from one location to another.

Predation: The effect of predation on social grouping depends on the type of predator, primate body size, and social structure. For instance, when predation pressure is high and body size is small, primates tend to live in large communities.

Relationships with other nonpredatory species: When primate species share habitats with other primate and nonprimate species with similar dietary needs, they attempt to exploit different resources. Predator avoidance is one reason species may coexist in the same habitat despite intense competition for food.

Dispersal: The dispersal of members of one sex at sexual maturity has a profound effect on social structure. The dispersing sex must join a new group or form one, which reduces inbreeding in the population in general. Members of the **philopatric** sex, those who remain in the natal group as adults, are able to create long-term bonds with relatives and other animals with whom they cooperate to protect resources and sometimes increasing their position in the group.

Life histories: **Life history traits** are characteristics or developmental stages that are typical for members of specific species and therefore influence potential rates of reproduction. They influence primates' **social structure**, which can be critical to species survival. Some examples of these traits include length of gestation, length of time between pregnancies, period of infant dependency, and age of sexual maturity, to name a few.

Strategies: **Strategies** are behaviors that have been favored by natural selection to increase individual reproductive fitness. Some examples include feeding strategies, **reproductive strategies**, and predator-avoidance strategies.

Distribution and types of sleeping sites: A primate's sleeping arrangement is related to social structure and to predator avoidance. Gorillas are the only nonhuman primates that sleep on the ground.

Activity patterns: Most primates are diurnal, that is, they are awake in the daytime, but some are nocturnal. Nocturnal species usually forage along or in groups of two or three and use concealment to avoid predators.

Human activities: Human encroachment on primate habitat has disrupted and isolated groups, reduced numbers, and can eventually cause extinction. Hunting has become a serious problem in recent years, and capture for trade also threatens primate habitats.

What is the benefit for nonhuman primates to be social? According to the Jurmain textbook, one widely accepted explanation is protection against predators, particularly in locales where predation pressure is high. More eyes searching for predators increases the chances for detection, and more individuals engaged in surveillance gives foraging individuals more time to eat, which increases reproductive success. Another benefit is that larger social groups can outcompete smaller groups of **conspecifics** (members of the same species) when searching for food in the same area. You should note, however, that not all primates live in large groups, and solitary foraging is typical in many species.

Many primate societies are organized into **dominance hierarchies**, meaning that individuals within the group are ranked relative to one another. Dominance hierarchies impose a degree of order within the group because they establish parameters of individual behavior. In other words, individuals know where they stand in the group and what is acceptable behavior with whom, so these hierarchies serve to reduce physical violence within the group. Dominant individuals have priority regarding food items and mating partners. Therefore, some primatologists believe dominance hierarchies increase reproductive success of high-ranking animals. However, it is well noted that lower-ranked individuals in some species also mate successfully.

Communication is universal among animals. It includes scents, unintentional or **autonomic** responses, and behaviors that convey meaning. In human and nonhuman primates, these behaviors include gestures, facial expressions, body posture, and vocalizations. While the ability to learn and perform such communication is genetically influenced, the context within which communication is used is learned. Communication makes living in social groups possible.

Affiliative behaviors are those that promote group cohesion, while aggressive behaviors often lead to group disruption. Affiliative behavior, such as reconciliation or consolation, often involves more than one form of physical contact and can strengthen peaceful relations in many primate groups. **Grooming**, for instance, is one of the most important affiliative behaviors among primates. Conflict in a group typically arises from competition for food or mating partners. But aggression isn't necessarily fighting; it might involve various signals and displays within the context of a dominance hierarchy.

Female primates spend most of their adult lives pregnant, lactating, and/or caring for offspring. The basic social unit among all primates is the female and her infant, a bond that begins at birth. Primates develop slowly and spend their long childhoods learning the rules of their groups within a social environment. The physical contact they experience with the mother is crucial for normal primate psychological and emotional development. A female's reproductive potential is limited by a biologically imposed interval between births. Therefore, female primates of many species work to maximize their resources and can be extremely competitive with other females and aggressively protect resources and territories. Male primates of many species have little involvement in raising offspring, so they maximize their reproductive success by producing as many offspring as possible. However, in some species of primates, such as gibbons, tamarins, and marmosets, males provide a great deal of parental care. In these species, males commit to one female in a mated pair or in a unit in which only one female reproduces. Among gorillas, males have been known to care for orphaned infants.

Sexual selection is a type of natural selection and is one outcome of different mating strategies. It operates on only one sex in a species, usually males. For males, the selective agent is male

*F*ew things draw attention like a baby, and much of that attention is in the form of the high-pitched "goo-goos" and "gah-gahs" that adults seemed compelled to use in the presence of an infant child.

Now it seems that we may not be alone in the practice of "baby talk." A recent study by Whitham, et al. (2007) that was published in the journal *Ethology*, indicates that rhesus monkeys also engage in such high-pitched vocalizations around infants, and the sounds have the same effect of capturing and holding the attention of those infants—the whole purpose of "baby talk."

But how did the researchers know the vocalizations were "baby talk"? One of the dangers of studying animal behavior, and particularly primate behavior, is the tendency of humans to interpret observations in light of our own behavior patterns. Consequently, scientists have to take special care to note the details surrounding behaviors before coming to conclusions about what they mean.

In this case, the researchers noted that female rhesus monkeys exhibited a variety of behaviors in the presence of another female's infant. The behaviors included the signs of arousal, including much tail-wagging and long strings of grunts, as well as high-pitched noises unique to rhesus monkeys, called "gimeys."

In the past, scientists had thought that the vocalizations were directed toward the infant's mother, but in this study, the researchers noticed that the monkeys were looking directly at the infant as they vocalized, rather than the mother. This led them to conclude that the grunts and "gimeys" were directed at the infants themselves and not the mother.

This interpretation is strengthened by the observation that these sounds were rarely made if an infant was not around. However, if an infant wandered away from the group, the other females would direct a series of grunts and "gimeys" toward the baby.

Finally, in a setting where females were approaching a mother with her infant, the vocalizations, even though directed toward the baby, seemed to have the effect of relaxing the mother and increasing the likelihood that she would allow the others to approach her child.

Interestingly, the mothers did not use such vocalizations with their own offspring.

Do the sounds carry meaning that is coded by the sender to be deciphered by the recipient? There is no way to know that, but the "goo-goos" and "gah-gahs" of human baby admirers don't seem to be meaningful either. It seems that "baby talk" is "baby talk" across species.

competition for mates; for females, it is mate choice. The long-term effect of sexual selection is an increase in the frequency of traits that lead to greater success in acquiring mates. In primate species in which competition for females is prominent, sexual selection produces dimorphism in several male traits, particularly in body size. On the other hand, in species that live in pairs or where male competition is less intense, dimorphism is reduced. Therefore, sexual dimorphism can be a reasonable indicator of the mating practices of primate groups.

Infanticide may be another way that males increase their chance of reproducing. Primatologist Sarah Hrdy explained this reproductive strategy when she was studying hanuman langurs in India during the late 1970s. Note that in a population, individual animals seek to maximize their own reproductive success, not the ultimate success of the population or species overall. Thus, if a "bachelor" male kills the offspring of another male, the mother stops lactating and within two or three months comes into estrus, which makes her sexually receptive to mating with the new male sooner than if the infant had lived.

We know that chimpanzees are genetically close to humans, but, once the human and chimpanzee lineages diverged from a common ancestor, they traveled different evolutionary paths and continued their separate evolution in response to different environmental pressures. This is why no living species can serve as the perfect representation of early hominin adaptations. However, primatologists agree that careful study of the complex factors that influence behavior in nonhuman primates, combined with a close analysis of fossil material, can help us acquire a better understanding of how human behaviors evolved. If we study the *patterns* of nonhuman primate behavior that have evolved and add this to what we know about the flexibility of primate behavior, it is believed that we can seek similar patterns in humans.

Relative brain size clearly differentiates humans from other animal species. **Encephalization** refers to the proportional size of the brain relative to some other measure, such as body weight. Modern humans have a brain size well beyond what is expected for a primate of similar body weight. Encephalization of modern humans is a critical component of recent human evolution. Besides brain size, certain areas of the brain are larger in humans than in other nonhuman primates. The **neocortex** is the part of the brain involved with higher mental functions, such as reasoning, complex problem solving, forethought, and language, and accounts for about 80 percent of total brain volume in humans.

Various hypotheses have been offered for why large brains evolved in humans. One prominent notion is that it is related to solving problems connected with obtaining food. Another hypothesis, the *social brain hypothesis*, says that primates' brains increased in size and capacity because they live in social groups. Having to use complex thinking to deal with complex social structures promoted brain growth. Most likely, group size and brain size coevolved. According to the Jurmain textbook, primatologist Craig Stanford proposes that meat eating was also important in the development of increased cognitive abilities in the human lineage. Some of these theories have been discounted for various reasons. For example, Stanford pointed out that other social carnivores, such as wolves and lions, have not developed relatively large brain sizes.

As noted on page 217 of the Jurmain textbook, "One of the most significant events in human evolution was the development of language." Humans are the only mammals who have evolved the necessary anatomical structures that make it possible to communicate using spoken language. Apes can learn to interpret visual signs and use them in communication, and chimpanzees have been taught to use symbols and signs to communicate specific meanings. Furthermore, some young chimps spontaneously began using symbols after accompanying their mother to training sessions, although they themselves weren't being taught.

It's quite possible that the last common ancestor humans shared with great apes had similar communication capabilities. However, for still-unknown reasons, communication became more important during human evolution, and natural selection favored anatomical and neurological changes that enabled early *Homo* species to learn to speak. More recent studies indicate that the gene FOXP2 regulates the expression of other genes. These other genes influence the embryological development of circuits in the brain that relate to language development in humans. All mammals probably have this gene, but it has nothing to do with language in species other than humans.

Some nonhuman primates, especially chimpanzees and bonobos, exhibit what may be called cultural behaviors. Most aspects of culture are uniquely human, but the cultural behavior of nonhuman primates can be cautiously studied as models for the behavior of early hominids. Culture is learned and taught. Humans deliberately teach their children, and, according to most observations, free-ranging nonhuman primates do not. However, learning in both human and nonhuman primates also occurs through observation, and young nonhuman primates do learn to forage for food, to make and use tools, and begin to learn their place in the dominance hierarchy from watching their elders as well as the behavior and treatment of their peers.

Chapter 8 of the Jurmain textbook picks up the subject of aggressive interactions between groups that was begun in Chapter 7. Many primates also have **territories**, which are portions of an individual's or group's home range that are actively defended when intruders wander in. This is particularly directed against conspecifics. The **core area** is the portion of territory where the group is most frequently found and where much of the group's resources are found. Not all primates are territorial, and many encounters between groups are nonaggressive. Male chimpanzees, on the other hand, can be very aggressive and have little tolerance for interlopers in their territory. Some scientists have suggested that chimpanzee aggression has implications for the evolution of human aggressive behavior. Primatologists had thought that lethal, unprovoked aggression in primates, between groups of conspecifics, only occurred among chimpanzees and humans, but a recent study has shown that it also happens among spider monkeys, but no killings have been observed.

Altruism is behavior that benefits another individual while involving some risk or sacrifice to oneself. The protection of dependent offspring is a common altruistic behavior, but other behaviors have been observed as well. Chimpanzees, for example, will often help relatives and friends, and female langurs will come forward to help protect an infant from an infanticidal male.

Regardless of increased brain size, the human ability to use spoken and written language to communicate, and our development of cultural adaptations that separate us from nonhuman primates, humans are still part of a biological continuum. This term refers to the fact that organisms are related through common ancestry and that behaviors and traits seen in one species are also seen in others to varying degrees. For example, our neurological processes are functionally the same. Bonding with one consistent caregiver is essential for physical and emotional development, infant dependence is similar, and we exhibit aggressive, affiliative, and altruistic behaviors. In many ways, many of our behaviors are elaborate extensions of our hominin ancestors and close primate relatives.

Review Exercises

Matching

Match each term with the appropriate definition or description.

1. __d__ affiliative
2. __c__ autonomic
3. __j__ core area
4. __i__ dominance hierarchies
5. __g__ free-ranging

6. __h__ neocortex
7. __b__ philopatric
8. __e__ polyandry
9. __f__ sympatric
10. __a__ social structure

a. The composition, size, and sex ratio of a group of animals.

b. Remaining in one's natal group or home range as an adult.

c. Pertaining to physiological responses not under voluntary control.

d. Pertaining to amicable associations between individuals.

e. A mating system wherein a single female constantly associates with more than one male with whom she mates.

f. Living in the same area; pertaining to two or more species whose habitats partly or largely overlap.

g. Pertaining to noncaptive animals living in their natural habitat.

h. The more recently evolved portions of the cortex of the brain that are involved with higher mental functions.

i. Systems of social organization wherein individuals within a group are ranked relative to one another.

j. The portion of a home range containing the highest concentration and most reliable supplies of food and water.

Completion

Fill each blank with the most appropriate term from the list below.

alloparenting	encephalization
altruism	home range
behavioral ecology	matriline
conspecifics	metabolism
display	ritualized behaviors
empathy	sexual selection

1. The total area exploited by an animal or social group is called their _home range_.

2. A _display_ is a repetitious behavior that communicates emotional state while _ritualized behaviors_ are exaggerated and may be removed from their original context.

3. The study of the evolution of behavior in an ecological context is called _behavioral ecology_.

4. _Sexual selection_ is a type of natural selection that can lead to sexual dimorphism.

5. Increases in brain size beyond that which would be expected given the body size of a particular species is called _encephalization_.

6. When individuals other than the parent(s) hold or carry infants it is called _alloparenting_.

7. Behaviors such as _altruism_ benefit another individual at a potential risk or cost to oneself.

8. A _Matriline_ is a grouping consisting of females who are all descended from the same female.

9. Members of the same species are called _Conspecifics_.

10. _Metabolism_ is the chemical process within cells by which nutrients are broken down and energy is released.

11. The ability to identify with the feelings and emotions of others is called
empathy

Self-Test

Select the best answer.

1. In multimale/multifemale primate groups, males and females
   - (a.) may form friendships and consortships.
   - b. always interact aggressively.
   - c. always avoid one another.
   - d. never interact unless the female is ready to mate.

2. Chimpanzees sometimes select a stem for eventual use in "termite fishing" and begin stripping its leaves even before the termite mound is in sight. This action indicates
   - a. nothing about chimpanzee intelligence.
   - (b.) that the chimpanzee has planned the making and use of the tool ahead of time.
   - c. that the chimp merely wants to eat the stem without its leaves.
   - d. none of the above.

3. A social grouping of one male mated to more than one female is said to be
   - a. monogamous.
   - b. polyandrous. → *only for females?*
   - c. sympatric.
   - (d.) none of the above.

4. The current view of communication in nonhuman primates is that
   - a. some species can use symbols to communicate with humans.
   - b. they are capable of conveying information about the external environment or their emotional state.
   - c. they often have different vocal calls with specific reference to external stimuli such as predators.
   - (d.) all of the above statements are true.

5. Examples of chimpanzee tool use in the wild include
   - a. using spears to kill other chimpanzees.
   - b. using a cart with wheels to move large objects.
   - (c.) using rocks to crack nuts.
   - d. all of the above.

6. Female primates
   a. usually assume most of the responsibility for infant care.
   b. are almost always larger than males.
   c. have the same nutritional requirements as males.
   d. do none of the above.

7. Large primate groups are advantageous because
   a. they increase the likelihood of early predator detection.
   b. they can outcompete smaller groups of conspecifics.
   c. they may help prevent infanticide by outside males.
   d. all of the above statements are true.

8. The primary goal of primate field studies is to
   a. teach other primates how to be more human-like.
   b. collect information on free-ranging primates.
   c. show that humans are superior to other nonhuman primates.
   d. do all of the above.

9. Which of the following statements is true about primate diets?
   a. Smaller primates tend to have a higher basal metabolic rate (BMR) so they have a higher-energy diet.
   b. Some monkeys eat primarily leaves and have evolved specialized digestive systems that help them to digest leaves.
   c. Most primates eat a large variety of foods.
   d. All of the above statements are true.

10. Male and female reproductive strategies may differ in that
    a. females usually invest more time and energy in each offspring.
    b. males may become larger than females due to male-male competition.
    c. female infanticide increases the reproductive opportunities of females.
    d. a and b are true.

11. Altruism
    a. never happens between nonrelatives.
    b. always involves males taking risks to benefit females.
    c. is any behavior that benefits another while involving some risk or sacrifice to the performer.
    d. is always reciprocal.

12. To understand what it is to be human, it is important to recognize that

    a. we are similar to our nonhuman relatives in our capacities for kindness and cruelty.
    b. many of our behaviors are extensions of those of our hominin ancestors and primate relatives.
    c. behavioral differences among humans and other primates are like to be more a matter of degree than kind.
    d. all of the above statements are true.

13. Male infanticide

    a. is thought to increase the reproductive success of males by bringing females into estrus earlier than they would have otherwise.
    b. incurs a large cost to females.
    c. rarely happens when it is possible that the male is the father of the infant.
    d. involves all of the above.

14. Lethal, unprovoked attacks between groups of conspecifics

    a. are unique to humans.
    b. have been observed among groups of chimpanzees, as well as humans.
    c. are primarily performed by females.
    d. have never been observed.

15. Language experiments in nonhuman primates

    a. have revealed a high degree of cognitive complexity in some individuals.
    b. show that they do not acquire and use language in the same way that humans do.
    c. show that humans are not the only species capable of some degree of symbolic thought.
    d. have shown all of the above.

16. Prosocial behaviors include

    a. sharing.
    b. agonism.
    c. assisting.
    d. both a and c.

Short-Answer Questions

1. List three types of primate communication.

   1. Crouching (body language)
   2. Sexual Behavior to relive tension or show dominance
   3. vocal calls.

2. How are diet and basal metabolic rate (BMR) related?

   Smaller Animals have a higher BMR, so they require more NRG-Rich diet than larger -Animals. So it changes how + when an animal gains/gathers food.

3. How does a "core area" differ from a "territory" or a "home range" among primate groups?

A core area is part of a/the home range and tends to be where a group will spend most of it's time + gather. While a territory is also part of the home range it is the defended area.

4. How do affiliative behaviors help to maintain group cohesion? Give two examples of affiliative behaviors and describe how they help group cohesion.

Affilative behavior helps to reinforce social bonds + Group solidarity. Grooming is the best example of this, but hugging/kissing are also examples.

5. What are the two main types of sexual selection? How do they contribute to sexual dimorphism in nonhuman primates?

Mate Choice + Mate Comp. Mate Comp. between males may result in greater strength + larger size + more agression.

6. Name the two primatologists profiled in the video who are best known for their observation of chimpanzees and describe some of their findings.

Jane Goodall + Toshisada Inishida. Who both Promoted Primate understanding in showing how Primates have a life history, social groupings + Personalitys.

Application Questions

1. What are the pros and cons of alloparenting from the perspective of the infant involved? How about the mother of the infant? Alloparenting gives an infant more social connections + if anything happens to it's mother, a new care giver. A mother than has an oppertunity for help in Providing for the child.

2. Do chimpanzees show cultural behaviors? If so, give examples. What are the criteria for cultural behavior in nonhuman primates?

Yes, various ways of gathering food, such as termites show cultural learning or using a rock to crack a nut, ect.

3. Discuss how humans fit into the "biological continuum." Do humans differ from other primates more in degree or in kind of anatomical and behavioral adaptations?

the represent a place on the biological Continum not seperate from it. We vary from Chimps more in degree then in kind. Such as cultural or language ect.

204 PHYSICAL ANTHROPOLOGY: THE EVOLVING HUMAN

Answer Key

Matching

1. d (video lesson, segment 2; objective 4)
2. c (objective 4)
3. j (objective 9)
4. i (video lesson, segment 2; objective 4)
5. g (video lesson, introduction; objective 2)
6. h (objective 10)
7. b (objective 4)
8. e (objective 5)
9. f (objective 4)
10. a (video lesson, introduction; objective 2)

Completion

1. home range (objective 4)
2. display; ritualized behaviors (objective 4)
3. behavioral ecology (objective 2)
4. Sexual selection (video lesson, segment 1; objective 5)
5. encephalization (objective 10)
6. alloparenting (objective 6)
7. altruism (objective 9)
8. matriline (objective 4)
9. conspecifics (objectives 4 & 7)
10. Metabolism (objective 3)
11. empathy (objective 9)

Self-Test

1. a. is the correct answer. Males and females often form friendship and/or consortship in multimale/multifemale groups. (objective 4)
2. b. is the correct answer. This indicates substantial forethought on the part of the chimpanzee. (objective 8)
3. d. is the correct answer. This is a one male/multifemale social grouping. (objective 4)
4. d. is the correct answer. All of these capabilities have been observed in nonhuman primates. (objective 7)
5. c. is the correct answer. Using a rock to crack nuts is an observed use of tools in chimpanzees. Using wheeled carts and spears to kill conspecifics has not been observed in the wild. (objective 8)

6. a. is the correct answer. In most species, female primates assume most of the responsibility for infant care. (objective 6)

7. d. is the correct answer. All of these are advantages of living in large groups. (objective 2)

8. b. is the correct answer. The goal of primate field studies is to study free-ranging primates with a minimum of human interference. (objective 1)

9. d. is the correct answer. All of these statements are true. (objective 3)

10. d. is the correct answer. Females usually invest more per offspring than males and males are often larger due to male-male competition (i.e., gorillas and baboons). Infanticide is thought to possibly increase the reproductive success of males but not females. (objective 5)

11. c. is the correct answer. Altruism is a behavior that benefits another at a cost to the performer. These behaviors are not restricted to relatives, or males and females, and altruism is not always reciprocal. (objective 9)

12. d. is the correct answer. All of these statements are true. (objective 10)

13. d. is the correct answer. Males who commit infanticide are thought to increase their reproductive success as long as the infant they are killing is not likely to be theirs. If a male has recently mated with a female, he is not likely to attempt to kill her infant. The loss of an infant in this manner is always very costly to the female. (objective 5)

14. b. is the correct answer. Lethal attacks on conspecifics have been observed in both chimpanzees and humans. (objective 9)

15. d. is the correct answer. Language experiments with nonhuman primates have shown remarkable cognitive abilities as a capacity for symbolic thought. Still, it is evident that they do not acquire and use language exactly like humans do. (objective 7)

16. d. is the correct answer. Prosocial behaviors are those behaviors that benefit another regardless of risk or reward to the performer. In humans, we say these are motivated in part by empathy and compassion. (objective 9)

Short-Answer Questions

Your answers should include the following:

1. Gestures, facial expressions, body posture, and vocalizations are all types of communication. (video lesson, segment 2; objective 4)

2. Larger animals have lower basal metabolic rates (BMR) and they can eat a higher proportion of lower quality foods such as leaves. Smaller animals have relatively higher BMRs. They need a diet that consists of higher-quality foods, such as insects, nuts, and fruits. (objective 3)

3. The core area is a part of the home range where a group is most often found. It is thought to be where most of the resources on the home range are found. A territory is the part of a home range that is defended against intrusion from others, especially conspecifics. (objective 9)

4. Affiliative behaviors help maintain group cohesion by building and maintaining friendly bonds between individuals in a group. Grooming is a very important affiliative behavior, as are reconciliation and consolation. Grooming serves both a hygienic function and a social function through bond building. Reconciliation happens between individuals who have had a conflict. It allows them to restore peaceful relationships. Consolation is reassurance by one group member to an individual that is upset for some reason. This shows support for the upset individuals and allows them to calm down. (video lesson, segment 2; objective 4)

5. The types of sexual selection are mate choice and mate competition. Male-male competition is likely to be responsible for the sexual dimorphism seen in many primates. Males who engage in aggressive physical contact with one another may become larger over time in order to be better competitors. (video lesson, segment 1; objective 5)

6. The two primatologists are Jane Goodall, who has worked in Gombe National Park in Tanzania, and Toshisada Inishida, who has worked in the Mahale Mountains just south of Gombe. As noted in the video, Goodall and Nishida have contributed to a greater recognition of chimpanzees as individuals with individual life histories and personalities whose intergroup interactions reveal various behaviors (including unprovoked aggression) that provide a theoretical framework for understanding the evolution of certain behaviors in humans. (video lesson, segment 3; objective 1)

Application Questions

Your answers should include the following:

1. Alloparenting may benefit the mother and the infant by increasing the number of individuals who will act toward the infant in a protective way. The "alloparent" benefits by learning to handle an infant. This is especially true if the alloparent is a young female. On the other hand, alloparents are not always very careful with the infant and may handle it roughly or neglect it. This has been known to result in the death of infants. This is, of course, very detrimental to both the infant and its mother. (objective 6)

2. Chimpanzees show many types of cultural behaviors, such as termite fishing, using leaves as sponges, and using stones to crack nuts. They also show intraspecific differences in grooming behavior, and regional dietary preferences. Table 8-1 on page 230 of the Jurmain textbook lists a number of cultural criteria. Chimpanzees groups regularly meet 6 to 8 of these criteria. (video lesson, segment 3; objective 8)

3. Humans represent a point on a biological continuum. They are not separate from it in any way. Many of our adaptations differ from our primate relatives more in degree than kind. This includes cultural behaviors, language capabilities, cognitive abilities, and developmental stages. (objective 10)

Lesson Review

Lesson 7: Primate Behavior

PLEASE NOTE: Use this matrix to guide your study and achieve the learning objectives of this lesson. It will also help you to view the video, which defines and demonstrates important concepts and principles as they relate to everyday life and actual case studies.

Learning Objective	Textbook	Student Guide	Video Lesson
1. Summarize the history of primate field studies, and list some of the scientists who initiated pioneering research.	pp. 184–185	Self-Test: 8; Short-Answer: 6.	Segment 3: *Primate Cultural Behavior*
2. Define primate behavioral ecology, and discuss how it is the current theoretical perspective in primate behavioral studies.	pp. 185–186	Key Terms: 1, 2, 3, 39; Matching: 5, 10; Completion: 3; Self-Test: 7.	Introduction
3. Describe the types of food primates eat and how species vary with regard to dietary preferences.	pp. 186–192	Key Terms: 4; Completion: 10; Self-Test: 9; Short-Answer: 2.	
4. Define the types of primate social interactions and communication methods, including grooming, dominance, and affiliative and aggressive behaviors.	pp. 192–200	Key Terms: 5, 6, 7, 8, 9, 10, 12, 13, 14, 15, 16, 17, 18, 19, 20; Matching: 1, 2, 4, 7, 9; Completion: 1, 2, 8, 9; Self-Test: 1, 3; Short-Answer: 1, 4.	Segment 2: *Life in a Social Group*
5. Differentiate between male and female reproductive strategies and their influence on sex-specific behaviors.	pp. 201–205	Key Terms: 11, 21, 22, 23, 24; Matching: 8; Completion: 4; Self-Test: 10, 13; Short-Answer: 5.	Segment 1: *Reproductive Strategies*

Learning Objective	Textbook	Student Guide	Video Lesson
6. Discuss the importance of the mother-infant bond in contributing to the normal social and psychological development of primate infants.	pp. 205–208	Key Terms: 25; Completion: 6; Self-Test: 6; Application: 1.	
7. Define language and describe the evolution of language and the results of ape language experiments.	pp. 217–224	Key Terms: 12, 30, 31; Completion: 9; Self-Test: 4, 15.	
8. List the criteria for cultural acts in nonhuman species, and discuss whether chimpanzees meet these criteria.	pp. 224–231	Key Terms: 32, 33; Self-Test: 2, 5; Application: 2.	Segment 3: *Primate Cultural Behavior*
9. Contrast between group aggression and altruism/cooperation among chimpanzees.	pp. 231–236	Key Terms: 34, 35, 36, 37, 38; Matching: 3; Completion: 7, 11; Self-Test: 11, 14, 16; Short-Answer: 3.	
10. From an anatomical and behavioral perspective, discuss how humans fit into the "biological continuum."	pp. 236–237	Key Terms: 26, 27, 28, 29; Matching: 6; Completion: 5; Self-Test: 12; Application: 3.	

LESSON 8

 Lesson 8:   Methods of Paleoanthropology

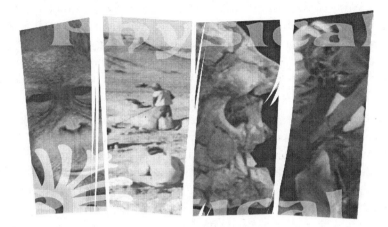

Methods of Paleoanthropology

Checklist

For the most effective study of this lesson, complete the following activities in this sequence.

Before Viewing the Video

❑ Read the Preview, Learning Objectives, and Viewing Notes below.

❑ Read Chapter 10, "Paleoanthropology: Reconstructing Early Hominin Behavior and Ecology," pages 282–309, in *Introduction to Physical Anthropology*.

What to Watch

❑ After reading the textbook assignment, watch the video for Lesson 8, *Methods of Paleoanthropology*.

After Viewing the Video

❑ Briefly note your answers to the questions listed at the end of the Viewing Notes.

❑ Review the Summary below.

❑ Review all reading assignments for this lesson, including the Viewing Notes in this lesson.

❑ Write brief answers to the "Critical Thinking Questions" at the end of Chapter 10 in the textbook.

❑ Complete the Review Exercises below. Check your answers with the Answer Key and review when necessary.

❑ Use the Lesson Review matrix found at the end of this lesson to review and assess your knowledge of each Learning Objective.

Preview

In previous lessons, you learned that humans are classified as primates with an evolutionary history shared with other primates. However, humans are a unique kind of primate and our hominin ancestors adapted to a particular way of life for millions of years. This lesson focuses on the quest to discover the anatomy, behavior, and the environments of early hominins. It is a big task, one that requires the multidisciplinary approach of **paleoanthropology**, the study of early hominins. This lesson introduces many specialists who contribute their expertise to the field of paleoanthropology in order to provide a picture of the physical and cultural nature of our ancestors.

There is evidence of hominins shortly after 5 million years ago (mya). The Jurmain textbook explains the different dating methods scientists use to help form the chronology of early hominins. Two sites rich in hominin artifacts are explored in this lesson: Olduvai Gorge is detailed in the textbook and video, and Koobi Fora in the video. Paleoanthropologists are interested in not just *how* early hominins evolved, but also *why* the evolution occurred in the manner it did. The Jurmain textbook offers some environmental explanations for hominin beginnings and some theories on why hominins became bipedal.

Concepts to Remember

❋ Lesson 1 introduced a number of subfields within the larger field of **physical anthropology**, including **paleoanthropology**, **archaeology**, and paleoecology. These disciplines, as well as related scientific fields, are represented in Lesson 8 as part of the academic background of the experts who appear in the video and who contribute to the site excavations at Olduvai Gorge in Tanzania and Koobi Fora in Kenya.

❋ Lesson 7 introduced the concept that nonhuman primates share some aspects of human culture, not because they are becoming human (an **anthropocentric** viewpoint), but because an aptitude for culture as a means of adapting to the natural environment is one of the behavioral patterns that human share with nonhuman primates as products of the same evolutionary forces. Researchers have selected several nonhuman primate species for comparison in the study of early hominin behavior and adaptation based on both behavioral ecology and biological relatedness. A good example from Lesson 7 involved chimpanzees, whose ability to use and modify sticks and stones as tools to better exploit existing resources can be seen as representing capabilities that would have been present among our earliest ancestors.

Learning Objectives

After you complete this lesson, you should be able to:

1. Define the term *hominin* and describe hominin characteristics. (pp. 283–287)

2. Give an overview of the multidisciplinary approach of paleoanthropology. (pp. 287–288)

3. Briefly describe how potential hominin sites are located, excavated, and analyzed. (pp. 287–293)

4. Compare and contrast relative and chronometric dating techniques and give examples. (pp. 293–298)

5. Summarize the types of hominin sites found at Olduvai Gorge and why Olduvai Gorge is an important location. (pp. 288–289, 292–293, 296–298)

6. Describe the types of experimental archaeology used to gain insights into hominin stone tool technology. (pp. 298–302)

7. Discuss the types of data used to create scenarios of the past, including the origins of bipedalism. (pp. 302–308)

At this point, read Chapter 10, "Paleoanthropology: Reconstructing Early Hominin Behavior and Ecology," pages 282–309.

Viewing Notes

The video for Lesson 8 details the multidisciplinary approach of paleoanthropology, showing the contributions of experts from many fields as they excavate a site and combine different analyses to provide a broader picture of our early ancestors.

In July of 1959, in a ravine in northern Tanzania known as Olduvai Gorge, Louis and Mary Leakey and their team found the remains of numerous extinct animals and stone tools. Although this team had been meticulously exploring this area for almost thirty years, it was the discovery made on this July day that became a major paleontological event and grabbed the attention of scientists and the general public alike. Mary Leakey discovered a 1.75-million-year-old skull of an early hominin, at first called *Zinjanthropus*, which means "East African man," but later classified as *Australopithecus boisei*. This discovery propelled Olduvai into the forefront of human origins research.

Mary Leakey's discovery reflects what many people imagine paleoanthropology to be like. Robert Blumenschine, a paleoanthropologist from Rutgers University who is featured in the video, points out that people think of human origins research as finding "the fantastic skull of a fossil hominid . . . the most famous figures in the history of paleoanthropology are those who have discovered spectacular hominid remains." Of course that is important, he says, but paleoanthropology shouldn't stop there. Olduvai Gorge is evidence of that. It is a site rich in geological and faunal history, all of which contributes valuable information about human origins.

The video focuses on two areas of vital importance for ongoing paleoanthropological research in East Africa: Koobi Fora and Olduvai Gorge. Koobi Fora, located in northern Kenya, lies on the eastern shores of Lake Turkana and stretches from the Ethiopian border south for 120 miles. Olduvai Gorge is situated in the Serengeti Plain of northern Tanzania. It is theorized that human origins can be traced to these regions, which is one of the main reasons for the intense focus on this area over the years. Because of volcanic activity, these sites contain neatly stratified layers of dirt and rock interspersed with datable volcanic ash and lava layers that hold a rich abundance of fossil and faunal material that can be extracted and analyzed. The ability to date the archaeological finds at Koobi Fora and Olduvai help us trace the anatomical evolution of early hominins as well as their behavior, including the earliest stages of manufacture and use of stone tools.

Because early hominins were part of an ecological community, paleoanthropologists explore the habitat in which they lived to learn what kind of food they ate, what fauna shared their area, and what predators threatened their survival. This study requires the collaboration of experts from different fields.

Another portion of the video examines the methods of dating fossils and the other materials found at the sites. One technique is **relative dating**, which is a way to date fossils in relationship to one another. The idea is that geological strata are deposited in chronological order, so that the older items are lower than more recent ones. Relative dating offers only relative age, not specific dates.

Another method of dating is **chronometric dating**. This technique is based on the process of radioactivity decay and can provide actual dates. The most common chronometric dating technique is carbon-14 (^{14}C) or **radiocarbon dating**. Carbon-14 (radioactive carbon) is created when nitrogen-14 in the upper atmosphere collides with radiation from the sun. Carbon-14 is absorbed by plants. Animals and humans eat the plants or other animals that have absorbed carbon-14 from the plants, and the carbon-14 is transferred into their bodies. The carbon-14 atoms are always decaying, but they are replaced by new carbon-14 atoms at a constant rate. When an organism dies, the process of replenishment of carbon-14 stops and, as paleoanthropologist Eric Delson says in the video, "The radioactive clock begins." Scientists can measure the amount of disintegration in a particular sample and calculate the number of years it took for that amount of decay to accumulate. According to the Jurmain textbook, the time period in which one-half the amount of a radioactive isotope is converted chemically into a daughter product is referred to as the **half-life** of the isotope. Carbon-14 is said to have a half-life of approximately 5,730 years. Simply put, this means that half of the original amount of carbon-14 in organic matter will have converted to a more stable isotope 5,730 years after the organism's death; half of the remaining carbon-14 will have converted after another 5,730 years, and so on. After about 50,000 years, the amount of carbon-14 remaining will be so small that the fossil can no longer be dated reliably.

Another method of chronometric dating mentioned in the video is **potassium-argon**, which is suitable for dating very old materials. Potassium-argon dating measures the *accumulation* of the gas argon (^{40}Ar) in a substance as a result of the decay of radioactive potassium-40 (^{40}K) into argon gas. When a volcano erupts, argon gas forms from the molten minerals. By comparing the amount of potassium to the amount of argon gas found in a sample of volcanic rock, and knowing the decay rate, scientists can date the sample. The half-life of radioactive potassium-40 as it converts into to argon-40 is about 1.3 billion years. This dating method becomes very valuable in areas of past volcanic activity, like that found at Olduvai Gorge in East Africa between 1 and 5 million years ago.

Questions to Consider

🌼 Why is Olduvai Gorge an important site for paleoanthropology?

🌼 How are the different dating methods used in the field to place sites and fossils into a specific time frame?

🌼 One expert comments that he is confident that we will find hominin remains in unexpected places. Based on what you learned in the video, what do you think?

Watch the video for Lesson 8, *Methods of Paleoanthropology.*

Segment 1: *Koobi Fora, Kenya*
Segment 2: *Olduvai Gorge, Tanzania*
Segment 3: *The Dating Game*

Key Terms and Concepts

Page references are keyed to *Introduction to Physical Anthropology,* 13th edition.

1. **mosaic evolution:** A pattern of evolution in which the rates of evolution in one functional system vary from that in other systems. For example, in hominin evolution, the dental system, locomotor system, and neurological system (especially the brain) all evolved at markedly different rates. (p. 284; objective 1)

2. **culture:** Behavioral aspects of human adaptation, including technology, traditions, language, religion, marriage patterns, and social roles. Culture is a set of learned behaviors transmitted from one generation to the next by nonbiological (i.e., nongenetic) means. (p. 284; objective 1)

3. **multidisciplinary:** Pertains to research involving mutual contributions and cooperation of experts from various scientific fields (i.e., disciplines). (p. 287; objective 2)

4. **artifacts:** Objects or materials made or modified for use by hominins. The earliest artifacts are usually made of stone or, occasionally, bone. (pp. 11, 289; video lesson, segment 1; objective 2)

5. **taphonomy:** (*taphos,* meaning "dead") The study of how bones and other materials came to be buried in the earth and preserved as fossils. Taphonomists study the processes of sedimentation, the action of streams, preservation properties of bone, and carnivore disturbance factors. (pp. 128, 291; objective 3)

6. **context:** The environmental setting where an archaeological trace is found. Primary context is the setting in which the archaeological trace was originally deposited. A secondary context is one to which it has been moved (such as by the action of a stream). (p. 291; video lesson, segments 1 & 2; objective 3)

7. **chronometric dating:** (*chrono*, meaning "time," and *metric*, meaning "measure") A dating technique that gives an estimate in actual numbers of years; also known as *absolute dating*. (p. 294; video lesson, segment 3; objective 4)

8. **stratigraphy:** Study of the sequential layering of deposits. (p. 294; video lesson, segment 1; objective 4)

9. **principle of superposition:** In a stratigraphic sequence, the lower layers were deposited before the upper layers. Or, simply put, the stuff on top of a heap was put there last. (p. 294; objective 4)

10. **half-life:** The time period in which one-half the amount of a radioactive isotope is converted chemically to a daughter product. For example, after 1.25 billion years, half the ^{40}K remains; after 2.5 billion years, one-fourth remains. (p. 295; video lesson, segment 3; objective 4)

11. **thermoluminescence (TL):** (ther-mo-loo-min-ess′-ence) Technique for dating certain archaeological materials (such as stone tools) that were heated in the past and that release stored energy of radioactive decay as light upon reheating. (p. 295; video lesson, segment 3; objective 4)

12. **paleomagnetism:** Dating method based on the earth's shifting magnetic pole. (p. 297; video lesson, segment 3; objective 4)

13. **biostratigraphy:** A relative dating technique based on regular changes seen in evolving groups of animals as well as presence or absence of particular species. (p. 297; objectives 4 & 5)

14. **blanks:** In archaeology, stones suitably sized and shaped to be further worked into tools. (p. 299; objective 6)

15. **flake:** Thin-edged fragment removed from a core. (p. 299; objective 6)

16. **core:** Stone reduced by flake removal. A core may or may not itself be used as a tool. (p. 299; objective 6)

17. **lithic:** (*lith*, meaning "stone") Referring to stone tools. (p. 299; objective 6)

18. **knappers:** People (frequently archaeologists) who make stone tools. (p. 300; objective 6)

19. **direct percussion:** Striking a core or flake with a hammerstone. (p. 300; objective 6)

20. **microliths:** (*micro*, meaning "small," and *lith*, meaning "stone") Small stone tools usually produced from narrow blades punched from a core; found especially in Africa during the latter part of the Pleistocene. (p. 300; objective 6)

21. **pressure flaking:** A method of removing flakes from a core by pressing a pointed implement (e.g., bone or antler) against the stone. (p. 300; objective 6)

22. **microwear:** Polishes, striations, and other diagnostic microscopic changes on the edges of stone tools. (p. 300; objective 6)

23. **phytoliths:** (*phyto*, meaning "hidden," and *lith*, meaning "stone") Microscopic silica structures formed in the cells of many plants, particularly grasses. (p. 301; objective 6)

24. **environmental determinism:** An interpretation that links simple environmental changes directly to a major evolutionary shift in an organism. Such explanations tend to extremely oversimplify the evolutionary process. (p. 303; objective 7)

25. **stable carbon isotopes:** Isotopes of carbon that are produced in plants in differing proportions, depending on environmental conditions. By analyzing the proportions of the isotopes contained in fossil remains of animals (who ate the plants), it is possible to reconstruct aspects of ancient environments (particularly temperature and aridity). (p. 303; objective 7)

26. **fossils:** The mineralized remains of plants and animals, usually found in deposits of ancient sediments. (video lesson, segment 1; objective 2)

27. **relative dating:** A dating technique that gives an estimated range of years based on stratigraphy, or the knowledge that fossil remains found in the lowest layers containing the oldest rock deposits will be older than those found in higher layers where younger rocks have been deposited. (video lesson, segment 3; objective 4)

28. **radiocarbon dating:** A chronometric dating technique based on the half-life of carbon-14, a radioactive isotope. (video lesson, segment 3; objective 4)

29. **optically stimulated thermoluminescence:** A dating technique based on radiometric decay by which inorganic artifacts, such as burned stone flakes or ceramic pots, are stimulated with light to measure their thermoluminescence and then calculate their age. (video lesson, segment 3; objective 4)

30. **potassium-argon dating:** A chronometric dating technique based on the half-life of the radioactive isotope potassium-40 (^{40}K) and its daughter product argon-40 (^{40}Ar). (video lesson, segment 3; objective 4)

31. **Oldowan:** The earliest stone tool industry for which evidence has been found, dating approximately from 2 to 1.8 million years ago and named after the site at Olduvai Gorge. (video lesson, segment 2; objective 5)

Summary

The Jurmain textbook and the video both emphasize that *paleoanthropology*, the study of ancient humans, is a team effort requiring the expertise of scientists from a variety of disciplines. Our understanding of our earliest ancestors emerges from the study of fossil remains; material culture, such as tools and living sites; remains of other animals and plants living at the same time; and evidence of the prevailing climate and environment. All of this evidence needs to be dated, or fixed in time, so that specialists in dating techniques also play an important role.

The chart on page 285 of the Jurmain textbook is a graphic depiction of the different rates of development of hominin characteristics. Paleoanthropologists agree that the evolutionary changes in hominin form through time did not occur all at once, but at difference rates, a process referred to as mosaic evolution. **Mosaic evolution** occurs when the rate of evolution in one functional system varies from that in other systems. For example, human dentition, locomotion, and brain size all evolved separately and the rate of change in each is different. According to the Jurmain textbook, the single most important defining characteristic of a hominin is *bipedal* locomotion, or walking upright on two feet. As hominin evolution progresses, other features develop, such as enlarged brain size relative to body size and tool use and manufacture.

The elaboration and transmission of **culture**, a form of adaptation to the environment that depends on learned behaviors that can be communicated to others, is the hallmark of our species. The evidence for early human culture has tended to focus on stone tools, which emerge in the archaeological record somewhat late—about 2.5 million years ago. Prior to that time, we are certain that hominins used tools made from natural materials and engaged in a number of cultural behaviors, but there is no evidence that remains to explain, in detail, how this behavior evolved. We are dependent on the archaeological record, and are limited by our technical skill in reconstructing early hominin culture. While stone tools are our primary window into the lives of early hominins, we must remember that culture is more than tools—it is an adaptive strategy that involves cognitive, political, social, and economic components. The material culture that remains in the archaeological record from this time gives us our clues about the more complex nature of early humans—their biocultural evolution.

The reconstruction of the behavior of early hominins requires the skills and labor of many specialists, who collect both direct and indirect evidence of hominin evolution and the context in which it took place. Paleoecologists study ancient environments, including animal and plant communities that exerted selective pressures on early hominins. Geologists help locate archaeological sites through their knowledge of earth movement and geological events and provide information that allows us to date artifacts and locations. Archaeologists and physical anthropologists search for bones and artifacts left behind by early populations, excavating them carefully through painstaking procedures that map the site and the excavation process.

The paleoanthropological work at Olduvai Gorge provides much of what we know about the origins of human culture between 2 and 1 million years ago. Located in the Serengeti Plain of northern Tanzania, Olduvai Gorge resembles a miniature version of Arizona's Grand Canyon. The surrounding countryside is grassland savanna with some scattered scrub bushes and acacia trees, and the semiarid climate today is believed to be similar to what it has been for the last 2 million years. The 350-foot-deep ravine is easy to date geologically because of its volcanic rock and lava layers. More than 150 species of extinct animals have been found at Olduvai, along with early hominin remains and stone tools.

According to the Jurmain textbook on page 293, Olduvai Gorge provides "an extremely well-documented and correlated sequence of geological, paleontological, archaeological, and hominin remains." This sequence provides the opportunity for dating objects using their position in the sequence related to other objects, a method known as **relative dating**. Relative dating methods can tell us that something is older or younger than something else, but cannot provide an absolute date, such as its age in number of years. A fossil found 70 feet beneath the surface is assumed to be older than a fossil found at 50 feet beneath the surface at the same site. This method of relative dating is based on **stratigraphy**, the study of the sequential layering of deposits. Stratigraphy is based on the **principle of superposition**, which states that a lower stratum is older than a higher stratum. One problem with this method is that the earth is frequently disturbed by geological events that can shift the strata, or layers, and the

*O*ne of the greatest challenges for paleoanthropologists is drawing conclusions about early humans from partial remains. A simple stone knife can tell a researcher much based on its style, its edge, and the wear patterns. But the scientist must combine this information with other evidence to tell a more complete story about its makers.

So imagine the impact of discovering a stone tool covered with the actual preserved remains of 2-million-year-old blood, fat, and other biological substances. The quartz knife was found in the *Sterkfontein* caves 60 kilometers northwest of Johannesburg, South Africa, and analyzed in 2004 by Australian molecular archaeologist, Dr. Tom Loy of the University of Queensland.

Under a microscope, Loy discovered red and white blood cells, fat cells, collagen, muscle fibers, and even degraded hair. He also found residue from wood, keratin such as that found in horns, and starch grains similar to those from a plant that still grows in the area.

One of the puzzles paleoanthropologists have been working to solve is what early hominids ate. There is an abundance of evidence that meat and bone marrow were a significant part of early hominids' diet, and the consensus is that, given the relatively small size of these people, they probably scavenged leftovers from the kills of predators.

But the blood on the knife Loy analyzed was fresh when preserved. Loy came to that conclusion by making replica tools and using them on a variety of substances. When he examined them under a microscope, he found that fresh blood formed a distinctively patterned matrix with the silica that bound it to the tool. The knife was then covered by clay that protected the biological molecules on the matrix from oxidation and moisture.

But where would fresh blood come from? Did the knife's owner scavenge a fresh kill? Or did he hunt down his dinner himself? The latter would show a level of sophistication that exceeds current opinions about hominids at this time. It will take more evidence to determine a precise answer.

To be sure, Loy's 2004 announcement of his find generated plenty of skepticism. Some scientists understandably found it hard to believe that blood and fat could be preserved for 2 million years.

However, another remarkable discovery in North Dakota may lay some of the skepticism to rest. In 2007, a 77-million-year-old dinosaur was unearthed still encased in its own mummified skin, complete with muscle tissue, foot pads, and even stomach contents. Perhaps finding those answers has just become a bit easier.

objects within them. Fluorine analysis is another method of relative dating that applies only to bones. Since bones in the earth are exposed to groundwater that usually contains fluorine and they absorb that fluorine in the process of fossilization, bones deposited in the same place at the same time should contain the same amount of fluorine. Again, this method can provide age relative to another bone, but cannot tell us precisely how old the bone is.

Bones or artifacts that are found in association with faunal remains can be dated if the dates for the animal species are known. For instance, if a certain species of extinct pig lived between 1.5 million and 1 million years ago, we know that the associated hominin remains or stone tools were also present during that time period. This is why careful mapping during excavation, plus the techniques of **taphonomy**, or the study of how bones and other materials came to be buried in the earth and preserved as fossils, are essential for paleoanthropological field research.

Chronometric dating is a dating technique gives an estimate of age, in actual number of years, using a variety of techniques based on the phenomenon of radioactive decay. **Radiocarbon dating**, a well-known radiometric method, is based on measuring the relative amounts of carbon-14 and carbon-12 in an organic object. Knowing the rate of decay from radioactive carbon-14 to carbon-12, it is possible to determine when the object died or stopped absorbing carbon. This method is used to date things that were once living (such as wood and bone) up to about 50,000 years ago. The half-life of carbon-14 (meaning the amount of time it takes for half of the carbon-14 to decay into carbon-12) is 5,738 years; another 5,738 years must elapse before half of the remaining carbon-14 decays, and then another 5,738 years, and so on. By 50,000 years, there is nothing left to measure. **Potassium-argon dating** uses the decay of radioactive potassium-40, which gets trapped in volcanic rock as it cools, to date volcanic layers or strata. (For more details on these methods, refer to the Viewing Notes on page 210 above.)

Paleoanthropologists put together clues from the work of many specialists to build an image of the hominins and the way they lived at various points in human evolutionary history. At Olduvai Gorge, we have several dozen hominin sites that have been surveyed, and over the years, a number of interpretations of the artifacts and animal bones have been offered.

Experimental archaeology involves reconstructing prehistoric techniques for making tools or butchering animals by actually making and using stone tools and then seeing what the remains of that activity might look like. Microscopic study of the marks left by various types of tools on bone can help us understand how early hominins butchered and prepared wild game. Wear patterns on ancient tools, likewise, tell us about how they were used. Flint-knapping, or actually making stone tools of various types, tells us about the technical expertise necessary to produce such tools, giving us insight into the cognitive skills of hominins at various stages of evolution.

The environment plays an important role in the evolution of any species, and so paleoanthropologists also consider ecological factors that were present during the evolution of early hominins. It is not easy to know definitively just what prehistoric environments were like. The Jurmain textbook describes three current theories about the climate and environment that existed during the evolution of early hominins. One idea, based on faunal remains and fossil pollen, sugests that in eastern and central Africa between 12 and 5 million years ago, the climate cooled, which resulted in the appearance of expanded transitional zones between forests and savanna grasslands. This argument posits that some Miocene hominoids may have adapted to the drier grassland areas, while others leading to the African apes remained in the wetter forested areas. Life in more open transitional areas may have selected for bipedalism, dietary changes, and tool use. Alternatively, scientists working with stable carbon isotopes argue that their evidence suggests grassland never predominated. (Carbon isotope analysis studies isotopes of carbon found in plants, which are ingested by the animals that eat the plants, and thus are measurable in the fossilized animal bones.) A third theory is based on evidence for repeated environmental fluctuations, which suggest that there were a number of arid periods during the time that the early hominins lived. As the Jurmain textbook points out, **environmental determinism**, in which a major environmental change produces a major change in a species' evolution, is an oversimplification of a very complex process. Instead, it is likely that several pressures were at work simultaneously and at different intensities over time. One current idea is that our ancestors evolved not because they made big changes every time the environment changed but because they were "flexible opportunists" that could thrive in many different ecological niches.

Looking to the climate and ecology of the period during which hominins emerged does not involve reliance on environmental determinism. Clearly, the selective pressures on our ancestral line were multiple and varied over time. Our attempts to understand how and, more important, why hominins became bipedal will always focus on the environmental pressures that may have favored that shift. The chart on page 306 of the Jurmain textbook lists a variety of hypotheses to explain why hominins initially became bipedal. The next lesson will delve further into these explanations for bipedal locomotion, particularly the anatomical evidence gleaned from fossil finds.

Review Exercises

Matching

Match each term with the appropriate definition or description.

1. ____ blank
2. ____ chronometric dating
3. ____ flake
4. ____ microlith
5. ____ microwear

6. ____ paleomagnetism
7. ____ phytolith
8. ____ stratigraphy
9. ____ taphonomy

a. The study of the sequential layering of deposits.
b. Microscopic silica structures formed in the cells of many plants, particularly grasses.
c. Thin-edged fragment removed from a core.
d. The study of how bones and other materials came to be buried in the earth and preserved as fossils.
e. A dating method based on the earth's shifting magnetic pole.
f. A dating technique that gives an estimate in actual numbers of years.
g. Polishes, striations, and other diagnostic microscopic changes on the edges of stone tools.
h. Small stone tools produced from narrow blades punched from a core.
i. In archaeology, a stone suitably sized and shaped to be further worked into a tool.

Completion

Fill each blank with the most appropriate term from the list below.

artifacts   hominin
bipedal locomotion   mosaic evolution
context   stable carbon isotopes
culture

1. A _____ is characterized by _____.

2. _____ is a set of learned behaviors transmitted from one generation to the next by nonbiological (i.e., nongenetic) means.

3. The secondary _____ of an archaeological trace is one to which it has been moved after leaving its original deposit site.

4. Objects or materials that are modified by hominins, such as stone tools, are called _____.

5. _____ are molecules that are produced in plants in different proportions depending on environmental conditions. The analysis of these molecules allows researchers to reconstruct aspects of ancient environments.

6. The appearance of bipedalism first and increased brain size much later in hominin evolution is an example of _____.

Self-Test

Select the best answer.

1. Knappers are people who
   a. like to sleep during the day.
   b. study the position of a fossil or an archaeological trace in its environmental context.
   c. make stone tools.
   d. carry objects in a sack on their back.

2. The half-life of a radioactive isotope is the time period in which
   a. all of the isotopes present in a sample are converted chemically into a daughter product.
   b. some of the isotopes present in a sample are converted chemically into a daughter product.
   c. one-fourth of the isotopes present in a sample are converted chemically into a daughter product.
   d. half of the isotopes present in a sample are converted chemically into a daughter product.

3. A hominin is distinguished from the pongid family by which of the following characteristics?

    a. large genetic differences

    b. a smaller brain relative to body size

    c. bipedal locomotion

    d. none of the above

4. Paleoanthropology projects often involve cooperation with researchers from many other disciplines or subdisciplines. These experts provide information in their area of expertise that helps to complete a picture of what is going on at a fossil site. These areas include

    a. paleontology.

    b. religious studies.

    c. linguistics.

    d. all of the above disciplines.

5. Which of the following is true about Mary Leakey?

    a. She worked in South Africa looking for hominin fossils.

    b. She was a paleoanthropologist who exposed Piltdown Man as a hoax.

    c. She found a 1.75-million-year-old skull at Olduvai Gorge.

    d. None of these statements are true.

6. Paleoanthropology research projects are conducted in which of the following ways?

    a. Potential fossil sites are extensively surveyed.

    b. Financing is secured.

    c. The contexts of all materials found are carefully recorded and analyzed.

    d. All of these things are done.

7. Hominins are thought to have evolved in the Late Miocene or Early Pliocene epoch, about 7 to 5 million years ago. During that time period, the climate in Africa was

    a. going through a warming period.

    b. becoming substantially wetter.

    c. going through a cooling period.

    d. becoming less seasonal.

8. The edges of stone tools

    a. sometimes contain microscopic striations that can give clues as to how the tool was used.

    b. are usually too marked up to discern any use pattern.

    c. may retain phytoliths that indicate what plant materials it came in contact with.

    d. include both a and c.

9. Chronometric dating methods include
   a. carbon-14 dating.
   b. potassium-argon dating.
   c. thermoluminescence dating.
   d. all of the above methods.

10. A taphonomic analysis of a fossil or artifact will yield which of the following results?
    a. exactly how old the specimen is
    b. whether the site it was found in was a primary or secondary context
    c. what other animal and plant species are present at the site
    d. none of these

11. Which of the following have been proposed as an influencing factor in the evolution of bipedal locomotion in hominins?
    a. long-distance walking
    b. feeding from bushes
    c. thermoregulation
    d. all of the above

Short-Answer Questions

1. What are the three components of culture? Do we share any of these components with other nonhuman primates?

2. How do relative and chronometric dating methods differ? List and describe two relative dating methods and two chronometric dating methods.

3. Out of the eight possible factors influencing the evolution of bipedal locomotion that are listed in Table 10-2 in the Jurmain textbook, choose the three most plausible factors in your opinion. What are the strengths and drawbacks of these proposed influences?

4. When stone tools are placed under a microscope, researchers may observe patterns of microwear and residues on the surface of the tools. Give three examples of these patterns and residues.

5. What types of fossils and artifacts have been found at Koobi Fora?

6. How is the excavation of paleoanthropological sites destructive? What to researchers do to try to get the most information from these sites?

Application Questions

1. What can we learn from experimental archaeology? How can reproducing and using stone tools tell us more about our hominin ancestors?

2. Discuss mosaic evolution in hominins. Describe the order in which certain hominin features are thought to have evolved. These features are thought to be adaptations to what kinds of environmental conditions?

3. Drawing on what you have learned about fossils and dating methods, discuss why is it so important to know the context in which a fossil is found. Include consideration of whether the context is primary or secondary, its position in the geological strata, what other material is found in the same area, and the presence or absence of volcanic materials in the area, and so on.

4. Imagine that you were walking through Olduvai Gorge and happened to locate a hominin fossil site. Using the information in the Jurmain textbook, outline the steps you would take to properly excavate and analyze the material found there and what kinds of experts would be useful to gain information of varying kinds from the site.

5. As a paleoecologist, how would you go about reconstructing the ecology of a hominin site? For example, what type of plants and animals were present, where was water found, and what the climate was like?

Answer Key

Matching

1. i (objective 6)
2. f (video lesson, segment 3; objective 4)
3. c (objective 6)
4. h (objective 6)
5. g (objective 6)
6. e (video lesson, segment 3; objective 4)
7. b (objective 6)
8. a (video lesson, segment 1; objective 4)
9. d (objective 3)

Completion

1. hominin; bipedal locomotion (objective 1)
2. culture (objective 1)
3. context (video lesson, segments 1 & 2; objective 3)
4. artifacts (video lesson, segment 1; objective 2)
5. Stable carbon isotopes (objective 7)
6. mosaic evolution (objective 1)

Self-Test

1. c. is the correct answer. Knappers is a term used to describe people who make stone tools. (objective 6)
2. d. is the correct answer. A half-life is the period of time in which half of a radioactive material decays into some other material. (video lesson, segment 3; objective 4)
3. c. is the correct answer. The main difference that sets hominins apart from pongids is bipedal locomotion. (objective 1)
4. a. is the correct answer. Paleontologists often work closely with paleoanthropologists at study sites. (objective 2)

5. c. is the correct answer. Mary Leakey discovered a 1.75 million-year-old skull at Olduvai Gorge. This is just one of many finds in her long, distinguished career. (objective 5)

6. d. is the correct answer. All of these steps are taken in the process of conducting a paleoanthropological research project. (objective 5)

7. c. is the correct answer. During the late Miocene and Early Pliocene, the climate in Africa was becoming cooler and drier. (objective 7)

8. d. is the correct answer. Marks on the edges of stone tools can reveal how the tool was used. Phytoliths retained on the tool indicate that it has probably been used for processing plants. (objective 6)

9. d. is the correct answer. All of the listed methods are chronometric dating methods. (video lesson, segment 3; objective 4)

10. b. is the correct answer. A taphonomic analysis will attempt show how the fossil came to be where it was found. (objective 3)

11. d. is the correct answer. All of the listed factors have been proposed to influence the evolution of bipedality in hominins. (objective 7)

Short-Answer Questions

Your answers should include the following:

1. The Jurmain textbook identifies material, social, and cognitive components of culture. Nonhuman primates share some degree of all three components of culture. They make tools, they have complex social interactions and signals, and they have some of the language capabilities exhibited by humans. (objective 1)

2. Relative dating methods can tell you what something is older or younger than, whereas chronometric dating methods can give an approximate age for certain materials. Relative dating methods include stratigraphy, biostratigraphy, and fluorine analysis. Chronometric dating methods include potassium-argon, carbon-14, thermoluminescence, and fission-track. (video lesson, segment 3; objective 4)

3. Eight factors are listed in the Jurmain textbook in Table 10-2, and all of them have their pros and cons. While there is no right or wrong answer in your choice of three of these factors, the following factors are currently considered to be the most plausible by many researchers: feeding from bushes, thermoregulation, and carrying. (objective 7)

4. Different striation patterns and polishes come from working various kinds of materials, such as bone, hides, wood, and other plant materials. Phytoliths from plants and amino acid residues have also been found on the surfaces of stones tools. The phytoliths indicate plant processing and the amino acids indicate animal processing in many instances. (objective 6)

5. Early hominin stone tools have been found at Koobi Fora, as well at the fossil remains of hominins such as *Homo erectus/Homo ergaster*. (video lesson, segment 1; objective 3)

6. The excavation of paleoanthropological sites involves the disturbance of those sites and the removal of material from those sites and researchers dig up entire areas and also sift

soil. Researchers try to get the most out of these disturbed sites by gleaning as much information as possible. They carefully survey the area and learn about its geology, they extract artifacts and the fossils of many animals and plants. Bones are analyzed for marks, and the ecology of the area is analyzed. (video lesson, segment 1; objective 3)

Application Questions

Your answers should include the following:

1. Experimental archaeology can help us to learn a great deal of information about stone tools and their use. By reproducing how to make them, we can get an idea of how hominins might have made them. By using stone tools on a variety of materials and analyzing the marks and residues that those materials leave behind on the tools, we can compare them to ancient stone tools to estimate how those tools were used. By reproducing cut marks, tooth marks, and striations on bones, we can look at these patterns on fossil bone specimens and make inferences about how they came to be at that place. (objective 6)

2. The features that distinguish hominins from the great apes include tooth and jaw dimensions, bipedal locomotion, a larger brain relative to body size, and to some degree, stone tool use, These features did not evolve simultaneously nor did they evolve in response to the same environmental pressures. In the Jurmain textbook, Figure 10-1 shows some of these features and the time periods in which they were thought to have evolved. A large brain is thought to have evolved in response to social pressures, or possibly the need to find and remember food resources; there are many possible ecological explanations for the evolution of bipedalism. Please see Table 10-2 in the Jurmain textbook for a list of these explanations. While we now know that most of these features evolved while hominins were living in forested areas, it is thought that hominin evolution was heavily influenced by the need to adapt to the cooler, drier climate that appeared in Africa during the Late Miocene/Early Pliocene. This change caused many forested areas to disappear, possibly pushing hominins into living in a more open environment. (objectives 1 & 7)

3. To use relative dating methods it is crucial to know exactly where a fossil was embedded in relation to other strata. This is true for geological strata and for biostratigraphy where the remains of other types of animals are used in analysis. Only if this is known, can we tell what material the fossil is older or younger than. It is also important to know if the fossil was found in the place where it died, or whether it was moved there from another place. If it was moved there from another place, i.e., through stream action, it could be of a very different age than the material around it so it is also important to know if it was found in a primary or secondary context.

   Most chronometric dating methods are not used on the fossils themselves. They are used to analyze geological strata above or below the fossil, so it is also important to know where the fossil was found to use these methods. Layers of volcanic materials are particularly useful in these analyses as they usually contain many radioactive molecules. Researchers can measure the half-life of these materials and estimate the age of a fossil. Paleomagnetic analyses can also be used if the strata is known. (objective 4)

4. Excavating a hominin site involves a great deal of teamwork. Teams usually consists of experts from many different areas of expertise and they take part in different aspects of the project. The first task at hand is to survey the site to get an idea of what might be there. Then funding for the project must be obtained as well as governmental permission to excavate at the site. Once excavation begins, geologists identify and analyze geological strata. Paleontologists analyze the remains of organisms found at the site. Archaeologists might examine any artifacts that are present, such as stone tools. Paleoecologists might reconstruct the environment and climate of the area during that time period. A taphonomist might tell you whether a bone has been marked by stone tools or chewed by a carnivore, or both. All remains and artifacts should be carefully handled, labeled and analyzed, usually offsite in a laboratory. The utmost care should be taken to be as precise as possible and to handle all materials very carefully as they are often very delicate. (video lesson, segments 1, 2, & 3; objective 2)

5. Paleoecologists examine fossilized remains of plants and animals as well as geological information to reconstruct an ancient landscape. Once they have an idea of what the ecology of the area was like, they then look at the plants and animals present in similar modern environments and study their interactions. In the video, Kari Prassack says that many of the bird species that were present two million years ago are the same ones that are seen today. This is also true for many other animal, plant, and insect species. The climate can be estimated from looking at the types of plants present in the fossil record and comparing them to environments they live in today. Analyses can also be done by looking at other organisms like birds. Geologic information can indicate the former presence of water and whether it was still as in a lake, or flowing like a river. (video lesson, segment 2; objective 3)

Lesson Review

Lesson 8: Methods of Paleoanthropology

PLEASE NOTE: Use this matrix to guide your study and achieve the learning objectives of this lesson. It will also help you to view the video, which defines and demonstrates important concepts and principles as they relate to everyday life and actual case studies.

Learning Objective	Textbook	Student Guide	Video Lesson
1. Define the term *hominin* and describe hominin characteristics.	pp. 283–287	Key Terms: 1, 2; Completion: 1, 2, 6; Self-Test: 3; Short-Answer: 1; Application: 2.	
2. Give an overview of the multidisciplinary approach of paleoanthropology.	pp. 287–288	Key Terms: 3, 4, 26; Completion: 4; Self-Test: 4; Application: 4.	Segment 1: *Koobi Fora, Kenya;* Segment 2: *Olduvai Gorge, Tanzania;* Segment 3: *The Dating Game*
3. Briefly describe how potential hominin sites are located, excavated, and analyzed.	pp. 287–293	Key Terms: 5, 6; Matching: 9; Completion: 3; Self-Test: 10; Short-Answer: 5, 6; Application: 5.	Segment 1: *Koobi Fora, Kenya;* Segment 2: *Olduvai Gorge, Tanzania*
4. Compare and contrast relative and chronometric dating techniques and give examples.	pp. 293–298	Key Terms: 7, 8, 9, 10, 11, 12, 13, 27, 28, 29, 30; Matching: 2, 6, 8; Self-Test: 2, 9; Short-Answer: 2; Application: 3.	Segment 1: *Koobi Fora, Kenya;* Segment 3: *The Dating Game*
5. Summarize the types of hominin sites found at Olduvai Gorge and why Olduvai Gorge is an important location.	pp. 288–289, 292–293, 296–298	Key Terms: 13, 31; Self-Test: 5, 6.	Segment 2: *Olduvai Gorge, Tanzania*

Learning Objective	Textbook	Student Guide	Video Lesson
6. Describe the types of experimental archaeology used to gain insights into hominin stone tool technology.	pp. 298–302	Key Terms: 14, 15, 16, 17, 18, 19, 20, 21, 22, 23; Matching: 1, 3, 4, 5, 7; Self-Test: 1, 8; Short-Answer: 4; Application: 1.	
7. Discuss the types of data used to create scenarios of the past, including the origins of bipedalism.	pp. 302–308	Key Terms: 24, 25; Completion: 5; Self-Test: 7, 11; Short-Answer: 3; Application: 2.	

LESSON 9

 Lesson 9:   The First Bipeds

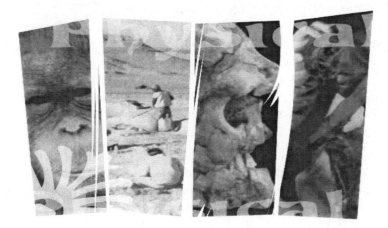

The First Bipeds

Checklist

For the most effective study of this lesson, complete the following activities in this sequence.

Before Viewing the Video

❑ Read the Preview, Learning Objectives, and Viewing Notes below.

❑ Read Chapter 11, "Hominin Origins in Africa," pages 310–339, in *Introduction to Physical Anthropology*.

What to Watch

❑ After reading the textbook assignment, watch the video for Lesson 9, *The First Bipeds*.

After Viewing the Video

❑ Briefly note your answers to the questions listed at the end of the Viewing Notes.

❑ Review the Summary below.

❑ Review all reading assignments for this lesson, including the Viewing Notes in this lesson.

❑ Write brief answers to the "Critical Thinking Questions" at the end of Chapter 11 in the textbook.

❑ Complete the Review Exercises below. Check your answers with the Answer Key and review when necessary.

❑ Use the Lesson Review matrix found at the end of this lesson to review and assess your knowledge of each Learning Objective.

Preview

Lesson 8 discussed various dating methods that are currently in use today. That lesson pointed out that fluorine analysis, a dating method useful only with bones, helped to solve the controversy that surrounded the discovery of the "Piltdown man" fossil in 1912. This "find" caused a sensation because the skull displayed the combination of a human cranium and an apelike jaw, and was considered a true "missing link" by many British scientists for forty years, when in the early 1950s, it was determined a fraud. However, the search for *the* missing link continued until it became clear, in science, that no ancestral fossil form is an even split between modern ones. Rather, each fossil represents its own unique adaptation. There are many "links" in the chain of evolution, and each fossil find expands our knowledge of how, when, where, and why humans evolved as they did.

Lesson 9, which is based on Chapter 11 of the Jurmain textbook, looks at the earliest hominin fossil finds and traces the evolutionary transition from the most primitive (possible) hominins, the pre-australopiths, through four million years of evolution, to the first members of our genus, *Homo*, who appeared 2.0 million years ago.

Concepts to Remember

※ Lesson 1 included the definition of a hominid, or hominin. **Hominin** is the colloquial term for members of the tribe Hominini, which includes all bipedal hominoids back to the divergence from African great apes. The video for Lesson 9 and Chapter 11 of the Jurmain textbook both concentrate on the evolutionary pattern of hominins.

※ Lesson 5 introduced the **geological time scale**, a method for organizing earth history in which large spans of time are broken down into eras and periods. Periods can be divided into epochs. There is evidence that primate evolution began in the late Mesozoic era. This lesson primarily concentrates on the later Cenozoic era and the Tertiary period, which is further divided into epochs discussed in the Jurmain textbook: Paleocene (began 68 million years ago), Eocene (55 million years ago), Oligocene (34 million years ago), Miocene (23 million years ago), and Pliocene (5 million years ago).

※ Lesson 5 also discussed the principles of animal classification. A **clade** is a group of organisms sharing a common ancestor and includes the common ancestor and all descendants. This lesson discusses how some of the fossil finds are evaluated so they can be classified.

※ Lesson 8 offered theories on factors that influenced the evolution of bipedal locomotion in hominins. Suggested advantages of **bipedalism** include freeing arms to carry objects and offspring, visual surveillance over tall grass to prevent predation, long-distance walking, and thermoregulation. For more details, refer to the chart on page 306 of the Jurmain textbook.

Learning Objectives

After you complete this lesson, you should be able to:

1. List and describe the major skeletal adaptations for full-time bipedalism and compare these with skeletal structures seen in quadrupedalism. (pp. 312–316)

2. Identify the geographic locations and the names of the major early hominin fossil sites in East and South Africa. (pp. 316–319)

3. Describe the pre-australopiths, with special attention to the environments and time period in which they were found. (pp. 319–322)

4. Describe the australopiths, with special attention to *Australopithecus afarensis*. (pp. 322–333)

5. Describe the morphological traits that characterize the later, more derived australopiths, with special attention to their relationship to other hominins living at the same time. (pp. 328–333)

6. Contrast the geological context of the East versus the South African hominin sites and discuss how it affects the reliability of the dates for these sites. (p. 317)

7. Contrast the morphology of the earliest members of the genus *Homo* with the morphology of the genus *Australopithecus*. (pp. 333–335)

8. Discuss the alternative approaches of explaining the early hominins. (pp. 335–337)

9. Discuss the impact of new discoveries on our understanding of hominins. (pp. 337–338)

At this point, read Chapter 11, "Hominin Origins in Africa," pages 310–339.

Viewing Notes

Our cultural adaptations have allowed us to live practically anywhere on this planet. Before the emergence of culture, early human forms depended to a great extent on biological adaptations, which develop much more slowly. In recent years, scientists have identified three main groups of *protohominins*, the term sometimes used for the earliest representative of human lineage, in Ethiopia, Kenya, and Chad. Fossil finds indicate that these animals looked very much like modern apes, but with several features that suggest an ancestral link to humans. These protohominins—*Sahelanthropus* in Chad, *Orrorin* from Kenya, and *Ardipithecus* from Ethiopia—may be the first of our kind to be bipedal, or to move about on two legs.

The video for Lesson 9 details several features that distinguish a quadruped from a biped. First is the **foramen magnum**, the opening at the base of the skull, where the spinal cord goes into the brain. In an ape, the foramen magnum is located more to the rear of the skull, while in a biped it is shifted anteriorly, so the head sits directly on the spinal column. Also, the pelvis in a quadruped is elongated and flat; in a biped, it is much shorter and curves toward the front of the body, providing a large area for the gluteus muscles to attach, which aids in bipedal locomotion. A biped's leg is longer, its femur is angled inward and is part of a modified knee anatomy, and its foot is more arched than a quadruped, three additional features that help humans walk on two feet.

Almost all scientists agree that humans first evolved in Africa. By about 4 million years ago, a genus called *Australopithecus* first appeared in East Africa and in South Africa. This early hominin genus is characterized by bipedal locomotion, a relatively small brain, and large back teeth. The most famous find of an *Australopithecus afarensis* is Lucy, a partial skeleton that was discovered at a site in Ethiopia in 1974.

About two and a half million years ago, there was a change in the evolutionary lineage. First, in *Australopithecus*, there is a distinction between gracile forms and robust forms. The South African *Australopithecus africanus* is an example of a gracile form. **Gracile** is a reference to the smaller dentition and jaw structure of this animal, whereas Paranthropus, an australopith from both South and East Africa, is referred to as **robust** because of its large teeth and jaw structure. Mary Leakey's discovery at Olduvai Gorge in Tanzania, in 1959, was at first named *Zinjanthropus*, and later classified as *Paranthropus boisei*. Note that this differentiation of robust and gracile does not refer to body size but to teeth and jaw size. *Australopithecus* seems to have been disappearing by about one million years ago.

Another evolutionary change, at this time, is the appearance of our own genus, *Homo*. Some scientists believe that *Australopithecus africanus* is a direct ancestor of early *Homo* while others believe it is a distinct lineage.

In 1960, the Leakey team at Olduvai Gorge discovered a new type of hominin at the same place where they had found *Paranthropus boisei* the year before. This new hominin was called **Homo habilis**, "the handy man." It appeared much more like a human, with the beginning of a larger brain, evidence of toolmaking, and evidence of an expanded diet. The video explores how these two species coexisted in the same geographic location.

Questions to Consider

❋ What kind of interaction may have existed between *Homo habilis* and *Paranthropus boisei*?

✹ To what genus and species did the famous "Lucy" fossil belong? Where was this fossil found and when?

✹ What is the difference between gracile and robust forms? To what do these physical characteristics refer?

Watch the video for Lesson 9, *The First Bipeds*.

Segment 1: *Biomechanics*
Segment 2: *"Would the First Biped Please Stand Up?"*

Key Terms and Concepts

Page references are keyed to *Introduction to Physical Anthropology*, 13th edition.

1. **morphological:** Pertaining to the form and structure of organisms. (p. 312; objective 1)

2. **habitual bipedalism:** Bipedal locomotion as the form of locomotion shown by hominins most of the time. (p. 315; objective 1)

3. **obligate bipedalism:** Bipedalism as the *only* form of hominin terrestrial locomotion. Since major anatomical changes in the spine, pelvis, and lower limb are required for bipedal locomotion, once hominins adapted this mode of locomotion, other forms of locomotion on the ground became impossible. (p. 315; objective 1)

4. **Sterkfontein:** (sterk´-fawn-tane) Site in South Africa that has yielded important fossil evidence of early hominin foot structure. (p. 316; video lesson, segment 2; objective 2)

5. **Aramis:** (air´-ah-miss) A site located along the Awash River in Ethiopia in East Africa in which a substantial collection of primitive hominin fossil remains have been excavated and been dated to 4.4 million years ago. (p. 321; objective 2)

6. **australopiths:** (os-tra-loh-piths) The colloquial name referring to a diverse group of Plio-Pleistocene African hominins. The group is made up of two closely related genera, *Australopithecus* and *Paranthropus*. Australopiths are the most abundant and widely distributed of all early hominins and are also the most completely studied. (p. 322; video lesson, segment 2; objective 4)

7. **sectorial:** Adapted for cutting or shearing; among primates, refers to the compressed (side-to-side) first lower premolar, which functions as a shearing surface with the upper canine. (p. 324 objective 3)

8. **sagittal crest:** A ridge of bone that runs down the midline of the cranium like a short Mohawk. This serves as the attachment for the large temporal muscles, indicating strong chewing. (p. 328; video lesson, segment 2; objective 5)

9. *Australopithecus africanus*: (os-tral-oh-pith´-e-kus af-ri-kan´-us) The name given to a species originally believed to form a kind of halfway "missing link" between modern apes and humans. Dated to between 2.5 and 2 million years ago, the first skull of *A. africanus* was excavated from a limeworks quarry at Taung near Johannesburg, South Africa, in 1924. (p. 331; objective 5)

10. **Plio-Pleistocene:** Pertaining to the Pliocene and first half of the Pleistocene, a time range of between 5 and 1 million years ago. For this time period, numerous fossil hominins have been found in Africa. (p. 333; objective 2)

11. ***Homo habilis:*** (hab´-ih-liss) A species of early *Homo* from Olduvai and the Turkana Basin. (p. 333; video lesson, segment 2; objective 7)

12. **postcranial:** (post, meaning "after") In a quadruped, referring to that portion of the body behind the head; in a biped, referring to all parts of the body beneath the head (i.e., the neck down). (video lesson, segment 2; objective 3)

13. **foramen magnum:** The large opening at the base of the human skull through which the spinal cord enters into the brain. It is positioned farther forward in the skulls of the early hominins than is the case in quadrupeds, and anthropologists make comparisons between the position of the foramen magnum in early hominin species to determine how likely such species were to have walked habitually upright (bipedally) rather than on four legs (quadrupedally). (video lesson, segment 1; objectives 1 & 3)

14. **robust:** Referring to large, heavily built body/anatomical structure. (video lesson, segment 2; objective 5)

15. **gracile:** Referring to smaller, more lightly built body/anatomical structure. In the case of *Australopithecus africanus*, it refers to their teeth, jaws and faces, not to their body size. (video lesson, segment 2; objectives 4 & 5)

Summary

The video and reading for Lesson 8 offered hypotheses of why biped locomotion evolved in hominins. Lesson 9 looks at how bipedalism evolved, and examines specific morphological (anatomical) evidence for this adaptation.

When humans walk, we stride; we step onto our heel, roll forward, and push off with our big toe as we swing the opposite leg forward to begin its step. A striding gait requires us to alternate our weight on a single, fully extended leg, shifting our center of gravity so we don't tip over or lurch from side to side. To maintain a stable center of balance, several major structural features emerged:

- The foramen magnum became repositioned farther under the skull to balance the head on the spine.

- The spine curved twice to keep the trunk centered above the pelvis.

- The pelvis became shortened and broad, providing attachment for the powerful gluteus maximus (buttock) muscle needed for extending the thigh and powering running.

- Lower limbs became longer.

- The femur angled inward, keeping the legs more directly under the body. The knee changed, permitting full extension of this joint.

- The big toe became larger and came in line with the other toes and the foot became arched, providing a stable platform to stand upright.

As explained in the Jurmain textbook, organisms do not undergo significant structural reorganization unless the changes, over generations, confer functional benefits. While bipedalism must have been a major benefit for hominins, we don't know precisely what behavioral stimuli contributed to its evolution. Several possibilities are suggested in Table 10-2 on page 306 of the Jurmain textbook. As the textbook authors state on pages 314–315, "once behavioral influences initiated certain structural modifications, the process [of bipedalism] gained momentum and proceeded irreversibly." Eventually, this mode of locomotion became habitual, meaning that it was the most efficient way of moving about, and obligate, meaning that hominins could not move efficiently any other way.

Pre-Australopiths (6.0+ to 4.4 million years ago): The earliest hominins are found in Africa. The oldest known candidate today is *Sahelanthropus*, dated by faunal correlation between 7 and 6 million years ago. *Sahelanthropus* is a complete cranium discovered in Chad (Central Africa) in 2001, with the brain size and skull resembling apes but the lower face and teeth resembling humans. Two other very early hominins have been found in East Africa: *Orrorin* from Kenya and *Ardipithecus* from Ethiopia. Limb bones suggest that around 6 million years ago, *Orrorin* is bipedal, as is *Ardipithecus*, which dates from 5.8 to 4.4 million years ago. These early specimens show a mixture of primitive and derived characteristics—just what would be expected for transitional periods. The sites yielding these fossils are continuing to be excavated, and as more material is discovered, our understanding of this initial period in our history will grow. On page 319, the Jurmain textbook describes these pre-australopiths as "the earliest and most primitive (possible) hominins," an acknowledgment of the fragmentary nature of the evidence and the unique and puzzling combinations of characteristics found in this group.

Australopiths (4.2 to 1.2 million years ago): These diverse hominins are grouped into two genera, *Australopithecus* and *Paranthropus*, and are found in South Africa, central Africa (Chad), and East Africa. They are all bipedal, they all have relatively small brains, and they all have large teeth, with thick enamel on the molars.

Early Australopiths (4.2 to 3.0 million years ago): *Australopithecus anamensis* is the earliest and most primitive species, appearing in East Africa between 4.2 and 3.0 million years ago, with clear evidence of bipedalism but with primitive features such as a large canine and a sectorial lower first premolar. *Australopithecus afarensis* is found slightly later, between 3.9 and 3.0 million years ago, and is a likely candidate for the ancestor of later australopithecines and early *Homo*. Two sites, Hadar in Ethiopia and Laetoli in Tanzania, have provided a treasure trove of specimens of *Australopithecus afarensis*, including the famous skeleton "Lucy," one of the three most complete individual hominin specimens from anywhere in the world dating before 100,000 years. As the textbook authors point out, several hundred specimens have come from these two sites, providing the opportunity to study variability in australopithecines. Based on the Laetoli footprints and leg bones from specimens such as Lucy, we know that *A. afarensis* was a habitual biped, although there is speculation that they also spent time in trees.

Later More Derived Australopiths (3.0 to 1.2 million years ago): Hominins from this time period show increased diversity as well as derived characteristics that distinguish them from their ancestors. The "robust" form of early hominin, *Paranthropus,* appears in East Africa around 2.5 million years, with its combination of small brain size and primitive traits plus a complex of derived traits including a very broad face, large palate, and massive back teeth and lower jaws. By 2 million years ago, there are two species in East Africa: the earlier *P. aethiopicus* and the later even more derived *P. boisei*. At the same time, there is a separate robust species in South Africa. By 1 million years ago, all have disappeared. Refer to Figure 11-16 on page 329 of the Jurmain textbook for a detailed visual representation of the different robust australopithecine specimens.

In East Africa, erosion caused by wind, rain, and gravity has exposed fossils on the ground, and the presence of volcanic activity there makes it possible to date specimens chronometrically. Thus, East Africa is the source of much of what we know about early hominin evolution. But the first *Australopithecus* fossil was actually found in South Africa. At the beginning of the twentieth century, most scientists thought that the likely origin of humans was Asia, because that was where the first skulls of an early *Homo* ("Java Man" in Indonesia) had been found. In 1924, anatomist Raymond Dart discovered the Taung child, the skull of a three- to four-year-old child encased in limestone from a quarry in Taung, South Africa. Dart christened it *Australopithecus africanus*, southern ape of Africa, and he believed this specimen was the "missing link" between modern apes and humans. While the concept of one link between apes and humans is not accurate, Dart was correct in identifying the hominin-like features of the fossils. Further discoveries cemented the idea of early hominin activity in South Africa. While the fossils are difficult to date there because of the absence of volcanic strata and the disturbance caused by commercial quarrying, it is estimated that *Australopithecus africanus* lived between 2.5 and 2 million years ago. As described in the video, Dart's *A. africanus* is an example of a gracile australopithecine, which refers to its smaller teeth and jaw structure relative to those of the robust form, *Paranthropus*.

Early *Homo*: Early *Homo* is distinguished primarily by larger cranial capacity (average 631 cm^3 compared to 520 cm^3 for *Paranthropus* and 442 cm^3 for *Australopithecus*) along with some difference in cranial shape and tooth proportions. There is reasonable evidence that one or more species of early *Homo* were present in East Africa by 2.0 million years ago, developing in parallel with at least one line of australopithecines. These two hominin lines lived as contemporaries for at least one million years, at which point the australopithecine lineage disappears. However, new evidence from South Africa has opened the possibility that the transition to *Homo* occurred there rather than in East Africa. The two partial skeletons of *Australopithecus sediba*, found in the Malapa Cave in South Africa, show a mix of *Australopithecus* and *Homo* characteristics, making it a possible transitional species.

The challenge of interpreting the early hominin data is significant—the time span is extensive and far in the past, the normal problems of dating fossil finds are exacerbated by the geologically complex South African limestone breccia in which the hominin remains are embedded, and the varied combinations of hominin characteristics in particular specimens obscure clear taxonomic distinctions. However, the extraordinary efforts that are being made to excavate and interpret the material from this time period—the end of the Miocene through the Plio-Pleistocene—provide us a wealth of data to work with. Despite gaps in the fossil record and limitations in the locations and paleoenvironments we can sample today, it is possible to make some inferences about the adaptive patterns that characterize the early part of human history. As summarized on pages 337–338 of the Jurmain textbook, we know something about where they lived, what they ate, their rates of development, and which hominin features emerged earliest.

Review Exercises

Matching I

Match each term with the appropriate definition or description.

1. _f_ *Australopithecus africanus*
2. _h_ foramen magnum
3. _b_ habitual biped
4. _d_ Laetoli
5. _c_ morphological
6. _e_ obligate biped
7. _a_ Plio-Pleistocene
8. _g_ Sterkfontein

a. The period of time that spans 5 to 1 million years ago.

b. Bipedal locomotion as the form of locomotion shown by hominins most of the time.

c. Pertaining to the form and structure of organisms.

d. An East African site that dates to the Plio-Pleistocene period.

e. Bipedalism as the only form of hominin terrestrial locomotion.

f. The first australopithecine species described.

g. A site in South Africa that has yielded important fossil evidence of early hominin foot structure.

h. The large opening at the base of the human skull through which the spinal cord enters into the brain.

Matching II

Match each term with the appropriate definition or description.

1. _b_ Aramis
2. _e_ australopiths
3. _c_ *Australopithecus*
4. _g_ gracile
5. _i_ *Homo habilis*
6. _a_ postcranial
7. _f_ robust
8. _h_ sagittal crest
9. _d_ sectorial

a. All the body parts below the head in a hominin.

b. A site in Ethiopia where a nearly complete skeleton of *Ardipithecus* was discovered.

c. An early hominin genus, known from the Plio-Pleistocene of Africa, that is characterized by bipedal locomotion, a relatively small brain, and large back teeth.

d. The compressed first lower premolar in primates that functions as a shearing surface with the upper canine.

e. A diverse group of Plio-Pleistocene African hominins.

f. Referring to a large, heavily built body or anatomic structure.

g. Referring to a smaller, more lightly built body or anatomic structure.

h. A structure on the skull that, when found in a fossil, indicates strong chewing muscles.

i. The earliest species of *Homo* described so far.

Completion I

Fill each blank with the most appropriate term from the list below.

Aramis	obligate bipedalism
Australopithecus	Plio-Pleistocene
habitual bipedalism	posteranial
morphology	Sterkfontein

1. Numerous hominin fossils have been found dating from the *Plio-Pleistocene*

2. The form and structure of an organism is its *Morphology*.

3. Bipedalism as the standard and most efficient form of locomotion is referred to as *habitual bipedalism*

4. An important fossil found at *Sterkfontein*, has added greatly to our knowledge of early hominin foot structure.

5. The term *postcranial* refers to all body parts located below the head in a biped.

6. *Aramis* is a site located in Ethiopia along the Awash River that has yielded a substantial number of early hominin fossils dated to 4.4 million years ago.

7. *Australophithecus* is an early genus of hominins found in both East and South Africa.

8. When hominins became committed to bipedal walking and were no longer capable of moving efficiently using other types of locomotion, they are said to show *Obligate bipedalism*

Completion II

Fill each blank with the most appropriate term from the list below.

australopiths	Homo habilis
Australopithecus africanus	robust
foramen magnum	sagittal crest
gracile	sectorial

1. A lower premolar that is adapted for shearing is called a *sectorial* premolar.

2. *Australopiths* is a colloquial term for a group of Plio-Pleistocene hominins living between 5 and 2 million years ago.

3. The type of australopith that has a heavily built skull has historically been referred to as *robust*.

4. The type of australopith that does not have exaggerated features of the skull, jaws, and teeth of *Paranthropus* has historically been referred to as *gracile*.

5. A ridge of bone that serves as an anchor for large temporalis muscles and runs down the middle of the skull is called a *sagittal crest*.

6. The earliest member of the genus *Homo* is _homo habilis_ .

7. _Australopithicus_ was first described in the 1920s by Raymond Dart.

8. The shift to bipedalism in hominins required the repositioning of the _Foramen Magnum_ toward the center of the bottom of the skull in order to balance the head.

Self-Test

Select the best answer.

1. Which of the following is **NOT** a major feature of hominin bipedalism?
   a. development of curves in the human vertebral column
   b. the divergence of the big toe to the side of the foot so that it can oppose the other toes
   c. the forward repositioning of the foramen magnum underneath the cranium
   d. the modification of the pelvis into a basin-like shape

2. Which of the following statements is true?
   a. The human vertebral column is fairly straight.
   b. The earliest hominin, *Homo erectus*, is completely bipedal.
   c. All the major structural changes required for bipedalism are seen in the early hominins from East and South Africa.
   d. The earliest hominins have all the major features of bipedalism, except that the os coxa is long and bladelike.

3. Which of the following is a hominin trait found in *Sahelanthropus*?
   a. evidence for bipedalism
   b. a cranial capacity of 550 cm^3
   c. a reduced canine
   d. curves in the vertebral column

4. *Orrorin* was recovered from
   a. Olduvai Gorge, Tanzania.
   b. Tugen Hills, Kenya.
   c. Toros-Menalla, Chad.
   d. Sterkfontein, South Africa.

5. Which hominin species has been recovered from Aramis?
   a. *Ardipithecus ramidus*
   b. *Australopithecus aethiopus*
   c. *Australopithecus africanus*
   d. *Homo habilis*

6. Which of the following has a sectorial or semisectorial premolar?

    a. *Ardipithecus*
    b. *Australopithecus afarensis*
    c. *Australopithecus aethiopus*
    (d) both a and b

7. Which of the following is **NOT** a characteristic of *Australopithecus afarensis*?

    a. small stature
    b. a small brain, averaging around 420 cm^3
    c. upper limbs that are longer relative to lower limbs
    (d) reduced canine size relative to the other teeth

8. Which of the following was found at or near Hadar, Ethiopia?

    a. "Lucy"
    b. the Dikika infant
    c. the Black Skull
    (d) both a and b

9. The earliest species of robust australopith is

    a. *Paranthropus boisei.*
    b. *Paranthropus robustus.*
    (c) *Paranthropus aethiopicus.*
    d. *Australopithecus africanus.*

10. Early *Homo* is distinguished from the australopiths largely by

    (a) larger cranial capacity.
    b. shorter stature.
    c. larger back teeth.
    d. the presence of a chin.

11. Louis S. B. Leakey's explanation for tools associated with *Paranthropus boisei* ("Zinj")
    is that

    a. this species made tools.
    (b) this species was dinner for the toolmaker.
    c. these were specialized tools used for breaking open nuts and crushing seeds.
    d. they were the result of geological processes, not intentional hominin modification.

12. Compared to *Australopithecus africanus, Paranthropus robustus*

    a. was larger, weighing up to 300 pounds (about the size of a gorilla).

    b. had megadont back teeth.

    c. had a sagittal crest and large projecting canines.

    d. had a relatively larger brain.

13. In South Africa, fossil-bearing geological deposits are composed of

    a. volcanic rock.

    b. granite.

    c. limestone.

    d. clay.

14. In South Africa, the limestone deposits in which hominin fossils are found do not allow as precise chronometric dating as is possible in East Africa. For instance, *Paranthropus* in South Africa is dated using

    a. paleomagnetism.

    b. potassium-argon dating.

    c. radiocarbon dating.

    d. tree ring dating.

15. Early *Homo* differs from the australopiths in that it has

    a. larger molars.

    b. altered cranial shape.

    c. wider premolars.

    d. a and c.

16. Which of the following is **NOT** a pre-australopith?

    a. *Sahelanthropus*

    b. *Orrorin*

    c. *Ardipithecus*

    d. *Paranthropus*

17. Assigning the generic and specific names to fossil finds comes *before* which of the following steps?

    a. selecting and surveying sites

    b. designating individual finds with specimen numbers for clear reference

    c. comparing with other fossil material

    d. None of the above; assigning the generic or specific name follows all of them.

18. Which of the following can be said regarding new discoveries of hominins?
    a. Almost all the material is redundant.
    b. We now know exactly who our ancestors were.
    (c) Because so much has been recovered recently, reaching any firm conclusions is premature.
    d. Both b and c are true.

19. Recent discoveries paint a picture that
    (a) early hominin species had restricted ranges, and this could have led to rapid genetic divergence.
    b. there was a great deal of overlap among the earliest hominins, and there was probably a great deal of gene flow between them.
    c. early hominins were only found in East Africa.
    d. hominins have been found in China, suggesting a non-African origin for humans.

20. Which of the following is a characteristic that can be used as a diagnostic feature of *Homo sapiens* to distinguish us from the early African hominins?
    a. bipedalism
    b. thick enamel caps on the molars
    (c) delayed development
    d. use of stone tools

Short-Answer Questions

1. List the major features of human bipedalism.

   foramen magum that is placed more underneath the skull, a great be that is para. to the other toes, an arch in the foot, the pelvis is more bowl shaped w/ shorter ilic blades.

2. Explain what is meant by habitual and obligate bipedalism.

   habitual bipedalism means that walking upright is the fastest locomotion. Obligate means that you can't move any other way.

3. Briefly comment on the cranial capacities of the earliest hominins.

   the earliest hominins had a brain the size of a modern African brain but was smaller in stature.

4. Offer a general outline that reviews the earliest appearance of the genus *Homo*.

2.4 - 2.3 mya First hominins appear. Better remains found date back to about 1.85 mya. Homo species are i.ded w/ larger brain capablities.

5. Compare and contrast the "robust" and "gracile" australopiths from South Africa. Why is *Paranthropus* considered the most derived australopith?

Paranthropus is larger w/ a broader face, reduced dentation w/ thicker enamal in back teeth. had a saggital crest and wide teeth suggest a tough Plant diet.

Application Questions

1. Explain the changes in human anatomy that accompanied the development of bipedalism in humans, using examples from the video and the Jurmain textbook.

With bipedalism ~~also~~ came a # of structual changes. The lower limbs became elongated, they developed a pelvis that acted more like a resting place for the internal organs. This helped to stabalize the low back + hip joint. This also change Muscel

2. Discuss the evidence for bipedalism in the earliest hominins.

Remains as early as 4 mya show bipedalism goups, but still shows a big toe capable of grasp- log. some remains also show an arch in the foot.

4 X Describe the appearance, development, and feeding niche of the "robust" australopiths and follow this lineage until its end. The First Stage, Paranthropes ~~Aethiopicus~~ are debated at being human but ~~are~~ show signs. the next stage Austral. are devent huminins. 3rd Stage is homo.

3 X Trace the appearance of the earliest hominins up through the appearance of *Homo*.

All seem to have a diet of tough Veg. They have broad/wide teeth/faces + smaller cranel) capabilites.

5. What are some of the evolutionary patterns that we can see in the evolution of the early hominin species (pre-australopiths, *Australopithecus*, *Paranthropus*, and early *Homo*)?

- had restricted geographic range
- Aborcal habatats
- accel. developement

6. Why was the hominin cranium discovered in East Turkana given the number ER 1470 rather than a name such as *Homo habilis* or *Homo erectus*?

Naming species is done by interpreating lots of data and anaylyzeltion. They have to match many characteristics to be in the same name group as others.

Answer Key
Matching I

1. f (video lesson, segment 1; objective 5)
2. h (video lesson, segment 2; objectives 1 & 3)
3. b (objective 1)
4. d (objective 2)
5. c (objective 1)
6. e (objective 1)
7. a (objective 2)
8. g (video lesson, segment 2; objective 2)

Matching II

1. b (objectives 2 & 3)
2. e (video lesson, segment 2; objectives 3, 4, & 5)
3. c (video lesson, segment 1; objective 4)
4. g (video lesson, segment 2; objective 5)
5. i (video lesson, segment 2; objective 7)
6. a (objective 1)
7. f (video lesson, segment 2; objective 5)
8. h (video lesson, segment 2; objective 5)
9. d (objective 3)

Completion I

1. Plio-Pleistocene (objective 2)
2. morphology (objective 1)
3. habitual bipedalism (objective 1)
4. Sterkfontein (video lesson, segment 2; objective 2)
5. postcranial (video lesson, segment 2; objective 1)
6. Aramis (objectives 2 & 3)
7. *Australopithecus* (video lesson, segment 2; objective 4)
8. obligate bipedalism (objective 1)

Completion II

1. sectorial (objective 3)
2. australopiths (video lesson, segment 2; objectives 3, 4, & 5)
3. robust (video lesson, segment 2; objective 5)
4. gracile (video lesson, segment 2; objective 5)
5. sagittal crest (video lesson, segment 2; objective 5)
6. *Homo habilis* (video lesson, segment 2; objective 7)
7. *Australopithecus africanus* (video lesson, segment 2; objective 5)
8. foramen magnum (video lesson, segment 1; objective 1)

Self-Test

1. b. is the correct answer. The human great toe is enlarged and in line with the other toes. It is unusual among primates in that it is not opposable. (video lesson, segment 1; objective 1)

2. c. is the correct answer. As of 2011, scientists have not yet found a hominin that was not bipedal. (video lesson, segment 1; objective 1)

3. c. is the correct answer. No postcrania of this species have yet been recovered, and the cranial capacity is estimated to be between 320 and 380 cm^3. (objective 3)

4. b. is the correct answer. The species name, *Orrorin tugenensis*, offers a clue to where this species was located. (video lesson, segment 1; objective 3)

5. a. is the correct answer. Aramis is located in Ethiopia. (video lesson, segment 1; objective 3)

6. d. is the correct answer. A sectorial premolar is a primitive trait among the hominins. (objective 4)

7. d. is the correct answer. The canines are actually large, pointed teeth. (objective 4)

8. d. is the correct answer. The Dikika infant is a mostly complete immature hominin and is dated at 3.3–3.2 million years ago. (objectives 2 & 4)

9. c. is the correct answer. *Paranthropus aethiopicus*, represented by the "Black Skull," dates to 2.5 million years ago. (objective 5)

10. a. is the correct answer. Cranial capacity in *Homo* is increased by about 20 percent as compared with the larger brained australopiths. One early representative, ER 1470 from Lake Turkana, is clearly outside the range of the australopiths at 775 cm³. (video lesson, segment 2; objective 7)

11. b. is the correct answer. Leakey suggested that *Homo habilis* was the hunter and "Zinj" was the hunted. (objective 6)

12. b. is the correct answer. The molars of *Paranthropus robustus* were large with a thick cap of enamel and adapted for grinding. (video lesson, segment 2; objective 5)

13. c. is the correct answer. The deposits are generally in limestone quarries. (video lesson, segment 2; objective 6)

14. a. is the correct answer. *Paranthropus* in South Africa has been dated at 2 to 1.2 million years ago using paleomagnetism. (objectives 5 & 6)

15. b. is the correct answer. In addition, early *Homo* has a larger brain and smaller and thinner molars. (video lesson, segment 2; objective 7)

16. d. is the correct answer. *Paranthropus* is a more derived australopith species, not an early primitive one. (video lesson, segment 1; objective 5)

17. d. is the correct answer. The taxonomic naming of fossils carries biological implications and occurs only after data is collected and comparative analyses are done. (objective 8)

18. c. is the correct answer. As would be expected in science, interpretation undergoes a series of discussions nationally and globally before any consensus is reached. (objective 9)

19. a. is the correct answer. Because these populations had restricted ranges, they became separated, and genetic drift and natural selection could have led to speciation. (objective 9)

20. c. is the correct answer. Rates of development can be accurately reconstructed by examining dental growth markers, and these data may provide a crucial window into understanding early hominin evolution. (objective 8)

Short-Answer Questions

Your answers should include the following:

1. These are the major features of hominin bipedalism: a foramen magnum repositioned farther underneath the skull, a vertebral column that has two major curves, a pelvis that is bowl shaped with shorter and broader iliac blades, lower limbs that are elongated, a femur that is angled inward and thus places the legs more directly under the body, a great toe that is parallel to the other toes, and a longitudinal arch in the foot that allows better shock absorption. (video lesson, segment 1; objective 1)

2. Habitual bipedalism means moving bipedally as the standard and most effective form of locomotion. Obligate bipedalism means being unable to locomote efficiently in any other way. (video lesson, segment 1; objective 1)

3. Cranial capacities of the earliest hominins were within the range of modern African apes. Modern gorillas have a bigger brain than most of the australopithecines, but relative to body size the australopithecine brain is 10 percent larger. Thus, we say that the australopithecines are more encephalized. (objectives 3, 4, 5, & 7)

4. The earliest *Homo* remains (dating between 2.4 and 2.3 million years ago in East Africa) are very fragmentary. Better representation appears at Olduvai between 1.85 and 1.6 million years ago. Koobi Fora also provides a specimen from the same time period. The earliest recognized species is *H. habilis*. The main criterion distinguishing *Homo* from the australopithecines is larger cranial capacity. The cranial capacity of the Koobi Fora specimen is well beyond the range of any australopithecine and actually overlaps the range for *H. erectus*. Based on evidence from Olduvai and Koobi Fora it can be reasonably postulated that one or more species of *Homo* was present in East Africa by 2.4 million years ago. (video lesson, segment 2; objective 7)

5. Historically the "robust" australopiths, *Paranthropus*, have been portrayed as significantly larger than the smaller "gracile," or *Australopithecus africanus*. *Paranthropus* is characterized by reduced anterior dentition associated with a flat and wide face, and large back teeth capped with thicker enamel than is present in the "gracile" form *Australopithecus africanus*. Nevertheless, these features are not as extreme the East African forms of *Paranthropus*. Despite these pronounced skull features, postcranially the robust forms are not particularly different from the gracile species, being about the same height and weight. Derived characteristics are modified from the ancestral condition and thus are diagnostic of a particular lineage. Large dentition is a derived characteristic of australopiths, and *Paranthropus* has the biggest teeth of all. The huge molars and premolars of *Paranthropus* require large chewing muscles and sites for attachment on the skull. The masseter muscles attach on the broad cheekbones and the temporal muscles that power the jaw cause a bony ridge, or saggital crest to develop along the midline of the top of the skull. All of these features indicate a diet of tough vegetable foods, although new studies indicate that *Paranthropus* ate a varied diet in addition. *Paranthropus boisei* in East Africa is the most derived member of this lineage, with massive back teeth and lower jaws. (video lesson, segment 2; objective 5)

Application Questions

Your answers should include the following:

1. A number of structural changes occurred with bipedalism. The pelvic girdle of quadrupeds tends to be long, bladelike, and to the side of the vertebral column. The shift to bipedalism required changes to the pelvis. The pelvis in hominins is broad, short, and extends to the sides forming a bowl shaped structure capable of holding the viscera. This alteration helps to stabilize the line of weight transmission from the lower back to the hip joint. The reconfiguration of the hominin pelvis also altered the relationships of several muscle groups. The most prominent of these is the gluteus maximus. This muscle assists in pulling the upper leg to the side in quadrupeds. In hominins it increases in size and is attached to the backside of the pelvis. Its action is to extend the thigh. Other effects on the axial skeleton include repositioning of the

foramen magnum so that the head balances atop the vertebral column. The vertebral column has to curve in order to redistribute the weight of the upper body over the feet. The legs lengthen causing an increase in stride length. The femurs angle inward so that both the knees and the feet are close together under the body. Finally, there are several anatomic changes to the foot, including the realignment of the great toe in parallel with the other toes (i.e., a nondivergent big toe). (video lesson, segment 1; objective 1)

2. There are some skeletal fragments dating before 4 million years ago that suggest bipedalism. Postcranial remains from the pre-australopith *Orrorin* dated around 6 million years ago indicate bipedal locomotion. And the recent reconstruction of the 4.4 million-year-old *Ardipithecus ramidus* from Awash suggests that with a short broad ilium and a foot modified to act as a prop for propulsion, *Ardipithecus* is likely a competent biped. However, the great toe is divergent and capable of grasping, so she clearly spent a lot of time in the trees. There is very good evidence for bipedalism after 4 million years ago. An ankle recovered from South Africa indicates the presence of a longitudinal arch and a heel adapted for bipedalism. *Australopithecus afarensis*, best represented by the "Lucy" skeleton, was definitely bipedal although the degree of bipedalism is debated. Lucy's pelvis, curved vertebral column, and angled femur are strong pieces of evidence. A trace fossil from roughly the same time period as Lucy, a hominin footprint in volcanic ash that appears more human rather than ape-like, has also been recovered. (video lesson, segment 1; objectives 1, 3, & 4)

3. *Paranthropus aethiopicus*, recovered from West Lake Turkana, Kenya, is the earliest representative found so far of the "robust" group of australopithecines. It is dated to approximately 2.5 million years ago. *P. aethiopicus* has a much more projecting face than found in the later robust species. Other features such as a broad face, very large palate, and a large area for the back teeth link it to later robust forms. This species has one of the smallest cranial capacities, 410 cm³, for any known hominin. By 2 million years ago, other varieties of robust australopithecines appear in both East and South Africa. These species are more derived with larger, broader, and flatter faces and very large teeth. Cranial capacities have increased to between 510 and 530 cm³, but still small for a hominin. The East African *P. boisei* is the more derived species possessing more extreme features than are found in the South African *P. robustus*. All members of the robust lineage appear to be specialized for a diet of hard food morsels, such as seeds, nuts, and other heavy vegetable foods. (objective 5)

4. It is difficult to give clear relationships among the different hominin taxa, but the earliest members go back to around 6 million years ago. *Sahelanthropus tchadensis* was recovered from Central Africa in the country of Chad. It has a derived hominin face and canine teeth, although the braincase is very primitive. Unfortunately, we do not have any postcrania of this genus, so it is not possible to determine whether it was bipedal or not. Another early hominin is *Orrorin tugenensis*, recovered from 5.8- to 5.2-million-year-old deposits in Ethiopia. This species has an angled femur indicative of bipedalism although the teeth are chimp-like. *Ardipithecus* appears at 4.4 million years ago and also has a mix of primitive cranial features with a suggested bipedal gait. These three genera can be grouped under a set referred to as pre-australopith hominins.

The next set of hominins is the *Australopithecus/Paranthropus* stage. These are undoubted hominins. The primitive member of this group is *Australopithecus afarensis*.

It has primitive features of the skull, but it is clearly bipedal although it does retain climbing abilities. The more derived forms of this set range from 2.4 to 1 million years ago. These later forms consist of at least two genera with several different species. These are best known from East and South Africa. All of these species have very large back teeth and show no appreciable encephalization compared to *A. afarensis*. *Paranthropus* is very specialized for feeding on tough vegetation and reflects a different adaptation than other contemporaneous hominins.

The third set is early *Homo*, existing from 2.0 to 1.8 million years ago. Specimens are found in both East and South Africa. This group is composed of possibly one, but probably more than one species. Compared to *Australopithecus* and *Paranthropus*, early *Homo* is characterized by greater encephalization, altered cranial shape, and smaller molars and narrower premolar teeth. (objective 5)

5. New discoveries have been made at a furious pace over the last decade. We can never know the entire picture because there are gaps because of bias in fossilization. What emerges, however, are several adaptive patterns.

    First, the early hominins had a restricted geographic range. They may have exploited a very small area and they could easily become separated from other populations of their own species. Genetic drift and natural selection could have led to rapid genetic divergence and eventual speciation.

    A second pattern is that most of these species appear to be at least partially tied to arboreal habitats, although this has been disputed for early *Homo*. *Paranthropus* was probably less arboreal than *Australopithecus* or *Ardipithecus*. This highly specialized megadont genus was probably feeding on tough fibrous food morsels such as roots and tubers.

    Third, there does not seem to be an evolutionary trend towards greater body size and encephalization. Early *Homo* is the exception.

    Finally, these African hominins appear to exhibit an accelerated development pattern, similar to that seen in the living apes, that is very different than the delayed pattern seen in modern humans. This is not only true for the pre-australopithecines and australopithecines, but early *Homo* as well.

    These African hominin predecessors were rather small, able bipeds, but still closely tied to arboreal niches. They had small brains and, compared to later *Homo*, matured rapidly. (objective 9)

6. The formal naming of specimens occurs as the result of a series of complex interpretations based on a comparative analysis of its features. Since the taxonomic name implies known biological relationships, it is important to wait until the specimen has been analyzed and compared to other known specimens before assigning it a genus and species name. Initially specimens are numbered; once the biological relationship is posited, a taxonomic name is proposed. The specimen ER 1470 is generally considered to be a member of the genus *Homo*, but its species has never been assigned. (objective 8)

Lesson Review

Lesson 9: The First Bipeds

PLEASE NOTE: Use this matrix to guide your study and achieve the learning objectives of this lesson. It will also help you to view the video, which defines and demonstrates important concepts and principles as they relate to everyday life and actual case studies.

Learning Objective	Textbook	Student Guide	Video Lesson
1. List and describe the major skeletal adaptations for full-time bipedalism and compare these with skeletal structures seen in quadrupedalism.	pp. 312–316	Key Terms: 1, 2, 3, 13; Matching I: 2, 3, 5, 6; Matching II: 6; Completion I: 2, 3, 5, 8; Completion II: 8; Self-Test: 1, 2; Short-Answer: 1, 2; Application: 1, 2.	Segment 1: *Biomechanics* Segment 2: *"Would the First Biped Please Stand Up?"*
2. Identify the geographic locations and the names of the major early hominin fossil sites in East and South Africa.	pp. 316–319	Key Terms: 4, 5, 10; Matching I: 4, 7, 8; Matching II: 1; Completion I: 1, 4, 6; Self-Test: 8.	Segment 2: *"Would the First Biped Please Stand Up?"*
3. Describe the pre-australopiths, with special attention to the environments and time period in which they were found.	pp. 319–322	Key Terms: 7, 12, 13; Matching I: 2; Matching II: 1, 2, 9; Completion I: 6; Completion II: 1, 2; Self-Test: 3, 4, 5; Short-Answer: 3; Application: 2.	Segment 1: *Biomechanics* Segment 2: *"Would the First Biped Please Stand Up?"*
4. Describe the australopiths, with special attention to *Australopithecus afarensis*.	pp. 322–333	Key Terms: 6, 15; Matching II: 2, 3; Completion I: 7; Completion II: 2; Self-Test: 6, 7, 8; Short-Answer: 3; Application: 2.	Segment 1: *Biomechanics* Segment 2: *"Would the First Biped Please Stand Up?"*

Learning Objective	Textbook	Student Guide	Video Lesson
5. Describe the morphological traits that characterize the later, more derived australopiths, with special attention to their relationship to other hominis living at the same time.	pp. 328–333	Key Terms: 8, 9, 14, 15; Matching I: 1; Matching II: 2, 4, 7, 8; Completion II: 2, 3, 4, 5, 7; Self-Test: 9, 12, 14, 16; Short-Answer: 3, 5; Application: 3, 4.	Segment 1: *Biomechanics* Segment 2: *"Would the First Biped Please Stand Up?"*
6. Contrast the geological context of the hominin sites located in East Africa with those located in South Africa and discuss how this context affects the reliability of the dates for these sites.	p. 317	Self-Test: 11, 13, 14.	Segment 2: *"Would the First Biped Please Stand Up?"*
7. Compare the morphology of the earliest members of the genus *Homo* to the morphology of the genus *Australopithecus*.	pp. 333–335	Key Terms: 11; Matching II: 5; Completion II: 6; Self-Test: 10, 15; Short-Answer: 3, 4.	Segment 2: *"Would the First Biped Please Stand Up?"*
8. Discuss the alternative approaches of explaining the early hominins.	pp. 335–337	Self-Test: 17, 20; Application: 6.	
9. Discuss the impact of new discoveries on our understanding of hominins.	pp. 337–338	Self-Test: 18, 19; Application: 5.	

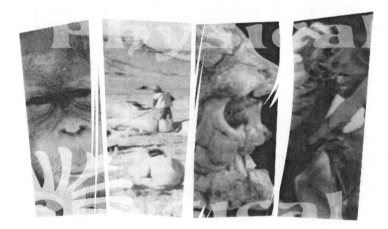

10

A New Hominin

Checklist

For the most effective study of this lesson, complete the following activities in this sequence.

Before Viewing the Video

❏ Read the Preview, Learning Objectives, and Viewing Notes below.

❏ Read Chapter 12, "The First Dispersal of the Genus *Homo*: *Homo erectus* and Contemporaries," pages 340–365, in *Introduction to Physical Anthropology*.

What to Watch

❏ After reading the textbook assignment, watch the video for Lesson 10, *A New Hominin*.

After Viewing the Video

❏ Briefly note your answers to the questions listed at the end of the Viewing Notes.

❏ Review the Summary below.

❏ Review all reading assignments for this lesson, including the Viewing Notes in this lesson.

❏ Write brief answers to the "Critical Thinking Questions" at the end of Chapter 12 in the textbook.

❏ Complete the Review Exercises below. Check your answers with the Answer Key and review when necessary.

❏ Use the Lesson Review matrix found at the end of this lesson to review and assess your knowledge of each Learning Objective.

Preview

As mentioned previously during this course, the earliest fossils that paleoanthropologists identify as hominins evolved in Africa. Lesson 10 focuses on *Homo erectus*, the first members of the human family to migrate out of Africa into other areas of the Old World. Remains of *Homo erectus* show that this hominin lived from at least 1.8 million years ago (mya) until 200,000 years ago, spanning a period of more than 1.5 million years.

Homo erectus artifacts are found on three continents, and every new discovery either confirms previous hypotheses or turns old ideas upside down. However, there is universal agreement that the hominins found outside of Africa are all members of the genus *Homo*. There seems to be less diversity in these hominins than is seen in their predecessors, although dispersed hominins differ anatomically and behaviorally from their African ancestors. There is some morphological variation among the different geographical groups of these successful hominins, and paleoanthropologists are still debating how to classify them. Lesson 10 explains what we know so far about *Homo erectus*, including their physical attributes and their toolmaking skills. This lesson also explains some of the alternative interpretations that call for splitting the fossil sample into more species.

Concepts to Remember

❀ Lesson 2 introduced the term **taxonomy,** the branch of science concerned with the rules of classifying organisms on the basis of evolutionary relationships. Later lessons explained that the term **genus** refers to a group of closely related species. The term **species** refers to a group of organisms that can interbreed to produce fertile offspring. Lesson 10 emphasizes that there is universal agreement among experts that all hominins found outside of Africa belong to the genus *Homo*. However, the debate focuses on how many species of *Homo* are represented.

❀ Lesson 8 explained that **taphonomy** is the study of how bones and other materials came to be buried in the earth and preserved as fossils. On pages 356–357 of the Jurmain textbook, the "Closer Look" section demonstrates how a better understanding of this branch of paleontology offers a new view of what deposits at Dragon Bone Hill, a fossil site located southwest of Beijing, China, tell us about the eating habits of early hominins.

Learning Objectives

After you complete this lesson, you should be able to:

1. Describe the morphology and geographical distribution of *Homo erectus* and the environmental changes during the Pleistocene. (pp. 341–365)

2. Discuss the taxonomic nomenclature for African and Asian *Homo erectus*. (pp. 344, 359)

3. Summarize the history of *Homo erectus* discoveries in Java and China. (pp. 351–359)

4. Discuss the cultural remains and other materials that pertain to the lifestyle of *Homo erectus* at Zhoukoudian, and note the alternate interpretations of Zhoukoudian regarding its status as a hominin habitation site. (pp. 354–356)

5. Discuss the significance of *Homo erectus* sites and important fossil discoveries from East Africa, with particular reference to WT 15000. (pp. 347–349)

6. Identify when the first hominins left Africa, and describe the supporting evidence. (pp. 349–351)

7. List the fossil discoveries from Europe and discuss how they relate to *Homo erectus*. (pp. 359–360)

8. Discuss the archaeological evidence for the increased reliance of *Homo erectus* on cultural adaptations. (pp. 361–364)

At this point, read Chapter 12, "The First Dispersal of the Genus *Homo: Homo erectus* and Contemporaries," pages 340–365.

Viewing Notes

In 1887, Dutch anatomist Eugene Dubois left Holland to search for "the missing link," that one fossil find that would serve as the missing puzzle piece of human evolutionary progression. The phrase "missing link" is still commonly used today for different purposes, but it remains misleading because it implies a single transitional form between apes and human. And as stated in Lesson 9, there is no fossil form that is an even split that serves this purpose. This course has repeatedly demonstrated that the evolutionary path to *Homo sapiens* is much more complex than that.

There are a number of early species within the genus *Homo*. The video for this lesson focuses on a well-documented one, **Homo erectus**, which existed during the **Pleistocene**, an epoch of the Upper Cenozoic period characterized by drastic and sometimes rapid climatic changes that created a diversity of habitats to which human and nonhuman species were required to adapt or perish. When the climate changes made some landscapes inhospitable, hominins were forced to move from one location to another. *Homo erectus* survived well on the arid plains, or savannas, of East Africa, and as climate changes occurred in southern Europe and southern Asia, conditions were created there that anthropologist John Shea refers to in the video as "savannaization." These were wide, grassy expanses that *Homo erectus* knew, having come from similar environments in East Africa. Furthermore, along with foraging and scavenging, it is likely that *Homo erectus*, on the savanna, incorporated hunting into their subsistence pattern.

The migration of *Homo erectus* from Africa to Asia and Europe occurred in waves. In the video, anthropologist John Shea likens it to waves pounding the beach as the tide rolls in. Waves advance on the beach and then roll back; they pound the shore again, this time advancing farther. The fossil finds of *Homo erectus* outside of Africa are almost all confined to the warmer parts of southern Europe and southern Asia. There may have been brief movements north of the Alps and the Himalayas, but this happened, it is thought, primarily during the warmer periods. Cold environments were a deterrent to any sustained settlement. Large quantities of *Homo erectus* fossils have been discovered at a site called Zhoukoudian in northeastern China, not far from Beijing. In the 1930s, anatomist Franz Weidenreich created detailed descriptions of crania, mandibles, and postcranial material from Zhoukoudian that have become the standard of comparison for other fossil finds that followed. The rich assortment of *Homo erectus* fossils from this site gave scientists the opportunity to try to understand the variation within the *Homo erectus* species, in the same way that humans from different parts of the world today have different physical attributes.

The fossils from Dmanisi, in the Republic of Georgia (formerly part of the Soviet Union), are generally considered *Homo erectus* remains, but they are much smaller in size and brain capacity than what was initially believed necessary for survival for the first *Homo erectus* migration from Africa. These fossils are approximately 1.8 million years old, indicating that the migration started very soon after the species appeared in Africa. While the prevailing theory is that *Homo erectus* first traveled north of the Anatolian Plateau about 900,000 years ago, the *Homo erectus* fossils found at Dmanisi indicate that migration happened much earlier. Of great interest to anthropologist Karen Babb, who speaks about the Dmanisi fossils in the video, is that they are not only much smaller, but the faces also have a more primitive look, reminiscent of *Homo habilis*. However, she explains that this would not be surprising if the Dmanisi fossils date to a period near the split with *Homo habilis*; they would then be expected to retain certain features of the earlier species.

As hominins dispersed geographically, they adapted to their local environments. The first stone tools appear with fossil discoveries about 2 million years ago in sites in Ethiopia. There was more than one hominin species existing in Africa at that time, so it is difficult to say which species produced which tool. The Oldowan tools, named after the sites at Olduvai Gorge in Tanzania, where the artifacts were found, were simpler than later tool industries. Associated with *Homo habilis*, approximately 2.5 million years ago, the Oldowan toolmaker would strike one rock against another until flakes broke off. The flakes were then used as cutting tools. By 1.6 million years ago, Acheulian tools appear. More sophisticated than the Oldowan tools, these are characterized by bifacial stones flaked on both sides. Many of the Acheulian tools look exactly alike, whether they are found in Europe, Africa, or Asia. These newer tools indicate a more complex range of activities associated with *Homo erectus*. Anthropologist John Shea points out that Acheulian tools are not replacements for the Oldowan industry. Rather, they are an additional technology manufactured along with Oldowan tools as needed.

Shea also mentions a link between the production of stone tools, meat eating, and the enlargement of the hominin brain. The theory is that if hominins were under selective pressure to grow a larger brain, they sought out the food sources necessary for brain growth and maintenance. More sophisticated stone tools helped them obtain animal proteins. Tools were more efficient than their teeth and fingernails.

The video demonstrates how scientists are still making new fossil discoveries, and how each one helps fill in the gaps of the stages of human evolution.

Questions to Consider

🌿 Who were the first members of the human family to disperse out of Africa?

🌿 What kinds of evidence have paleontologists used to support the idea that Acheulian tool industries developed alongside and as a supplement to Oldowan tools?

🌿 What major questions do the *Homo erectus* fossils from Dmanisi pose for paleoanthropologists regarding which species of *Homo* migrated first and when?

Watch the video for Lesson 12, *A New Hominin.*

> Segment 1: *Homo erectus*
> Segment 2: *Location, Location*
> Segment 3: *Tool Time*

Key Terms and Concepts

Page references are keyed to *Introduction to Physical Anthropology,* 13th edition.

1. **grade:** A grouping of organisms sharing a similar adaptive pattern. Grade is not necessarily based on closeness of evolutionary relationship, but it does contrast organisms in a useful way (e.g., *Homo erectus* with *Homo sapiens*). (p. 344; objective 2)

2. **nuchal torus:** (nuke´-ul, pertaining to the neck) A projection of bone in the back of the cranium where neck muscles attach. These muscles hold the head upright. (p. 345; objective 1)

3. **Nariokotome:** (nar´-ee-oh-koh´-tow-may) A site in the Lake Turkana region of Kenya where a nearly complete skeleton of a young hominin boy was discovered in 1984. (p. 347; video lesson, segment 1; objectives 1 & 5)

4. **Dmanisi:** (dim´-an-eese´-ee) A site located in the present-day Caucasus region of the Republic of Georgia where early fossil remains of *Homo erectus* have been found and dated to 1.81 million years ago. (p. 350; objectives 1 & 6)

5. **Acheulian:** (ash´-oo-lay-en) Pertaining to a stone tool industry of the Early and Middle Pleistocene; characterized by a large proportion of bifacial tools (flaked on both sides). Acheulian tool kits are common in Africa, Southwest Asia, and western Europe, but they are thought to be less common elsewhere. Also spelled *Acheulean*. (p. 350; video lesson, segment 3; objective 8)

6. **Pleistocene:** The epoch of the Cenozoic from 1.8 million until 10,000 years ago. Frequently referred to as the Ice Age, this epoch is associated with continental glaciations in northern latitudes. (p. 352; video lesson, segment 1; objective 1)

7. **Zhoukoudian:** (Zhoh´-koh-dee´-en) A cave site located near Beijing, China, where fossil remains of *Homo erectus*, historically known as Peking Man, were discovered in the 1920s and 1930s. Although early excavators believed that the cave deposits showed evidence of cannibalism, later observations led scientists to believe that bone remains show patterns of damage consistent with scavenging by hyenas. (p. 355; video lesson, segment 2; objectives 1, 3, & 4)

8. *Homo erectus*: A hominin that first appears around 1.8 million years ago and may have persisted until 25,000 years ago. It was the most widely distributed hominin, ranging from Africa to the islands of Southeast Asia, until modern humans. (video lesson, segment 1; objective 1)

Summary

Hominins were restricted to Africa for the first 5 million years of evolution. Close to 2 million years ago, they began to disperse from that continent into Asia and Europe, and every new discovery forces a new discussion on which hominin species migrated out of Africa first. The species for which there is the most evidence is *Homo erectus*.

According to the Jurmain textbook, paleoanthropologists consider *Homo erectus* to represent a different grade of evolution than their more ancient African predecessors. A **grade** is an evolutionary grouping of organisms that share a similar adaptive pattern. Increase in body size, robustness, longer limbs, and bigger head size all indicate an evolutionary move in the direction of modern humans.

Recent discoveries at the **Dmanisi** site in the Republic of Georgia show that *Homo erectus* migrated from Africa soon after first appearing there. The Dmanisi fossils are smaller in body and brain size than their typical African counterpart. They do not have the adaptations believed to be essential for hominin migration, such as taller stature and larger brains. This indicates to some anthropologists that there were possibly two migrations from Africa at almost the same time—the smaller-brained, diminutive species to Dmanisi and the larger hominins that established the well-recognized *Homo erectus* population of Java and China.

The video and the Jurmain textbook discuss some of the historical discoveries of *Homo erectus* fossils that have been found widely distributed over three continents. Since the 1891 discovery of the Java fossils, *Homo erectus* has been considered our ancestor. While not exactly the "missing link" Dutch anatomist Eugene Dubois was hoping for, the discovery of the Java skulls represented a previously unidentified species. It is believed, from the *Homo erectus* fossils found in Java, that this species survived in this area long after it had disappeared elsewhere, but since very few artifacts have been found in Java, anthropologists are limited in their ability to reconstruct their life patterns with any certainty.

Unlike Java, the **Zhoukoudian** site in China has yielded more that 100,000 artifacts. This rich record helps scientists reconstruct the life of *Homo erectus* as hunters and gatherers. It is surmised that *Homo erectus* wore some sort of clothing, probably in the form of animal skins, since winters in Beijing were bitter during the Middle Pleistocene. Furthermore, one

Did *Homo erectus* control fire?

One of the most important technological achievements of hominins is the use of fire. Fire provides a number of benefits. Cooked meat is more tender than raw meat, making it easier to chew. The heat denatures proteins, including metabolic defensive chemicals found in many plants. Tool points can be "fire-hardened," making them harder and stronger than those not similarly treated. Finally, fire provides warmth, light, and frightens any dangerous animals that might come near.

Making fire requires some type of starter. For Paleolithic humans, this could have included striking stones to create sparks or rubbing wood together to create enough friction for combustion.

Another more likely way for early hominins to have obtained fire is from natural brush fires started by lightning. When humans capture fire and keep it burning, it is referred to as "control of fire." The 1981 film, *Quest for Fire*, told a compelling story about this topic.

The earliest use of fire is equivocal. Two sites in Africa initially seemed to have evidence for hominin-controlled fire. The site at *Chesowanja* in southern Kenya contained burned clay associated with stone tools dated 1.4 million years ago. This is the time period of *Homo erectus*. However, there is no proof that the fire was used by hominins; it could have been naturally occurring.

The other African site, *Swartkrans* in South Africa, has yielded burned bones in association with stone tools dated 1 to 1.3 million years ago. But again, the burning could have been from natural occurrences rather than hominin activities.

The most promising site for evidence of *Homo erectus* using fire is *Zhoukoudian*, China, which boasts an accumulation of stone tools, charred animal bones, burned stone artifacts, and layers of ash. However, the site has been reassessed by a number of researchers who suggest that this assemblage is actually the result of natural occurrences. Researchers discovered that the bones were burned after fossilization, and so could not have been the remains of cooked *Homo erectus* meals. Furthermore, the thick layer of ash is actually organic sediment, and what appeared to be "hearths" are naturally occurring pits created by water action.

So, the earliest use of fire that can currently be supported by the archaeological record is somewhat later, during the Middle Pleistocene about 125,000 years ago. Neandertals built hearths made of cobbles arranged in circles and ovals. A hearth such as this is the best evidence for fire, and one that was lacking at the older sites.

of the bone tools found at the Zhoukoudian site may have been a needle. It has been assumed that the hominins at Zhoukoudian had learned how to control and use fire. However, some newer evidence challenges that assumption. Soil samples indicate that previously identified ash samples are actually naturally accumulated organic sediment and what were once considered hearths may be simply round depressions formed in the past by water collecting in the cave.

Generally, African *Homo erectus* fossils are older and different in form in comparison with the Asian fossil remains found in Java and China. Some of the cranial variations between the two are striking, and some researchers believe they should be regarded as separate species. However, the current consensus is to refer to all of these hominins as *Homo erectus*.

Larger brains most likely meant that *Homo erectus* developed more sophisticated tools. The **Acheulian** tool artifacts show the first evidence that raw materials were being constantly transported around the landscape, indicating that *Homo erectus* understood that a good stone found in one spot was worth holding onto for toolmaking in the future. The tool kits created by *Homo* *erectus* feature bifaces, which are known as hand axes or cleavers. They have a flatter core with sharper, straighter edges than the earlier Oldowan tools and the edges are worked on both sides, forming a narrow, sharp edge. Butchering sites are common. It has been assumed that *Homo erectus* were regular hunters, but cut marks on bones are often found on top of carnivore teeth marks, which indicates scavenging on the part of these hominins. It hasn't been conclusively proven that *Homo erectus* were scavengers rather than hunters, but the potential for both a hunting and scavenging culture exists. These hominins probably obtained 80 percent of their daily calories from plant materials.

New discoveries don't necessarily answer old questions. Did *Homo erectus* hunt? Did they control fire? Was the evolution to later hominins gradual or rapid? New fossils help scientists reevaluate old theories and create new hypotheses. Past theories suggested that *H. erectus* migrated from Africa because of a more advanced culture and a more modern anatomy. The fossils found in Dmanisi put that theory into question. They indicate that at least some of the earliest hominins that migrated out of Africa were small and had smaller cranial capacity than the more robust forms found elsewhere. However, the evidence does support enormous achievements, overall, of this ancient ancestor. *Homo erectus* increased in body size, with more efficient bipedalism than their earlier counterparts; they embraced culture as an adaptive strategy, became better scavengers and, very likely, hunters, and established more permanent settlements as time progressed.

Review Exercises

Matching I

Match each term with the appropriate definition or description.

1. __d__ Acheulian   4. __c__ nuchal torus
2. __e__ grade   5. __f__ Pleistocene
3. __b__ *Homo erectus*   6. __a__ sagittal keel

a. A small ridge of bone running along the midline of some *Homo erectus* skulls.

b. The most widely distributed species of *Homo* before modern humans.

c. A projection of bone in the back of the neck that serves as a site of attachment for the neck muscles responsible for holding the head upright.

d. A stone tool industry of the Lower and Middle Pleistocene characterized by bifacial tools.

e. A grouping of organisms sharing a similar adaptive pattern.

f. The epoch of the Cenozoic from 1.8 million until 10,000 years ago.

Matching II

Match each hominin site with the appropriate definition or description.

1. __j__ Ceprano
2. __h__ Daka
3. __a__ Dmanisi
4. __i__ Gran Dolina
5. __f__ Hexian

6. __b__ Nariokotome
7. ____ Olduvai
8. ____ Sangiran
9. ____ Trinil
10. ____ Zhoukoudian

a. A site in the Caucasus region that forced a reevaluation of when hominins left Africa.

b. An African site that yielded the most complete skeleton of a *Homo erectus*.

c. The village near the Solo River from which the first *Homo erectus* fossil was recovered.

d. This site has produced some of the largest brained individuals from among *H. erectus*.

e. This is the most famous *Homo erectus* site and was inhabited 780,000 years ago.

f. The population here ranks as one of the among the more recent members of *H. erectus*.

g. The first African *Homo erectus* find was made here by Louis Leakey,

h. A cranium from this site is very similar to the Asian *Homo erectus* finds and is used as evidence against separate species in African and Asia.

i. The fossils from this site have been provisionally classified as *Homo antecessor*, but further analysis may reveal a *Homo erectus* population.

j. This site provides the best evidence for *Homo erectus* in Europe.

Completion I

Fill each blank with the most appropriate term from the list below.

Acheulian	~~Dmanisi~~
~~adolescent growth spurt~~	Java
~~braincase~~	missing link
~~breadth~~	~~nuchal~~
cranial capacity	Sangiran Dome

1. The Nariokotome skeleton indicates a developmental pattern closer to apes than to modern humans, with no _adolescent growth spurt_

2. *Homo erectus* is said to have a distinctive cranial shape. The characteristics that give *H. erectus* this distinct shape include large browridges above the eyes, a _nuchal_ torus, long and low _braincase_, little forehead development, and maximum cranial _breadth_ below the ear opening.

3. Hominins are found outside of Africa at 1.6 million years ago in Indonesia, and around 1.75 million years ago at _Dmanisi_, Republic of Georgia.

4. The Dmanisi fossils differ from other early hominin finds outside of Africa in that they have a very small __Cranial cap__.

5. *Homo erectus* is broadly associated with the __Acheulian__ tool industry in Africa after 1.4 million years ago.

6. The first *H. erectus* was found by Eugene Dubois on the island of __Java__.

7. Eugene Dubois left Holland for Sumatra in 1887 in search of the "__Missing link__

8. The site of __Sangiran Dome__ on Java has yielded more than 80 different fossil hominin individuals, representing a long and thriving population, some of whom had the largest cranial capacities found among *Homo erectus*.

Completion II

Fill each blank with the most appropriate term from the list below.

biface	100,000
East Turkana	separate
hunters and gatherers	Sima del Elefante
Ngandong	Zhoukoudian

1. The largest collection of *Homo erectus* fossils has been recovered from the site of __Zhoukoudian__, near Beijing, China.

2. The youngest group of *Homo erectus* fossils from Java are found at the site __Ngandong__ suggesting that *Homo erectus* lasted a very long time in Java, even as it disappeared elsewhere.

3. The traditional view of Chinese *Homo erectus* was that they lived as __hunters & gatherers__.

4. The Zhoukoudian Cave has yielded the remains of 40 individuals and more than __100,000__ artifacts have been recovered.

5. ER 3733 is a cranium recovered from __East Turkana__ that is the oldest *Homo erectus* recovered so far at 1.8 million years ago. Its cranial capacity is 848 cm^3, which is at the lower end of the range for *H. erectus* cranial capacity.

6. Bernard Wood proposes that African and Asian *Homo erectus* finds are __Separate__ species.

7. The __Sima del Elefante__ site at Altapuerca in northern Spain is dated at 1.2 million years ago, making it the oldest hominin find in Western Europe.

8. During the existence of *Homo erectus* in Africa, a new tool kit was developed with the addition of the __biface__.

Self-Test

Select the best answer.

1. A grouping of organisms that share a similar adaptive pattern defines a
   - (a) grade.
   - b. clade.
   - c. family.
   - d. species.

2. Compared to earlier members of the genus *Homo*, *H. erectus* cranial capacity
   - a. was double the relative size of early *Homo*.
   - b. was less encephalized, relative to body size.
   - (c.) is about 25 percent larger, relative to body size, when compared to the large-bodied early *Homo*.
   - d. both a and b are correct.

3. A physical characteristic distinct to *Homo erectus* that distinguishes it from other hominins is
   - a. cranial height.
   - b. degree of encephalization.
   - c. high forehead.
   - (d) the maximum cranial breadth is below the ear.

4. The earliest *H. erectus* fossils from Java are dated as
   - a. 1 million years old.
   - (b.) 1.6 million years old.
   - c. 2 million years old.
   - d. none of the above.

5. Which of the following statements is **NOT** correct?
   - a. There may have been two migrations out of Africa around 1.8 million years ago, with one being a small-brained member of *Homo*.
   - b. The Dmanisi hominins had a typical Oldowan stone tool culture.
   - (c.) A large cranial capacity and a sophisticated tool culture was required to emigrate from Africa.
   - d. The Dmanisi hominins were only 4 feet, 6 inches tall.

6. The first fossil human found outside of Europe or Africa was recovered from

    a. Japan.
    b. Australia.
    c. China.
    (d.) Java.

7. The first *Homo erectus* find consisted of a

    (a.) skullcap.
    b. clavicle.
    c. tibia.
    d. femur.

8. If the date range of 50,000 to 25,000 years ago for the Ngandong hominins from Java is confirmed, it would show

    a. that *H. erectus* lived contemporaneously with *H. sapiens*.
    b. that *H. erectus* had art.
    c. that *H. erectus* were among the last of their species.
    (d.) both a and c.

9. Which of the following has been conclusively demonstrated for *Homo erectus* at Zhoukoudian?

    a. They made and controlled fire.
    b. They were proficient hunters of deer and horses.
    c. They lived in a cave.
    (d.) None of the above; recent research has cast doubt on all three propositions.

10. The importance of WT 15000, found at Nariokotome on the west side of Lake Turkana, is

    a. the remarkable old age of the specimen at death.
    (b.) the completeness of the skeleton.
    c. the estimated stature of a twelve-year-old boy.
    d. both b and c are correct.

11. Which of the following statements describe *Homo ergaster*?

    a. It was suggested as an alternative species for all African *H. erectus*.
    b. It is not supported by the Daka cranium.
    c. As a separate African species, it is now losing support.
    (d.) All of the above statements are true.

12. European hominin finds that are at least 700,000 years old have been discovered in

    a. the Republic of Georgia.
    b. Italy.
    c. Spain.
    d. all of the above locations.

13. Fossil remains from the Gran Dolina site in northern Spain

    a. are dated from approximately 850,000 to 780,000 years ago.
    b. are agreed by all paleoanthropologists to represent *Homo erectus*.
    c. are the oldest fossils of *Homo sapiens*.
    d. are evidence of *Homo habilis* in Europe.

14. The Acheulian stone biface, which was the standard tool for *Homo erectus* for more than a million years,

    a. served to cut, pound, scrape, and dig.
    b. is only found in southern Africa.
    c. was hafted onto spear shafts as an effective throwing weapon.
    d. is first found in the archaeological record of China.

15. Which of the following applies to the Acheulian culture?

    a. A suitable piece of stone would be taken from one place to another by toolmakers.
    b. Stone tools are found near the raw material source.
    c. Acheulian toolmakers had foresight.
    d. Both a and c are correct.

16. Which of the following applies to *Homo erectus*?

    a. This species embraced culture.
    b. It is notable for its increased body size and more efficient bipedal locomotion.
    c. Its brain was reshaped and increased in size.
    d. all of the above

Short-Answer Questions

1. Describe the physical characteristics of *Homo erectus*.

has a larger body and brain size than all other Previous hominis. Has thick cranial bones + a thick brow ridge above the eyes. has a unique Pentagon shaped cranium. with max width below the ear hole.

2. Describe *Homo erectus* evolution in East Africa.

appears 1.7mya, had a light build than asian counterparts. By 1.4mya we see the largest cranial cap. in African speciese

3. Briefly discuss the presence of *Homo erectus* in Europe.

In Europe the first traces found date back to 1.8mya w/ first findings in 1990 in N. Spain. These, though are placed in a different species cause they do not have the same chraeterichics.

4. How does the Acheulian stone tool culture differ from the Oldowan tool culture?

Oldowan is also called pebble stone tools from around 2.mya. By 1.4mya Acheulian stone tools came to light with something called a biface (hand ax) which is flaked on both sides.

Application Questions

1. Briefly discuss the migration of different types of animals and how this might relate to early *Homo*.

Homo like most other mammals probably went along paths that would lead them to the most resources and food. By following animal herds Homo s species would be led to many new areas, ie: Africa and the such until they split

2. What fundamental questions of interpretation do the fossil hominins from Dmanisi raise? How does this fit in with the dates for *Homo erectus* in China and Java?

Dmanisi proves that Homo erectus migrate off. out of africa well over a1Mya and dates from Java also show that remains discovered date from at least 1.6mya.

3. Was Zhoukoudian *Homo erectus* a hunter? Why or why not?

No, it is now believed that they were scavangers, their believed shelter could not be accessed except vertically, and bones appear to be done/ carried by Hyenas.

4. Why was it suggested that the African early Pleistocene large-bodied *Homo* were a separate species from *Homo erectus* in Asia? What is the current thinking regarding *H. erectus?* They have a smaller build and brain capacity with less defined browridges and a nuchal tori with thinner bones. Leading some researchers to believe they are not the same species.

Answer Key

Matching I

1. d (video lesson, segment 3; objective 8)
2. e (objective 2)
3. b (video lesson, segment 1; objective 1)
4. c (objective 1)
5. f (video lesson, segment 1; objective 1)
6. a (objective 1)

Matching II

1. j (objectives 1 & 7)
2. h (objectives 1 & 5)
3. a (video lesson, segment 2; objectives 1 & 6)
4. i (objectives 1 & 7)
5. f (objectives 1 & 3)
6. b (video lesson, segment 1; objectives 1 & 5)
7. g (objectives 1 & 5)
8. d (objectives 1 & 3)
9. c (objective 3)
10. e (video lesson, segment 2; objectives 1, 3, & 4)

Completion I

1. adolescent growth spurt (objective 1)
2. nuchal; braincase; breadth (video lesson, segment 1; objective 1)
3. Dmanisi (video lesson, segment 2; objective 6)
4. cranial capacity (video lesson, segment 2; objectives 1 & 6)
5. Acheulian (video lesson, segment 3; objective 8)
6. Java (video lesson, segment 2; objectives 2 & 3)
7. missing link (video lesson, segments 2 & 3; objective 3)
8. Sangiran Dome (objective 3)

Completion II

1. Zhoukoudian (video lesson, segment 2; objective 3)

2. Ngandong (objective 4)

3. hunters and gatherers (objective 4)

4. 100,000 (objective 4)

5. East Turkana (objective 5)

6. separate (objective 5)

7. Sima del Elefante (objective 7)

8. biface (video lesson, segment 3; objective 8)

Self-Test

1. a. is the correct answer. Members of a grade share a similar adaptive pattern and, as such, seem more closely related than they may actually be. The prosimians, for example, represent a grade. (objective 2)

2. c. is the correct answer. In addition to having an absolutely larger cranial capacity, *Homo erectus* also had a larger brain compared to its body size than earlier hominins. (objective 1)

3. d. is the correct answer. *Homo erectus* is the only hominin that has the maximum cranial breadth below the ear. (objective 1)

4. b. is the correct answer. The earliest *H. erectus* fossils from the island of Java date from 1.6 million years ago. (objectives 1 & 3)

5. c. is the correct answer. There may have been two migrations out of Africa. One was the large-bodied *Homo erectus*. The other migration may have been a pre-erectus *Homo* or else a very early member of *H. erectus*. These would be represented by the Dmanisi hominins, who were small in stature and in cranial capacity. They also only had the simple Oldowan tool culture. (objective 6)

6. d. is the correct answer. The first fossil human remains found outside of Europe or Africa were the *Homo erectus* specimens recovered by Eugene Dubois in Java. (video lesson, segment 2; objective 2)

7. a. is the correct answer. Dubois find a skullcap along the Solo River near the village of Trinil. (video lesson, segment 2; objective 3)

8. d. is the correct answer. There appears to have been some relict populations of *Homo erectus* that survived until 40,000 years ago and would have coexisted with modern humans. (objective 3)

9. d. is the correct answer. Earlier views were that *Homo erectus* lived in caves and controlled fires in hearths where they cooked the large mammals that they hunted. Now all of these ideas are disputed. (objective 4)

10. b. is the correct answer. WT 15000 is the most complete hominin skeleton found before hominins begin burying their dead. Original estimates, based on modern growth curves,

predicted that this boy would have been around six feet tall had he lived to adulthood but new analysis has found that *H. erectus* growth patterns are more ape-like and lack the adolescent growth spurt typical of modern humans. (video lesson, segment 1; objective 5)

11. d. is the correct answer. *Homo ergaster* means "working man," and this species was proposed to include all African *H. erectus*. However, the similarities between the Daka cranium and the Asian *H. erectus* has led to a decline in support for this species recognition. (objective 5)

12. d. is the correct answer. European hominin finds greater than 700,000 years old have been found in the Republic of Georgia, Italy, and Spain. (video lesson, segment 2; objectives 1 & 7)

13. a. is the correct answer. The Gran Dolina site has been dated to between 850,000 and 780,000 years ago. (objective 7)

14. a. is the correct answer. The Acheulian biface, sometimes referred to as a "hand ax," was a multipurpose tool. (video lesson, segment 3; objective 8)

15. d. is the correct answer. Acheulian toolmakers appear to have been looking for good raw material and when they found it they took it with them. This implies forethought. (objective 8)

16. d. is the correct answer. *H. erectus* had larger body and brain sizes, was more efficient at bipedal locomotion (possibly transiting to long duration running), and wholeheartedly embraced culture as a means of adaptation. (objectives 1 & 8)

Short-Answer Questions

Your answers should include the following:

1. *Homo erectus* has a larger body size than all previous hominins. Accompanying this size increase is an increase in the size of the braincase and brain. The cranial bones are thick. There is a heavy browridge (supraorbital torus) above the eyes, and there is a thick nuchal torus where the heavy neck muscles would have inserted. The posterior teeth are large. The shape of the cranium of *Homo erectus* is also unique among hominins, being pentagonal when viewed from behind. Maximum cranial width is below the earhole, a feature not seen in any other hominin. The braincase is long and low, resulting in a receding forehead. (video lesson, segment 1; objective 1)

2. *H. erectus* first appears in the fossil record of East Africa about 1.7 million years ago. These hominins were more lightly built than their Asian counterparts. They had less pronounced supraorbital and nuchal tori, and the cranial bones were not as thick. One example from East Turkana of an early *H. erectus* is an almost complete skull that, at 848 cm^2, is at the lower end of cranial capacity for the species. The largest cranial capacity of the African specimens, 1067 cm^2, is found in OH 9 (approximately 1.4 million years ago; see Figure 12-2 on page 346 of the Jurmain textbook). OH 9 also has the most robust supraorbital torus of any *H. erectus* known, although the cranial bones are still thin. These differences with Asian *H. erectus* have led some authorities to suggest a separate species designation, *H. ergaster*. However, a younger find (1 million years ago) from Daka, Ethiopia, has thick cranial bones, more like its Asian

conspecifics, suggesting that the populations in Africa and Asia are all one species. (objective 6)

3. Until the discovery of the Dmanisi hominins, it was believed that *H. erectus* never made it to Europe. However, these are among the earliest members of *H. erectus*, having been present in eastern Europe at roughly 1.81 million years ago. In the 1990s, hominin materials dating from 850,000 to 780,000 years ago were recovered from the Gran Dolina site in northern Spain. These fossils have been assigned to a different species, *H. antecessor*, because they appear to be different from *H. erectus*, based on initial analysis of fragmentary evidence. However, the Ceprano cranium, a hominin fossil recovered in Italy that has been dated at 450,000 years, does bear strong resemblance to *H. erectus* from elsewhere. Around 400,000 years ago, the fossil record of Europe improves, but the hominins recovered are considered by most authorities to be immediate predecessors to modern humans. (objective 7)

4. The Oldowan tool culture is a pebble tool culture first found approximately 2 million years ago in East Africa. The tools are made quickly with a hammerstone by knocking flakes off one side of the "blank." The flakes were held between the thumb and forefinger. Around 1.4 million years ago, a new tool kit supplements this technique in the Acheulian tool culture. A biface (sometimes called a "hand ax") is produced, in which the core is flaked on both sides. It will be the standard tool kit for almost a million years. Another major difference between Oldowan and Acheulian cultures is that Oldowan tools were produced at the location of the raw materials, whereas Acheulian toolmakers transported choice materials with them. This suggests foresight and planning that was not evident with Oldowan toolmakers. (video lesson, segment 3; objective 8)

Application Questions

Your answers should include the following:

1. Mammals, such as the wildebeest, travel along preferred paths that supply them with resources to which they are adapted. Hominins probably dispersed along similar paths as they scavenged animals that had died on the migration rather than hunting from the herd for food. Following migratory herds would have led some hominins out of Africa. They most likely left and returned many times over several thousand generations. However, as hominin populations grew larger, some groups may have split off and wandered farther from the origin, eventually making their way into Europe and Asia. (video lesson, segment 1; objective 6)

2. Historically, it was thought that *H. erectus* did not leave Africa until around one million years ago. The fossil hominin finds from Dmanisi in the Republic of Georgia are dated at 1.81 million years ago, meaning that the emigration from Africa must have been much earlier than a million years ago. Dates from Java corroborate this; there, *H. erectus* remains are found at the Sangiran Dome around 1.6 million years ago. The Dmanisi specimens also challenge the assumption that the large body size and relatively large brains would have been necessary for hominin migrations of this scope. The hominins found at Dmanisi are extremely short in stature and have small cranial capacities. However, they show the body proportions, sagittal keel, and low braincase

typical of *Homo erectus*. One possible interpretation is that the Dmanisi hominins are a small-brained early form of *Homo erectus* and were the first hominins to leave Africa. Others have suggested that there may have been two migrations. The Dmanisi hominins represent the first migration, while the founding population of the larger-brained Asian *H. erectus* leave slightly later. The Jurmain textbook also raises a third possibility—that Dmanisi may represent the center of origin for the species rather than Africa. (video lesson, segment 2; objective 6)

3. Traditionally, the Zhoukoudian *H. erectus* was believed to be a hunter and gatherer. In addition to hunting deer, horses, and other animals and gathering fruits and berries, they were also believed to have controlled fire and used it to heat their cave dwellings and to cook meat. This view has now been challenged because an alternative interpretation of the materials at Zhoukoudian paints a very different picture, according to several researchers. It appears that *H. erectus* may have been a scavenger rather than a hunter. The accumulated materials at the site may have been the result of hyena activity, including the collection of hominin bones that could have been the refuse of hyena meals. The bones may have been burned long after they were deposited. Also, the layers of ash previously thought to be the remains of *H. erectus* fire could actually have come from naturally accumulated organic matter. Finally, reassessment of the geology now reveals that the cave could only have been accessed vertically. As one researcher put it, "It wouldn't have been a shelter. It would have been a trap." (objective 4)

4. The earliest *H. erectus* from Africa (about 1.8 million years ago) are different than the later members of the species from Asia. They are not as strongly buttressed, with more gracile browridges and nuchal tori. Cranial capacities are smaller. The cranial bones are not as thick. Around 1.4 million years ago, the African populations begin using a new tool industry called the Acheulian. In the past, Acheulian tools were not found in Asia. The tools recovered from Zhoukoudian, for example, were crude and shapeless although they do become more sophisticated with time. This suggested that the Asian *H. erectus* was not capable of making Acheulian tools. All of these factors suggested to some that the African hominins were a different species and so they were given the name *H. ergaster*. More recent discoveries, such as the fossil cranium from Daka, provide a different picture. The Daka cranium bears a strong resemblance to Asian *H. erectus*. There have been Acheulian tools found in some of the Chinese sites dating to 800,000 years ago. Thus, current thinking is that African and Asian *H. erectus* represent one species. (objective 5)

Lesson Review

Lesson 10: A New Hominin

PLEASE NOTE: Use this matrix to guide your study and achieve the learning objectives of this lesson. It will also help you to view the video, which defines and demonstrates important concepts and principles as they relate to everyday life and actual case studies.

Learning Objective	Textbook	Student Guide	Video Lesson
1. Describe the morphology and geographical distribution of *Homo erectus* and the environmental changes during the Pleistocene.	pp. 341–365	Key Terms: 2, 3, 4, 6, 7, 8; Matching I: 3, 4, 5, 6; Matching II: 1, 2, 3, 4, 5, 6, 7, 8, 10; Completion I: 1, 2, 4; Self-Test: 2, 3, 4, 12, 16; Short-Answer: 1.	Segment 1: *Homo erectus* Segment 2: *Location, Location*
2. Discuss the taxonomic nomenclature for African and Asian *Homo erectus*.	pp. 344, 359	Key Terms: 1; Matching I: 2; Completion I: 6; Self-Test: 1, 6.	Segment 2: *Location, Location*
3. Summarize the history of *Homo erectus* discoveries in Java and China.	pp. 351–359	Key Terms: 7; Matching II: 5, 8, 9, 10; Completion I: 6, 7, 8; Completion II: 1; Self-Test: 4, 7, 8.	Segment 2: *Location, Location* Segment 3: *Tool Time*
4. Discuss the cultural remains and other materials that pertain to the lifestyle of *Homo erectus* at Zhoukoudian, and note the alternate interpretations of Zhoukoudian regarding its status as a hominin habitation site.	pp. 354–356	Key Terms: 7; Matching II: 10; Completion II: 2, 3, 4; Self-Test: 9; Application: 3.	Segment 2: *Location, Location*

© 2012 Cengage Learning. All Rights Reserved. May not be scanned, copied or duplicated, or posted to a publicly accessible website, in whole or in part.

Learning Objective	Textbook	Student Guide	Video Lesson
5. Discuss the significance of *Homo erectus* sites and important fossil discoveries from East Africa, with particular reference to WT 15000.	pp. 347–349	Key Terms: 3; Matching II: 2, 6, 7; Completion II: 5, 6; Self-Test: 10, 11; Application: 4.	Segment 1: *Homo erectus*
6. Identify when the first hominins left Africa, and describe the supporting evidence.	pp. 349–351	Key Terms: 4; Matching II: 3; Completion I: 3, 4; Self-Test: 5; Short-Answer: 2; Application: 1, 2.	Segment 1: *Homo erectus* Segment 2: *Location, Location*
7. List the fossil discoveries from Europe and discuss how they relate to *Homo erectus*.	pp. 359–360	Matching II: 1, 4; Completion II: 7; Self-Test: 12, 13; Short-Answer: 3.	Segment 2: *Location, Location*
8. Discuss the archaeological evidence for the increased reliance of *Homo erectus* on cultural adaptations.	pp. 361–364	Key Terms: 5; Matching I: 1; Completion I: 5; Completion II: 8; Self-Test: 14, 15, 16; Short-Answer: 4.	Segment 3: *Tool Time*

LESSON 11

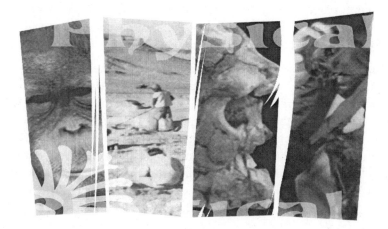

Premodern Humans

Checklist

For the most effective study of this lesson, complete the following activities in this sequence.

Before Viewing the Video

- ❑ Read the Preview, Learning Objectives, and Viewing Notes below.

- ❑ Read Chapter 13, "Premodern Humans," pages 366–401, in *Introduction to Physical Anthropology*.

What to Watch

- ❑ After reading the textbook assignment, watch the video for Lesson 11, *Premodern Humans*.

After Viewing the Video

- ❑ Briefly note your answers to the questions listed at the end of the Viewing Notes.

- ❑ Review the Summary below.

- ❑ Review all reading assignments for this lesson, including the Viewing Notes in this lesson.

- ❑ Write brief answers to the "Critical Thinking Questions" at the end of Chapter 13 in the textbook.

- ❑ Complete the Review Exercises below. Check your answers with the Answer Key and review when necessary.

- ❑ Use the Lesson Review matrix found at the end of this lesson to review and assess your knowledge of each Learning Objective.

Preview

A popular television commercial, which spawned a television series in 2007, featured a Neandertal of the typical depiction—the sloping forehead, bony brow ridge over the eyes, large nose, and muscular build. The ad, for an insurance company, touted the company's website as so easy to use that "even a caveman could do it." The joke was that the "caveman" in the ad was insulted by this derogatory comment about his intelligence.

Despite a popular misconception, Neandertals weren't dumb. Their brains were at least as large as modern humans and they displayed many sophisticated cultural capabilities. Also, the television counterparts walked upright (as the earlier *Homo erectus* did), not stooped over as Neandertals have been incorrectly depicted in the past. In the last lesson, you learned how *Homo erectus* were clearly moving closer on the evolutionary scale toward becoming human; they were larger than earlier hominins with bigger brains and the ability to make more sophisticated tools. Lesson 11 looks at what are referred to as "premodern humans"—hominins who continue the evolutionary journey and in some ways are very much like modern humans, but still retain major differences. This lesson tackles an intriguing question: When were our predecessors obviously human?

Concepts to Remember

❋ Lesson 5 covered the principles of classification and the definition of species. Recall that a **species** is a group of interbreeding or potentially interbreeding organisms that is reproductively isolated from other such groups. Another term introduced in Lesson 5 is **phylogenetic species concept**, a classification technique based on an identifiable parental pattern of ancestry. Phylogenetic analysis is used to determine evolutionary relationships among organisms. Although a few samples of ancient DNA have been extracted from fossils, for extinct groups the evidence mostly comes from phenotypic characteristics, or the physical properties of the organism determined from morphology. This lesson discusses how scientists attempt to classify premodern humans.

❋ Lesson 10 discussed the **Acheulian** stone tool industry, the toolmaking artifacts and techniques dating from the Lower and Middle Pleistocene that were characterized by a large proportion of bifacial tools (flaked on both sides). The hominins discussed in Lesson 11 lived during the Middle and Upper Pleistocene and the tools featured in this lesson show advancing sophistication.

Learning Objectives

After you complete this lesson, you should be able to:

1. Discuss the most important physical characteristics, the major sites, and the time range of early premodern *Homo sapiens*. (pp. 368–377)

2. Contrast the evolutionary development of premodern *Homo sapiens* in Africa, Asia, and Europe, emphasizing the evidence that Neandertals evolved in Europe. (pp. 369–377)

3. Discuss key cultural innovations during the Middle Pleistocene, emphasizing advances in tool technologies and possible hunting activities. (pp. 377–378)

4. Describe the distinctive features of Neandertals. (pp. 378–380)

5. Describe the temporal and geographic distribution of the Neandertals. (pp. 380–387)

6. Discuss the culture of Neandertals, including their technology, settlement patterns, subsistence behaviors, and symbolic behaviors. (pp. 387–392)

7. Use the Neandertals to illustrate the problems anthropologists have encountered in attempting to distinguish the different species among the various extinct hominins. (pp. 392–401)

At this point, read Chapter 13, "Premodern Humans," pages 366–401.

Viewing Notes

Why do we have the view of Neandertals as stoop-shouldered, thick-headed cavemen? Part of this misconception came when early examination of Neandertal fossils, which had bone malformations caused by spinal osteoarthritis, were interpreted as normal skeletal configurations. Subsequent fossil discoveries contradict this erroneous interpretation. Neandertal gets it name from the Neander Valley in Germany, the area where the first fossils were found. They were the first clue of an extinct species of premodern humans living in Europe.

Following in the footsteps of *Homo erectus*, new hominins begin to emerge as far back as 780,000 years ago. Among these hominins was a species known today as *Homo heidelbergensis*, which appears more human than other hominin predecessors. They settled into Europe and western Asia and are believed to have evolved into Neandertals.

Neandertals and *Homo sapiens* emerged about the same time, but there isn't clear evidence that they interacted. However, in western Europe, there seems to be some chronological overlap of the stone tool industries of the two groups. Fossil remains of Neandertals and modern humans have yet to be found together, but similar tool artifacts used by both groups have been discovered at the same sites. This circumstance supports the notion that some kind of contact or interaction may have occurred between the two species.

The muscular build and thick bone structure of Neandertals lead scientists to hypothesize that these hominins lived a physically demanding lifestyle in the extremely cold climate of the Pleistocene period at northern latitudes. However, the video is careful to point out that biological adaptations are not the only reasons Neandertals were able to survive a harsh climate. Archaeological finds indicate that this species developed culturally as well. They developed an advanced tool technology, they controlled fire extensively, they were successful in hunting large game, and they most likely developed some type of clothing for protection against the elements.

Nevertheless, the Neandertals disappear from the archaeological record beginning about 30,000 years ago, just when modern humans begin to disperse about the earth. In this way, Neandertal extinction and modern human dispersal correlate in time. Neandertal extinction may have nothing to do with *Homo sapiens* dispersal; perhaps their numbers dwindled because of extreme climate changes. On the other hand, perhaps *Homo sapiens* did have some sort of active role in driving Neandertals to extinction, but so far there seems to be no evidence to support this notion. Did Neandertals interbreed with modern humans and become absorbed by *Homo sapiens*, or was the Neandertal a species that went extinct before giving rise to something else? Many questions have yet to be answered regarding the disappearance of this fascinating species of hominin.

Questions to Consider

❋ What does the term "Paleolithic Era" refer to?

❋ During what time frame did the Mousterian tool industry develop? What early hominin species developed this industry?

❋ What scenarios have paleoanthropologists devised to help explain why the Neandertal disappeared from the archaeological record?

Watch the video for Lesson 11, *Premodern Humans*.

Segment 1: *Age of the Caveman*
Segment 2: *Clan of the Caveman*
Segment 3: *Death of a Caveman*

Key Terms and Concepts

Page references are keyed to *Introduction to Physical Anthropology*, 13th edition.

1. **Middle Pleistocene:** The portion of the Pleistocene epoch beginning 780,000 years ago and ending 125,000 years ago. (p. 368; video lesson, segment 1; objective 1)

2. **Late Pleistocene:** The portion of the Pleistocene epoch beginning 125,000 years ago and ending approximately 10,000 years ago. (p. 368; video lesson, segment 1; objective 1)

3. **glaciations:** Climatic intervals when continental ice sheets cover much of the northern continents. Glaciations are associated with colder temperatures in northern latitudes and

more arid conditions in southern latitudes, most notably in Africa. (p. 368; video lesson, segment 1; objective 1)

4. **interglacials:** Climatic intervals when continental ice sheets are retreating, eventually becoming much reduced in size. Interglacials in northern latitudes are associated with warmer temperatures, while in southern latitudes the climate becomes wetter. (p. 368; video lesson, segment 1; objective 1)

5. **Neandertal (*Homo neanderthalensis*):** A Late Pleistocene premodern human that occupied Europe and southwestern Asia. Contemporary with modern humans. (video lesson, segment 1; objectives 4 & 5)

6. **flexed:** The position of the body in a bent orientation, with arms and legs drawn up to the chest. (p. 380; objective 6)

7. **Upper Paleolithic:** A cultural period usually associated with modern humans, but also found with some Neandertals, and distinguished by technological innovation in various stone tool industries. Best known from western Europe, similar industries are also known from central and eastern Europe and Africa. (p. 383; video lesson, segment 1; objective 6)

8. **Chatelperronian:** Pertaining to an Upper Paleolithic industry found in France and Spain, containing blade tools and associated with Neandertals. (p. 383; objectives 5 & 6)

9. **Mousterian:** Pertaining to the stone tool industry associated with Neandertals and some modern *H. sapiens* groups, also called Middle Paleolithic. This industry is characterized by a larger proportion of flake tools than found in Acheulian tool kits. (p. 387; video lesson, segment 1; objectives 5 & 6)

Summary

The **Middle Pleistocene** (between 780,000 and 125,000 years ago) was a period of great transition in human evolution. Hominin fossils from this time period share characteristics with both *Homo erectus* and *Homo sapiens*. But these hominins also show several significant differences from modern humans that set them apart. Most paleoanthropologists are comfortable identifying Middle Pleistocene hominins as "human," but they qualify this recognition by referring to them as "premodern humans."

The Pleistocene is also called the Ice Age, although, as the Jurmain textbook and the video point out, it was marked by periodic advances and retreats of massive glaciations and interglacial periods. **Glaciations** are climatic intervals when enormous ice sheets cover much of the northern continents, and they are associated with cold temperatures. **Interglacial** periods are the climatic intervals when continental ice sheets retreat, and these intervals are associated with warmer temperatures. During the Pleistocene, numerous major cycles of cold and warm climates occurred that affected huge areas of Europe, Asia, and North America. Hominins living in these areas during this time period were severely affected by the changing climate, flora, and animal life.

The premodern humans found in the Old World during the Middle Pleistocene (after 780,000 years ago) followed *H. erectus*, although there is evidence that premodern humans and *H. erectus* did coexist for a long period of time, especially in Asia. A growing consensus classifies most of the fossils found as *Homo heidelbergensis*, named after a fossil found in

Germany in 1907. While most researchers no longer consider this species as simply archaic *H. sapiens*, according to the Jurmain textbook, most agree that *Homo heidelbergensis* is a very closely related species to modern humans as well as to Neandertals. It is still debated whether they represent a fully separate species.

Fossils found in Africa exhibit traits of both *H. erectus* and more modern humans. The large supraorbital torus, low vault, and prominent occipital torus of the skull more closely resembled *Homo erectus*. But the occipital region is less angled, the cranial vault bones are thinner, and the cranial base is essentially modern. Most of the fossils found in the Kabwe (Broken Hill) site in Zambia are dated from 600,000 to 125,000 years ago. Bodo, located in Ethiopia, is the site of one of the most significant fossil finds in Africa. A nearly complete cranium found there has been dated to the Middle Pleistocene, approximately 600,000 years ago, making it one of the oldest specimens of *Homo heidelbergensis* from the African continent.

Europe has provided more premodern hominin fossils dating to the Middle Pleistocene than any other region, and, like the African finds, these fossils show a mix of traits of both their predecessors and successors. In China, fossil remains are not as similar to the ones found in Europe and Africa, leading some paleoanthropologists to hypothesize that the remains are a regional variant of *Homo heidelbergensis*. The environmental challenges of the Pleistocene meant that many small populations of premodern humans became geographically isolated from one another. Some became extinct; others evolved. In Africa, *Homo heidelbergensis* is hypothesized to have evolved into modern *H. sapiens*. In Europe, *H. heidelbergensis* evolved into Neandertals. The Chinese premoderns may have all become extinct, although this theory is under considerable debate.

The Acheulian tool industry of *H. erectus* was prominent during the Lower and Middle Pleistocene. Some of the later premodern humans in Africa and Europe invented a toolmaking method called the Levallois technique, which controls the size and shape of the flakes by employing several coordinated steps in the manufacturing process. This sophistication suggests that the toolmakers had gained increased cognitive abilities. Different stone tool industries coexisted in some areas for quite some time, perhaps because they were produced by different groups of hominins, or because the differing tools represented varied activities at separate locales, or perhaps because some areas lacked the stone resources to create all the tools the people were capable of making.

Archaeological finds support the idea that the Middle Pleistocene hominins built temporary habitations and subsisted on many different food sources such as fruits, vegetables, seeds, nuts and bird eggs, but evidence of their hunting abilities is less clear-cut.

As the Jurmain textbook points out, **Neandertals** fit into the general scheme of human evolution, and yet they are misfits. In classifying Neandertals as *H. sapiens*, they are included as a subspecies, *Homo sapiens neanderthalensis*, but not all scientists agree with this interpretation.

The Jurmain textbook concentrates on the Neandertal populations that lived during the last major glaciation, which began about 75,000 years ago and ended about 10,000 years ago. The textbook authors are careful to note that the descriptions of Neandertals found in Chapter 13 are based primarily on those fossils that have been found in Europe, called *classic* Neandertals.

Was There Cannibalism in the Middle Pleistocene?

*O*ccasionally, paleoanthropologists find specimens that seem to show evidence of cannibalism, the consumption of fellow human beings. There are two types of cannibalism: gustatory and ritual. Gustatory cannibalism is the consumption of other humans for calories and protein. As a regular practice, gustatory cannibalism is rare. A more common practice is "cannibalism by necessity" of a person who has already died and is subsequently consumed by others for survival. Ritual cannibalism may be a mortuary practice or a religious rite such as the consumption of slain enemies.

There are numerous well-known examples of cannibalism by necessity. Two most prominent cases are the *Donner Party* of 1840s who were lost in the Sierra Nevada Mountains and, more recently, the survivors of an Andean plane crash in 1972. Ritual cannibalism is known among the *Fore* of Papua, New Guinea.

While no one denies that cannibalism occasionally occurs, there have been disputes as to whether reports of it are exaggerated. Invariably, the reported cannibals are from a different group than the individual reporting the behavior. At one time, anthropologists suggested that the *Homo erectus* remains found at *Zhoukoudian* near Beijing, China, showed evidence of cannibalism, noting that the foramen magnum had been removed to reach the brain. One anthropologist denied cannibalism at *Zhoukoudian* and suggested the skull had been used as a soup bowl! It is now believed that the enlarged foramen magnum in these fossils occurred postmortem and was caused by natural processes.

In the Jurmain textbook, two cases of possible cannibalism are mentioned. The *Bodo* cranium appears to have been "scalped." It is hard to say what happened to this individual. Scalping may have been a ritual act or an act of warfare. It does not appear to be the result of natural weathering or any other natural process. The Neandertal site of *Moula-Guercy Cave* in southeastern France provides evidence that is more suggestive of cannibalism. Markings on the remains suggest that these individuals were butchered. The long bones were broken open to expose the yellow marrow, which is high in calories. This evidence appears to support the practice of gustatory cannibalism.

Other Neandertal specimens reveal cuts and scratches that appear to be butchering marks. When these fossils were first discovered, researchers suggested cannibalism, but this was rejected. However, new analytical methods have resurrected the cannibalism hypothesis. Material from *Gran Dolina* in northern Spain has "butchering marks," and it may be that cannibalism goes back as far as 780,000 years ago, which is the date given to the earliest hominin remains found at *Gran Dolina*.

As pointed out in the video, the brain size of Neandertals was actually larger than that of *H. sapiens* today, and that this may be associated with the metabolic efficiency of a larger brain in cold weather. Interestingly, the Inuit (Eskimo), who also live in very cold climates, have a brain that is larger than that of other modern human populations. The classic Neandertal cranium is large, long, and low; the forehead rises more vertically than that of *H. erectus*; and the body is robust, with shorter limbs than are seen in most modern *Homo sapiens* populations.

More recent fossil finds in western Europe suggest that anatomically modern humans were living in central and western Europe by about 35,000 years ago or a bit earlier, making it possible that Neandertals and modern *H. sapiens* lived in close proximity to one another for several thousand years. In fact, as the Jurmain textbook points out on page 393, "we now are able to conclude with confidence that Neandertals interbred with modern *Homo sapiens*."

Neandertals lived in the cultural period known as the Middle Paleolithic and are associated with the **Mousterian** tool industry, characterized by a larger proportion of flake tools than is found in Acheulian tool kits. They improved on previous Levallois techniques, and there is some archaeological evidence to suggest that they made specialized tools for meat preparation, hunting, and woodworking. What is clear is that they were successful hunters, as evidenced by the large amounts of animal bones at their sites. Spear-throwers, or atlatls, and bows and arrows weren't developed until later, so the close-proximity spears the Neandertals probably used exposed them to serious injury. The high proportion of head and neck injuries evident in Neandertal fossils is a pattern that matches the injuries seen in modern rodeo performers, causing researchers to conclude that the Neandertals had close encounters with their large prey. Besides meat, Neandertals also consumed berries, nuts, and other plants. New evidence from the island of Gibraltar shows they also gathered shellfish and hunted seals and dolphins. Many scholars believe that Neandertals could speak, but not necessarily with the same language capabilities of modern humans. New evidence of the use of pigment and perforated shell jewelry as body adornment points to advanced cognitive abilities in Neandertals and blurs the line of demarcation between Neandertals and early modern *Homo sapiens*. At some point, Neandertals became an evolutionary dead end, but as Jurmain points out, some of their genes can be found today in modern humans.

While the Middle Pleistocene hominins are a diverse group, they still reveal some general trends. For instance, in many respects, they were transitional between the hominin grade that preceded them (*Homo erectus*) and that which followed (*Homo sapiens*). Most likely, some of them are ancestral to the earliest fully modern humans. But, as you have seen throughout this course, classification is not an easy task. A number of species names have been proposed. One thought is to recognize only one species for all premodern fossils, *Homo sapiens*, and place them in the modern humans group, albeit with distinctive terminology such as archaic *H. sapiens*. Other paleontologists have identified at least three species distinct from *H. sapiens*: *H. heidelbergensis*, *H. neanderthalensis*, and *H. helmei*. This last species is suggested as a possible African ancestor of both modern humans and Neandertals. While there is disagreement among scholars, there is also consensus that all these hominins are quite closely related to each other as well as to modern humans. Moreover, the different species are seen by most researchers as paleospecies rather than as fully biological ones.

Review Exercises

Matching I

Match each term with the appropriate definition or description.

1. __j__ Chatelperronian
2. __i__ flexed
3. __g__ glaciations
4. __d__ interglacials
5. __f__ Late Pleistocene
6. __h__ Levallois technique

7. __b__ Middle Pleistocene
8. __c__ Mousterian
9. __e__ Neandertals
10. __a__ premodern human
11. __k__ Upper Paleolithic

  a. The immediate predecessors to modern humans.
  b. The period that begins 780,000 years ago and ends around 125,000 years ago.
  c. Pertaining to the stone tool industry associated with the Neandertals and some moderns.
  d. When ice sheets are retreating and climate in the northern latitudes becomes warmer.
  e. A Late Pleistocene premodern human that lived in Europe and southwestern Asia.
  f. The period encompassing 125,000 to 10,000 years ago.
  g. Intervals when continental ice sheets cover much of the northern continents.
  h. A technique developed by premodern humans for controlling the size and shape of flake tools.
  i. The position of the body in a bent orientation often seen in Neandertal burials.
  j. Pertaining to an Upper Paleolithic industry found in France and Spain, containing blade tools and associated with Neandertals.
  k. A cultural period associated with modern humans and some Neandertals distinguished by technological innovation in various stone tool industries.

Matching II

Match each term with the appropriate definition or description.

1. __f__ Atapuerca
2. __c__ Bodo
3. __g__ Jinniushan
4. __h__ Kabwe
5. __d__ La Chapelle-aux-Saints

6. __i__ Schöningen
7. __b__ Steinheim
8. __e__ Tabun
9. __a__ Terra Amata

  a. Hunter-gatherer premoderns visited this site seasonally, built shelters, and obtained resources from the ocean.
  b. An almost complete *Homo heidelbergensis* cranium was recovered from this site in Germany.
  c. This site yielded a cranium that may be the earliest evidence of *Homo heidelbergensis* in Africa, perhaps in the world.

d. This site produced the idea of what a Neandertal looked like.

e. An important early Neandertal site that provides evidence of Neandertals in the Near East.

f. A cave in which the earliest evidence of Neandertal morphology is present.

g. Chinese scientists claim that a *Homo sapiens* skeleton is found at this site from 200,000 years ago.

h. A complete *Homo heidelbergensis* cranium recovered from Zambia.

i. A site in Germany from which wooden throwing spears were recovered.

Completion I

Fill each blank with the most appropriate term from the list below.

Atapuerca
Bodo
glaciations
Homo heidelbergensis
interglacials
Jinniushan

Kabwe
Late Pleistocene
Middle Pleistocene
premodern humans
Steinheim

1. The Middle Pleistocene people who were the immediate predecessors to modern *Homo sapiens* are referred to as ___Premodern Humans___

2. *Homo heidelbergensis* lived during a period called the ___Middle Pleistocene___.

3. The Neandertals lived well into the ___Late pleistocene___.

4. During ___glaciations___, hominin migratory routes in northern regions were greatly affected and some key passages were blocked by glaciers.

5. Rainfall increased in Africa during ___interglacials___.

6. The transitional species between *Homo erectus* and *Homo sapiens* was ___Homo heidelbergensis___

7. The ___Kabwe___ cranium was found in Zambia and has one of the most massive supraorbital torus ever found in a hominin.

8. ___Bodo___ is a cranium found in Africa that shows evidence that it was defleshed by other humans.

9. ___Atapuerca___ is a site in Spain from which a large sample has been recovered including the earliest evidence of the Neandertal morphology.

10. An almost complete cranium of *Homo heidelbergensis* was recovered from a site in Germany called ___Steinheim___.

11. A partial skeleton, including a cranium, recovered from ___Jinniushan___ is controversial because Chinese scientists assign it to *Homo sapiens*, while others consider it to be *H. heidelbergensis*.

Completion II

Fill each blank with the most appropriate term from the list below.

Chatelperronian   Neandertals
classic Neandertals   Schöningen
flexed   Tabun
La Chapelle-aux-Saints   Terra Amata
Levallois technique   Upper Paleolithic
Mousterian

1. The _Levallois tech._ is a toolmaking technique that allows for control of the size and shape of flake tools.

2. Premoderns constructed shelters, obtained food from the sea, and returned year after year to _Terra Amata_.

3. Wooden throwing spears were found at _Schöningen_, Germany.

4. The Late Pleistocene premodern humans that occupied Europe were the _Neandertals_.

5. The Neandertal populations of western Europe showed extreme development of the species characteristics and were termed _Classic Neandertals_.

6. The remains of an older Neandertal male recovered from a burial site at _La Chapelle-aux-Saints_ constitute one of the most important Neandertal finds.

7. A feature of Neandertal burials was that the deceased was placed in a _Flexed_ position.

8. The cultural period usually associated with modern humans is the _Upper Paleolithic_.

9. An Upper Paleolithic tradition that is associated with Neandertals is the _Chatelperronian_.

10. Evidence that Neandertal populations were in the Near East comes from the site of _Tabun_.

11. A stone tool industry that is mainly associated with Neandertals and is characterized by flake tools is the _Mousterian_.

Self-Test

Select the best answer.

1. Which of the following events occur during a glacial period?
   a. Africa becomes wetter.
   b. Sea levels drop.
   c. The Sahara desert contracts.
   d. Northern regions open up for migration of humans.

2. Which of the following are considered to be premodern humans?
   a. *Homo erectus*
   b. *Homo heidelbergensis*
   c. *Homo neanderthalensis*
   d. both b and c

3. The premodern humans of the Middle Pleistocene immediately succeeded
   a. *Homo habilis.*
   b. *Homo heidelbergensis.*
   c. *Homo erectus.*
   d. *Homo neanderthalensis.*

4. Which of the following *Homo erectus* traits are found in premodern humans?
   a. large browridges
   b. rounded braincase
   c. reduced face
   d. both b and c

5. Which of the following is **NOT** a derived morphological change found in premodern humans?
   a. brain expansion
   b. increase in molar size
   c. rounder cranial vault
   d. less angled occipital bone

6. Which of the following applies to *Homo heidelbergensis*?
   a. It was the first hominin to use stone tools.
   b. It represents a transition between *Homo erectus* and *Homo sapiens.*
   c. It was the first hominin to leave Africa.
   d. It had a larger brain than found in modern humans.

7. Which of the following applies to the Kabwe cranium from Zambia?

    a. Its foramen magnum was enlarged to remove the brain, suggesting cannibalism.

    b. It was found in association with Acheulian tools.

    c. Its cranial base is essentially modern.

    d. It has a short, flat face.

8. Which of the following crania may be the earliest evidence of *Homo heidelbergensis*?

    a. Kabwe

    b. Shanidar I

    c. Steinheim

    d. Bodo

9. The Atapuerca (Sima de los Huesos) site is important because it

    a. yielded the largest sample of premodern humans from anywhere in the world.

    b. documents the appearance of premodern humans in Mexico.

    c. is where Neandertal toolmakers first used the Levallois technique.

    d. involves a and c.

10. Modern Chinese populations retain certain premodern human traits, including

    a. extreme postorbital constriction and sagittal crests.

    b. projecting canines and diastemata.

    c. sagittal keels (or ridges) and flattened nasal bones.

    d. receding forehead.

11. Which of the following statements is **NOT** correct?

    a. The premodern human African and European fossils resemble one another more than they do the Asian hominins from the Middle Pleistocene.

    b. All premodern humans from the Middle Pleistocene resemble one another.

    c. Some researchers consider the Asian premodern humans to be a regional branch of *Homo heidelbergensis*.

    d. Chinese paleoanthropologists consider the specimen from Jinniushan to be an early member of *Homo sapiens*.

12. The tool technology of *Homo heidelbergensis* in the Middle Pleistocene in Europe and Southwest Asia

    a. differed considerably from the Acheulian tools of *H. erectus*.

    b. continued to be the Acheulian tradition of *H. erectus*.

    c. incorporated the use of bone and antler for the first time.

    d. involved the use of finely made, bifacially flaked blades and points.

13. Which of the following has been offered as an explanation of why different Acheulian traditions coexisted in close proximity?

   a. They were made by different groups of people.
   b. The same group of people made them while performing varied activities at different sites.
   c. They represent a trade network.
   d. Both a and b have been offered as explanations.

14. Classic Neandertals are found in

   a. Israel.
   b. Iraq.
   c. Europe.
   d. all of the above locations.

15. Which of the following is **NOT** typical of Neandertal crania?

   a. The skull is long and low.
   b. The browridges are arched over the orbits and do not form a bar-like supraorbital torus.
   c. The occipital bone is sharply angled.
   d. The forehead begins to appear and rises more vertically.

16. Based on the crania recovered, Neandertal brain size

   a. was smaller, on average, than that of modern humans.
   b. was larger, on average, than that of modern humans.
   c. was smaller than that of *Homo erectus*.
   d. averaged around 1,100 cm^3.

17. The La Chapelle-aux-Saints Neandertal was buried with

   a. flint tools.
   b. broken animal bones.
   c. a bison leg.
   d. all of the above.

18. The La Chapelle-aux-Saints skeleton was found in

   a. Germany.
   b. Croatia.
   c. France.
   d. Switzerland.

19. The Neandertal site at St. Césaire dates to

    a. *circa* 35,000 years ago.
    b. 125,000 years ago.
    c. the Upper Paleolithic.
    d. both a and c.

20. Which site has yielded Neandertals with smaller browridges and slight chin development, suggesting a possible evolutionary link with modern humans?

    a. St. Césaire
    b. Kebara
    c. Vindija
    d. Krapina

21. The Kebara skeleton is the first Neandertal fossil to preserve which bone?

    a. patella
    b. turbinate bone
    c. hyoid bone
    d. calcaneus

22. The easternmost Neandertal site yet discovered is

    a. Kebara.
    b. Tabun.
    c. Shanidar.
    d. Teshik Tash.

23. The physical condition of Shanidar I suggests which of the following?

    a. Neandertals at this site practiced cannibalism.
    b. Neandertal bones were used for tools.
    c. This male could only have survived through assistance from others.
    d. Both a and b are true.

24. Neandertals are almost always associated with

    a. cannibalism.
    b. the Mousterian tool industry.
    c. throwing spears.
    d. both b and c.

25. The Neandertal subsistence base was
    a. hunting and gathering.
    b. strictly vegetarian.
    c. herding domesticated animals.
    d. scavenging.

26. Neandertals appear to have been prone to serious injury. Why?
    a. They only had thrusting spears and had to get close to the dangerous animals they were hunting.
    b. They lived in areas with a lot of cliffs and appear to have fallen often.
    c. It appears they were raging war with each other and this is evidenced by the bone injuries on their remains.
    d. They were clumsy.

27. Neandertal hunting
    a. utilized bows and arrows.
    b. probably required close contact with their prey.
    c. was probably rare and generally successful.
    d. was learned by copying from early modern human hunters.

28. What advantage do many researchers believe modern humans had over Neandertals?
    a. an expanded ability to symbolize and communicate
    b. an expanded ability to organize social activities
    c. more elaborate technology
    d. All of these have been suggested.

29. Which of the following statements is true regarding the replacement of Neandertals by modern humans?
    a. Direct anatomic evidence suggests that the Neandertal vocal track hampered them in verbal communication.
    b. Direct anatomic evidence indicates that the Neandertal brain organization was more like a chimpanzee.
    c. Direct anatomic evidence does not provide any conclusive evidence.
    d. Both a and b are true.

30. Deliberate burial of the dead
    a. was characteristic of Neandertals.
    b. is first observed in the archaeological record among *Homo erectus*.
    c. is only a modern behavior.
    d. was infrequent among European Neandertals.

31. Recent analysis of the entire Neandertal genome suggests that

    a. Neandertals should be viewed as a subspecies of *Homo sapiens, viz., H. sapiens neanderthalensis.*

    (b.) Neandertals and modern lineages separated between 440,000 and 270,000 years ago.

    c. Neandertals and modern humans did not interbreed.

    d. they were unable to make any conclusions because of contamination from saber-toothed cat mtDNA.

32. Which of the following statements applies to Neandertals?

    a. They can be viewed as a side branch of later hominin evolution.

    b. They are our ancestors.

    c. There is good evidence that they interbred with modern humans.

    (d.) Both a and c are true.

33. Neandertals can be interpreted as a(n)

    a. atavism.

    (b.) incipient species.

    c. anachronism.

    d. cryptic species.

34. Why is Neandertal DNA evidence important to human evolutionary studies?

    a. The place of Neandertals in human evolution has been and continues to be a topic of contention.

    b. It is of interest to researchers to know if Neandertal DNA can shed light on whether this hominin was a separate species or not.

    c. Being able to compare Neandertal DNA with the first modern *Homo sapiens* would be enlightening as to whether Neandertals and early moderns were distinct.

    (d.) It is important for all of the above reasons.

Short-Answer Questions

1. Describe the anatomy of Middle Pleistocene premodern humans.

had some chara. relating to Homo erectus. W/ large facial structures. They ~~robust to~~ have robust traits such as thick bones. But they share a larger brain and skull shape W/ modern humans.

2. What is the place of *Homo heidelbergensis* in hominin evolution?

They are known as a transitional phase between Homo erectus and AMH. They are found in both Europe & Africa. They also show both M. Human and Neanderantal traits.

3. Compare and contrast premoderns in Africa and Europe. What did each lead to?

African speciamen Retain a Prominant occipital torus and externly large supraorbital torus. While in Europe they have a larger cranial cap. and reduced tooth size, they aulso have a rounded occipital region.

4. Describe the anatomy of a classic Neandertal.

They have a large Cranium Capacity. They also have a Projecting Face, and elongated occipital region. Though there foreheads are more like M. Humans in the way that they rise.

5. What is significant about the Chatelperronian stone tool culture?

It shows interaction with M. Humans. Originally it was much less advanced w/ teck. being based on flaking. But w/ Contact came advance. such as the advent of blades.

Application Questions

1. Neandertals are often depicted as stupid, brutish, and not capable of walking in a fully upright position. Discuss the evidence that none of these depictions is accurate.

This insight is based on a paticular speciman who was actually quite old (40ish) he suffered a spinal problem and is more robust than others found.

2. Does Shanidar I represent an example of Neandertal compassion for the disabled?

Yes, in the Cave 9 skeletons were found, of those 9 one was found w/ many disabilites, such as a limb, brain damage and a usless arm, yet he was about 30-40. he would have needed help.

3. Could Neandertals speak? Explain your conclusion using examples from your reading.

There is no Conclusive evidence for this. In Modern Humans speech is determined by the soft tessiues and it is impossible to know if this in the fossil record. But by looking at placements of hard tissues + fixation of the Brain

4. Why is the extraction and sequencing of mtDNA from Neandertal fossils so significant?

Because it helps to place where they it seem are in the human Evo. flow likely Chart. Weather or Nalhay interacted W/ M. Humans. and where they Migrated from.

5. Discuss the taxonomic philosophies of "splitting" and "lumping" in the context of premodern humans and Neandertals. Splitters' like to break things done not only for physical / genitic difference, but also for culture. Where as 'lumpers' try to condense Species and base it only on Physical/genetic differences.

Answer Key

Matching I

1. j (objectives 5 & 6)
2. i (objective 6)
3. g (video lesson, segment 1; objective 1)
4. d (video lesson, segment 1; objective 1)
5. f (video lesson, segment 1; objective 1)
6. h (objective 3)
7. b (video lesson, segment 1; objective 1)
8. c (video lesson, segment 1; objectives 5 & 6)
9. e (video lesson, segment 1; objectives 4 & 5)
10. a (objective 1)
11. k (video lesson, segment 1; objective 6)

Matching II

1. f (objective 1)
2. c (objective 1)
3. g (objective 1)
4. h (objective 1)
5. d (objective 5)
6. i (objective 3)
7. b (objective 1)
8. e (objective 5)
9. a (objective 3)

Completion I

1. premodern humans (objective 1)
2. Middle Pleistocene (video lesson, segment 1; objective 1)
3. Late Pleistocene (video lesson, segment 1; objective 1)
4. glaciations (video lesson, segment 1; objective 1)

LESSON 11: PREMODERN HUMANS   297

5. interglacials (video lesson, segment 1; objective 1)
6. *Homo heidelbergensis* (objective 1)
7. Kabwe (objectives 1 & 2)
8. Bodo (objective 1)
9. Atapuerca (objectives 1 & 2)
10. Steinheim (objective 1)
11. Jinniushan (objective 1)

Completion II

1. Levallois technique (objective 3)
2. Terra Amata (objective 3)
3. Schöningen (objective 3)
4. Neandertals (video lesson, segment 1; objective 5)
5. classic Neandertals (objective 4)
6. La Chapelle-aux-Saints (objective 5)
7. flexed (objective 6)
8. Upper Paleolithic (video lesson, segment 1; objective 6)
9. Chatelperronian (objective 6)
10. Tabun (objective 5)
11. Mousterian (video lesson, segment 1; objective 6)

Self-Test

1. b. is the correct answer. During an ice age, water is held in ice on the land. Consequently, as water becomes glaciers there is less in the oceans and sea level drops. (video lesson, segment 1; objective 1)
2. d. is the correct answer. *Homo heidelbergensis* appears around 600,000 years ago. This species appears to be the ancestor of the other premodern human, the Neandertals. (objective 1)
3. c. is the correct answer. *Homo erectus* is the previous hominin in terms of appearance. It should be pointed out that *H. erectus* populations continue to be present in the world during the Middle Pleistocene. (video lesson, segment 1; objective 1)
4. a. is the correct answer. The premodern humans retain the large browridges, but they differ from the condition in *H. erectus* in that the browridges are arched and not the straight bar that *H. erectus* possessed. (objective 1)
5. b. is the correct answer. Molar size does not increase in premodern humans. In fact, molar size decreases in *H. heidelbergensis*. (objective 1)
6. b. is the correct answer. *Homo heidelbergensis* was an intermediate form between *H. erectus* and modern *H. sapiens*. (objective 1)

7. c. is the correct answer. Kabwe was not found in association with any tools, it has a projecting face, and its foramen magnum is not intact, but it does have a modern cranial base. (objectives 1 & 2)

8. d. is the correct answer. Bodo is definitely the earliest evidence of *H. heidelbergensis* in Africa. (objective 1)

9. a. is the correct answer. More than 4,000 fossil fragments have been recovered from Atapuerca, and at least 28 individuals have been identified. (objective 1)

10. c. is the correct answer. The presence of these traits in the modern Chinese populations has led Chinese paleoanthropologists to hypothesize that they are directly descended from those populations that occupied China in the Middle Pleistocene. This fits with the multiregional evolution model of human evolution. (objective 1)

11. b. is the correct answer. While the African and European *Homo heidelbergensis* resemble one another, those from Asia are different. (objective 2)

12. b. is the correct answer. The appearance of a new species was not accompanied by the appearance of a new tool industry. (objective 3)

13. d. is the correct answer. The different traditions may represent different groups of people who made them. However, it has been noted that modern hunters and gatherers make tools depending on the season, the type of animals they might be hunting, or the area that they migrate to. (objective 3)

14. c. is the correct answer. The classic Neandertals, the first discovered by paleontologists, are found mainly in Europe. Those found elsewhere are sometimes referred to as "progressives." (objective 5)

15. c. is the correct answer. Neandertals have an occipital bone that is "bunned." An angled occipital is found in *H. erectus*. (objective 4)

16. b. is the correct answer. The average cranial capacity of Neandertals is 1,520 cm³, whereas that of modern humans is 1,340 cm³. (objective 4)

17. d. is the correct answer. This Neandertal was also in a flexed position. (objectives 4 & 5)

18. c. is the correct answer. This skeleton was found in 1908 in southwestern France. (objective 5)

19. d. is the correct answer. The St. Césaire Neandertals were among the last Neandertals and had an Upper Paleolithic tool culture. (objective 5)

20. c. is the correct answer. Vindija is a central European site dating between 42,000 and 32,000 years ago. (objective 5)

21. c. is the correct answer. The tongue (a muscle) originates from the hyoid. The size and shape can give us an idea about the capability of the tongue attached to it (and its potential for language). (objective 5)

22. d. is the correct answer. Teshik Tash is in Central Asia and, if this is indeed a Neandertal site, it expands the range of Neandertals to around 4,000 miles. (objective 5)

23. c. is the correct answer. This implies that Neandertals had compassion. (objective 5)

24. b. is the correct answer. The Mousterian is an advancement over the Acheulian. (video lesson, segment 1; objective 6)

25. a. is the correct answer. There is a great deal of evidence that indicates Neandertals were a hunting and gathering people. (video lesson, segment 2; objective 6)

26. a. is the correct answer. Based on injuries sustained by rodeo riders, it appears that fractures found on Neandertal skeletons were caused by animals. (objective 6)

27. b. is the correct answer. It appears that Neandertals only had thrusting spears, which means they had to get very close to some very dangerous animals. (objective 6)

28. d. is the correct answer. It is believed that the modern behavioral repertoire gave modern humans a competitive edge over the Neandertals. (objective 6)

29. c. is the correct answer. There is no conclusive evidence as to why modern humans replaced Neandertals. (objective 6)

30. a. is the correct answer. Burials are a common practice of the Neandertals. (video lesson, segment 2; objective 6)

31. b. is the correct answer. The ability to sequence the entire Neandertal genome has provided evidence for a much more recent separation between moderns and Neandertals, somewhere between 440,000 and 270,000 years ago. The former date of 800,000 years ago was as less complete analysis, based largely on mtDNA evidence. (objective 7)

32. d. is the correct answer. There is still a great deal of contention regarding the place of Neandertals in human evolution, but they do appear to have been a side branch. With new molecular evidence, we can now say with some certainty that they did interbreed with modern humans. (objective 7)

33. b. is the correct answer. While some researchers believe that Neandertals should be interpreted as a separate species, there is no way to know this for certain. However, they were evolving in their own direction which makes it legitimate to refer to them as an incipient species. (objective 7)

34. d. is the correct answer. All of these reasons are important to answering questions about the Neandertals. (objective 7)

Short-Answer Questions

Your answers should include the following:

1. The earliest premodern humans retain some *Homo erectus* features: large browridges, a receding forehead, and a large face. Often the cranial bones are still thick. However, premodern humans also share derived traits with modern humans: relatively larger brain, more rounded braincase, and more vertical nose. The back of the skull of premodern humans has a shallower angle than that of *Homo erectus*, and the maximum width of the braincase is above the ear hole (auditory canal). (objective 1)

2. *Homo heidelbergensis* is found in Africa and Europe. It occupies a place between *Homo erectus* and modern humans (*Homo sapiens*) and is often referred to as a transitional or even archaic *H. sapiens*. Early *H. heidelbergensis* in Spain shows

© 2012 Cengage Learning. All Rights Reserved. May not be scanned, copied or duplicated, or posted to a publicly accessible website, in whole or in part.

some Neandertal-like morphology. It is very likely that *H. heidelbergensis* is the ancestor to both modern humans and Neandertals. There is some dispute whether *H. heidelbergensis* is represented at Asian sites. Although Chinese paleoanthropologists consider Middle Pleistocene fossils from Jinniushan and Dali to be early representatives of modern humans, other researchers believe that these fossils represent a regional variant of *H. heidelbergensis*. (objective 2)

3. The earliest premodern humans of both Europe and Africa retain a number of *Homo erectus* features including large browridges, a receding forehead, often thick cranial bones, and a large face. The African specimens retain a prominent occipital torus. Bodo is an African cranium recovered from Ethiopia, *c.* 600,000 years ago. It is the earliest representative of *Homo heidelbergensis* in Africa, and possibly the world. The age of the Kabwe cranium from Zambia is not well determined, but it is believed to be younger than Bodo. It has an extremely massive supraorbital torus, that arches over the orbits rather than the straight bar in *H. erectus*. The similarities in the African specimens indicate a single species. European premoderns are very similar. Like the African specimens they retain some *H. erectus* traits. However, they also have derived traits. These derived traits include increased cranial capacity, a more rounded occipital region, parietal expansion, and reduced tooth size. Current views are that the African *H. heidelbergensis* led to modern humans, while the Middle Pleistocene *H. heidelbergensis* of Europe led to the Neandertals. Indeed, fossils from Atapuerca, Spain, show early Neandertal morphology. (objective 2)

4. Classic Neandertals were found in Europe. Some of the traits observed in *Homo heidelbergensis* are further elaborated in Neandertals. The cranium is large, long, low, and bulging at the sides enabling it to accommodate the larger Neandertal brain. The occipital region is elongated (called an "occipital bun" in reference to the way Victorian women wore their hair). The forehead is more vertical than the forehead of *Homo erectus*, but not the rising forehead of modern humans. Two separate browridges arch over each orbit. Neandertals have a projecting face. The postcranial skeleton is robust with shorter limbs than other hominins (possibly an adaptation to a cold environment). (objective 4)

5. Neandertals are usually associated with a tool industry called the Mousterian, which is less advanced than the tool cultures that are developed by moderns in the Upper Paleolithic but more advanced than the previous Acheulian tool industry. Mousterian tool industry is characterized by a larger proportion of flakes than Acheulian. However, Neandertals and anatomically modern humans came into contact with one another in Europe around 35,000 years ago. The Neandertal Chatelperronian stone tool culture reflects the influence of this contact. Many of the Chatelperronian tools are blades that are not found in Mousterian cultures and are most likely modifications based on borrowing from tools of modern human design. (objective 6)

Application Questions

Your answers should include the following:

1. The stereotype of Neandertals as a slouched-over, dim-witted caveman comes mainly from a reconstruction of the La Chapelle-aux-Saints "old man" by French paleontologist Marcellin Boulé. This specimen suffered from osteoarthritis of the spine, was around 40 years of age (extremely old for a Late Pleistocene human), and was particularly robust. Boulé did not consider the Neandertals to be human because they differed from the norm for a modern human. Today the "old man of La Chapelle" is not even considered to be typical of Neandertals. (objectives 4 & 5)

2. Shanidar is a cave site in northeastern Iraq. Nine skeletons were found here. One of the skeletons, cataloged as Shanidar 1, is an older male (somewhere between 30 and 45 years old) showing evidence of a number of debilitating injuries. His right arm was injured long before death and had withered. He also had suffered a blow to the side of the head that fractured the orbit, probably causing blindness in that eye. He also had endured injuries to his legs and probably walked with a limp. Because the life of a hunter-gatherer is strenuous and requires being able to move quickly, to be able to have full use of both arms in attempting to spear a large mammal, and to be able to perceive depth (which requires the use of both eyes), it is difficult to see how this individual survived without support. The two researchers who have studied these remains most thoroughly suggest that other members of his band must have cared for him. If this is the case, then the Shanidar Neandertals show evidence for possessing compassion. (objective 6)

3. This is not a question that can be answered definitively. Modern human speech is largely enabled by soft tissue anatomy of the brain and the vocal tract. We do have endocasts of fossil brains and can identify areas such as the motor speech area (Broca's area). However, this is incomplete information and subject to varying interpretations. One approach to reconstructing the ancestral vocal tract is by looking at the hard tissues near it. In modern humans the larynx is located low in the throat. One way to determine the placement of the larynx in the throat is by the degree of flexion of the cranial base. Thus, the degree of flexure at the cranial base has been compared between modern humans and fossil hominins. Cranial base flexure like modern humans is not present in fossil hominins until *Homo heidelbergensis* so Neandertals would have met this condition. Another approach is to look at the hyoid, the bone to which the tongue attaches. Hyoid bones are rarely recovered. An australopithecine hyoid is known and it resembles the bone found in chimpanzees rather than in humans. A Neandertal hyoid recovered from Kebara is indistinguishable from a modern hyoid, suggesting that Neandertals had the potential for speech.

   In summary, several of the anatomic features found in modern humans are present in Neandertals. This suggests that they had the potential for spoken language. However, this does not mean they spoke a language comparable to modern language. (objective 6)

4. The position of Neandertals in human evolution has been contested ever since they were first recognized 150 years ago. Over the years Neandertals have alternated between being our immediate ancestors and being another species of humans altogether. The question could not be settled by analysis of skeletal evidence alone because physical features are profoundly influenced by environment and do not accurately disclose phylogenetic relationships. Since Neandertal fossils are relatively young, it is possible to extract both nuclear and mitochondrial DNA from some of them and use this information to determine evolutionary distances between Neandertals and both early and modern *H. sapiens*. Using mtDNA extracted from more than twelve Neandertal fossils, scientists discovered that Neandertal mtDNA is somewhat distinct from both modern humans and the early modern *H. sapiens* populations in Europe. In 2010, scientists from the Max Planck Institute announced they had succeeded in mapping the entire Neandertal genome using nuclear DNA from three individuals from Vindija, Croatia. They compared the Neandertal genome with the genomes of five modern individuals (from Africa, China, France, and New Guinea) and learned that the individuals from China, France, and New Guinea all retained Neandertal genes, while the African individuals did not. From this data it is hypothesized that modern *H. sapiens* migrants from Africa may have interbred with Neandertals in the Middle East sometime between 80,000 and 50,000 years ago. (video lesson, segment 3; objective 7)

5. Taxonomists can often be placed into two camps. A lumping philosophy occurs when a paleoanthropologist condenses, or "lumps," a larger number of species into a smaller group, perhaps only one species. A splitter, by contrast, believes that any anatomic difference could be grounds for specifying a new species. For an extreme splitter (not necessarily in human paleontology, but in evolutionary studies in general), any new discovery is potentially a new species.

    Lumpers have often dominated Middle Pleistocene taxonomy. Fossils from this time period are often lumped into a non-taxonomic group referred to as "transitions." This refers to the fact that these specimens are in between *Homo erectus* and *Homo sapiens*. Another lumping approach is to refer to the non-*Homo erectus* (which is living at this time also) Middle Pleistocene specimens to "archaic *Homo sapiens*." Often lumpers consider Neandertals to be a subspecies of *H. sapiens*.

    Splitters consider at least three, sometimes more, species of hominins during the Middle Pleistocene. The three species usually recognized include *Homo heidelbergensis*, *Homo sapiens*, and *Homo neanderthalensis*. Some splitters further divide *H. heidelbergensis* into *H. rhodesiensis*, *H. helmei*, *H. florisbadensis*.

    The approach of these different taxonomic philosophies regarding the Neandertals is for lumpers to consider them as *Homo sapiens* or as a subspecies, *Homo sapiens neanderthalensis*. Splitters divide the contemporary Late Pleistocene humans into two species, *H. sapiens* and *H. neanderthalensis*. (objectives 2 & 7)

Lesson Review

Lesson 11: Premodern Humans

PLEASE NOTE: Use this matrix to guide your study and achieve the learning objectives of this lesson. It will also help you to view the video, which defines and demonstrates important concepts and principles as they relate to everyday life and actual case studies.

Learning Objective	Textbook	Student Guide	Video Lesson
1. Discuss the most important physical characteristics, the major sites, and the time range of early premodern *Homo sapiens*.	pp. 368–377	Key Terms: 1, 2, 3, 4; Matching I: 3, 4, 5, 7, 10; Matching II: 1, 2, 3, 4, 7; Completion I: 1, 2, 3, 4, 5, 6, 7, 8, 9, 10, 11; Self-Test: 1, 2, 3, 4, 5, 6, 7, 8, 9, 10; Short-Answer: 1.	Segment 1: *Age of the Caveman*
2. Contrast the evolutionary development of premodern *Homo sapiens* in Africa, Asia, and Europe, emphasizing the evidence that Neandertals evolved in Europe.	pp. 369–377	Completion I: 7, 9; Self-Test: 7, 11; Short-Answer: 2, 3; Application: 5.	
3. Discuss key cultural innovations during the Middle Pleistocene, emphasizing advances in tool technologies and possible hunting activities.	pp. 377–378	Matching I: 6; Matching II: 6, 9; Completion II: 1, 2, 3; Self-Test: 12, 13.	
4. Describe the distinctive features of Neandertals.	pp. 378–380	Key Terms: 5; Matching I: 9; Completion II: 5; Self-Test: 15, 16, 17; Short-Answer: 4; Application: 1.	Segment 1: *Age of the Caveman*

Learning Objective	Textbook	Student Guide	Video Lesson
5. Describe the temporal and geographic distribution of the Neandertals.	pp. 380–387	Key Terms: 5, 8, 9; Matching I: 1, 8, 9; Matching II: 5, 8; Completion II: 4, 6, 10; Self-Test: 14, 17, 18, 19, 20, 21, 22, 23; Application: 1.	Segment 1: *Age of the Caveman*
6. Discuss the culture of Neandertals, including their technology, settlement patterns, subsistence behaviors, and symbolic behaviors.	pp. 387–392	Key Terms: 6, 7, 8, 9; Matching I: 1, 2, 8, 11; Completion II: 7, 8, 9, 11; Self-Test: 24, 25, 26, 27, 28, 29, 30; Short-Answer: 5; Application: 2, 3.	Segment 1: *Age of the Caveman* Segment 2: *Clan of the Caveman*
7. Use the Neandertals to illustrate the problems anthropologists have encountered in attempting to distinguish the different species among the various extinct hominins.	pp. 392–401	Self-Test: 31, 32, 33, 34; Application: 4, 5.	Segment 3: *Death of the Caveman*

LESSON 12

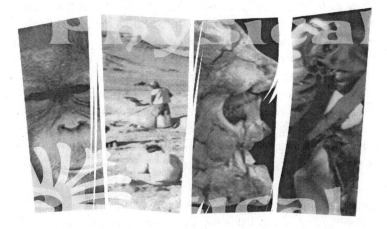

LESSON

12

Origin & Dispersal of Modern Humans

Checklist

For the most effective study of this lesson, complete the following activities in this sequence.

Before Viewing the Video

❏ Read the Preview, Learning Objectives, and Viewing Notes below.

❏ Read Chapter 14, "The Origin and Dispersal of Modern Humans," pages 402–431, in *Introduction to Physical Anthropology*.

What to Watch

❏ After reading the textbook assignment, watch the video for Lesson 12, *Origin & Dispersal of Modern Humans*.

After Viewing the Video

❏ Briefly note your answers to the questions listed at the end of the Viewing Notes.

❏ Review the Summary below.

❏ Review all reading assignments for this lesson, including the Viewing Notes in this lesson.

❏ Write brief answers to the "Critical Thinking Questions" at the end of Chapter 14 in the textbook.

❏ Complete the Review Exercises below. Check your answers with the Answer Key and review when necessary.

❏ Use the Lesson Review matrix found at the end of this lesson to review and assess your knowledge of each Learning Objective.

Preview

You have learned that the Pleistocene epoch saw the human species evolve from our very early ancestors to modern *H. sapiens*. Within approximately 150,000 years, our ancestors inhabited much of the Old World, expanding as far as Australia. Lesson 12 examines the questions that still puzzle experts today. Where did modern *H. sapiens* originate, and how did they disperse to other geographical locations around the world? What happened to the other populations that our species encountered? This lesson explores several different models that have been proposed to explain this dispersal. One theorizes that all modern humans arose in Africa, migrated out of Africa, and replaced populations of Europe and Asia. Another theorizes that local populations in Africa, Europe, and Asia existed and evolved simultaneously in those regions. Yet another is a combination of the two, that modern humans originated in Africa, migrated out to areas of the Old World, and that some interbreeding occurred with local populations. Each model gains support from fossil discoveries and genetic theory advances, and the Jurmain textbook details the debates linked to all three hypotheses.

Lesson 11 concentrated on the evolution of premodern humans during the Lower and Middle Pleistocene. This lesson focuses on the archaeological evidence of the Upper Pleistocene, when technological advances, in a sense, exploded. This is the period when modern humans arose and quickly came to dominate the planet.

Concepts to Remember

- ❊ Lesson 3 explained cell function, which is instrumental in understanding genetic and evolutionary principles. Each cell contains a variety of structures called **organelles**. Each organelle performs a specific function. The **mitochondria** is an organelle that converts energy into a form that is used by the cell. Mitochondria contain their own distinct DNA. In recent years, **mitochondrial DNA** has attracted much attention, in part because of its significance in studies for certain evolutionary processes. The video for this lesson further details the significance of mitochondrial DNA.

- ❊ Recall that expansion of the brain presumably enabled *Homo sapiens* to develop ever more sophisticated tool kits. Lesson 10 discussed the **Acheulian** tool industry characterized by bifacial stones flaked on both sides which dominated the Lower Paleolithic.

- ❊ Lesson 11 discussed the **Mousterian** tool industry, which pertains to the Middle Paleolithic and is associated with Neandertals and some modern *H. sapien* groups. The Paleolithic cultural period discussed in this lesson is concerned with the Upper Paleolithic and extends roughly between 40,000 and 10,000 years ago. The term "Paleolithic" means "Old Age of the Stone" from the Greek words *paleos* (old) and *lithos* (stone). The workmanship exhibits tools with flakes in more forms, such as scrapers, points, and knives. This lesson explores the leaps in technology that took place during the Upper Paleolithic.

Learning Objectives

After completing this lesson, you should be able to:

1. Discuss the hypotheses regarding the appearance of anatomically modern *Homo sapiens*. (pp. 404–407)

2. Compare and contrast the skeletal differences between anatomically modern *H. sapiens* and premodern *H. sapiens*. (pp. 407–423)

3. Summarize the geographic distribution and dates of early fossil members of *H. sapiens*. (pp. 407–423)

4. Describe the climatic, technological, and subsistence changes evident in the Upper Paleolithic. (pp. 423–428)

5. Compare and contrast the cultural innovations during the late Pleistocene in Europe with those in Africa. (pp. 423–428)

6. Discuss the appearance and significance of "art" in Eurasia and Africa, especially with regard to cave paintings and their possible cultural significance. (pp. 423–428)

At this point, read Chapter 14, "The Origin and Dispersal of Modern Humans," pages 402–431.

Viewing Notes

Previous lessons have detailed some of the important advances that have been made in genetic research within the last 20 to 30 years, and how these advances have contributed to the knowledge of our evolutionary history. At one time, the common assumption was that Neandertals were no older than 80,000 years, and that modern humans evolved as recently as 40,000 years ago. The video explains that new DNA findings indicate that Neandertals and modern humans most likely existed much further back in time, are far older than previously thought, and very likely evolved from a common ancestor several hundred thousand years ago "as two separate branches of the human family tree."

The origins of this common ancestor causes considerable debate in paleoanthropology today. There are three hypotheses presented in the video that attempt to explain hominid dispersal out of Africa. The **complete replacement model** postulates that modern humans evolved in Africa, and then, from 40,000 to 60,000 years ago, migrated into other regions and replaced all other existing archaic hominids. According to Katerina Harvati, a paleoanthropologist interviewed in the video, there was little (if any) interbreeding among the archaic groups and this meant that modern humans coming out of Africa outcompeted the Neadertals in Europe, as well as other groups they encountered. A different theory, called the **regional continuity model**, is also referred to as the multiregional hypothesis of human evolution. It hypothesizes that premodern humans migrated out of Africa and a general evolution of all human populations then took place simultaneously in different regions. Gene flow also took place between the groups. A main difficulty with this model is that it does not allow for an expected divergence of these groups. The **partial replacement models** provide various alternative perspectives on human dispersal. They also suggest that modern humans originated in Africa and, when their populations increased, they expanded out of Africa into various regions of the Old World and some interbreeding took place between the emigrating African groups and premodern populations they encountered elsewhere. This is considered a middle ground between the first two theories.

The video states that some genetic studies focus on the DNA found in the mitochondria of the cell. Mitochondrial DNA (mtDNA) is genetic material that is inherited solely from our mothers, and this is where the name, "mitochondrial Eve," comes from. The premise is that all humans today can be traced back to a mitochondrial ancestor in Africa between 100,000 and 200,000 years ago. This does not mean there was only one ancestor. As paleoanthropologist Katerina Harvati states in the video, "If we take all the modern people living today and look at the mitochondria being made, we can reconstruct all the lineages and eventually they come to an African lineage we date to between 200,000 and 100,000 years before now. So, this is the mitochondrial Eve." The video is careful to point out that because mitochondrial DNA contains around 16,000 base pairs, and nuclear DNA contains around 3 billion, and contains most of the material that makes humans the way they are, most of the research today is on nuclear DNA. For example, research is being conducted on large piece of a recently recovered chunk of Neandertal remains that could provide a complete genetic blueprint of this interesting ancestor.

Mitochondria are organelles considered separate from the cell because they have their own DNA, which is unaffected by other genetic exchanges. As you learned in Lesson 3, an offspring is the genetic mix of his or her parents, who in turn are genetic mixes of their own parents, and so on. But mitochondrial DNA, through the generations, is not altered in the offspring. It remains intact through the female line. Mitochondrial DNA can be altered by natural mutation, but the rate is so slow that it can still be used to effectively trace this genetic heritage. Mitochondrial DNA from African populations was compared to European populations, and the mutation difference between the two populations was calculated to establish a timescale which indicates when the ancestors of modern Europeans first left Africa. But researchers also took genetic samples from people around the world. The mitochondrial DNA compared suggest that all living humans contain genetic material from a single woman who was living in Africa perhaps 200,000 years ago. Note that this does not mean that one woman populated the whole planet. It suggests instead that members of the lineage of this particular woman contained specific advantages to survive over the rest of the population. It also suggests a genetic bottleneck, an evolutionary event in which a large proportion of the population dies or is unable to reproduce; those who survive (the descendants of "mitochondrial Eve") pass on their genetic heritage. The theory of mitochondrial Eve would support a complete replacement model.

The oldest fossils of our species were found in Omo Kibish in southern Ethiopia and date back to 195,000 years ago. Omo I refers to a fragmentary skull found at this site. Africa is a vast continent, however, and archaeological exploration is still in the early stages of researching the origins of *H. sapiens*. A strategy to track the origin and dispersal of *H. sapiens* is to explore other regions in Africa (and around the globe) and compare the fossils found to those at Omo Kibish. What is certain, according to the video, is that as early humans evolved, so too did their culture and capabilities, allowing them to expand their territories and adapt to a variety of environmental challenges. Stone tools have always provided hints on the activities of our ancestors. Scientists today can lift plant and animal residue from the surface of tools, which offers information on what the tools could have been used for.

Differences in the way humans crafted their tools during the Upper Paleolithic in Europe have been classified into five different industries. Artifacts from the **Magdalenian** period, from 17,000 years ago, show craft specialization. During the Middle Paleolithic, the tools were simplistic enough for anyone to create, but in the Magdalenian period, the more specialized tool-making most likely required instruction from an expert. That is not to say that each society had a craft specialist. As paleoanthropologist John Shea points out in the video, having craft specialists is not particularly feasible in a hunter-gatherer society where the groups are necessarily small and where the loss of such specialists would be immediately felt. More likely, the group ensured that everyone had a basic knowledge of essential skills, but some people may have spent more time honing a particular skill or talent.

There is also evidence during this period of what we might classify as art—drawings, carvings, and decorations. The items clearly go beyond a purely functional use, but it is not clear that they simply fall under a modern definition of art for aesthetic expression and pleasure. Perhaps this art was used for signaling, a principle in which humans and other organisms signal to potential reproductive partners or social allies by putting more effort into a task than is necessary. Cave paintings may have been a method of communication, both between humans and between our world and the spiritual world.

As Shea says, this art is "a very important development because it tells us that humans are constructing their identities in social ways, in ways that we are quite familiar with from the record of recent human behavior."

Questions to Consider

✻ What research in the video supports the complete replacement model? The regional continuity model? The partial replacement models?

✻ According to John Shea in the video, what is the significance of the fossil finds at Omo I?

✻ What characteristics mark the facial morphology transition as *Homo sapiens* evolved from premodern to modern forms?

Watch the video for Lesson 12, *Origin & Dispersal of Modern Humans*.

Segment 1: *The Hominin Hypotheses*
Segment 2: *Who's On First?*
Segment 3: *Hi-Tech, Fine Art & the Modern Human*

Key Terms and Concepts

Page references are keyed to *Introduction to Physical Anthropology*, 13th edition.

1. **Cro-Magnon:** (crow-man´-yon) A site in southern France where fossil remains of anatomically modern humans were excavated that have been dated to 30,000 years ago. (p. 417; objective 3)

2. **Aurignacian:** Pertaining to an Upper Paleolithic stone tool industry in Europe beginning at about 40,000 years ago. (p. 417; objective 4)

3. **Magdalenian:** Pertaining to the final phase of the Upper Paleolithic stone tool industry in Europe. (p. 425; video lesson, segment 3; objective 4)

4. **burins:** Small, chisel-like tools with a pointed end; thought to have been used to engrave bone, antler, ivory, or wood. (p. 425; video lesson, segment 3; objective 4)

5. **complete replacement model:** A hypothesis that modern humans came "out of Africa" and replaced previous human populations throughout Asia and Europe. (video lesson, segment 1; objective 1)

6. **partial replacement models:** Hypotheses proposed by several researchers that state that modern humans came "out of Africa," but they interbred with previous human populations that lived in Asia and Europe. (video lesson, segment 1; objective 1)

7. **regional continuity model:** A hypothesis that humans left Africa more than one million years ago and those migrants to Asia and Europe evolved in place. Gene flow between groups prevented speciation from occurring and all premodern humans should be considered *Homo sapiens*. (video lesson, segment 1; objective 1)

Summary

Approximately 200,000 years ago, the first modern *Homo sapiens* evolved in Africa. Then, 50,000 years later, they were traversing across the Old World.

There are two major hypotheses that explain modern human origins: the complete replacement model and the regional continuity model. The **complete replacement model** suggests that anatomically modern populations arose in Africa, then migrated to Europe and Asia, and replaced populations there. This model proposes that the transition from premodern form to modern *H. sapiens* occurred only in Africa; the populations in other locales would therefore be different species of *Homo* with no interbreeding possible between them. For instance, Neandertals would be classified as *H. neanderthalensis*. According to the Jurmain textbook on page 406, "This speciation explanation fits nicely with, and in fact helps explain, *complete replacement*." Advances in molecular techniques have expanded opportunities to investigate genetic patterning of humans. New data that has come from studying mitochondrial DNA (mtDNA) and the Y chromosome, neither of which is significantly recombined during sexual reproduction, has shown that indigenous African populations show a far greater diversity than populations from elsewhere in the world. Therefore, this data strongly supports an African origin for modern humans. But the recent discovery that modern humans from Europe and Asia (and not those from Africa) have some Neandertal DNA is evidence that while modern humans originated in Africa, some interbreeding did take place between modern humans and Neandertals outside of Africa. This new evidence favors the **partial replacement model**. The **regional continuity model** puts forth the idea that local populations in Europe, Asia, and Africa continued their indigenous evolutionary development from premodern Middle Pleistocene forms to anatomically modern humans (See pages 404–405 in the Jurmain textbook). It suggests that anatomically modern humans arose separately in different continents and ended up very similar both physically and genetically to one another. It supports this view by denying that the earliest modern *H. sapiens* populations originated *exclusively* in Africa and challenges the notion of complete replacement. It also asserts that some interbreeding occurred between the African populations and others elsewhere. Through gene flow and natural selection, populations would not have evolved totally independently and speciation would have been prevented. Therefore, this theory assumes that all hominins from *H. erectus* through modern humans should be considered members of the *H. sapiens* species.

In face of the new evidence of recent years, paleontologists are turning away from the regional continuity model. Instead, they believe that the research points to one or more major migrations from Africa, which dispersed that population worldwide, and that there was some interbreeding between the African migrants and the local populations. Regardless of whether they did or did not interbreed, the general consensus is that the point of origin for modern humans is Africa.

The Jurmain textbook discusses some of the geographical areas that have offered important fossil evidence in regards to human dispersal. The earliest of these specimens come from Omo Kibish, mentioned in this lesson's video, in southern Ethiopia. With the use of sophisticated argon radiometric dating ($^{40}Ar/^{39}Ar$), paleoanthropologists have demonstrated that this material may be the earliest modern human yet found in Africa, at 195,000 years old. However, the findings are questioned by others. But more recent finds in Ethiopia (known as the Herto remains) were subject to radiometric dating, which placed the remains between 160,000 and 154,000 years ago. Currently, these are the best-dated hominin fossils from this time period anywhere in the world, and their morphology strongly points to their relationship to modern humans. Interestingly, the Herto fossils are the most conclusive evidence yet supporting an African origin of modern humans.

The Tianyuan Cave skeletal material, dated at 40,000 years ago, shows mostly modern features, but with a few archaic characteristics as well. This has been interpreted to confirm the African origins hypothesis while also suggesting interbreeding with resident premodern populations. Similarly, in Portugal, a recently discovered child's skeleton, the Lagar Velho child, exhibits features of both modern humans and Neandertals. Some paleoanthropologists argue that this too is evidence for the partial replacement model. As outlined in the Jurmain textbook, new discoveries and research offer ever more compelling clues to the debate on how, when and to where humans dispersed around the globe. The chart on page 420 of the Jurmain textbook illustrates the discoveries of early modern *H. sapiens* from Europe and Asia. The textbook authors are also careful to note that the proponents of each dispersal model are not dogmatic regarding their views because new evidence, found unexpectedly, can change the course of the debate in favor of one model over the other. While new genetic techniques offer us the ability to examine the question of human origins through study of genetic patterning, the samples are small in number and interpretation is complex. At this point in time, data supports some form of the partial replacement model, but we have a long way to go to understand how it may have played out geographically and through time.

The examination of archaeological evidence allows scientists to better understand the technological and social developments that occurred as modern humans dispersed during the Upper Paleolithic, approximately 40,000 years ago. The Upper Paleolithic, according to Figure 14-16 on page 423 of the Jurmain textbook, is divided into five cultural periods (the approximate beginning dates are in parentheses): Chatelperronian and Aurignacian (40,000), Gravettian (27,000), Solutrean (21,000) and Magdalenian (17,000). A warming trend after the last glacial period, about 30,000 years ago, led to several thousand years of partially melted glacial ice, which provided the ideal environment for the growth of vegetation. These areas served as huge pastures for herbivorous animals, and carnivorous animals fed off the herbivores. The Jurmain textbook describes the region as a hunter's paradise. Humans exploited fish and fowl systematically for the first time. Upper Paleolithic people spread all over Europe, living in caves and open-air camps and building shelters. In Eurasia, cultural innovations allowed humans to occupy areas where the climate was less hospitable. Artifacts at sites, including bone needles, indicate that humans had learned to sew clothing.

Increasingly sophisticated technology aided the human adaptation to changing climates and environmental conditions. Interestingly, the textbook authors report that this period of the Late Pleistocene was probably one of the greatest challenges facing numerous mammals because they had to survive the threat of ever more dangerously equipped humans. Solutrean tools demonstrate skill and perhaps aesthetic appreciation as well. Some lance heads were expertly flaked on both surfaces, with delicate points; they most likely were never intended to serve utilitarian purposes. The later **Magadelenian** stage, the last stage of the Upper Paleolithic, saw further developments in tool-making. A spear-thrower, or atlatl, is a wooden piece that extended the hunter's arm and enabled him to throw the spear further. Harpoons aided in catching fish, and there is some evidence that a bow and arrow was used for the first time. Some scientists hypothesize that the development of such sophisticated tools limited the need for large front teeth in modern *H. sapiens*. Notably, modern *H. sapiens* have reduced dentition and facial features in comparison to earlier populations.

Western Europeans of the Upper Paleolithic are well known for their symbolic representation, or what we would refer to as "art." It is impossible for us to know if these early people truly created the symbols as artistic representations, or whether they served a more utilitarian function. One archaeologist refers to cave paintings and sculptures as "visual and material imagery," although for convenience, the Jurmain textbook refers to it as art. You may be most familiar with cave art, but there are also numerous examples of small sculptures excavated from sites around Europe, along with engravings on tools. Innovations in art came from the development of new methods of mixing pigments and more precise tools for carving and engravings. There have been many examples of small sculptures found. Perhaps the most famous of these are known as "Venuses," found at such sites as Brassempouy, France, and Grimaldi, Italy. Some were realistically carved, and the faces seem to be modeled on actual women. Other figurines have been found with sexual characteristics quite exaggerated and perhaps were used for fertility or other ritual purposes.

While nuclear DNA can provide much information about individuals, it is not very helpful in tracing evolutionary relationships. Most of this DNA is shuffled around during the process of meiosis. This has created the genetic diversity necessary for a species' survival. But mitochondrial DNA, or mtDNA, is another story. It is passed down from mother to child relatively intact through many generations.

However, mutations do occur over time, allowing scientists to trace and date evolutionary change by analyzing mtDNA. This analysis has revealed that all humans today descended from a single African woman who lived 143,000 years ago, "mitochondrial Eve." It's not that there was only a single female alive at that time, only that the lines of other females came to dead ends at one point or another.

A similar situation exists on the male side. Like mtDNA, the Y chromosome that exists only in males is not part of meiotic shuffling so it, too, remains relatively intact over many generations, except for time-based mutations. Analysis has revealed that we also descend from a single African male ancestor, "Y-chromosome Adam," whose Y chromosome is the only one to have "made the cut" over the millennia.

While our genetic Adam and Eve both lived in Africa, they did not know each other. Adam's Y chromosome dates to 59,000 year ago, making him 84,000 years younger than his female counterpart.

However, "Eve" dates to a time period that coincides with *Omo I*, discovered near the Omo River in southwestern Ethiopia, and the *Herto* remains, discovered in Ethiopia's Afar Triangle. As for Adam, the modern population that has the most ancient Y chromosomes is the *Khoisan Kung* peoples of sub-Saharan Africa. Both lend support to the complete replacement model.

The Y chromosome also lends some interesting support to people's history of themselves. One group is the African tribe called the *Lemba*, which claims Jewish ancestry and, indeed, practices a variety of rituals and dietary customs similar to those of the Jewish people. They also have Semitic sounding clan names.

Researchers compared the Y chromosome of the *Lemba* with samples from Sephardic Jews and Azhkenazi Jews, as well as to other *Bantu* groups, and an Arab group from Yemen. The results showed that one out of every ten *Lemba* shared a chromosomal type that appears to be a signature of a Jewish priesthood dating back to Moses' brother, Aaron, and one of the clans had an even higher frequency of individuals carrying this signature. The frequency is similar to that found in major Jewish populations.

Are the *Lemba* one of lost tribes of Israel? Only the Y chromosome knows for certain.

During the final phases of the Upper Paleolithic, particularly during the Magdalenian, that it seems that prehistoric art reaches a climax. Cave art is known from more than 150 separate sites, mostly in southwestern France. Other cultures in central Europe, China, and Africa also created sophisticated art work on rock faces in the open that have long since eroded. However, some peoples in western Europe chose to create images in deep caves, which was instrumental in preserving this art. Striking examples of cave art were discovered at the Grotte Chauvet and Lascaux in France, and also at Altamira in Spain. Some representations are typical Paleolithic subjects, such as bison, horses, and mammoths, but there are also images rarely seen, such as rhinos, lions, and bears.

Throughout the years, attempts have been made to interpret this ancient art. One of the early explanations links the paintings to hunting rituals. Other hypotheses view the art from a male/female perspective. Some view the stylized dots, such as those found in the Grotte Chauvet, as some kind of notational system associated with language. There is no single definitive interpretation of the meaning of these images.

Upper Paleolithic *Homo sapiens* displayed amazing development in culture and technology in a relatively short period of time. In Europe and central Africa particularly, innovations such as big game hunting, new weapons (such as harpoons and spear-throwing), body ornaments, needles, and sewn clothing was the culmination of a burst of creative development. Approximately 10,000 years ago, when temperatures slowly rose and glaciers retreated, animal and plant species were seriously affected, which, in turn, affected humans as well. As traditional prey animals were depleted, humans discovered others ways of obtaining food. Familiarity with plant propagation increased, followed by the domestication of plants and animals. Such domestication increased the need for permanent settlements, new technology, and more complex social organization. The following lessons will explore this next phase of human evolution in more detail.

Review Exercises

Matching I

Match each term with the appropriate definition or description.

1. _e_ atlatl
2. _b_ Aurignacian
3. _d_ burins
4. _h_ complete replacement model

5. _c_ Magdalenian
6. _g_ partial replacement models
7. _f_ regional continuity model
8. _a_ Venuses

a. A small female figurine.

b. The earliest Upper Paleolithic tool culture associated only with modern humans.

c. The latest Upper Paleolithic tool culture.

d. Small chisel-like tools.

e. A spear thrower.

f.   Hypothesis about human evolution that requires gene flow and considers all premodern humans to represent a single species.

g.   Hypotheses that humans evolved in Africa, migrated out, and interbred with some populations, while replacing others.

h.   The idea that modern humans evolved in Africa, migrated out, and replaced the earlier premodern humans of Asia and Europe.

Matching II

Match each term with the appropriate definition or description.

1. __k__ chin
2. __g__ Cro-Magnon
3. __b__ Herto remains
4. __f__ Kow Swamp
5. __j__ insular dwarfism
6. __i__ Lagar Velho child

7. __e__ Lake Mungo
8. __h__ "Little Lady of Flores"
9. __a__ Omo I
10. __d__ Qafzeh Cave
11. __c__ Skhul Cave

a.   A fragmentary skull with a chin, recovered in Ethiopia, and dated to 195,000 years ago.

b.   Includes a cranium with a cranial capacity of 1,450 cm^3.

c.   A site dated around 115,000 years ago that was contemporary with Neandertals.

d.   A cave in Israel dated to around 110,000 years ago.

e.   The oldest human site yet found in Australia.

f.   A modern human site in Australia dated between 14,000 and 9,000 years ago.

g.   A famous site from southern France that dates to around 30,000 years ago.

h.   A small skeleton that resembles *Homo erectus* from Dmanisi.

i.   A young child that appears to be a hybrid between moderns and Neandertals.

j.   Selection for small body size.

k.   Its presence means a mandible belongs to a modern human.

Completion I

Fill each blank with the most appropriate term from the list below.

complete replacement model   partial replacement models
mitochondrial DNA   regional continuity model
mitochondrial Eve

1.   The idea that modern humans originated in central Africa and migrated into Eurasia is called the _Complete Rep. Model_ of human origins.

2.   The model of modern human origins that posits that local Old World human populations evolved in the places that they are found today is called _regional Continuity Model_

3. The several different ideas of modern human origins that considers interbreeding with premodern humans to be a reality are grouped together as _Partial Rep. Model_.

4. Genetic material that is inherited only from our mothers is _Mitochondrial DNA_

5. A small group of women who lived in central Africa that are the ancestors of all living humans; sometimes referred to as a single individual, _Mitochondrial Eve_ .

Completion II

Fill each blank with the most appropriate term from the list below.

atlatl   Lake Mungo
Aurignacian   "Little Lady of Flores"
burins   Magdalenian
chin   Omo I
Cro-Magnon   Qafzeh Cave
Herto remains   Skhul Cave
Kow Swamp   Venus
Lagar Velho child

1. A specimen that is around 195,000 years old and has several modern features, such as a chin, is _Omo I_ .

2. An anatomic structure that is only found in the midline of the modern human mandible is the _Chin_ .

3. A fossil population called the _Herto Remains_ lived between 160,000 and 154,000 years ago and is clearly *Homo sapiens.*

4. _Skhul Cave_ is a site in Israel where modern humans lived near the Neandertal population at Tabun.

5. Another site in Israel that also is contemporary with Neandertals and from which 20 *Homo sapiens* were recovered is _Qafzeh Cave_ .

6. _Lake Mungo_ is the oldest site yet found in Australia.

7. A population of modern humans from only 14,000 to 9,000 years ago, yet present archaic traits such as receding foreheads, heavy browridges, and thick bones, have been found at _Kow Swamp_ .

8. The best-known sample of western European *Homo sapiens* is from _Cro-Magnon_ .

9. The _Lagar velho Child_ child possesses traits found in both modern humans and Neandertals.

10. The type specimen for *Homo floresiensis* is the _little lady of Flores_ .

11. The _Aurignacian_ is a stone tool industry of the Upper Paleolithic that began around 40,000 years ago.

12. The final phase of the Upper Paleolithic culture is called _Magdalenian_ .

13. The _atlatl_ was a tool invented by Upper Paleolithic hunters that enhanced the force and distance of a hurled spear.

14. _Burins_ are small, chisel-like tools that were believed to have been used to engrave bone, antler, ivory, or wood.

15. A _venus_ is a small figurine made in the form of a woman that some authorities believe represent real woman; some had exaggerated features and may have also been used as fertility figures.

Self-Test

Select the best answer.

1. The most likely ancestors of modern humans, appearing 195,000 years ago, were premodern populations of
   a. European *Homo heidelbergensis*.
   b. African *Homo heidelbergensis*.
   c. Chinese *Homo erectus*.
   d. Neandertals from southwest Asia.

2. According to the complete replacement model, modern *Homo sapiens*
   a. first appeared in Africa.
   b. migrated out of Africa and replaced the premodern populations.
   c. interbred with premodern populations in Europe and Asia.
   d. did a and b.

3. Comparisons of the genome of Neandertals with that of modern humans supports
   a. the complete replacement model.
   b. the partial replacement model.
   c. the regional continuity model.
   d. both b and c.

4. Which of the following is **NOT** a model of modern human origins?
   a. the complete replacement model
   b. the regional replacement model
   c. the partial replacement model
   d. the regional continuity model

5. According to the partial replacement models,

    a. modern humans evolved in Africa and Europe at the same time.
    b. premodern humans first evolved into modern *Homo sapiens* in southern Africa.
    c. the dispersal of modern humans was relatively rapid.
    d. modern humans interbred occasionally with premodern humans in Eurasia.

6. Which of the following is an assumption of the partial replacement model?

    a. Modern humans arose in different parts of the world.
    b. No speciation event occurred that led to *Homo sapiens*.
    c. There was no interbreeding between modern and premodern humans.
    d. This model is supported by mtDNA studies.

7. The regional continuity model of modern *Homo sapiens* origins proposes that

    a. modern humans did not evolve only in Africa.
    b. premodern populations in Africa, Europe, and Asia all evolved into modern humans.
    c. there was gene flow between the premodern populations of Eurasia and Africa.
    d. all of the above are true.

8. What factor of evolution is required if regional continuity is to be considered viable?

    a. founder effect
    b. genetic drift
    c. gene flow
    d. mutation

9. Which of the following is **NOT** an anatomic trait found in modern humans?

    a. projecting midface
    b. vertical forehead
    c. pyramidal mastoid process
    d. canine fossa

10. Which of the following features is found **ONLY** in anatomically modern humans?

    a. large cranial capacity
    b. canine fossa
    c. chin
    d. b and c

11. The main differences between modern humans and Neandertals are found in the

    a. legs.
    b. brain case.
    c. pelvis.
    d. feet.

12. A perplexing aspect of the modern finds at Omo is

    a. *Homo erectus* individuals living amongst moderns.

    b. the lack of variation in the population.

    c. the large amount of variation between the contemporary specimens.

    d. the presence of Mousterian tools.

13. In June of 2003, near-modern human fossils dating between 160,000 and 154,000 years ago were announced that had been recovered from

    a. Herto, Ethiopia.

    b. Lake Mungo, Australia.

    c. Omo, Ethiopia.

    d. Kebara, Israel.

14. The Herto remains have been classified as *Homo sapiens*

    a. *sapiens.*

    b. *neanderthalensis.*

    c. *heidelbergensis.*

    d. *idaltu.*

15. A site that provides some support for the partial replacement model is

    a. Cro-Magnon.

    b. Tabun.

    c. Niah Cave.

    d. Herto, Ethiopia.

16. What is the most likely manner by which modern humans reached Australia?

    a. bamboo rafts

    b. exposed areas of land that are currently submerged

    c. accidentally falling into the water and being swept by currents to Australia

    d. swimming

17. Which of the following statements describe the Kow Swamp people?

    a. They date between 14,000 and 9,000 years ago.

    b. They are robust, displaying thick bones.

    c. They exhibit premodern cranial traits such as receding foreheads.

    d. all of the above

18. Which site in central Europe has yielded fossils classified as modern humans even though they have some premodern features? This site has been referred to as supporting the partial replacement model.

    a. Cro-Magnon

    b. Terra Amata

    c. Mladec

    d. Oase Cave

19. A modern human site in the Dordogne region of France that yielded eight individuals who were associated with Aurignacian tools is

    a. La Chapelle-aux-Saints.

    b. Cro-Magnon.

    c. Combe Chapelle.

    d. Fillet Mignon.

20. Which site provides some support for the partial replacement model?

    a. Oase

    b. Lagar Velho

    c. Cro-Magnon

    d. Predmosti

21. A group of recent hominins that resemble the Dmanisi *Homo erectus* is the

    a. Flores hominins.

    b. Kow Swamp people.

    c. Mungo Lake hominins.

    d. Herto people.

22. What unusual evolutionary event appears to have occurred on the Indonesian island of Flores?

    a. A new hominin species, *H. floresiensis*, evolved.

    b. Insular dwarfing occurred.

    c. A modern *H. sapiens* population migrated there and became tiny in stature over time.

    d. both a and b.

23. The term "Aurignacian" refers to a

    a. tool assemblage associated with France's earliest anatomically modern humans.

    b. site in western Spain that yielded 10 skeletons.

    c. burial site in Portugal that yielded a four-year-old child showing both modern and Neandertal traits.

    d. tool tradition associated with premodern humans in western Asia.

24. During the Upper Paleolithic, humans in Eurasia relied heavily on

    a. marine resources.
    b. hunting.
    c. small-scale farming.
    d. herding of domesticated animals.

25. At the site in Sungir, Russia, excavators found

    a. burials that included ivory beads, spears made from mammoth tusks, ivory engravings, and jewelry.
    b. sand paintings.
    c. caches of weapons, including bows and arrows.
    d. Chatelperronian tools, including atlatls and copper spear tips.

26. An atlatl

    a. is a type of projective point.
    b. was used for starting fires.
    c. is used to increase the distance that a spear can be thrown.
    d. is a type of drill.

27. Which of the following is a tool that was **NOT** developed during the Magdalenian?

    a. burin
    b. barbed harpoon
    c. spear
    d. serrated knives

28. What is unusual about the technology of the Upper Paleolithic?

    a. It is superior to iron tools of some modern cultures.
    b. It only uses stone as a medium.
    c. It appears abruptly after a thousands of years of inertia.
    d. It is only found in Europe.

29. According to anthropologist C. Loring Brace,

    a. more effective tools and use of fire for food processing led to smaller teeth and facial skeletons.
    b. more advanced tools led to cave art.
    c. Solutrean hunters migrated into North America.
    d. use of the atlatl led to the limb proportions of modern humans.

30. Incised ochre fragments, various bone tools, and tick shell beads dated to 77,000 years ago have been found in
    a. Blombos Cave, South Africa.
    b. Altamira, Spain.
    c. Sungir, Russia.
    d. Grotte Chauvet, France.

31. Artistic endeavor in Africa has been dated
    a. to 2,000 years ago.
    b. as far back as 20,000 years ago.
    c. to 40,000 years ago by carbon-14 analysis.
    d. as far back as 80,000 years ago using electron spin resonance and thermoluminescence.

32. Early rock art, in the form of painted slabs, has been found at
    a. Altamira, Spain.
    b. Lascaux, France.
    c. Blombos Cave, South Africa.
    d. Apollo 11 rock shelter, Namibia.

33. Factors that influenced the demise of Upper Paleolithic culture probably included
    a. climatic change.
    b. extinction of many prey species.
    c. shift from hunting to domesticated plants.
    d. all of the above.

34. Prismatic blades have the advantage of
    a. being the easiest stone tool to make.
    b. having a longer cutting edge.
    c. being the lowest technology of the Stone Age.
    d. a and c.

35. John Shea suggests in the video that the elaborate art of the Upper Paleolithic can be explained by
    a. Marxist economic theory.
    b. Keynesian economic theory.
    c. signaling theory.
    d. second-messenger theory.

36. In the video, what does John Shea say allowed individuals to be identified by their status in a group?

   (a.) personal adornment

   b. stone tools

   c. whether they use an atlatl or a bow

   d. the length of hair

Short-Answer Questions

1. Compare and contrast the complete replacement model with the regional continuity model of modern human origins. How do these models differ in their interpretation of Neandertal taxonomy and fate? Complete Replacement states that as Modern Humans expanded out of Africa they took over the areas Previously inhabidated by Premodern humans which then died off w/ no desenderdents. Regional continuity states that Homo erectus started in Africa and slowly evolved over time into M. Human, this includes Neanderthals.

2. What are the major anatomic differences between modern and premodern humans? Major differences are seen in the skull. Premodern humans lack the chin and canine fossa that Modern humans have, while modern humans have a reduced brow ridge. And vertical foreheads.

3. What might account for the tiny stature of *Homo floresiensis* on the island of Flores in Indonesia? On islands there are sig. less resources that can be Produced or found so the species living on these island naturally grow smaller since that is the best way to survive on the island. it is Darwins theroy in action.

4. Describe the child from Lagar Velho. What does this child's anatomy suggest regarding the origins of modern humans? She is a 4yr old who shows many traits that lean towards interbreeding between M. Humans + Neanderthals. For one she lacks a Chin and had limb developement simeler to Neanderthals.

5. What were burins used for by Upper Paleolithic people?

They were used as a chisel for engraving, one end was flat white the other was pointed. They would use it to carve bone, wood, ather, ect.

Application Questions

1. Compare and contrast the complete replacement, partial replacement, and regional continuity models of modern human evolution. What evidence supports, or would support, each hypothesis?

Complete replacement is supported by Mitochondrial Eve but has recently been debated based on new findings. The Partial replacement is the idea that M. Humans evolved from Africa and that they may have interbreel with locals as they migrated. Some Remains support this. Regional Continuity is the idea that M. Humans + Pre modern Humans did interbreed.

2. If you were analyzing an incomplete skeleton that could be an early modern *Homo sapiens*, which parts of the skeleton would be most useful to your analysis? Explain why.

The Skull is what shows the most tell tale characteristiscs. It would lack the excgerated brow ridges and have a virtical forehead, plus a chin. One would also look at the jaw size (which would be shorter) and the teeth would also be smaller.

3. Compare the lifestyle (subsistence, habitation, technology, evidence for ritual, religion, art, and so forth) of modern *Homo sapiens* of the Upper Paleolithic to that of premodern humans, especially Neandertals.

Neanderthals were overall a hunting/gathering group they used specialized stone tools developed from flaking. They lack long distence weapons. M. Humans had long Range weapons and tools used as decoration not just Purpose. In terms of Burit Neanderthals did have Practice but w/ no written evidence this can not be accurathy informed.

4. Compare art from the Late Pleistocene of Europe with the same time period in Africa.

In Europe there are many examples of "Art" on artifacts and cave walls, but this does not make them more artistically advance. Europe has been excavated for longer and Remains protected w/in caves. Africa has been subject to the elements but beads + eggs have been uncovered.

5. Why did "art" develop?

Art developed along side culture. Humans feel the need to express themselves and to spread their ideas. Cave art may have been a type of history or story while figurens, such as the venus are symbolic messeages. Basically art developed to tell others something.

Answer Key

Matching I

1. e (objective 4)

2. b (objective 4)

3. d (video lesson, segment 3; objective 4)

4. h (video lesson, segment 1; objective 1)

5. c (video lesson, segment 3; objective 4)

6. g (video lesson, segment 1; objective 1)

7. f (video lesson, segment 1; objective 1)

8. a (objective 6)

Matching II

1. k (objective 2)

2. g (objective 3)

3. b (objective 3)

4. f (objective 3)

5. j (objectives 1, 2, & 3)

6. i (objective 3)

7. e (objective 3)

8. h (objective 3)

9. a (objective 3)

10. d (objective 3)

11. c (objective 3)

Completion I

1. complete replacement model (video lesson, segment 1; objective 1)

2. regional continuity model (video lesson, segment 1; objective 1)

3. partial replacement models (video lesson, segment 1; objective 1)

4. mitochondrial DNA (objective 1)

5. mitochondrial Eve (video lesson, segment 1; objective 1)

Completion II

1. Omo I (video lesson, segment 2; objectives 2 & 3)

2. chin (objective 2)

3. Herto remains (objectives 2 & 3)

4. Skhul Cave (objective 3)

5. Qafzeh Cave (objective 3)

6. Lake Mungo (video lesson, segment 2; objective 3)

7. Kow Swamp (objective 3)

8. Cro-Magnon (objective 3)

9. Lagar Velho child (objective 3)

10. "Little Lady of Flores" (objective 3)

11. Aurignacian (objective 4)

12. Magdalenian (video lesson, segment 3; objective 4)

13. atlatl (objective 4)

14. Burins (video lesson, segment 3; objective 4)

15. Venus (objective 6)

Self-Test

1. b. is the correct answer. By answering "b," we are suggesting that either the complete replacement model, or one of the partial replacement models, are more likely to have occurred. (video lesson, segment 1; objective 1)

2. d. is the correct answer. Complete replacement asserts that the ancestors of modern humans originated in Africa, migrated out, and completely replaced all other humans in the world. This does not necessarily mean that modern humans exterminated the previous humans in any sort of warfare. (video lesson, segment 1; objective 1)

3. b. is the correct answer. The evidence that modern humans from Europe and Asia, but not Africa, retain some Neandertal DNA, suggests that there was interbreeding in the past and that modern humans originated in Africa. (video lesson, segment 1; objective 1)

4. b. is the correct answer. There is no regional replacement model (which doesn't actually make sense). (video lesson, segment 1; objective 1)

5. d. is the correct answer. Partial replacement asserts that there was some interbreeding between premodern populations and modern humans migrating from Africa, although it rarely occurred. This is not one model, but several that are similar. (objective 1)

6. b. is the correct answer. You may recall that part of the definition of a biological species includes populations that can interbreed. If moderns and premoderns could interbreed and produce viable, fertile offspring, that would suggest that they belonged to the same species. Therefore, there would be no speciation event. (objective 1)

7. d. is the correct answer. Regional (or local) continuity posits that, ultimately, premodern humans evolved from *Homo erectus* that had migrated to different parts of the Old World. Thus, they did not evolve only in Africa, but evolved in place. (video lesson, segment 1; objective 1)

8. c. is the correct answer. If modern humans are descended from earlier premodern populations in local areas, why haven't they speciated? This would be expected if small populations were isolated from one another inhabiting very different environments. The answer is gene flow, the non-Darwinian mechanism that actually prevents speciation by "exchanging" alleles between populations (video lesson, segment 1; objective 1)

9. a. is the correct answer. A projecting midface is characteristic of premodern humans. (objective 2)

10. d. is the correct answer. The canine fossa is a depression in the maxilla just above and behind the upper canine. (objective 2)

11. b. is the correct answer. While there are some differences in the postcranial skeleton, it is in the brain case that the most dramatic differences exist. (video lesson, segment 2; objective 2)

12. c. is the correct answer. There is a great deal of variation in this population. This should not be considered that unusual, especially in a population undergoing a change. (objective 3)

13. a. is the correct answer. This is considered to be the first completely modern population, even though they still have some primitive traits. (objective 3)

14. d. is the correct answer. The Herto humans are classified as a subspecies of *Homo sapiens*. (objective 3)

15. b. is the correct answer. The fact that Neandertals are living in this site during the same time period as moderns and geographically so close, suggests that *Homo sapiens* likely did interbreed with the premodern Neandertals who were contemporaries. (objectives 1 & 3)

16. a. is the correct answer. At the lowest sea levels, Australia still lay across sixty miles of water. For populations (rather than individuals) to get across would require some sort of watercraft. (objective 3)

17. d. is the correct answer. Kow Swamp was occupied between 14,000 and 9,000 years ago. Surprisingly, they possess traits that are more primitive than the Lake Mungo people that lived anywhere from 30,000 to 60,000 years ago. Yet Jurmain cites genetic evidence suggesting that all native Australians are descendants of a single migration dating to around 50,000 years ago. (objectives 1 & 3)

18. c. is the correct answer. Some of these people exhibit large browridges. (objective 3)

19. b. is the correct answer. The Cro-Magnon cave is one of the most famous paleontological sites. (objective 3)

20. b. is the correct answer. Lagar Velho is said to be a hybrid child. If this is the case, then it appears that some Neandertals produced offspring with modern humans. (objectives 1 & 3)

21. a. is the correct answer. The Flores hominins are very small. There currently is debate about whether they are evolved from *Homo erectus* or if they are *Homo sapiens* that underwent an unusual evolution. (objective 3)

22. d. is the correct answer. The morphology of the Flores hominins are quite distinct from *H. sapiens* in several ways and evidence points to their evolution as a separate species, *H. floresiensis*. This discovery is very recent and there are still a number of explanations that have been proposed. (objective 3)

23. a. is the correct answer. The Aurignacian is the first Upper Paleolithic tool industry associated exclusively with *Homo sapiens*. (objective 4)

24. b. is the correct answer. The Upper Paleolithic was the heyday of hunting in Eurasia with large numbers of herds inhabiting the lush grasslands. (objective 4)

25. a. is the correct answer. This is a spectacular find of the burial of two teenagers. (objective 4)

26. c. is the correct answer. This tool is also called a spear-thrower. (objective 4)

27. c. is the correct answer. Spears go back at least to 400,000 years ago (recall the wooden spears recovered at Schöningen). (objective 4)

28. c. is the correct answer. Physically, anatomically modern humans were around for tens of thousands of years when, suddenly, there were major advances in technology. (objective 4)

29. a. is the correct answer. By this, Brace means that there is an interaction between genetics and environment and a less rigorous lifestyle can lead to smaller muscles and more gracile bone structure. This means less energy is required for maintenance and energy may be a major selective factor. (objective 4)

30. a. is the correct answer. The exquisite art associated with the European Upper Paleolithic is already well established before it ever appears in Europe. (objective 5)

31. d. is the correct answer. There is discrepancy between carbon dating and electron spin resonance and thermoluminescence, but we can safely say that, in Africa, art was well established sometime between 40,000 and 80,000 years ago. (objective 5)

32. d. is the correct answer. European painting has survived because it was protected in deep caves. However, rock art was probably widespread, but exposed to the elements. (objective 5)

33. d. is the correct answer. The decline of the Upper Paleolithic cultures coincide with the mass extinction of the megafauna (e.g., saber-toothed cats, American mammoths, and others). (objective 4)

34. b. is the correct answer. Middle Paleolithic cultures were characterized by flakes. While the Upper Paleolithic cultures still retain flakes, the more advanced blades now make their appearance. (video lesson, segment 3; objective 4)

35. c. is the correct answer. Signaling theory, when applied to humans, is the idea that all art is performed to attract mates. (video lesson, segment 3; objective 6)

36. a. is the correct answer. Even today, personal adornment may reflect an individual's status in society. A wedding band, for example, indicates that the wearer is not available as a potential mate. (video lesson, segment 3; objective 6)

Short-Answer Questions

Your answers should include the following:

1. Complete replacement is the idea that the earliest modern humans evolved only in Africa, and then expanded from central Africa into Asia and Europe. As they migrated, they replaced groups of premodern humans who had inhabited the regions. According to this model, the Neandertals in Europe went extinct with no descendents. They are considered to be a separate species from modern humans.

    Regional continuity is an alternative model to complete replacement. According to the regional continuity model, *Homo erectus* evolved in Africa and migrated into Eurasia some 1.8 million years ago. These populations then slowly evolved into modern humans, with the species kept stable via gene flow. From the perspective of this model, Neandertals evolved into modern humans and are considered to be *Homo sapiens.* (video lesson, segment 1; objective 1)

2. The major differences between modern and premodern humans are found in the skull. Two features unique to modern humans are the chin and the canine fossa. The forehead, long and receding in premoderns, is vertical in moderns. The browridges, prominent in premodern humans, are relatively small in modern humans. (video lesson, segment 2; objective 2)

3. One possible explanation for the small stature of the Flores Island hominins is based on the principle of insular dwarfism. On islands, natural selection can favor smaller body size in response to reduced resource availability. Once underway, such selection can work rapidly owing to the isolation of the gene pool. The discovery of dwarfed elephants on Flores Island adds credence to this possible explanation. Alternatively, the small stature and small brain size could be the result of pathology. If so, the Flores

Island hominins are not a separate species (*Homo floresiensis*) but are actually *Homo sapiens* afflicted with a serious disorder. (objective 3)

4. The fossil recovered from a burial site at Lagar Velho is that of a four-year-old female who appears to have a mix of both modern and Neandertal traits. She lacks a chin and has limb proportions and muscle insertions reminiscent of Neandertals. This suggests interbreeding between modern humans and Neandertals, which weakens the case for the complete replacement model and supports partial replacement. However, most scientists are cautious about accepting one child's skeleton as sufficient evidence for interbreeding. (objective 1)

5. Burins were blade tools of the Upper Paleolithic. One end was flat like a chisel and the other end was pointed. These tools were used for engraving. The carvings found on wood, ivory, antler, and bone were made by burins. (video lesson, segment 3; objective 4)

Application Questions

Your answers should include the following:

1. According to the complete replacement model, the earliest *Homo sapiens* evolved from existing *H. heidelbergensis* populations living in Africa during the Middle Pleistocene. As the population expanded, modern humans migrated out of Africa into Asia and Europe. Neandertals were living in Europe when the first modern humans arrived. Soon after, the Neandertals disappear from the fossil record. In Asia, the African modern human migrants replaced populations of *Homo erectus* and some premodern humans (such as the population at Jinniushan). The complete replacement model was originally based on mtDNA and was once referred to as the "mitochondrial Eve" hypothesis. According to this model, modern humans were a separate species and therefore could not have interbred with Neandertals or other premodern human populations. Studies of Neandertal mtDNA suggest that this group of humans was very different and possibly a different species from both ancient *Homo sapiens* and living humans. However, more recent evidence based on comparisons of the entire genomes of Neandertals (using nuclear DNA) with modern humans indicates that there was interbreeding between Neandertals and *H. sapiens*. Evidence for an African origin for *H. sapiens* can be found in the fossil record since the oldest *H. sapiens* fossils are found in Africa. Also, studies of both mtDNA and Y chromosomes suggest that African populations are the most genetically diverse human populations, which is interpreted to mean that these are the oldest human populations.

   The partial replacement model takes a middle course between complete replacement and regional continuity. Its proponents recognized that the earliest *H. sapiens* evolved and came from Africa. However, they allow that the African migrants may have interbred with existing local populations in the regions that they entered. Generally, very little interbreeding occurs with partial replacement. Nevertheless, enough interbreeding occurs that no speciation event is recognized and that all premoderns should be considered *Homo sapiens*. Evidence that supports partial replacement is the Lago Velho hybrid child as well as several other possible hybrids. In Asia, the Chinese and American team working on the Tianyuan remains, dated at 40,000 years ago, claim that there was some interbreeding between resident archaic populations and modern *H. sapiens*. And in the Near East, the chronological overlap of premodern and modern humans in adjacent sites (Skuhl and Tabun) suggests the possibility that the interbreeding between moderns and Neandertals occurred there rather than in Europe.

The regional continuity model posits that *Homo erectus* left Africa around 1.8 million years ago and migrated into different regions. Fossils found in Gran Dolina, Dmanisi, Zhoukoudian, and Java suggest that they adapted to their regions and, some argue, left descendents, namely those human living in these regions today. In order to explain the overall similarity of humans across the world at this time, the regional continuity model posits that gene flow occurred among neighboring groups so that over time alleles were exchanged throughout the entire human population. In this scenario, speciation did not occur. Evidence supporting regional continuity is the appearance of physical features of premodern populations (such as flattened nasal bones and sagittal keel) in modern populations of the same locality. For example, Chinese paleoanthropologists believe that regional continuity from Zhoukoudian *Homo erectus* to modern Chinese can be seen in the physical features of both. However, fossil evidence from other sites such as Skhul and Tabun which show modern and Neandertal populations living next to each other at roughly the same time, contradicts the regional continuity model, as does the evidence of Neandertal genes in modern human populations outside of Africa. (video lesson, segment 1; objective 1)

2. If you were analyzing a potential *Homo sapiens* skeleton, the most useful diagnostic features would be found on the skull. These would include a vertical forehead, rather than a receding one, relatively small browridges instead of the heavy arched ridges found in premoderns, and a more prominent mastoid process than found in premoderns. Two traits unique to modern humans are the presence of a chin and a canine fossa above the maxillary canine. Other features include smaller teeth, a shorter jaw, and a flatter midface. Although there are some differences in the postcrania, it is the skull that gives us the most information about the species. (Figure 14-3; video lesson, segment 2; objective 2)

3. Neandertals were hunters and gatherers who used a flake-based tool technology referred to as Mousterian. It appears that they used simple thrusting spears that required close proximity to dangerous prey (possibly accounting for the large number of injuries that are found on Neandertal skeletons). They had no weaponry to allow striking from a distance (i.e., bows and arrows, or spear-throwers). This probably made them less efficient than *Homo sapiens* who had both bows and spear-throwers. Upper Paleolithic tools were blade based. Blades provided a longer cutting edge than flake-based tools. Many of them were "microliths" that could be hafted onto arrows or spears. Throwing weapons such as the barbed harpoon also make their appearance in the Upper Paleolithic. The Neandertals were principally limited to stone and wood as their mediums for tool working. Upper Paleolithic humans also utilized bone, antler, and ivory and the tools are often serve a specific function, whereas Neandertal tools are often general purpose. *Homo sapiens* tools often have intricate designs, whereas Neandertal art is either lacking or only very rudimentary.

Neandertals practiced deliberate burial. This is sometimes used as evidence of ritual, belief in the afterlife and religious beliefs. However, this is an interpretation only. We cannot know for certain whether Neandertals had such beliefs. Neandertal burials are stark compared to Upper Paleolithic burials, with very few or no grave goods. *Homo sapiens* burials, by contrast, are very elaborate (e.g., the Sungir burial that included thousands of artifacts). From the historical records of our own species, we know that many cultures had beliefs that objects placed with the individual were for that person to use in an afterlife.

Art among the Neandertals is equivocal. If it exists it is very rudimentary, and while one researcher may interpret scratches on a Neandertal artifact as art, another does not. In the case of Upper Paleolithic modern humans, artwork is indisputable. It is found on portable objects, on rock slabs, and on cave walls. Personal adornment such as jewelry is part of Upper Paleolithic artwork. (video lesson, segment 3; objectives 4 & 6)

4. An abundance of artwork has been found from the Upper Paleolithic of Europe. Even practical tools like atlatls often have intricate engravings on them. In some cases, tools have been extensively reworked so that they themselves become an expression of art. In France and Italy, small figurines called Venuses have been recovered at archaeological sites. It is believed that the faces on these figures represent real women who were the models for them. Portable art such as jewelry and beadwork has been uncovered. The most spectacular artwork comes from deep caves where exquisite representation of animals is painted on the walls. In Africa rock art has been discovered, as well as portable art such as incised ostrich eggs and tick shell beads. At first glance, it might appear that Europe was the "art center" of the Late Pleistocene. However, there are two reasons why this is probably a false impression. First, for nearly one hundred and fifty years, people in Europe have been looking for evidence of earlier humans (e.g., Altamira was discovered in 1868). This has resulted in a large collection of artifacts from the Upper Paleolithic. Second, the spectacular paintings from Lascaux, Altamira, and Grotte Chauvet were all safely protected in deep caves. It is now believed that a great deal of rock painting, not just in Africa, but elsewhere as well, has disappeared over time as a result of weathering. If recent dating is correct, art has an earlier appearance in Africa than anywhere else in the world, perhaps as early as 80,000 years ago. (video lesson, segment 3; objective 6)

5. Before this question can be answered, it must be recognized that we need a definition. The Jurmain textbook quotes Berkeley anthropologist Margaret Conkey in defining art as "visual and material imagery." This definition covers a wide variety of forms, from the scratches on the stone from Blombos cave (see Figure 14-21 on page 429) to the tattoos on a person's body as art. We now know that art appeared in Africa about as early as it did in Europe, if not earlier. But what led to art? The textbook authors state that the Upper Paleolithic was the culmination of previous cultures and traditions as well as reorganization of the brain. Whether this is led to art or not, we do know that art appears in its most developed form with *Homo sapiens*. (In the video, John Shea flatly says it appears with us.) The Venus figurines represent one type of art that is found in Europe. These figurines may have more meaning than just a stone portrait of a woman in the hunting-gathering band. Many researchers believe that these are fertility fetishes, particularly the ones with exaggerated female characteristics. Therefore, these

go beyond art and have a supernatural significance to their creators. John Shea cites signaling theory as the motivation behind the development of art. He suggests that art is made by individuals who are trying to attract mates (i.e., art is communication between potential mates). He also states that personal adornment is symbolic and serves to identify a person's status (e.g., a wedding band identifying the wearer as a married individual). Jean-Jacques Hublin also suggests communication is why art develops, but he thinks that it may be developed to distinguish individuals as belonging to certain groups. Use of pigments or objects can indicate what group a person belongs to. He does not think art developed because of creativity, but rather to convey stories about who we are and why we are here. However, as the researchers in the video point out, we can recognize symbolic behavior in the archaeological record, but we can only offer theories as to why it developed. (video lesson, segment 3; objective 6)

Notes:

Lesson Review

Lesson 12: Origin & Dispersal of Modern Humans

PLEASE NOTE: Use this matrix to guide your study and achieve the learning objectives of this lesson. It will also help you to view the video, which defines and demonstrates important concepts and principles as they relate to everyday life and actual case studies.

Learning Objective	Textbook	Student Guide	Video Lesson
1. Discuss the hypotheses regarding the appearance of anatomically modern *Homo sapiens*.	pp. 404–407	Key Terms: 5, 6, 7; Matching I: 4, 6, 7; Matching II: 5; Completion I: 1, 2, 3, 4, 5; Self-Test: 1, 2, 3, 4, 5, 6, 7, 8, 15, 17, 20; Short-Answer: 1, 4; Application: 1.	Segment 1: *The Hominin Hypotheses*
2. Compare and contrast the skeletal differences between anatomically modern *H. sapiens* and premodern *H. sapiens*.	pp. 407–423	Matching II: 1, 5; Completion II: 1, 2, 3; Self-Test: 9, 10, 11; Short-Answer: 2; Application: 2.	Segment 2: *Who's On First?*
3. Summarize the geographic distribution and dates of early fossil members of *H. sapiens*.	pp. 407–423	Key Terms: 1; Matching II: 2, 3, 4, 5, 6, 7, 8, 9, 10, 11; Completion II: 1, 3, 4, 5, 6, 7, 8, 9, 10; Self-Test: 12, 13, 14, 15, 16, 17, 18, 19, 20, 21, 22; Short-Answer: 3.	Segment 2: *Who's On First?*
4. Describe the climatic, technological, and subsistence changes evident in the Upper Paleolithic.	pp. 423–428	Key Terms: 2, 3, 4; Matching I: 1, 2, 3, 5; Completion II: 11, 12, 13, 14; Self-Test: 23, 24, 25, 26, 27, 28, 29, 33, 34; Short-Answer: 5; Application: 3.	Segment 3: *Hi-Tech, Fine Art & the Modern Human*

Learning Objective	Textbook	Student Guide	Video Lesson
5. Compare and contrast the cultural innovations during the late Pleistocene in Europe with those in Africa.	pp. 423–428	Self-Test: 30, 31, 32.	
6. Discuss the appearance and significance of "art" in Eurasia and Africa, especially with regard to cave paintings and their possible cultural significance.	pp. 423–428	Matching I: 8; Completion II: 15; Self-Test: 35, 36; Application: 3, 4, 5.	Segment 3: *Hi-Tech, Fine Art & the Modern Human*

LESSON 13

LESSON

13

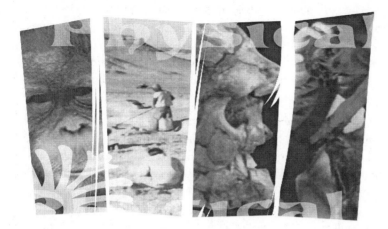

Patterns of Variation

Checklist

For the most effective study of this lesson, complete the following activities in this sequence.

Before Viewing the Video

☐ Read the Preview, Learning Objectives, and Viewing Notes below.

☐ Read Chapter 15, "Modern Human Biology: Patterns of Variation," pages 432–459, in *Introduction to Physical Anthropology*.

What to Watch

☐ After reading the textbook assignment, watch the video for Lesson 13, *Patterns of Variation*.

After Viewing the Video

☐ Briefly note your answers to the questions listed at the end of the Viewing Notes.

☐ Review the Summary below.

☐ Review all reading assignments for this lesson, including the Viewing Notes in this lesson.

☐ Write brief answers to the "Critical Thinking Questions" at the end of Chapter 15 in the textbook.

☐ Complete the Review Exercises below. Check your answers with the Answer Key and review when necessary.

☐ Use the Lesson Review matrix found at the end of this lesson to review and assess your knowledge of each Learning Objective.

Preview

As discussed in Lesson 2, the evolutionary process takes a great deal of time. Humans rarely witness the appearance of a new species; an exception would be new microorganisms that evolve at relatively rapid rates. The emergence of resistant strains of some bacteria because of human overuse of antibiotics is one example of this. Even though we don't see ourselves changing, humans continue to evolve. Lessons 3 and 4 discussed how our phenotypes reflect both the genetic code (DNA) we inherited and its unique expression through the developmental process. This lesson continues the study of genetics and how it contributes to human variation at the population level.

Both the Jurmain textbook and video examine the concept of race and racial variation. Most people think it is an easily recognizable phenotypic variation in humans, but what does race mean in relation to biology and evolution? An anthropologist featured in the video offers insight into the complexity of this subject. He says, "The concept of race is not the same as the concept of difference. The fact that people from one part of the world look different from people of another part of the world doesn't necessarily mean that there are two kinds of people or four kinds of people or six kinds of people." Skin color is a biological variation in *Homo sapiens* that develops in response to environmental conditions, but as a characteristic to define human races it is problematic. The Jurmain textbook states, "Most people don't seem to understand the nature of human diversity, and worse yet, many seem quite unwilling to accept what science has to contribute on the subject." This lesson explores human phenotypic diversity and racial classifications and examines modern methods of interpreting diversity.

Concepts to Remember

- Lesson 3 introduced the term **alleles**, which are alternate forms of a gene that can direct the cell to produce slightly different forms of the same protein and ultimately different expressions of traits.

- Lesson 3 also focused on the basic mechanisms of inheritance and their importance in the processes of evolution. It also offered a genetic definition of **evolution** as a change in allele frequency from one generation to the next. This lesson will offer a more detailed account of genetic variation.

Learning Objectives

After you complete this lesson, you should be able to:

1. Trace the historical views of human variation, emphasizing early (eighteenth and nineteenth century) scientific classifications. (pp. 434–435)

2. Discuss the typological concept of race and whether it has any biological validity. (pp. 435–440)

3. Draw on knowledge of natural selection and other evolutionary factors to discuss the population patterning of human genotypic and phenotypic variation. (pp. 440–445)

4. Explain the application of population genetics to the study of human diversity. (pp. 445–447, 452–453)

5. Calculate allele frequencies using the Hardy-Weinberg equilibrium formula. (pp. 447–452)

6. Discuss examples of human biocultural evolution. (pp. 453–456)

At this point, read Chapter 15, "Modern Human Biology: Patterns of Variation," pages 432–459.

Viewing Notes

While visible differences in the way people look are not usually meaningful to anthropologists in regard to biological diversity, the video demonstrates that in many cultures, such variations can lead to tragic and catastrophic consequences in human relations. For example, in Somalia, lighter-skinned Somalis violently discriminate against darker-skinned Bantus because of the color of their skin. This persecution resulted in the genocidal deaths of millions of Bantus and has caused millions more to flee the country.

In everyday usage, the word *race* refers to a group that is distinguished by physical characteristics, culture, and geography. Biologically, *race* defines a taxonomic category of a subspecies. In that sense, the word and concept of race cannot apply to *Homo sapiens* because, as is well understood, there are no subspecies of *Homo sapiens*. In the sixteenth century, during the Age of Exploration, European explorers traveled to distant locales, and they encountered groups of people who looked and acted vastly different from them, and from one another. The Europeans developed a system of classification based on the physical differences they witnessed. This system simplified the task of identifying people by visible characteristics (phenotypes), and skin color, because it is the most visible human characteristic of all, defined a group's "race." Today, anthropologists and scholars in other disciplines use genetics, a field not available to the early European explorers, to study variation in humans. A genotype is an individual's personal genetic make-up, and DNA, which is the cornerstone of genetic studies, provides a much more accurate picture of human diversity.

Alleles of genes, or different forms of genes, that cause different phenotypic expressions in people within the same group are called **polymorphisms**. Polymorphisms are common in humans, so we are sometimes referred to as a polymorphic species. In Somalia, just a few polymorphisms can create a chasm in race relations. As Halima Lamungu, a Bantu refugee explains, "This Somali we have two people different. We have Somali Bantu and Somali. Somali people they have long hair, they have long nose, you know. We are different." People use skin color to define a racial group because it is so visible; in actuality, however, it is an arbitrary distinction. As anthropologist Ann Stone points out in the video, people could be classified according to their height, eye color, blood type, or just about anything.

Another difficulty with using skin color to classify people into races has to do with how polymorphisms are spread across the world. As the narrator in the video points out, skin color does not go from black in Africa, to brown in southern Europe, to white in northern Europe. Rather, there are gradual changes in the frequency of genotypes as one travels in various geographical regions. These gradual changes are called **clines**. A montage of images in the video and another montage on page 439 of the Jurmain textbook indicate the phenotypic variation of skin tones in Africa; there is no one definitive black skin color.

Rather than using superficial physical characteristics to categorize people, scientists prefer to study the biological processes that shape differences in humans. Natural selection acts on variations that arise from DNA mutations, and mutations are happening all the time. The video features Gregory Lanzaro, a medical entomologist who is working to eradicate malaria. Chapters 3 and 4 of the Jurmain textbook explained that sickle-cell anemia is a severe, inherited hemoglobin disorder that results when a person inherits two copies of a mutant allele. However, in areas where malarial mosquitoes are common, people who carry the sickle-cell allele have protection from malaria because the organism that causes malaria cannot flourish in these cells. Being a carrier of sickle-cell anemia is a positive situation for people living in tropical regions where malaria is prominent. If an individual inherits this allele from both parents, he or she will suffer from sickle-cell anemia and probably will not live long enough to produce offspring. However, individuals with just one allele will have a greater resistance to malaria and will pass some of their immunity to their offspring, with the result that the allele becomes more widespread in the population. So, in areas where malaria is common, there is a measurable difference in the genetic make-up of the population. Natural selection interacts with environmental factors to accomplish this. Scientists who study groups of people from a genetics standpoint are involved in population genetics.

Human beings survive by evolving both biologically and culturally in their environments. **Biocultural evolution** can act in both positive and negative ways. While Americans in general are being diagnosed with type 2 diabetes at alarming rates today, Native Americans suffer from the disease at a disproportionately high rate relative to the general population of the United States. Lifestyle changes, especially changes in diet, are one culprit, but other reasons for the high rate of type 2 diabetes among Native Americans are being evaluated. The "thrifty gene" hypothesis theorizes that for thousands of years many populations, including Native Americans, experienced alternating periods of feast and famine. In order to adapt to these extreme changes in caloric needs, a **thrifty genotype** developed that allowed these people to store fat during times of plenty so that they would not starve during times of famine. Today, however, this ability to store fat is detrimental for several reasons; Native Americans have stopped cooking traditional fare because of busier lifestyles, their lives have become less strenuous and more sedentary, and they have greater access to an abundance of high-fat, high-sugar foods.

Questions to Consider

※ Historically, how was the concept of race developed in the Western world?

※ Since the twentieth century, how has the scientific study of human diversity changed from the more traditional approach?

※ What is a cline, and how do they help dispel misconceptions regarding racial differences based on phenotypic differences?

※ How is the concept of polymorphism defined in the video?

Watch the video for Lesson 13, *Patterns of Variation*.

    Segment 1: *Phenotype vs. Genotype*
    Segment 2: *Looking at Human Variation*
    Segment 3: *Microevolution at Work*

Key Terms and Concepts

Page references are keyed to *Introduction to Physical Anthropology*, 13th edition.

1. **biological determinism:** The concept that phenomena, including various aspects of behavior (such as intelligence, values, and morals) are governed by biological (genetic) factors; the inaccurate association of various behavioral attributes with certain biological traits, such as skin color. (p. 434; objective 1)

2. **eugenics:** The philosophy of "race improvement" through forced sterilization of members of some groups and increased reproduction among others; an overly simplified, often racist view that is now discredited. (p. 435; objective 1)

3. **polytypic:** Referring to species composed of populations that differ in the expression of one or more traits. (p. 435; objectives 2 & 3)

4. **polymorphisms:** Loci with more than one allele. Polymorphisms can be expressed in the phenotype as the result of gene action (as in ABO), or they can exist solely at the DNA level with noncoding regions. (p. 441; video lesson, segment 2; objective 3)

5. **population genetics:** The study of the frequency of alleles, genotypes, and phenotypes in populations from a microevolutionary perspective. (p. 443; video lesson, segment 3; objectives 3 & 4)

6. **gene pool:** All of the genes shared by reproductive members of a population. (p. 445; objective 4)

7. **breeding isolates:** Populations that are clearly isolated geographically and/or socially from other breeding populations. (p. 445; objective 4)

8. **endogamy:** Mating with individuals from the same group. (p. 446; objective 4)

9. **exogamy:** Mating pattern whereby individuals obtain mates from groups other than their own. (p. 446; objective 4)

10. **Hardy-Weinberg theory of genetic equilibrium:** The mathematical relationship expressing—under conditions in which no evolution is occurring—the predicted distribution of alleles in populations; the central theorem of *population genetics*. (p. 446; objectives 4 & 5)

11. **nonrandom mating:** Pattern of mating in which individuals choose mates preferentially, with mate choice based on criteria such as social status, ethnicity, or biological relationship. In nonrandom mating, an individual doesn't have an equal chance of mating with all other individuals in their group. (p. 452; objective 4)

12. **inbreeding:** A type of nonrandom mating in which relatives mate more often than predicted under random mating conditions. (p. 452; objective 4)

13. **incest avoidance:** In animals, the tendency not to mate with close relatives. This tendency may be due to various social and ecological factors that keep the individuals apart. There may also be innate factors that lead to incest avoidance but these aren't well understood. (p. 453; objective 4)

14. **slash-and-burn agriculture:** A traditional land-clearing practice involving the cutting and burning of trees and vegetation. In many areas, fields are abandoned after a few years and clearing occurs elsewhere. (p. 453; objective 6)

15. **balanced polymorphism:** The maintenance of two or more alleles in a population due to the selective advantage of the heterozygote. (p. 454; objective 6)

16. **lactase persistence:** In adults, the continued production of lactase, the enzyme that breaks down lactose (milk sugar). This allows adults in some human populations to digest fresh milk products. The discontinued production of lactase in adults leads to lactose intolerance and the inability to digest fresh milk. (p. 454; objective 6)

17. **race:** As used in biology, a taxonomic category of subspecies. In common usage, it can also refer to a group that is distinguished by physical characteristics, culture, and geography. (video lesson, segment 1; objective 2)

18. **cline:** A gradual change in the frequency of genotypes and phenotypes from one geographical region to another. (video lesson, segment 2; objective 3)

19. **biocultural evolution:** The mutual, interactive evolution of human biology and culture. (video lesson, segment 3; objective 6)

20. **thrifty genotype:** Human genotype that permits efficient storage of fat to draw on in times of food shortage and conservation of glucose and nitrogen. (video lesson, segment 3; objective 4)

Summary

People tend to categorize each other based on the external traits they see. The video has explained, quite thoroughly and poignantly, why categorizing human beings according to their phenotypic differences not only has no scientific validity, but more often reflects social and cultural beliefs, not biology. The desire to categorize humans and to treat individuals as representatives of a racial group has a long history and persists even today in spite of efforts by anthropologists and others to explain the scientific evidence that says it is futile.

The Jurmain textbook recounts several notable attempts over the years to classify human diversity, starting with the ancient Egyptians and their idea of four geographically oriented skin colors. Explorations during the Age of Discovery provided even more evidence of the scope and scale of human diversity, not only in appearance but also in behavior. Numerous systems for classifying people ensued, based on skin color, head shape, head size, and body type, to name only a few. In the mid-nineteenth century, the concept of **biological determinism**, which includes the idea that physical characteristics are connected to attributes such as morals, intelligence, and even economic conditions, was widely accepted among educated people as well as the public. People with darker skins and non-European facial features were placed in racial categories that included their "primitive" behavior among their defining characteristics, and behavior was viewed as inheritable along with biological factors. Racial categories were ranked, with Europeans at the top and sub-Saharan Africans at the bottom.

In fact, some Europeans feared that "civilized society" was being weakened by the failure of natural selection to eliminate inferior individuals. Francis Galton, an English intellectual and scientist who was a cousin and contemporary of Charles Darwin, wrote and lectured on the need for "race improvement." He suggested that governments regulate marriage and family size. He called this approach **eugenics**, a program of selective breeding promoted with the intention of improving humanity, not only by regulating marriages between people but also by measures such as forced sterilization of people considered unfit and inferior. People of color, mentally challenged individuals, people of varying sexual orientations, and even people who were considered poor housekeepers could be targeted during the later phases of this movement in the United States. Conversely, people who were considered exemplary—the patriotic, the very religious, individuals of high moral standing within the mainstream white community— would be encouraged to procreate and perpetuate these characteristics within the population. The eugenics movement flourished during the last two decades of the nineteenth century and the first three decades of the twentieth century. Eventually, scientists began to shift from a focus on racial classification to more of an evolutionary approach, reflecting the increased understanding and knowledge of genetics and the process of natural selection.

Many people erroneously use the word *race* as synonymous with species, as in "the human race." People also refer to culturally defined groups, such as African Americans or Latinos, as races. These are actually social categories, defined by ethnic or national or cultural features, and may or may not reflect shared biology. Biologically speaking, race, or subspecies, is the category below the species and refers to geographically patterned phenotypic variations within a species. This is a category that exists in the eye of the beholder—there is no established criteria to assess whether a population constitutes a biological race, and the distinction itself is of interest primarily to taxonomists.

Picture a man who proudly asserts, "I am the original Seoul Brother." What do you immediately "know" about him? What does he look like? What are his values? His educational level?

Next, pretend you are blindfolded and hearing him say the same sentence. Now what do you "know" about him?

The man who made this statement was born of a Korean mother and African-American father. "Everyone sees me as black," he is quoted as saying in the book, *On Being Different*, written by Conrad Phillip Kottak and Kathryn A. Kozaitis. "But I'm more than that; my nature is mixed and my culture is rich." As it turns out, this person is cosmopolitan, well traveled, well-spoken, and far more complex than one might imagine upon reading—or hearing—his original statement.

Why would we think otherwise? Psychologists call it social categorization. It's the way we make quick judgments about people in the absence of time, opportunity, or desire to know them in depth. We place people in boxes that are full of associations that may or may not be accurate.

One of the categories into which we quickly place people is race. But research into the human genome now tells us that there is, in reality, no such thing. There is more genetic variation within ethnic groups than between so-called races. And the physical differences that define race have turned out to be purely cosmetic—the color of skin, the shape of eyes, the texture of hair.

In fact, ancient peoples did not have a concept of race. That category was created with the birth of the American republic. The proposition that "all men are created equal" conflicted with the young country's economic dependence upon slavery. The idea of race—based upon the physical attributes shared by all slaves—rationalized treating some people as less entitled to rights and liberties than others.

Once established, the idea of race has been consistently reinforced—both by those who use race as an excuse to discriminate as well as by those who work to stop it. Kottak and Kozaitis point out that affirmative action programs designed to stop discrimination themselves depend upon making racial distinctions. In doing so, they perpetuate the idea of linking privilege, or lack thereof, to a person's appearance.

Perhaps the answer is to remember what the analysis of mtDNA and the Y chromosome have already revealed: that we are direct descendants from a single male and a single female, both of whom lived many years apart, in Africa. If there were such a thing as race, we would all belong to the same one.

Anthropologists are interested in human biological variation and its geographic distribution, but find that it is too complex to fit into categories such as race. For example, studies show there is more genetic variation within groups than between them. Given that, how could we define a group biologically? Instead, anthropologists focus on the distribution of phenotypic traits and seek to understand that distribution, as a result of adaptation, genetic drift, mutation, and gene flow. When studying processes of evolution in modern human populations, anthropologists focus on **polymorphisms**, or traits that exist in more than one form (allele). We have learned a great deal about polymorphic traits, such as ABO blood types; various types of hemoglobin, including sickle cell or human leukocyte antigens (HLA), helping us to understand the movement of human populations over time; and the impact of selective factors, such as disease or nutrition in human society. The recent work of the *Human Genome Project* takes our understanding of human polymorphisms to a new level, using mitochondrial DNA (mtDNA) and chromosomal (nuclear) DNA to answer questions about our species' genetic history. In their attempt to map the species genome of *Homo sapiens*, scientists from the Human Genome Project are examining DNA polymorphisms whose evolution can be studied in the same way that phenotypic polymorphisms are. The DNA polymorphism research confirms what we have learned by studying traditional polymorphic traits, which is that, as the Jurmain textbook says on page 438, "the amount of genetic variation accounted for by differences *between* groups is vastly exceeded by the variation existing *within* groups." The newest research on geographically patterned genetic clusters is leading us back to some of the old issues about races and racial variation, and it remains to be seen how DNA polymorphisms will advance that discussion.

Forensic anthropologists do rely on phenotypic criteria associated with human populations or races to help them identify human remains, although they fully understand the limitations of relying on any single trait or set of criteria.

The study of **population genetics**, which looks at the distribution of allele frequencies within populations, can tell us much about how evolution has occurred in our species. A *population* is a group of interbreeding individuals that constitute a **gene pool**, or the total complement of alleles shared by reproductive members of a population. Strictly speaking, the entire species of *Homo sapiens* can be described as a population. Each member has the potential to mate with another member, but in practice, this doesn't happen because there are geographical, ecological, and social factors that determine mate choice. In past centuries, as the video points out, boys really did marry the girl next door. Parish records in Europe indicate that most people married someone living within three miles of their home. When bicycles were invented, the radius changed to within ten miles of home. Modern transportation makes it easier for a wider range of potential mates. However, as pointed out on page 102 of the Jurmain textbook, actual mating patterns are still somewhat restricted. Data from Ann Arbor, Michigan, show the average distance between birthplaces of partners to be about 160 miles, which indicates that many people do not find mates from distant locales. Geography also plays a part in mating patterns in **breeding isolates**, populations living in remote areas, such as a Pacific island, where there is little chance of finding a mate from outside.

Exogamy, which refers to marrying or mating outside the group, is prevalent in many societies for many reason, one of which is the benefit of wider social bonds and obligations of reciprocity, and another, the avoidance of inbreeding. Social, ethnic, and religious boundaries can create smaller population segments who practice **endogamy**, or marrying or mating within the group. The Amish in North America are a religious group who share a common ancestry, customs, and religious beliefs. Amish men and women are only permitted to marry within their community and stand as a good example of a population that practices strict endogamy.

Once a population is identified, population geneticists attempt to determine the evolutionary forces that might be operating on the group by measuring allele frequencies for specific traits against the **Hardy-Weinberg theory of genetic equilibrium**, a mathematical model that gives a baseline set of evolutionary expectations under known conditions. Essentially, the Hardy-Weinberg theory says that allele frequencies in a population will remain the same over time as long as there is nonrandom mating, and no mutation, no gene flow, no genetic drift, and no natural selection. Since the allele frequencies remain the same, the population is said to be in equilibrium. This is a hypothetical situation against which scientists can compare the real allele frequencies in a population. By examining the differences from the theoretical expectation (no change), it is possible to measure how much change has taken place and evaluate the source of that change (gene flow, genetic drift, rapid mutation, natural selection, or mate choice). See pages 447, 450–451 in the Jurmain textbook for an explanation of how scientists calculate allele frequencies using the Hardy-Weinberg theory of genetic equilibrium.

A number of factors initiate changes in allele frequencies: mutation, gene flow, natural selection, and nonrandom mating. **Nonrandom mating**, in which individuals choose their mates preferentially rather than at random, should change allele frequencies, but in most human populations, it appears to have little influence. **Inbreeding** is a type of nonrandom mating in which individuals have a higher likelihood of mating or marrying close relatives. Since relatives are more likely to have the same alleles than are nonrelatives, inbreeding can increase the possibility of homozygous recessive traits, which can have medical and evolutionary consequences. Hence, all societies have some sort of incest taboo, although the definition of "close" relatives or prohibited mating patterns varies from society to society. The biological ramifications of incest are also highly variable, depending on other factors in the population.

The Jurmain textbook refers to culture as the human strategy of adaptation. Natural selection operates within specific environmental settings, and adaptation can take place through either biological or cultural means. Often, biology and culture interact in this process. The textbook authors cite two examples of human polymorphisms that demonstrate this interaction: the sickle-cell allele and lactose intolerance. In both cases, variant alleles that are normally occurring variants in the population are favored under circumstance that are created by culture. In the first example, the recessive sickle-cell allele is highly deleterious, even in the heterozygous condition. Individuals with two recessive alleles rarely live to reproductive age, and those with one allele have frequent and debilitating episodes of anemia. The sickle-cell allele rose in frequency among certain populations in West Africa because it conferred an advantage against malaria—the malarial parasite is unable to complete its reproductive cycle in the human red blood cell because the cell is shaped like a sickle (a crescent or hook), rather than being rounded. The selective pressure that favored the sickle-cell allele was the adoption of slash-and-burn agriculture in the tropical rain-forest belt. In clearing the rain forest for agriculture, people provided roosting places, water, and hosts for mosquitoes that carried the organism that causes malaria. Those individuals in the population who happened to have inherited the sickle-cell allele were suddenly favored against the selective pressure of malaria, so that a balanced polymorphism emerged. The negative effects of having sickle-cell alleles, in the form of red blood cells that couldn't carry hemoglobin properly, were balanced by the benefits of those cells in resisting parasitism by the malarial parasite. This resulted in higher than expected frequencies of the recessive allele for sickle cell in those populations practicing slash-and-burn agriculture in Africa. Thus, a biological variation made possible a cultural adaptation that, in turn, increased the frequency of the biological variant by maintaining the selective pressure.

Lactose intolerance is a condition in humans that refers to the inability to digest fresh milk products. One ingredient in milk is lactose, a sugar that is broken down in humans and other mammals by the enzyme lactase. In most mammals, including humans, the gene that codes for lactase production turns off in adolescence. If an adult drinks too much milk, various unpleasant intestinal symptoms occur. However, not all humans lose the ability to break down lactose. The geographical distribution of **lactase persistence** mirrors the worldwide distribution of cultures that depend on dairying and consume large amounts of fresh milk products. In those populations, selection has favored individuals who do not turn off lactase production at adolescence. During the last few thousand years, according to the Jurmain textbook, cultural factors have initiated evolutionary changes in human groups that are reflected in their biology.

Review Exercises

Matching

Match each term with the appropriate definition or description.

1. _b_ balanced polymorphisms
2. _d_ biocultural evolution
3. _a_ biological determinism
4. _e_ breeding isolates
5. _c_ cline
6. _g_ endogamy
7. _j_ eugenics
8. _h_ exogamy
9. _i_ gene pool
10. _k_ Hardy-Weinberg theory
11. _m_ incest avoidance
12. _n_ lactase persistence
13. _p_ nonrandom mating
14. _f_ polytypic
15. _l_ polymorphisms
16. _o_ population genetics
17. _s_ race
18. _q_ slash-and-burn agriculture
19. _r_ thrifty genotype

a. The concept that phenomena, including aspects of behavior, are governed by biological (genetic) factors.

b. The maintenance of two or more alleles in a population due to the selective advantage of the heterozygote.

c. A gradual change in the frequency of genotypes and phenotypes from one geographical region to another.

d. The mutual, interactive evolution of human biology and culture.

e. Populations that are clearly isolated geographically or socially from other breeding populations.

f. Species composed of populations that differ in the expressions of one or more traits; the expression of genetic variants in different frequencies in different populations of a species.

g. Mating with individuals from the same group.

h. Mating with individuals from other groups.

i. The total complement of genes shared by reproductive members of a population.

j. The philosophy of race improvement through forced sterilization of members of some groups and increased reproduction among others.

k. The mathematical relationship expressing—under ideal conditions—the predicted distribution of alleles in populations.

l. Characteristics or traits caused by different forms of genes, or alleles, with different expressions in the phenotype.

m. The tendency to avoid mating with close relatives.

n. The continued production of the enzyme lactase in adults, thus allowing them to digest fresh milk.

o. The study of the frequency of alleles, genotypes, and phenotypes in populations.

p. Patterns of mating in a population in which individuals choose their preferred mates.

q. An agricultural land-clearing practice in some cultures whereby trees and vegetation are cut and burned.

r. Human genotype that permits efficient storage of fat to draw on in times of food shortage and conservation of glucose and nitrogen.

s. As used in biology, a taxonomic category of subspecies. In common usage, it can also refer to a group that is distinguished by physical characteristics, culture, and geography.

Completion

Fill each blank with the most appropriate term from the list below.

balanced polymorphism   lactase persistence
changing   no
clines   polymorphic
hypothetical   polytypic
inbreeding

1. The human species is said to be ___Polytypic___ because local populations differ in the expression of one or more traits.

2. The ABO blood group system is said to be ___Polymorphic___ because the gene for blood type has three different alleles.

3. Today anthropologists study biological diversity in terms of ___Clines___, or the continuous gradation over space in the form or frequency of a trait.

4. The Hardy-Weinberg theory of genetic equilibrium establishes a set of conditions where ___no___ evolution occurs; in other words, the theory is based on an idealized ___hypothical___ state.

5. The Hardy-Weinberg formula provides a tool to determine whether allele frequencies are ___changing___.

6. An example of human biocultural evolution involving the ability to digest milk is called ___lactase Persistence___

7. The precise evolutionary mechanism in the sickle-cell trait (that provides a reproductive advantage to the heterozygote in certain environments) is called ___balanced polymorphism___

8. ___Inbreeding___ is a type of nonrandom mating in which relatives mate more often than predicted.

Self-Test

Select the best answer.

1. The first scientific attempt to classify humans based on biological variation was made by
   a. Christopher Columbus.
   b. the ancient Egyptians.
   c. J. F. Blumenbach.
   d. C. Linnaeus.
   e. none of the above.

2. The application of evolutionary principles to the study of human variation
   a. reinforced traditional views of races as fixed biological entities that do not change.
   b. helped replace earlier views based solely on phenotypes.
   c. allowed scientists to divide the human species precisely into well-defined races.
   d. allowed scientists to ignore the adaptive significance of most traits.
   e. has been of little value for understanding human variation.

3. Which of the following describes the main problem with using the concept of race to understand polytypic variation in humans?
   a. The traits that are used to define race are arbitrary; they could include shape of ear lobes, number of fingers, or skin color.
   b. The traits used to define race do not always go together; the genes for dark skin color, for example, may exist in a person who has genes for straight hair and blue eyes.
   c. Alleles usually exist in all populations; what varies is the frequency.
   d. all of the above
   e. none of the above

4. When a polymorphic species is divided into geographically dispersed populations, it usually is _____; that is, the store of genetic variability is unevenly expressed.
   a. polysynthetic
   b. polytypic
   c. polygala
   d. polychromatic
   e. polynomial

5. The person responsible for popularizing eugenics among nineteenth-century Europeans was
   a. Charles Darwin.
   b. Francis Galton.
   c. Georges Cuvier.
   d. Gregor Mendel.
   e. Charles Lyell.

6. The modern biological usage of the term race
   a. refers to the geographically patterned phenotypic variation within a species.
   b. refers only to IQ.
   c. refers only to skin color.
   d. refers to a person's nationality.
   e. has precise definitions agreed upon by all anthropologists.

7. The total complement of genes shared by reproductive members of a population is
   a. a cline.
   b. a breeding isolate.
   c. a gene pool.
   d. an endogamy
   e. none of the above.

8. Which of the following statements explains why the ABO system of blood types is interesting from an anthropological viewpoint?
   a. The frequencies of the *A, B,* and *O* alleles varies tremendously among humans.
   b. Most contemporary human populations are polymorphic for all three alleles.
   c. The large number of human leukocyte antigen (HLA) alleles are useful in showing patterns of human population diversity.
   d. Natural selection has influenced the evolution of HLA alleles in humans, particularly as related to infectious disease.
   e. all of the above

9. Under idealized Hardy-Weinberg conditions, which of the following statements is **FALSE**?
   a. No new alleles will be added to a population's gene pool.
   b. No alleles will be removed from a population's gene pool.
   c. There will be no change in the allele frequencies in a population over time.
   d. There are no molecular changes in the gametes.
   e. Mutation rates will increase with each generation.

10. The Hardy-Weinberg genetic equilibrium formula assumes that
    a. the population under study is infinitely large.
    b. there is constant mutation of alleles in the population under study.
    c. the population under study is very small.
    d. a and b are true.
    e. b and c are true.

11. A genetic trait (such as sickle-cell trait) that provides a reproductive advantage to the heterozygote in certain environments is a clear example of
    a. natural selection.
    b. evolutionary interactions.
    c. new alleles being added by molecular changes in gametes.
    d. balanced polymorphism.
    e. a and d.

12. An example of biocultural evolution is
    a. bulky body development.
    b. lactase persistence.
    c. patterns of genetic differences in human populations.
    d. slash-and-burn agriculture.
    e. none of the above.

13. Endogamy refers to
    a. marrying/mating outside of a group.
    b. marrying/mating inside of a group.
    c. advantageous traits that evolve in a population over time.
    d. disadvantageous traits that evolve in a population over time.
    e. none of the above.

14. In the video, Dr. Lauren Breihan is shown treating Navajo patients at a clinic run by Native Americans for Community Action. She routinely screens her patients for type 2 diabetes because of the increased health risk they have for this type of diabetes—a vulnerability that may be explained by which of the following theories?
    a. the Hardy-Weinberg theory
    b. the sickle-cell hypothesis
    c. the polymorphism theory
    d. the thrifty genotype hypothesis
    e. none of the above

Short-Answer Questions

1. What is meant when it is said that humans are members of the same polytypic species?

   There is only one species of Human and all humans are Polytypic. This means they Belong to one population, But have more than one expression of traits.

2. How are the concepts of population, gene pool, and breeding isolates related to one another?

   A population is comprised of a group of individuals whom can interbreed w/ each other. The gene Pool is the total # of genes and our relatedness to one another. But environment determines that Pop. Gene Pool.

3. Write the equation for the Hardy-Weinberg theory of genetic equilibrium and list four of the five assumptions that must be met in an idealized population at equilibrium.

   $$(p+q) \times (p+q) = p^2 + 2pq + q^2$$
   1. larg Pop.
   2. No genetic Muttation
   3. No gene Flow
   4. Random mating

4. What is the physiological mechanism of lactose intolerance? Why is the ability to digest milk sugars, or lactase persistence, an example of biocultural evolution?

   After weaning the Body Switches Off the ability to drink Milk. But some People Must relay on Animals that Produce dairy Products and the Cbility to eat/drink Milk Products to survive.

5. What have scientists learned about the history of the San people in Africa through studies of molecular evidence?

   They have the highest Genetic diversity in the known pop. They differ greatly compared to Europeans. This seems to point to the Possibility that the Sans people are the original decendents of the 1st Homo Sapians.

Application Questions

1. An anthropology teacher who has taught human variation courses for fifteen years tells you about her dilemma. Each semester she takes much time and effort to explain and demonstrate the difference between "race" and "ethnicity," emphasizing that the perception of distinct "races" in human populations does not exist. Only a few students, however, demonstrate their understanding of the distinction between "race" and "ethnicity" and the fact that "race" is no longer a useful term to refer to human diversity. She commonly hears students continue to refer to the "race" of other people and groups in their general conversation. How do you explain the students' lack of comprehension and application to their daily life of the facts about the inaccuracy of the "race" concept?

   Race in todays socity is the belife that People are different based on outside apperences such as Skin Color, Rather than on biological evidence. Genetically speaking Humans for the most part share the majority of genes w/ one another and many outside apperences are based soley on bioculture evolution.

2. The health care workers in an emergency room of a hospital in Los Angeles County are highly confused and angered by the claim of a white male in his twenties. The young man is writhing in pain as he begs for painkiller to alleviate his sickle-cell anemia. His girlfriend argues with the health care staff because they do not believe it is possible for a white person to have sickle-cell anemia. What could you say to the staff about sickle-cell anemia, given what you have learned about biocultural evolution and balanced polymorphisms, in an attempt to motivate them to treat the suffering of the young man?

   Sickel-cell is carried in many Humans due to the emergence of the slash/burn tech. in the early development of Agriculture. Though it is true that African pop. Are the more common carriers. But as long as Both Parents carry the resive gene they can develope the disease.

3. Describe the case of the refugee Somali Bantu family, the Lumungus, in relation to the concepts of race and racism. What would you suggest to policy makers in Somalia to prevent such displacement of people as a result of racism?

   They were driven out of because they were darker skinned. What the Somalians really must do is educate people as to the true Meaning of "Race" it is a purly Psychological ideology that has nothing to do with Fact.

Answer Key

Matching

1. b (objective 6)
2. d (objective 6)
3. a (objective 1)
4. e (objective 4)
5. c (video lesson, segment 2; objective 3)
6. g (objective 4)
7. j (objective 1)
8. h (objective 4)
9. i (objective 4)
10. k (objectives 4 & 5)
11. m (objective 4)
12. n (objective 6)
13. p (objective 4)
14. f (objectives 2 & 3)
15. l (video lesson, segment 2; objective 3)
16. o (video lesson, segment 3; objectives 3 & 4)
17. s (video lesson, segment 1; objective 2)
18. q (objective 6)
19. r (video lesson, segment 3; objective 4)

Completion

1. polytypic (objectives 2 & 3)
2. polymorphic (objective 3)
3. clines (video lesson, segment 2; objective 3)
4. no; hypothetical (objectives 4 & 5)
5. changing (objectives 4 & 5)
6. lactase persistence (objective 6)
7. balanced polymorphism (objective 6)
8. inbreeding (objective 4)

Self-Test

1. d. is the correct answer. The ancient Egyptians had a system for classifying humans based on their skin color as early as 1350 B.C.E., but Linnaeus' taxonomic system was the first scientific attempt at classifying humans. (objective 1)

2. b. is the correct answer. This genetic emphasis has dispelled previously held misconceptions that races are fixed biological entities that don't change over time and that are composed of individuals who all conform to a particular type. (objective 1)

3. d. is the correct answer. Trait-based classification is problematic because typologies can be inherently misleading; most racial classifications are based on polygenic characteristics that have a continuous range of expression, which makes the creation of distinct boundaries nearly impossible. (objective 1)

4. b. is the correct answer. A polytypic species is composed of local populations that differ in the expression of one or more traits. (objectives 2 & 3)

5. b. is the correct answer. Francis Galton was a cousin of Charles Darwin who wrote and lectured widely on the philosophy of "race improvement"—a now-discredited approach that he called eugenics. (objective 2)

6. a. is the correct answer. In its most common biological usage, the term *race* refers to geographical patterned phenotypic variation within a species. (video lesson, segment 1; objective 2)

7. c. is the correct answer. This is the definition of a gene pool. (objective 3)

8. e. is the correct answer. All four statements are described in the Jurmain textbook as reasons why anthropologists study the polymorphic expression of blood types among humans. (objective 3)

9. e. is the correct answer. The Hardy-Weinberg theory assumes that no mutation occurs, so no new alleles are being added by molecular changes in gametes. (objectives 4 & 5)

10. a. is the correct answer. This statement is the first hypothetical condition described in the Hardy-Weinberg model. (objectives 4 & 5)

11. e. is the correct answer. The sickle-cell allele is referred to as a balanced polymorphism in malarial regions because it occurs at a higher frequency in these environments as a result of the action of natural selection. (objective 6)

12. b. is the correct answer. The Jurmain textbook offers a detailed explanation for why lactase persistence is an example of biocultural evolution. (objective 6)

13. b. is the correct answer. This is the definition of endogamy. (objective 4)

14. d. is the correct answer. The video lesson is the source of the definition of the thrifty genotype. (video lesson, segment 3; objective 4)

Short-Answer Questions

Your answers should include the following:

1. There is only one species of humans on the planet and all humans are polytypic. Being polytypic means that all humans belong to local populations that have different expressions of one or more traits. (objective 1)

2. A population is a group of people who interbreed with one another. Therefore, people within a population share a common gene pool and have a degree of relatedness. Most likely, people choose their mates from candidates within their same local population. However, geography, ecology, and social factors also determine mate choice. If a

group of people are geographically isolated or adhere to certain types of mating rules (endogamy, for example), they are restricted from finding mates outside the immediate vicinity or immediate local population. These isolated populations are referred to as breeding isolates. However, people who are in isolated populations, for whatever reason, can still interbreed with people from outside their populations if barriers (geographical, ecological or social) are removed because all humans, everywhere, belong to the same polytypic species. (objective 4)

3. The Hardy-Weinberg theory of genetic equilibrium depends on a simple Mendelian pattern that has only two alleles: "A," or, the frequency of the dominant allele, and, "a," or the frequency of the recessive allele. Their combined total frequency must represent all possibilities, or, in other words, be equal to 1:

$$p + q = 1$$

In this formula, "A" $= p$, and "a" $= q$. Using these two alleles, the formula looks like this:

$$(p + q) \times (p + q) = p^2 + 2pq + q^2$$

In this case, p^2 is the frequency of the AA genotype, $2pq$ is the frequency of the Aa genotype, and q^2 is the frequency of the aa genotype, where p is the frequency of the dominant allele and q is the frequency of the recessive allele in a population. The model assumes that the following hypothetical conditions are met: large population, no mutations, no gene flow, and random mating. (objectives 4 & 5)

4. The physiological mechanism of lactose intolerance is a gene that codes for lactase production, which typically "switches off" after weaning. Lactase is the enzyme required for breaking down the sugar lactose into a usable form by the body. So, after weaning, the individual no longer produces lactase and becomes lactose intolerant.

Humans are said to be the result of interactions between their culture and their biology. This is what we refer to as biocultural evolution. It is thought that some people continue to tolerate milk and milk products because we are descended from Middle Eastern populations who were economically dependent on pastoralism, the raising of cows, sheep, and goats, and consumed large quantities of milk products. This cultural environment imposed strong selective pressure to shift allele frequencies in the direction of lactase persistence through time. The geographical distribution of lactase persistence is related to a history of cultural dependence on fresh milk products. In groups who are lactose intolerant, however, and who still rely on dairying for economic purposes, groups in Africa and Asia, for example, tolerate certain types of milk products because their consumption is restricted to cheese and yogurt products that are already broken down by bacteria. (objective 6)

5. A genome-wide scan of more than 100 indigenous African populations found that the San population in South Africa has the highest genetic diversity and the greatest number of unique alleles of any African group. A second study confirmed this; in fact, two San individuals are more genetically diverse from each other than a European would be from an Asian. This high genetic diversity confirms the African origin theory for modern humans, and points to the San, formerly known as the Bushmen, as the closest living descendants to the original modern *Homo sapiens*. (objective 6)

Application Questions

Your answers should include the following:

1. The concept of race is understood by anthropologists and scientists within the specific context of the evolutionary principles of human variation. It is one thing to convey to individuals fundamental scientific principles and another thing to persuade them to change their long-ingrained cultural perspectives and habits as a result. As stated by the textbook authors on page 433, "Unfortunately, there are probably hundreds (if not thousands) of popular misconceptions regarding human diversity, and to make matters worse, many people seem quite unwilling to accept what science has to contribute on the subject." Being exposed to evolutionary perspectives on human variation does not preclude people from retaining their old behaviors and attitudes toward race. Students are surprised to hear that there is no biological validity behind human variation, and it takes a while for them to devise a way to incorporate this information and share it with others. It is the task of educators to keep conveying this information as clearly as possible. In doing this, we can expect change to come, but slowly. (objective 2)

2. There are several ways to answer this question. Useful examples can be selected from among human polymorphisms discussed on pages 441–445 in the Jurmain textbook. The answer below explores the concept of balanced polymorphisms that is covered as part of the textbook authors' explanation of the mechanism that causes sickle-cell anemia.

    An individual does not have to have black skin to inherit the two recessive alleles, one from each parent, necessary for sickle-cell disease. Both parents would have to be carriers of the trait. While it is true that certain African populations have higher frequencies of the sickle-cell allele, the alleles that code for sickle cell are simple mutations that exist in many human populations. It all started about 2,000 years ago with the introduction of slash-and-burn agriculture in tropical rain forests. This subsistence method caused the environment to change to one that provided prime conditions for mosquitoes, ones that carried the organism responsible for malaria, to breed close to human settlements. The sickle-cell allele was already present in the human population, a result of a point mutation, a common occurrence that supplies diversity for natural selection to act upon. After slash-and-burn agriculture was introduced, this allele became widespread in the population.

    In malarial regions, the sickle-cell allele is a biological adaptation to this cultural innovation that has negative consequences for many people, as can be seen from the example of the patient described in this question. If a person inherits two recessive alleles from his parents, he is afflicted with the disease, can be very sick most of his life, and probably will not live to reproduce offspring himself. In tropical regions, the trait has become a balanced polymorphism because it provides reproductive advantages to the people who carry it. Being a carrier of the trait is not fatal, so these individuals usually live to reproduce offspring, and they are somewhat immune from the ravages of malaria. (video lesson, segment 3; objective 3)

3. The Somali Bantu family, the Lumungus, were persecuted and driven out of Somalia because they were darker skinned than the lighter skinned Somalis. Racism sparked a genocidal mania in Somalia that wiped out millions of people, including many

members of the Lumungus' immediate family. The racism exhibited in Somalia was based on the nineteenth-century concept of "race," one that categorized people intellectually, morally, and physically solely on phenotypic differences. The Somalis need to be exposed to the current knowledge that this perspective on "race" has no biological validity in human beings. Today, scientific opinion operates from the position that there are evolutionary principles of human diversity based on genetic variation, not phenotypic differences. The authority figures in Somalia must be educated in the latest concepts regarding human variation and biocultural diversity, and then they must implement and foster major educational programs to convey twenty-first century evolutionary principles to both factions, the lighter-skinned Somalis and the Somali-Bantu people. (video lesson, segment 1; objective 6)

Notes:

Lesson Review

Lesson 13: Patterns of Variation

PLEASE NOTE: Use this matrix to guide your study and achieve the learning objectives of this lesson. It will also help you to view the video, which defines and demonstrates important concepts and principles as they relate to everyday life and actual case studies.

Learning Objective	Textbook	Student Guide	Video Lesson
1. Trace the historical views of human variation, emphasizing early (eighteenth and nineteenth century) scientific classifications.	pp. 434–435	Key Terms: 1, 2; Matching: 3, 7; Self-Test: 1, 2, 3; Short-Answer: 1.	
2. Discuss the typological concept of race and whether it has any biological validity.	pp. 435–440	Key Terms: 3, 17; Matching: 14, 17; Completion: 1; Self-Test: 4, 5, 6; Short-Answer: 5; Application: 1.	Segment 1: *Phenotype vs. Genotype*
3. Draw on knowledge of natural selection and other evolutionary factors to discuss the population patterning of human genotypic and phenotypic variation.	pp. 440–445	Key Terms: 3, 4, 5, 18; Matching: 5, 14, 15, 16; Completion: 1, 2, 3; Self-Test: 4, 7, 8; Application: 2.	Segment 2: *Looking at Human Variation* Segment 3: *Microevolution at Work*
4. Explain the application of population genetics to the study of human diversity.	pp. 445–447, 452–453	Key Terms: 5, 6, 7, 8, 9, 10, 11, 12, 13, 20; Matching: 4, 6, 8, 9, 10, 11, 13, 16, 19; Completion: 4, 5, 8; Self-Test: 9, 10, 13, 14; Short-Answer: 2, 3.	Segment 3: *Microevolution at Work*

Learning Objective	Textbook	Student Guide	Video Lesson
5. Calculate allele frequencies using the Hardy-Weinberg equilibrium formula.	pp. 447–452	Key Terms: 10; Matching: 10; Completion: 4, 5; Self-Test: 9, 10; Short-Answer: 3.	
6. Discuss examples of human biocultural evolution.	pp. 453–456	Key Terms: 14, 15, 16, 19; Matching: 1, 2, 12, 18; Completion: 6, 7; Self-Test: 11, 12; Short-Answer: 4, 6; Application: 3.	Segment 1: *Phenotype vs. Genotype* Segment 3: *Microevolution at Work*

LESSON 14

 Lesson 14:   Patterns of Adaptation

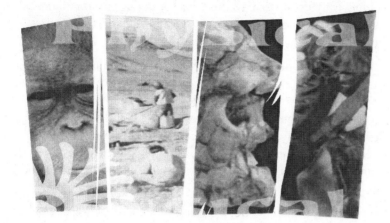

Patterns of Adaptation

Checklist

For the most effective study of this lesson, complete the following activities in this sequence.

Before Viewing the Video

❑ Read the Preview, Learning Objectives, and Viewing Notes below.

❑ Read Chapter 16, "Modern Human Biology: Patterns of Adaptation," pages 460–481, in *Introduction to Physical Anthropology*.

What to Watch

❑ After reading the textbook assignment, watch the video for Lesson 14, *Patterns of Adaptation*.

After Viewing the Video

❑ Briefly note your answers to the questions listed at the end of the Viewing Notes.

❑ Review the Summary below.

❑ Review all reading assignments for this lesson, including the Viewing Notes in this lesson.

❑ Write brief answers to the "Critical Thinking Questions" at the end of Chapter 16 in the textbook.

❑ Complete the Review Exercises below. Check your answers with the Answer Key and review when necessary.

❑ Use the Lesson Review matrix found at the end of this lesson to review and assess your knowledge of each Learning Objective.

Preview

Lesson 14 is primarily focused on biological issues but considers the influence of cultural practices on human adaptive responses as well because cultural adaptation has played a critical part in the evolution of *Homo sapiens*. Physiological responses to changing environments and innovative cultural practices, together, enabled human beings to colonize almost the entire planet except for the oceans, the highest mountains, and Antarctica.

Skin color is commonly cited as an example of adaptation by natural selection in response to the pressures of ultraviolet radiation. The textbook authors and the video explain that, in the Old World especially, pigmentation follows a particular geographical pattern. The most pigmentation is found in the tropics, while lighter skin colors are associated with northern latitudes. This lesson also notes the physiology of skin color and the three substances that influence it: hemoglobin, carotene, and melanin. It also takes a detailed look at how skin color changes in response to environmental stressors, which can take many generations to become widespread in a population.

The textbook and the video explain what is understood regarding *H. sapiens'* physiological response to heat, cold, and high altitude. For example, Lesson 14 describes how body shape and size, and the production of increased numbers of red blood cells reflect adaptations to the environmental stress imposed by high altitude. If you have ever gone skiing and had the unfortunate experience of mountain sickness, which includes symptoms from headache and fatigue to life-threatening lung congestion and fluid build-up in the brain, it is because your rate of ascent into higher altitudes outpaced your body's ability to adjust to the higher elevation. However, people who are natives of the Himalayas or the Andes, for example, don't experience such symptoms, because of their long-standing physical adaptations to the altitude in which they were born.

Finally, Lesson 14 explains the adaptations that *H. sapiens* have developed to infectious diseases. An individual's elaborate immune system protects against infectious disease, and we learn why, in some instances, the immune system of *H. sapiens* fails to protect.

Concepts to Remember

❀ Lesson 4 introduced the term **polygenic**, which refers to traits or characteristics that are influenced by genes at two or more loci. Skin color, height, and eye color are three polygenic traits. Many polygenic traits in humans are influenced by environmental factors, and thus may be products of adaptation to changing environmental conditions.

❀ Lessons 3 and 4 explained how evolutionary factors, such as **mutation**, **gene flow**, **genetic drift**, and **recombination**, all interact to produce variation in humans and to distribute genes within and between populations. In addition, **natural selection** provides directional change in allele frequencies relative to specific environmental factors. If the environment changes, then selection pressures also change and the resulting shift in allele frequencies is what is meant by adaptation.

Learning Objectives

After completing this lesson, you will be able to:

1. Describe the adaptations known as acclimatization, and distinguish among the different types. (pp. 461–462)

2. Discuss the population patterning of human skin color variation and possible adaptive explanations. (pp. 463–467, 470–471)

3. Contrast human physiological responses to heat and to cold. (pp. 468–472)

4. Describe the body's responses to high altitude. (pp. 473–475)

5. Define and give examples of infectious disease, pathogens, and vectors, and discuss their interaction with human cultural behavior. (pp. 475–478)

6. Describe the recent reemergence of infectious disease, and identify the factors that have contributed to this phenomenon. (pp. 478–481)

At this point, read Chapter 16, "Modern Human Biology: Patterns of Adaptation," pages 460–481.

Viewing Notes

You're cold and you shiver; you're hot and you sweat. What you notice is the change in temperature. What your body notices is the stress on its physiological mechanisms, and it compensates in some way to maintain internal constancy, or **homeostasis**. The video points out that our reaction to stress in the environment—changes in temperature, light, noise, food production, disease—is the process of adaptation. Skin color is an example of adaptation. It is likely that the first humans had a dark skin color because they originated in Africa around the equator. Dark skin is produced by the skin pigment **melanin**, which protects us from ultraviolet radiation from the sun.

It is thought that as humans migrated out of the tropics, and into climates where they were exposed to less UV radiation, they ultimately produced less melanin. This enabled them to synthesize more vitamin D. The body can easily produce vitamin D when stimulated by ultraviolet light. But in northern latitudes, where humans receive less exposure to direct sunlight, too much melanin interfered with the production of vitamin D. Vitamin D is needed to maintain normal blood levels of calcium and phosphorus, which helps form and maintain strong bones. Research also suggests that vitamin D may help maintain a healthy immune system. Nina Jablonski, an anthropologist interviewed in the video, explains that it was essential that early humans evolved "depigmented" skin as they moved away from the equator into eastern Asia and Europe so they could produce vitamin D in their skin. (For a reminder why, read pages 463–468 of the Jurmain textbook.)

The video introduces the term **acclimatization,** which refers to the human body adapting to environmental conditions that occur during an individual's lifetime.

Throughout human evolution, infectious disease has exerted enormous selective pressures on populations. The video points out the important relationship between **pathogens** and the human immune system that creates **antibodies** to fight them. Antibodies are proteins that attach to the pathogen when it enters the body. According to Wendy Birky, an anthropologist interviewed in the video, disease is one of the biggest challenges for human beings. The video provides information about **zoonoses**, diseases that are transmitted to humans through contact with nonhuman animals. Three zoonoses—HIV/AIDS, tuberculosis, and malaria—are the top fatal diseases today, resulting largely from humans manipulating the natural environment. The video points to a recent zoonosis in the United States, the West Nile virus, which was first detected in New York City in 1999. By 2006, the Center for Disease Control reported human cases in every state except Vermont, New Hampshire, Maine, Delaware, Alaska, and Hawaii.

The video interestingly notes that science had high hopes that having antibiotics available to cure infectious diseases would wipe them out completely. However, pathogens become resistant to antibiotics when they are used too often, and human populations have seen a return of diseases once thought eradicated because of the overuse of antibiotics.

Questions to Consider

❀ What is the action of melanin within the theory of skin color adaptations?

❀ What temporary responses to environmental conditions are mentioned in the video? Can you name some developmental adaptations that humans acquire in response to specific environmental conditions?

❀ Why haven't antibiotics wiped out infectious diseases?

Watch the video for Lesson 14, *Patterns of Adaptation*.

> Segment 1: *Genetic Adaptation*
> Segment 2: *Short-Term Adaptation*
> Segment 3: *Infectious Disease*

Key Terms and Concepts

Page references are keyed to *Introduction to Physical Anthropology*, 13th edition.

1. **stress:** In a physiological context, any factor that acts to disrupt homeostasis; more precisely, the body's response to any factor that threatens its ability to maintain homeostasis. (p. 462; video lesson, introduction; objective 1)

2. **homeostasis:** A condition of balance, or stability, within a biological system, maintained by the interaction of physiological mechanisms that compensate for changes (both external and internal). (p. 462; video lesson, introduction; objective 1)

3. **acclimatization:** Physiological responses to changes in the environment that occur during an individual's lifetime. Such responses may be temporary or permanent, depending on the duration of the environmental change and when in the individual's life it occurs. The *capacity* for acclimatization may typify an entire species or population, and because it is under genetic influence, it is subject to evolutionary factors such as natural selection and genetic drift. (p. 462; video lesson, segment 2; objective 1)

4. **neural tube:** In early embryonic development, the anatomical structure that develops to form the brain and spinal cord. (p. 465; objective 2)

5. **spinal bifida:** A condition in which the arch of one or more vertebrae fails to fuse and form a protective barrier around the spinal cord. (p. 465; objective 2)

6. **evaporative cooling:** A physiological mechanism that helps prevent the body from overheating. It occurs when perspiration is produced from sweat glands and then evaporates from the surface of the skin. (p. 468; objective 3)

7. **vasodilation:** Expansion of blood vessels, permitting increased blood flow to the skin. Vasodilation permits warming of the skin and facilitates radiation of warmth as a means of cooling. Vasodilation is an involuntary response to warm temperatures, various drugs, and even emotional states (blushing). (p. 469; objective 3)

8. **vasoconstriction:** Narrowing of blood vessels to reduce blood flow to the skin. Vasoconstriction is an involuntary response to cold and reduces heat loss at the skin's surface. (p. 472; objective 3)

9. **hypoxia:** A condition in which there is insufficient oxygen reaching body tissues. (p. 473; video lesson, segment 2; objective 4)

10. **vectors:** Agents that serve to transmit disease from one carrier to another. Mosquitoes are vectors for malaria, just as fleas are vectors for bubonic plague. (p. 475; video lesson, segment 3; objective 5)

11. **endemic:** Continuously present in a population. (p. 475; video lesson, segment 3; objective 5)

12. **zoonotic:** (zoh-oh-no´-tic) Pertaining to a zoonosis (*pl.* zoonoses), a disease that is transmitted to humans through contact with nonhuman animals. (p. 475; video lesson, segment 3; objective 5)

13. **melanin:** The pigment that gives color to the skin, hair, and parts of the eye, and provides protection against the damaging effects of ultraviolet radiation. (video lesson, segment 1; objective 2)

14. **antibodies:** Proteins that are produced by some types of immune cells and that serve as major components of the immune system. Antibodies recognize and attach to foreign antigens on bacteria, viruses, and other pathogens. Then other immune cells destroy the invading organism. (video lesson, segment 3; objective 5)

15. **pathogens:** Substances or microorganisms, such as bacteria, fungi, or viruses, that cause disease. (video lesson, segment 3; objective 5)

Summary

More than 99 percent of Antarctica is covered by ice. There is no indigenous human population and no animal life except around the coastal areas. The summer mean temperatures range from □5 to □31°F; winter temperatures are □40 to □94°F. During the winter months, there is no sun, and no planes are able to take off or land. However, there are numerous Antarctic stations in the southern part of the continent that allow some scientists to remain in the field year round, braving the cold, the blackness, and the isolation to conduct their research. Cultural adaptations, such as survival clothing, secure housing, and food brought in by plane, are critical to human survival in regions that experience extremes of heat and cold.

Throughout the human evolutionary past, survival depended on physiological adaptations as well as cultural ones. This lesson explores the biological adaptations that have facilitated human survival through time. Importantly, the Jurmain textbook points out, on page 462, that to survive, "all organisms need to maintain the normal functions of internal organs, tissues, and cells. What's more, they must accomplish this task in the context of an ever-changing environment." In other words, the human body maintains **homeostasis**. It accommodates environmental changes, such as changes in external temperatures in the environment, by compensating in some way to maintain a constant internal temperature. All life-forms have evolved mechanisms that achieve homeostasis and the ability to do this is influenced by genetic factors. The Jurmain textbook states on page 462 that "adaptation refers to long-term evolutionary (that is, genetic) changes that characterize all individuals within a population or species." Examples of long-term adaptations in *H. sapiens* are our physiological response to heat by sweating and our response to excessive UV light by tanning.

Acclimatization refers to physiological responses to changes in the environment that occur during an individual's lifetime. It can be short-term, long-term, or permanent. An example of a temporary and rapid physiological adjustment is the increase in red blood cells when the individual travels to locations in higher altitudes. After returning to a lower altitude, an individual's red blood cell count returns to his or her normal range. A developmental acclimatization is one that results from exposure to an environmental challenge during growth and development. This type of acclimatization is incorporated into an individual's physiology, and can be permanent. An example is the larger chest circumference and greater lung volume found in lifelong residents of higher altitudes. The people who live in the Andes Mountains of Peru are a good example of this type of acclimatization.

A visible example of adaptation by natural selection is skin color. The Jurmain textbook and video explain how the pigment **melanin**, a granular substance, is produced by specialized cells called melanocytes, which are located in the outer layer of the skin. All humans have approximately the same number of melanocytes, but they vary in the amount of melanin and the size of the melanin granules they produce. Melanin acts as a built-in sunscreen by absorbing potentially dangerous ultraviolet (UV) rays from the sun. People with fair skin produce small amounts of melanin and, when exposed to sunlight, their cells have little ability to increase production.

Natural selection has favored dark skin in regions near the equator, where the UV rays are most direct. It has been suggested that one reason for this is because increased melanin production around the equator helped protect them from the harmful effects of ultraviolet light. In this case, the selective mechanism is posited to be skin cancer. One objection to this theory harks back to an idea learned in Lesson 4: that natural selection can act only on traits that affect reproduction. In one African study, however, it was shown that all albino individuals in dark-skinned populations had either precancerous lesions or skin cancer by the age of twenty. It is certainly possible that in early human populations, individuals with little melanin may have succumbed to skin cancer, reducing their reproductive fitness.

Another theory suggests that dark skin may have helped early humans maintain a healthy level of folate, a B vitamin required for many developmental processes. UV radiation depletes folate serum levels in light-skinned individuals. Dark skin could have evolved as a protective response to this risk.

As populations migrated to different parts of the earth, especially to environments that exposed humans to less sunlight in the winter, the advantages of deeply pigmented skin no long applied. Since vitamin D is necessary for normal bone growth and because it is most easily produced through human's exposure to sunlight, it is hypothesized that a lighter skin color, or less melanin, was favored in those regions.

According to the Jurmain textbook, humans cope better with heat than with cold, a testimony to the long-term adaptations to heat that likely evolved during our early evolution in the tropics. In humans, sweat glands are distributed throughout the skin which makes it possible to lose heat at the body's surface. This mechanism for cooling, evolved to the greatest degree in humans, is called **evaporative cooling**. **Vasodilation,** another mechanism for radiating body heat, is the expansion of blood vessels, permitting increased blood flow to the skin where it is emitted from the skin's surface to the surrounding air. **Vasoconstriction** is a physiological response to cold. It is a short-term response in which the blood vessels narrow to reduce blood flow to the skin, reducing heat loss. Body size and proportions also play a part in regulating body temperature. *Bergmann's rule* states that among mammals, body size tends to be greater in populations that live in colder climates. Because heat is lost at the surface, increased mass allows for greater heat retention. *Allen's rule* maintains that in colder climates shorter appendages are more adaptive because their increased mass-to-surface ratios are more effective at preventing heat loss. In warmer climates, longer appendages encourage heat loss, which is adaptive there. Both the video and the Jurmain textbook offer graphic illustrations of these concepts although it is important to remember that, because of multiple selection pressures, not all populations may conform precisely to these rules.

*P*aul Farmer, an M.D. and a Ph.D. in anthropology, has found that healing a sick child is sometimes more a matter of confronting his own profession's cultural roadblocks than prescribing treatment. Farmer is a co-founder of Partners in Health (PIH), a charity committed to universal health care for those living in poverty, and he has spent much of his time in Haiti over the past two decades caring for thousands of the island's poorest inhabitants.

One illness that runs rampant among the poor is tuberculosis (TB). Resistant strains of TB have arisen in many parts of the world because of the erratic care that patients receive, especially those who live in impoverished, overcrowded communities under unsanitary conditions and lack access to or the financial resources to pay for a complete course, or regime, of "first-line" drugs commonly prescribed to treat the disease. Farmer noted that the World Health Organization treatment regime was contributing to the ability of the TB pathogen to mutate into a drug-resistant strain, and he undertook the difficult task of convincing the organization to change the regime.

In doing so, he ran up against a cultural attitude that has a strong impact on which populations are likely to get effective treatment for TB and other diseases—the belief on the part of the medical community that it isn't economically or logistically feasible to provide medical care for large masses living in poverty.

Farmer confronted those cultural attitudes with action. When told that there weren't enough doctors, he trained them. When the cited obstacle was high drug prices, he negotiated with pharmaceutical companies to make drugs more affordable. Misguided policies were met head on with successful arguments for change—including the change in the TB treatment regime.

Another common cultural practice Farmer has confronted is cost-benefit analysis, which is often used by Western medical organizations and insurance companies to determine who receives treatment. In one case, PIH hired a Medevac helicopter for $19,000 to take a 12-year-old cancer victim from Haiti to the United States for treatment. When doctors examined him there, his cancer was too widespread to treat and he died within weeks.

The result generated much criticism of PIH for spending this amount of money to save a single child when it could have provided food or drugs for many children. But PIH's action underscores a different cultural value: the importance of an individual life. Would the critics have been so quick to condemn if the child had been their own?

Small wonder that Farmer has won many awards and honors, including the MacArthur Foundation "genius" award, and has had a book written about him. *Mountains Beyond Mountains* written by Tracy Kidder, narrates the story of Farmer's work among Haiti's peasants and beyond. Can the movie be far behind?

Perhaps you have read books or seen documentaries about individual mountain climbers who are determined to scale Mount Everest, the highest point on the earth. It becomes a struggle between life and death because the physiological mechanisms that maintain homeostasis in humans evolved at lower altitudes. Therefore, humans are physically compromised by the conditions at higher altitudes, and Mount Everest is 27,500 feet above sea level. Above 9,000 feet, according to the Jurmain textbook, most people start to suffer from **hypoxia,** a lack of sufficient oxygen. The oxygen at higher elevations is less concentrated than it is at lower altitudes and so the body has to make certain physiological adjustments that increase its ability to use oxygen efficiently.

Yet, according to the Jurmain textbook, many millions of people live at altitudes above 10,000 feet. In the Andes, for example, human settlements exist as high as 17,000 feet. Interestingly, people born at lower altitudes and high-altitude natives differ somewhat in how they adapt to hypoxia. Some adaptations are temporary and occur during exposure to high altitudes. Other adaptations are developmental, or acquired during their residence at high altitude, while other physiological adaptations are genetic, and have evolved in certain populations over many generations. For example, the people of Tibet seem to have made evolutionary (genetic) accommodations to hypoxia. Infant birth weights of highland Tibetans are no lower than lowland populations, suggesting a biological adaptation to the stresses of high-attitude hypoxia that would otherwise favor small size at birth.

Infectious diseases are caused by **pathogens**, which are microorganisms in our environment, such as viruses, bacteria, and fungi, that enter the body and cause disease. They are important agents of natural selection and have always exerted selective pressures on human populations. With the domestication of plants and animals, people began to settle in one area rather than move about as nomadic hunters and gatherers.

As the Jurmain textbook points out, gradually, villages became towns, and towns became densely populated cities. This cultural shift created environmental conditions, such as high densities and poor sanitation, that gave rise to disease **vectors**, agents that serve to transmit disease from one carrier to another. In Chapter 4, the textbook authors described the dynamics of malaria and the role of sickle-cell hemoglobin in protecting individuals from the disease, an excellent example of natural selection. Nowadays, we seek cultural solutions to the problems of disease. In 2005, the Gates Foundation began giving large grants to several organizations to enable them to develop a vaccine for malaria. Another grant was given to the University of Leeds in 2006 to develop a new type of mosquito netting that will use the actual material and structure of the net to kill the mosquito rather than chemicals applied to the net. Chemically treated nets need to be retreated or replaced approximately every twenty washings. Moreover, a move away from insecticides avoids the problem of mosquitoes becoming resistant to the chemicals.

As long as humans lived in small bands, the opportunities for infectious diseases to affect large numbers of people was minimal. But when humans began a sedentary lifestyle and started raising animals for food, populations increased and infectious diseases became **endemic**, or continuously present within them. With exposure to domestic animals, such as cattle and fowl, opportunities developed for the spread of **zoonotic** diseases such as tuberculosis. Another example of the selective role of infectious disease, according to the Jurmain textbook, is AIDS (acquired immune deficiency syndrome).

Pathogens can become immune to the agents humans develop and use to combat them. Antibiotics place selective pressures on bacterial species that have, over time, evolved antibiotic-resistant strains. This has caused the reemergence of bacterial diseases in forms that are less responsive to the medications humans manufacture, as we see with tuberculosis and some of the resistant strains of streptococcus and staphalococcus plaguing modern hospital.

A final note in the Jurmain textbook, and in the video, concerns the effect of global warming on the emergence and spread of infectious diseases. The destruction of natural environments contributes to global warming and allows for the spread of disease vectors out of their restricted local areas thus facilitating the expansion of the geographical range of vectors, such as mosquitoes, to new habitats. And, as the human population continues to grow, we increase the effect of global warming through the increased intensity and pace of human activity. In developing countries, where 50 percent of mortality is a result of infectious disease, overcrowding and unsanitary conditions also contribute to increased rates of communicable diseases.

In February of 2007, the Intergovernmental Panel on Climate Change of the United Nations issued an assessment of the causes and consequences of climate change. It was their fourth report since 1990, and it was the first time the group asserted, with more than 90 percent confidence, that carbon dioxide and other heat-trapping greenhouse gases from human activities are the main causes of global warming. The group concluded that there should be no more debate on whether humans have contributed to warming since 1950. Instead, they challenged policy-makers to find solutions to slow down global warming. The implications of this for human evolution in the future is profound.

Review Exercises

Matching

Match each term with the appropriate definition or description.

1. __e__ acclimatization
2. __h__ antibodies
3. __d__ endemic
4. __g__ homeostasis

5. __a__ pathogens
6. __f__ vasoconstriction
7. __c__ vasodilation
8. __b__ zoonoses

a. Substances or microorganisms, such as bacteria, fungi, or viruses, that cause disease.

b. Diseases that are transmitted to humans through contact with nonhuman animals.

c. Expansion of blood vessels, permitting increased blood flow to the skin.

d. Continuously present in a population.

e. Physiological responses to changes in the environment that occur during an individual's lifetime.

f. Narrowing of blood vessels to reduce blood flow to the skin.

g. A condition of balance or stability within a biological system.

h. Proteins that are produced by some types of immune cells and that serve as major components of the immune system.

Completion

Fill each blank with the most appropriate term from the list below.

antibodies
evaporative cooling
homeostasis
neural tube

pathogens
spinal bifida
stress
vectors

1. Folate deficiency may cause _Neural tube_ defects such as _Spinal bifida_

2. A disruption of _homeostasis_ in the body may result in physical _stress_ .

3. _evaporative cooling_ helps keep the body from overheating.

4. Attack by _pathogene_ may stimulate the production of _antibodies_ in the body.

5. Agents that transmit disease organisms, such as the one that causes malaria, from one individual to another are called _vectors_ .

Self-Test

Select the best answer.

1. It is thought that melanin pigments in the skin
   a. can screen the skin from a excess of UV radiation that may cause skin cancer.
   b. in excess, may cause a shortage of folates in the body.
   c. in excess, may cause a shortage of vitamin D production in the body.
   d. can cause all of the above.

2. Rickets is caused by a
   a. folate deficiency.
   b. virus.
   c. vitamin D deficiency.
   d. bacterial pathogen.

3. West Nile virus is transmitted by
   a. birds.
   b. mosquitoes.
   c. bacteria.
   d. none of the above.

4. In terms of worldwide distribution, darker skin colors occur at their highest concentration at which of the following locations?
   a. near the poles
   b. in areas with the highest UV radiation
   c. near the equator
   d. b and c

5. Until the twentieth century, infectious disease was the leading cause of death
   a. among all humans.
   b. in the developing world.
   c. in Europe only.
   d. in Africa only.

6. The incidence of infectious disease in the world is increasing as a result of
   a. overuse of antibiotics.
   b. increasing pathogen resistance.
   c. the destruction of natural environments by human action and changes caused by global warming.
   d. all of the above.

7. Zoonotic diseases may be transmitted to humans
   a. from certain plants.
   b. through contact with nonhuman animals.
   c. only through endemic means.
   d. by none of the above.

8. Which of the following is true of a population that is genetically adapted to high altitudes?
   a. The population has lived at high altitudes for many generations, long enough for certain adaptations to evolve and spread throughout the population.
   b. The population has developmentally acclimatized to a high-altitude area after being raised there from a young age.
   c. The population has acclimatized to a high-altitude area after being exposed to it for a short period of time.
   d. none of the above

9. People with tall, linear body types are expected to be adapted to warm climates because
   a. according to Bergmann's rule, the surface area to body mass ratio is relatively large and it allows heat to dissipate.
   b. according to Allen's rule, the limbs of people from warm climates should be relatively short and thick.
   c. according to Bergmann's rule, the surface area to body mass ratio is relatively small and it allows heat to dissipate.
   d. a and b are true.

10. Vasodilation
   a. occurs when an individual is exposed to excessive cold.
   b. occurs when an individual is exposed to excessive heat.
   c. is a way that the body tries to maintain homeostasis.
   d. involves a and c.

11. Human responses to high altitude include
   a. lower birth weights for infants.
   b. late maturation.
   c. better diffusion of oxygen into the bloodstream.
   d. all of the above.

12. High-altitude stressors on the human body include
   a. excessive heat.
   b. strongly reduced solar radiation.
   c. hypoxia.
   d. high humidity.

13. According to the Jurmain textbook, which of the following peoples are thought to have genetic adaptations to living at high altitudes?

    a. Australian Aborigines
    b. highland Tibetans
    c. the Quechua of Peru
    d. b and c

14. Changes that occurred between 10,000 and 12,000 years ago that are thought to have encouraged the spread of disease organisms and vectors to larger population groups include

    a. a sedentary settlement pattern.
    b. the domestication of plants.
    c. the domestication of animals.
    d. all of the above.

15. HIV

    a. is a zoonotic disease in origin.
    b. is a deadly bacteria.
    c. evolves very slowly, so it is easy to treat.
    d. is none of the above.

Short-Answer Questions

1. What is the difference between acclimatization and genetic adaptation in relation to high altitudes? How do humans acclimate to high altitudes? What genetic adaptations are known? In which populations do they occur?

   Acclimatization is the short-term adaptation of to higher altitudes. It Produces more red-blood cells increase in heart Rate, + an increase in the bodies resperation Rate. Genetic adaption happens to those who live there. They have a slower maturation period, Produce more Red Blood cells and have larger lungs.

2. List a zoonosis and describe how it has been aided and spread by human cultural practices.

   Malaria is a 1 celled organism that is passed to humans through mosquitoes. As agriculture Progressed as a movement and Populations became denser the ability for it to spread grew.

3. How are body shape and size related to adaptations to heat and cold? Explain how these adaptations are related to Bergmann's rule and Allen's rule.

When living in colder environments the body tends to be "fatter" or stouter so as to conserve heat. Where as warmer climates tend to produce humans that are taller and linear. This matches what Allen + Bergmann's rules state regarding biocultural evo.

4. How do Australian aborigines use vasoconstriction as a long-term adjustment to cold?

Vasoconstriction is the narrowing of the blood vessels to conserve heat. Since the Aborigine people in Australia experince a wide range of temps. They use this rather than build shelters or clothes.

5. Explain how melanin helps to protect the skin from ultraviolet radiation.

Melanin absords certian wave lengths of UV radiation which reduces the radiation that actually touches the skin.

6. What are disease vectors? List three of these vectors and briefly explain how they transmit disease to humans.

Organisms that carry diseases from one carrier to another. Fleas and masquitoes transmite by biting other animals including humans.

Application Questions

1. What is the relationship between solar radiation and skin color? How does melanin protect the skin? What may be result from too much solar radiation on the skin? What deficiencies may result if not enough ultraviolet radiation is absorbed through the skin? How do these issues connect to the global patterning of skin color?

   Malanian changes the color the skin. The more Melanin Present the darker the skin. So it makes since that those who have more exposur to the sun and its radation to have darker skin. The Shortage of such results in a lack of Vitamin D.

2. How are stress and adaptation related to one another? Please use at least three examples from the Jurmain textbook and the video lesson.

   Outside stres results in adaptation. like cold inflicing the body type of those who live there, short term adaption on a higher altitude. or Melanin in the skin.

3. What is the contribution of culture in the development of zoonotic diseases?

   Zoonotic diseases spread easier in dense Populations and agriculture so as culture tends to bring large Pop. together. It makes spreading easier.

4. What are some reasons that some disease organisms are becoming immune to certain antibiotics? What are some possible solutions? Please use examples from the Jurmain textbook and video lesson about disease organisms that have become immune to some antibiotics.

   Organisms evolve to suite their enviroment. So as antibiotics are placed their to kill them they evolve to work around them. Such as HIV/AIDs, tuber-colusious ect.

Answer Key

Matching

1. e (video lesson, segment 2; objective 1)
2. h (video lesson, segment 3; objective 5)
3. d (video lesson, segment 3; objective 5)
4. g (video lesson, introduction; objective 1)
5. a (video lesson, segment 3; objective 5)
6. f (objective 3)
7. c (objective 3)
8. b (video lesson, segment 3; objective 5)

Completion

1. neural tube; spinal bifida (objective 2)
2. homeostasis; stress (video lesson, introduction; objective 1)
3. Evaporative cooling (objective 3)
4. pathogens; antibodies (video lesson, segment 3; objective 5)
5. vectors (video lesson, segment 3; objective 5)

Self-Test

1. d. is the correct answer. The amount of melanin pigment in the skin may have an effect on all three conditions. (video lesson, segment 1; objective 2)
2. c. is the correct answer. Rickets is caused by a vitamin D deficiency. (objective 2)
3. b. is the correct answer. Mosquitoes are the vector for West Nile virus. (video lesson, segment 3; objectives 5 & 6)
4. d. is the correct answer. The darkest skin colors are found near the equator, which also receives the greatest UV radiation. (video lesson, segment 1; objective 2)
5. a. is the correct answer. Until recently, infectious diseases were the number one cause of death among all humans. (objective 6)
6. d. is the correct answer. All three factors are thought to contribute to the increasing incidence of infectious disease. (video lesson, segment 3; objective 6)
7. b. is the correct answer. Zoonotic diseases are transmitted to humans by other animals. (video lesson, segment 3; objective 5)
8. a. is the correct answer. Genetic adaptations spread through a population over generations so a population would have to be living at high altitudes for many generations for a genetic adaptation to become common in the population. (objective 3)
9. a. is the correct answer. According to Bergmann's rule, warm climate people are expected to have a large surface to volume ratio. Allen's rule would predict long, thin extremities under the same circumstances. (objective 3)

10. b. is the correct answer. Vasodilation allows the release of heat by opening up capillaries near the surface of the skin. This helps to cool the body when it is exposed to excessive heat. (objective 3)

11. d. is the correct answer. All three are adaptive responses to high-altitude living. (objective 4)

12. c. is the correct answer. High-altitude environments have a lower concentration of oxygen, which can cause hypoxia. They also tend to be cold, dry, and to have a great deal of solar radiation. (video lesson, segment 2; objective 4)

13. d. is the correct answer. Genetic adaptations to high altitude have been observed in both Tibetan highlanders and the Quechua of Peru. (objective 4)

14. d. is the correct answer. All of these factors are thought to have contributed to the spread of infectious disease during this time period. (objective 5)

15. a. is the correct answer. HIV is considered to be a zoonotic disease because it was probably passed to humans by other primates. (video lesson, segment 3; objective 6)

Short-Answer Questions

Your answers should include the following:

1. Acclimatization is a short-term adaptation to a change in environmental conditions. At high altitudes, short-term responses include an increase in respiration rate, an increase in heart rate, and an increase in the production of red blood cells.

   Developmental acclimatizations by people who grow up at high altitudes include slower growth and later maturation, a larger chest, greater lung volume, and better diffusion of oxygen from the blood to the tissues of the body. Reproduction is affected in the following ways: lower birth weights, an increase in miscarriages, and an increase in infant mortality rates.

   Genetic adaptation to high altitude have been studied in Tibetan highlanders and the Quechua of Peru. Tibetan highlanders have nearly normal birth weights, probably due to changes in blood flow to the uterus. Both groups utilize glucose in a way that uses oxygen more efficiently and they also have some skeletal adaptations to high-altitude living. (video lesson, segment 2; objective 4)

2. Malaria is a one-celled organism that is passed to humans by mosquitoes. Humans have become more common prey of these mosquitoes through a sedentary settlement pattern, high population densities, and the creation of more pools of water, which is essential to the development of mosquito young.

   HIV is a virus that was probably spread from the human practice of hunting and consuming other primates. It has become a worldwide epidemic because of the human ability to engage in unprotected sexual intercourse with multiple partners and a tendency to travel over long distances, allowing the disease to spread in a wider area.

   Bubonic plague is a bacterium that uses fleas as a vector. During large outbreaks, these fleas were carried by the rats that infested towns and cities. Humans then came in contact with the fleas, and they contracted bubonic plague. The presence of fleas and rats was influenced by the often unsanitary, crowded conditions of towns and cities. (video lesson, segment 3; objectives 5 & 6)

3. Bergmann's rule states that the bodies of individuals living in warm climates should have a larger surface to volume ratio than those from cold climates. People from cold climates should then have a larger mass, relative to their height, than people from warmer climates. Allen's rule addresses the shape of the body and appendages. It states that people from warmer climates should have tall, thin bodies and long, thin appendages relative to people from cold climates who would be expected to have short, stocky bodies, and short, thick appendages to conserve heat. (objective 3)

4. Australian Aborigines experience wide variations in daytime and nighttime temperatures. Since traditionally they did not wear clothing or build shelters, they conserved heat by continuous vasoconstriction during cold periods. (objective 3)

5. Melanin absorbs certain wavelengths of UV radiation, which reduces the amount of UV radiation that reaches the under layers of the skin. (objective 2)

6. Disease vectors are organisms that transmit disease form one carrier to another. Fleas act as a vector for the bacteria that causes bubonic plague, certain mosquitoes are vectors that carry the organism that causes malaria, and some nonhuman primates may have been the vectors that transmitted HIV to humans. (video lesson, segment 3; objective 5)

Application Questions

Your answers should include the following:

1. The degree of melanin pigment in the skin affects skin color. The more melanin present, the darker the skin. Melanin helps to protect the skin from ultraviolet radiation. So higher concentration of melanin pigment are found in areas of high UV radiation, mainly in areas close to the equator. Native people in those areas will have darker skin. Without the protection of melanin in the skin, people in those areas would be more susceptible to skin cancer caused by UV radiation damage to the skin. UV radiation can also reduce the concentration of folates in the body. Some folates are B vitamins and they are essential to many bodily functions. Depletion of folates can negatively affect the health of individuals and may result in birth defects such as spinal bifida. However, the body does require some exposure to UV radiation. UV radiation is important in the stimulation of the metabolic pathway that produces vitamin D in the body. A shortage of vitamin D in the body can product rickets and other conditions. In areas without high UV radiation, such as higher latitudes, a high concentration of melanin might screen out too much UV radiation resulting in vitamin D deficiency. The balance between too much and too little UV radiation is maintained, in part, by melanin concentrations. This is why lighter skin tends to be found in areas of low UV radiation, where too much melanin might cause vitamin D deficiencies, and darker skin is found in areas of high UV radiation, where an excess of UV radiation might cause skin cancer and/or a folate deficiency. (video lesson, segment 1; objective 2)

2. Stress is the result of pressures from outside the body. Adaptation is often a response to stress. Adaptations may be short-term, like getting a tan in response to being exposed to UV radiation, or they may be long-term genetic adaptations, like a population characterized by darker or lighter skin color in response to the level of UV radiation.

If a particular stress is steady over a long period of time it can drive evolution by acting as a selective factor. Cold, for example, causes physiological stress, so any heritable variation that would reduce susceptibility to cold stress would be selected for and would spread throughout the population. One such adaptation might be selection for a body that has a high volume-to-surface ratio, in other words a body that is stocky and relatively short. Disease challenges can also cause stress and over time adaptations for disease resistance will become common in a population. (video lesson, segment 2; objective 1)

3. Zoonotic diseases are diseases transmitted to humans through contact with nonhuman animals. There are a variety of ways in which culture brings humans and animals into contact, and most can be traced back to domestication of plants and animals. The direct and sustained contact involved in managing domesticated animals provides the opportunity for diseases to be transmitted directly between livestock and people. Close proximity to cattle resulted in the transmission of the tuberculosis bacterium between cattle and humans many thousands of years ago, and it has moved apparently in both directions over time. Domestic swine and fowl are the source of influenza viruses. Domesticated plants and animals provided reliable year-round food sources, resulting in human population growth and sedentary settlement patterns. Such populations provided suitable hosts for the development of endemic diseases. For example, slash-and-burn agriculture provided conditions favorable to mosquitoes that transmitted malarial parasites to human hosts in the settlements near by. Even wild animals can be vectors for disease if there is some mechanism to bring them into contact with humans. It appears that the hunting and butchering of chimpanzees may have spread the simian immunodeficiency disease (SIV) to African human populations through blood-blood contact, where it mutated into HIV. (video lesson, segment 3; objective 5)

4. Disease organisms evolve just like all other organisms. From the point of view of the pathogen, antibiotics represent a selective pressure that selects variants that are resistant to the antibiotics while susceptible variants die off. This causes the resistant variants to increase in the population and eventually the antibiotic is no longer effective. The stronger the pressure from the antibiotic, the faster the process is likely to happen. Overuse of antibiotics is a factor that speeds up this process. If a pathogen is rarely exposed to an antibiotic, it will take longer for resistance to evolve. Some pathogens that have evolved resistance to many antibiotics include the bacterium that causes tuberculosis, the one-celled parasite that causes malaria, and the HIV virus that causes AIDS. Possible solutions to the evolution of antibiotic resistance are to use antibiotics more sparingly so as to reduce the selective pressure to evolve resistance. Another is to try to reduce the ways in which the disease is transmitted. If the transmission rate can be slowed down then the organisms may evolve to be less virulent. (video lesson, segment 3; objective 6)

Lesson Review

Lesson 14: Patterns of Adaptation

PLEASE NOTE: Use this matrix to guide your study and achieve the learning objectives of this lesson. It will also help you to view the video, which defines and demonstrates important concepts and principles as they relate to everyday life and actual case studies.

Learning Objective	Textbook	Student Guide	Video Lesson
1. Describe the adaptations known as acclimatization, and distinguish between the different types.	pp. 461–462	Key Terms: 1, 2, 3; Matching: 1, 4; Completion: 2; Application: 2.	Introduction; Segment 2: *Short-Term Adaptation*
2. Discuss the population patterning of human skin color variation and possible adaptive explanations.	pp. 463–467, 470–471	Key Terms: 4, 5, 13; Completion: 1; Self-Test: 1, 2, 4; Short-Answer: 5; Application: 1.	Segment 1: *Genetic Adaptation*
3. Contrast human physiological responses to heat and to cold.	pp. 468–472	Key Terms: 6, 7, 8; Matching: 6, 7; Completion: 3; Self-Test: 8, 9, 10; Short-Answer: 3, 4.	
4. Describe the body's responses to high altitude.	pp. 473–475	Key Terms: 9; Self-Test: 11, 12, 13; Short-Answer: 1.	Segment 2: *Short-Term Adaptation*

Learning Objective	Textbook	Student Guide	Video Lesson
5. Define and give examples of infectious disease, pathogens, and vectors, and discuss their interaction with human cultural behavior.	pp. 475–478	Key Terms: 10, 11, 12, 14, 15; Matching: 2, 3, 5, 8; Completion: 4, 5; Self-Test: 3, 7, 14; Short-Answer: 2, 6; Application: 3.	Segment 3: *Infectious Disease*
6. Describe the recent reemergence of infectious disease, and identify the factors that have contributed to this phenomenon.	pp. 478–481	Self-Test: 3, 5, 6, 15; Short-Answer: 2; Application: 4.	Segment 3: *Infectious Disease*

LESSON 15

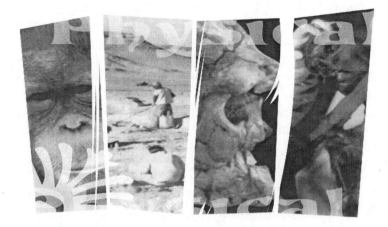

Legacies of Human Evolutionary History

Checklist

For the most effective study of this lesson, complete the following activities in this sequence.

Before Viewing the Video

- ❏ Read the Preview, Learning Objectives, and Viewing Notes below.

- ❏ Read Chapter 17, "The Human Life Course," pages 482–505, and Chapter 18, "Conclusion: Why It Matters," pages 506–517, in *Introduction to Physical Anthropology*.

What to Watch

- ❏ After reading the textbook assignment, watch the video for Lesson 15, *Legacies of Human Evolutionary History*.

After Viewing the Video

- ❏ Briefly note your answers to the questions listed at the end of the Viewing Notes.

- ❏ Review the Summary below.

- ❏ Review all reading assignments for this lesson, including the Viewing Notes in this lesson.

- ❏ Write brief answers to the "Critical Thinking Questions" at the end of Chapter 17 in the textbook.

- ❏ Complete the Review Exercises below. Check your answers with the Answer Key and review when necessary.

- ❏ Use the Lesson Review matrix found at the end of this lesson to review and assess your knowledge of each Learning Objective.

Preview

Previous lessons have shown how human biological evolution and adaptation has made us into the humans we are today. As you know by now, one big difference between humans and other mammals and primates is our ability to adapt through culture. Modern human beings have been shaped by biocultural evolution. Lesson 15 looks at the legacies of human evolution, how everything from our brain size to our nutritional needs to our reproductive functioning are the result of millions of years of biological evolution and cultural evolution. This lesson also explores the impact human behavior has on our planet. A Native American proverb says "We do not inherit the earth from our ancestors; we borrow it from our children." This saying begs the following questions: How are we caring for the planet? How will our behaviors today affect the resources that humans will need for the future? Unlike any other species, humans have profound influences on almost all life-forms. Lesson 15 encourages you to consider the kind of legacy humans are leaving for the generations to come.

Concepts to Remember

- Lesson 7 introduced the term **behavioral ecology**, the study of the evolution of behavior, emphasizing the role of ecological factors as agents of natural selection. This does not suggest that anthropologists believe that there are specific genes for specific behavior. On the contrary, science currently does not know the degree to which genes influence behavior in humans and other species. Because of human culture, behaviors are mostly learned and some are partly influenced by our biology. However, behavior is said to be "selected for" when it increases reproductive fitness.
- Lesson 7 also introduced the concept of **life history traits**, which are characteristics and developmental stages that contribute to social structure. These characteristics, such as length of gestation, period of infant dependency, and age of sexual maturity, influence potential reproductive rates. This lesson will study more closely the life history traits of humans, including why humans have longer periods of infancy and childhood compared with other primates and what are the differences in the life cycles of closely related species, such as humans and chimpanzees.

Learning Objectives

After completing this lesson, you will be able to:

1. Discuss human biocultural evolution in terms of life history theory. (pp. 483–484, 494–495)
2. Describe the general patterns of growth and development of human infants, children, and adolescents, including the effects of genes, environment, and hormones. (pp. 484–487, 491–498)
3. Discuss the effects of nutrition and nutritional stress on growth and development. (pp. 488–491)
4. Compare modern diet and lifestyle with preagricultural diet and lifestyle using an evolutionary perspective. (pp. 488–491, 498–504)

5. Describe the general patterns of human reproductive functioning. (pp. 498–504)

6. Discuss the impact of humans on the ecology and biodiversity of Earth. (pp. 508–517)

At this point, read Chapter 17, "The Human Life Course," pages 482–505, and Chapter 18, "Conclusion: Why It Matters," pages 506–517.

Viewing Notes

The video for Lesson 15 begins with an important example of human biocultural evolution—the birth of a human infant. The narrator states, "In each human birth, we see living evidence of an exchange between biology and culture. And the technology used to bring this child into the world represents thousands of years of cultural adaptations that have extended humans' capacity to meet nature's challenges. For example, the size and shape of the human infant's body and the timing of its development represents millions of years of evolution." One biological constraint in regard to human reproduction is that females have a narrow pelvis that evolved for efficient bipedality. However, humans also have large brains relative to body size, which is crucial to our evolution as well. To accommodate both biological traits, human infants are born at an immature stage when the head is small enough to pass through the birth canal. These small brains increase significantly with age, necessitating prolonged and intense parental care, which is a cultural adaptation. This pattern of brain growth is unusual among primates and other mammals, whose infants are born at a more mature stage of development.

The video explores other examples of the evolutionary interaction between biology and culture. **Menarche**, a girl's first menstruation, is clearly affected by genetic variation as well as a variety of environmental factors. Girls typically begin menstruation at approximately the same age their mothers did. However, over the last 150 years, the age of menarche has dropped from an average of 16 to around 12.5 years of age as a result of improved nutrition and the reduction in disease. **Menopause**, or the end of menstruation, which occurs in women around the age of 50, does appear to be a product of evolution, and it is a stage not found in primates and other mammals. For instance, a female chimp usually lives only a few years after her reproductive years are over. There are several theories to explain why women live 25 to 35 years after the birth of their last child. The video mentions several theories but explains one called "the grandmother hypothesis" in more detail. This hypothesis argues that natural selection may have favored this extended period in women's lives because postmenopausal women provide high-quality care for their daughters and grandchildren, thus increasing the reproductive success of women with whom they share genes. The video points out that **senescence**, or the decline in physiological functioning associated with the end of the life course, is looked upon by some researchers as a "disease," or a condition to be "fixed" by advanced scientific technologies.

Nutrition has a huge impact on our health. Until very recently in human history, humans foraged for their food, and the video refers to the diet of food foragers as the "**ancestral diet**." This diet contained a variety of nutrients, such as animal protein, complex carbohydrates, and fiber, and it was low in fats and salt. The development of agriculture was a major human cultural adaptation that led to the availability of increased calories but may have lacked the variety of the ancestral diet. As a result, some societies that depended chiefly on grains, like maize or rice, experienced nutritional deficiencies that can be seen in bone and teeth from agricultural sites. The easy availability of abundant calories, as the video also points out, conflicts with our "feast and famine" biological disposition, which evolved to allow us to take advantage of superabundance in times of plenty and use stored calories in times of famine. In industrial societies today, the continual supply of calories that cannot be used efficiently by the body, so they are stored as fat. As a result, we see increased incidence of obesity and the conditions that accompany it, such as heart disease, and type II diabetes. The "feast or famine" model was originally proposed by J. V. Neal in 1962 to explain the high incidents of the diseases mentioned above.

In addition to nutritional deficits for some groups, the development of agriculture posed environmental problems as well. Cultivating large tracts of land meant that habitats were being altered, affecting not only humans but also plant and animal species. Unlike foraging, crops require that people remain in one place, which allows the possibility of storing any surplus. Food storage, according to the video, allows populations to grow faster because there is a surplus of available calories. Today, perhaps the biggest problem facing humans is overpopulation. In 1950, there were 3 billion people on the earth. Today, there are almost 7 billion, and it is predicted that by 2040, the human population of the planet will be 10 billion.

The question for science is, how will the earth support such numbers? The reduction of the earth's **biodiversity**, which refers to the numbers of species of plants and animals with whom we share the planet, is almost entirely caused by the expansion of the human population and the resulting need for more resources, such as land for agricultural and living areas. The video mentions that the struggle for fresh water may become a cause for war in the future. Already, the World Health Organization estimates that 1 out of 6 people (or 1.1 billion people) lack access to safe drinking water. During the last century, the population may have increased three-fold, but water use increased six-fold. Population growth, industrialization, and urbanization increases the demand for all resources on the planet.

Sometimes our medical and scientific advances actually get in the way of good health. Overuse of antibiotics has created strains of bacteria that survive antibiotics that formerly killed them. In 2005, the FDA released a study that indicated that soaps and lotions that contain antibacterial agents have no benefits over ordinary soap and water. Moreover, many physicians are concerned that the use of products that contain antibacterial agents could increase antibiotic resistance. Another scientific breakthrough with mixed results is pesticides, which have helped to produce abundant crops, but at the expense of the animals and people who eat them.

Humans have spent much of their evolutionary history attempting to tame nature. Today, the challenge is to see whether we can live in accord with nature in order to ensure our survival.

Questions to Consider

- ❀ What is "the grandmother hypothesis" and what are its proposed advantages for children and their mothers?

- ❀ According to expert Douglas Crews in the video, why was the development of agriculture an example of cultural evolution? What were the benefits of agricultural innovations as well as the consequences to humans, animals, and the environment?

- ❀ What impact has human overpopulation had on the biodiversity of our planet?

Watch the video for Lesson 15, *Legacies of Human Evolutionary History*.

> Segment 1: *Diet, Lifestyle & Consequences*
> Segment 2: *Human Impact*

Key Terms and Concepts

Page references are keyed to *Introduction to Physical Anthropology*, 13th edition.

1. **growth:** Increase in mass or number of cells (p. 484; objective 2)

2. **development:** Differentiation of cells into different types of tissues and their maturation. (p. 484; objective 2)

3. **ossification:** The process by which cartilage cells are replaced by bone cells in normal growth. (p. 484; objective 2)

4. **distal:** Referring to the part of a bone that is farthest from the point of attachment to the central skeleton. (p. 485; objective 2)

5. **proximal:** Referring to the part of a bone that is closest to the point of attachment to the central skeleton. (p. 485; objective 2)

6. **adolescent growth spurt:** The period during adolescence when well-nourished teens typically increase in stature at greater rates than at other times in the life cycle. (p. 485; objective 2)

7. **essential amino acids:** The 9 (of 22) amino acids that must be obtained from the food we eat because they are not synthesized in the body in sufficient amounts. (p. 489; objective 3)

8. **evolutionary medicine:** The application of principles of evolution to aspects of medical research and practice. (p. 490; objectives 3 & 4)

9. **undernutrition:** A diet insufficient in quantity (calories) to support normal health. (p. 491; objective 3)

10. **malnutrition:** A diet insufficient in quality (i.e., lacking some essential component) to support normal health. (p. 491; objective 3)

11. **epigenome:** The instructions that determine what and how genes are expressed in cells. (p. 492; objectives 2 & 3)

12. **epigenetics:** Changes in phenotype that are not related to changes in underlying DNA. (p. 492; objectives 2 & 3)

13. **menopause:** The end of menstruation in women, usually occurring at around age 50. (p. 495; video lesson, introduction; objectives 1 & 5)

14. **menarche:** The first menstruation in girls, usually occurring in the early to mid-teens. (p. 495; video lesson, introduction; objectives 1, 2, & 5)

15. **senescence:** Decline in physiological function usually associated with aging. (p. 502; video lesson, introduction; objectives 1 & 5)

16. **pleiotropic genes:** Genes that have more than one effect; genes that have different effects at different times in the life cycle. (p. 503; objective 5)

17. **Holocene:** The most recent epoch of the Cenozoic. Following the Pleistocene, it is estimated to have begun 10,000 years ago. (p. 512; objective 6)

18. **ancestral diet:** The nutrients consumed by our early human ancestors, who supplemented newly cultivated food crops with fruit and grains gathered in the wild and meat from wild game animals they hunted. The resulting diet was high in animal protein, complex carbohydrates, and fiber and was low in fat and salt when compared to our modern diet. (video lesson, segment 1; objective 4)

19. **biodiversity:** The totality of genes, species, and ecosystems found on the earth. (video lesson, segment 2; objective 6)

20. **mass extinction event:** A period of time when a large number of species die out in a relatively quickly or there is a sharp drop in the rate of speciation, or the evolution of new biological species. (video lesson, segment 2; objective 6)

Summary

Previous lessons in this course have shown that humans have a basic evolutionary history that has much in common with other primates. Yet, as has also been emphasized throughout this course, modern humans have been shaped by a long history of biocultural evolution, or the evolutionary interaction of biology and culture. According to the Jurmain textbook, it would be impossible to understand human evolution without considering that human beings evolved within the context of culture. The human life course is an excellent place to examine the interaction of culture and biology, given that "patterns of human growth and nutritional requirements result from millions of years of biological evolution and thousands of years of cultural evolution" (page 505). There is a great deal of variation in the extent to which culture interacts with genes to produce behavior, and the full extent of this interaction has yet to be fully understood. Some genetically based characteristics occur regardless of the cultural environment. For example, Chapter 4 of the Jurmain textbook explained that albinism will always appear if a person inherits the two alleles for albinism. However, other characteristics, such as intelligence, body shape, and growth, are affected by an interaction between environment and genes. The **epigenome** is part of that interaction. The epigenome is the instructions that determine what and how genes are expressed in each body cell, and is itself influenced by lifestyle factors such as diet and smoking. The Jurmain textbook describes studies suggesting that the short stature of African Efe pygmies is affected both by genes (coding for altered levels of human growth hormones) and nutrition and infectious diseases which affect how those genes are expressed. Both biology and culture interact to produce short stature.

Nutrition is one of the lifestyle factors that affects our health and life expectancy, and the video detailed the nutritional changes from ancestral diets to contemporary ones. The "Closer Look" section on page 489 of the Jurmain textbook explains the health epidemic of diabetes and explains that type 2 diabetes is a disorder that is clearly linked with dietary and lifestyle behaviors.

Primatologists and other physical anthropologists study primate and human growth and development from an evolutionary perspective, considering how natural selection has operated on the life cycle from birth to death. This perspective is known as *life history theory*. Life history theory offers the premise that an organism has only a certain amount of energy available for growth, maintenance of life, and reproduction. Energy needed for one of these processes is not available for another. So, according to the Jurmain textbook on page 494, "the entire life course is a series of trade-offs among life history traits such as length of gestation, age at weaning, time spent in growth to adulthood, adult body size, and length of life span." This theory provides the basis for understanding how fast an organism will grow and to what size, how many offspring can be produced, how long gestation will last, and how long an individual will live. One must understand the evolutionary process in order to understand life history theory, as it is natural selection that shapes life history traits. Lesson 7 pointed out that for species living in unpredictable habitats, shorter life spans can be advantageous for survival. These species mature early and have short gestation periods, meaning reproduction can occur at a quick pace, as befits their short lives. Conversely, organisms with longer life spans, such as primates, benefit from stable environmental conditions. It is unclear about how applicable life history theory is to modern human populations, but for understanding our life cycle in terms of our evolutionary past, it is very useful.

One characteristic that humans and other primates share is a relatively large brain compared with body size. The combination of a large brain and a somewhat small pelvis makes childbirth a challenge for all primates, but the narrowing of the pelvis in support of bipedalism makes it especially difficult. One adaptation humans evolved is that human infants are born at an earlier stage of brain development than are other primates. Human neonates have brains that are one–quarter of their eventual size; three-quarters of the brain growth in humans occurs outside the womb. The Jurmain textbook notes that there is value to having most brain growth occur in the more stimulating environment outside the womb because humans are dependent on language. It is theorized that delayed brain growth may be particularly important for language skills, and in humans, the first three years are a crucial time for developing language.

Humans have long childhoods and a slowed growth process compared with most primates. According to the Jurmain textbook, this reflects the importance of learning for our species. Humans, and some nonhuman primate species, experience a growth phase between childhood and adulthood called *adolescence*. This is the time in the individual's life when he or she may be mature in some ways and immature in others. For example, a girl who is age 13 may have started her period and be able to bear a child, but she may not be mature enough to raise the child alone. The onset of menarche in girls is affected by genetic patterns, nutrition, stress, and disease. A certain amount of body fat is needed for menstruation as well. Until humans began living in settlements, it is likely that females became pregnant as soon as they were biologically able. Since life expectancy was low, early reproduction was advantageous. It is theorized that an early hominid female's chances of raising an offspring to the age in which it could survive on its own increased if she reproduced at a young age. In contrast, in many contemporary societies there are disadvantages to early reproduction. Younger mothers are often less socially mature and less self-sufficient than older mothers. They also suffer higher infant mortality rates than older mothers.

The end of a woman's reproductive cycle is called **menopause**. The Jurmain textbook asks on page 500, "Why do human females cease reproducing and then live such a long time when they can no longer reproduce?" One theory, relates to parenting. Since it takes 12 to 15 years before a child becomes independent, it has been proposed that women are biologically "programmed" to live at least that long after the reproduction cycle ends so she can raise her last child. Another theory is known as the "grandmother hypothesis." This idea argues that menopause is a result of natural selection, in that those women who have mothers or grandmothers to help provide care for their grandchildren and great grandchildren may be more successful reproductively than are women whose female kin are not so long lived.

The maximum life-span potential of humans has been about 120 years for probably the last several thousand years. However, human life expectancy (the average length of life) doesn't match the life span. Life expectancy has increased significantly in the last century as a result of advances in medical care, the most important being the prevention and treatment of infectious diseases.

As pointed out in earlier lessons, most causes of death that have their effects after the reproductive years aren't subject to natural selection. In evolutionary terms, reproductive success is measured by how many offspring we produce, not by how long we live. So, in evolutionary terms, organisms need to live only long enough to reproduce offspring and raise them to maturity.

One of the most pressing challenges for modern medicine is what to do when the antibiotics fail. As pointed out in the Jurmain textbook, the overuse of antibiotics has resulted in pathogens that have evolved a resistance so these antibiotics are no longer effective. Until now, the answer has been to develop the next generation of antibiotics, which precipitates the evolution of a new generation of drug-resistant pathogens.

One approach suggested by evolutionary medicine is to take control of a pathogen's evolution, directing it to become less virulent. This is the approach taken by Paul Ewald and other researchers. The work is based on the fact that a pathogen is only successful when it can pass from person to person. Pathogens that kill their host before being passed on are failures, as their genetic line dies with the host. More successful diseases keep their hosts mobile so they can be passed along when infected people move around; this is how colds and flu are spread. But the most successful pathogens are those that can be transmitted without the need for the host to be mobile.

This is why waterborne pathogens are often the most virulent. The toxins from the bacterium that causes cholera, for instance, induce diarrhea and vomiting in the host. The infected material is washed out into the water supply, often by people caring for the sick person, where it soon reaches new hosts. Because the pathogen can infect many people very quickly, it can afford to kill its host, which is why cholera epidemics have been so devastating to humans.

Ewald and other researchers have been investigating ways to control cholera by directing the pathogen to mutate in a direction that makes it less transmittable, with some unexpected results. Ewald has shown that if a water supply is cleaned up so that the cholera bacterium cannot be easily transmitted, the toxins produced by the organism decrease and evolve into milder forms that rarely kill people and may only cause minor discomfort. If all cholera strains could be directed to evolve in a similar direction, the pathogen would cease to be a threat to life.

The success of this method may cause modern medicine to reconsider its approach to treating disease from one of an "evolutionary arms race" between pathogen and antibiotic, to being more like an "evolutionary traffic cop" that pushes a pathogen in an alternative direction, one that will no longer harm humans.

One explanation as to why humans age and why they are affected by chronic diseases such as cancer, atherosclerosis, and hypertension is that genes that help reproductive success in earlier years and were thus favored by natural selection may be damaging to us in our later years. These are referred to as **pleiotropic genes**, which means they have multiple effects; these could occur at different times during the life span. The Jurmain textbook gives the example of genes that help the immune system when we are younger but may also damage tissues so that we are more susceptible to cancer later. Pleiotropy may help us understand evolutionary reasons for aging, but lifestyle factors such as smoking, physical activity, diet, and medical care are far more important in the aging process. Life expectancy at birth differs greatly in different countries and in different socioeconomic classes within the same country. A stark statistic from the Jurmain textbook states that before the AIDS epidemic, a person in Zimbabwe had a life expectancy of 65 years; since the advent of AIDS, the average is less than 37 years.

The last part of this lesson addresses the impact of humans on our planet and how that affects our future. Our success as a species (there are currently 7 billion humans on the planet) is dwarfed by the success of bacteria, if measured in terms of numbers of cells. However, our impact on the planet has been significant and the environment in which we and other life forms are now evolving has been altered extensively through our actions.

Human beings have an enormous impact on the **biodiversity** of the planet. Global warming is one grave example of this impact. Two major naturally occurring extinction events have occurred in the last 250 million years. A third one is occurring now, but unlike the others, the current extinction is caused not by continental drift or collisions with asteroids, but by the human activity.

The factor most instrumental in extinction is habitat reduction. The growing human population and the need for building materials and agricultural land to support this population has put many other species at risk. At present, the greatest threat to biodiversity is the destruction of the rain forest. Agriculture, wood collection for fuel, and extensive logging are some of the key activities responsible for the destruction of large sections of rain forest around the globe. Mining, industrial development, and large dams also affect rain-forest habitats. Humans benefit from continued research into potentially useful rain-forest products, but there are important ethical issues to be considered. Do humans have the right to destroy the planet's biodiversity to obtain these products when every other creature living within these rain-forest environments depends on their diverse resources for life?

Certainly the latter part of this lesson and its accompanying video both offer depressing news on the state of the natural environment and the impact that human beings have on the earth. Nevertheless, many people around the world want to change some of self-defeating actions of humans. The Jurmain textbook emphasizes the importance of global efforts to cooperate in addressing the impact of human activity on the planet. The United Nations conference on biological diversity held in Nagoya, Japan in October 2010 produced agreements with specific targets for reducing loss of natural habitat, lowering pollution levels, restoring degraded ecosystems, and preventing extinction of known species. The same must occur for climate change. Our evolutionary history offers us a roadmap as well as hope for our future. For example, Jurmain points out on page 517, "despite occasional evidence to the contrary, cooperation may have been more important in human evolution than conflict." Ultimately, it is human culture that has created these problems and it will be human culture that will solve them.

Review Exercises

Matching I

Match each term with the appropriate definition or description.

1. _____ adolescence

2. _____ childhood

3. _____ infancy

4. _____ menarche

5. _____ menopause

6. _____ senescence

7. _____ adolescent growth spurt

a. A time of life, after reproductive functioning begins, when individuals may be mature in some ways but immature in others.

b. In mammals, the period of life when nursing takes place.

c. The first menstruation in girls.

d. The time of life between weaning and puberty.

e. The process of physiological decline in body function that is usually associated with aging.

f. A time of life characterized by the end of menstruation for women.

g. The period during adolescence when well-nourished teens typically increase in stature at greater rates than at other times in the life cycle.

Matching II

Match each term with the appropriate definition or description.

1. ____ ossification
2. ____ distal
3. ____ growth
4. ____ proximal
5. ____ essential amino acids

6. ____ epigenetics
7. ____ development
8. ____ undernutrition
9. ____ malnutrition
10. ____ epigenome

a. Increase in mass or number of cells.

b. Differentiation of cells into different types of tissues and their maturation.

c. The process by which cartilage cells are replaced by bone cells in normal growth.

d. Referring to the part of a bone that is farthest from the point of attachment to the central skeleton.

e. A diet insufficient in quantity (calories) to support normal health.

f. Referring to the part of a bone that is closest to the point of attachment to the central skeleton.

g. The 9 (of 22) amino acids that must be obtained from the food we eat because they are not synthesized in the body in sufficient amounts.

h. Changes in phenotype that are not related to changes in underlying DNA.

i. A diet insufficient in quality (i.e., lacking some essential component) to support normal health.

j. the instructions that determine what and how genes are expressed in cells.

Completion

Fill each blank with the most appropriate term from the list below.

adolescent growth spurt   menopause
childhood   pleiotropic genes
evolutionary medicine   Pleistocene
fat   pregnancy
Holocene   protein
infancy   transgenerational
menarche

1. Genes that have multiple effects or that have different effects at different times of the life cycle are called _____.

2. The extinction event that is occurring now started in the late _____ or early _____.

3. The "grandmother hypothesis" proposes that women live beyond _____ because they can provide benefits to their grandchildren.

4. The age at first _____ has been decreasing for more than 100 years in many human societies.

5. Dietary comparisons show that contemporary Americans eat more _____ and less _____ than those who ate a preagricultural diet in the past, as a percentage of their total dietary energy intake.

6. The human brain grows very rapidly as a percentage of its adult size during _____ and _____.

7. Deficiencies of nutrients during _____ affect fetal development and can have _____ effects.

8. The _____ occurs approximately two years earlier in girls than in boys.

9. _____ provides insight into the prevalence of diabetes in our contemporary life through an examination of the selective factors that affected human diet in the past.

Self-Test

Select the best answer.

1. Humans are considered to be a highly generalized species because they
   a. can live in a great variety of climates.
   b. eat a large variety of foods.
   c. have a wide array of responses to environmental challenges.
   d. do all of the above.

2. Examination of the skeleton can give us information about

    a. an individual's age and sex.
    b. an individual's height.
    c. an individual's health.
    d. all of the above.

3. Which of the following are among the characteristics that reflect the interaction of environment and genes?

    a. albinism
    b. body shape and height
    c. intelligence
    d. b and c

4. Compared to most other animals, humans have

    a. fewer life cycle stages.
    b. the same number of life cycle stages.
    c. more life cycle stages.
    d. none of these; stages vary depending on the animal.

5. Evolutionarily, humans are thought to have long childhoods with slow growth

    a. because it was adaptive to limit the number of fully adult people in a foraging group.
    b. in order to delay reproduction.
    c. because a long period for learning is very important in the human species.
    d. mothers are reluctant to let their children grow up.

6. Is it possible for one monozygotic twin to have a genetically based cancer while the other is disease free?

    a. Yes, because structural changes to the DNA and associated proteins can occur in an individual as a result of lifestyle factors.
    b. No, because they are 100% genetically identical.
    c. Yes, because epigenetic differences result in different phenotypes from identical genotypes.
    d. Both a and c are true.

7. As discussed in the video by Douglas E. Crews and as mentioned in the Jurmain textbook, some of the "negative" aspects of our "feast or famine" biology in the constant feast that many industrialized nations enjoy today include an increase in

    a. type 2 diabetes.
    b. obesity.
    c. cardiovascular disease.
    d. all of the above.

8. Which one of the following statements about the hormone cortisol is **FALSE**?

    a. Cortisol influences growth and development.

    b. Cortisol levels are elevated during stress.

    c. Chronic high cortisol levels can have negative effects on health by suppressing normal immune functioning.

    d. Chronic high cortisol levels can have positive effects on health by increasing TSH (thyroid secreting hormone) production.

9. About 95 percent of the growth in world populations is occurring in

    a. the United States.

    b. other developed/industrialized nations.

    c. the nations that control the majority of the world's resources.

    d. developing nations.

10. Humans have a relatively long life span compared to many other animals, but they have a shorter maximum life span than which of the following organisms?

    a. a blue whale

    b. a gorilla

    c. a tortoise

    d. an Indian elephant

11. During senescence, a physiological decline occurs in the body's systems, including

    a. immune system function.

    b. muscle mass.

    c. bone density.

    d. all of the above.

12. According to Melvin Konner in the video, human activities have an impact on the earth in which of the following ways?

    a. There has been a reduction in biodiversity as a result of habitat destruction.

    b. Through the use of antibiotics and pesticides, humans have become a selective force in the evolution of many pathogens.

    c. There have been changes in ecosystems as a result of global warming.

    d. All of the above are human impacts.

13. Which of the following are possible consequences of nutrient deficiency during human growth and development?

    a. A deficiency of vitamin D may cause rickets.

    b. Calcium deficiency may cause sickle-cell anemia.

    c. Folate deficiency during gestation may cause albinism.

    d. Both a and c are true.

14. Modern agricultural diets differ from preagricultural diets in that they contain more

    a. protein.

    b. fiber.

    c. fats.

    d. calcium.

15. The growth patterns of human infants and children include

    a. a long period of dependency compared to other primates.

    b. a slow period of brain growth from birth to about 5 years of age.

    c. the ability to cling to mothers immediately after birth.

    d. all of the above.

Short-Answer Questions

1. What are some possible explanations for the long post-reproductive period in human females?

2. In what ways does culture shape the pregnancy and birth experience?

3. How do the life cycle stages for humans differ from monkeys and apes? How do they differ from those of other mammals?

4. What is the connection between type 2 diabetes, diet, and obesity?

5. Discuss childhood from a life history perspective.

6. What is a "thrifty genotype"? Why might it have evolved? How is it associated with obesity?

7. What basic nutrients and food types are important to proper development?

Application Questions

1. Are humans still evolving? What are some of the selective pressures that humans in urban settings must contend with?

2. Discuss the evolutionary conflict between narrow hips in women and the brain size of infants. How does the diameter of the human birth canal vs. the head size of an infant compare to other primates? How has this affected the timing of brain development in human infants compared to other primates?

3. Discuss the effects of human activities and high human population growth rates on the environment. Include examples of the effects of pesticides, habitat destruction, extinction rates, and human contributions to global warming.

4. Discuss the impact of agricultural practices on diet, population growth rates, human settlement patterns, and human culture. Why did agriculture have so many wide-ranging effects?

5. How does the "contemporary diet" of many modern people differ from the "preagricultural diet" discussed in the Jurmain textbook? Outline each type of diet and discuss the impacts of the main differences in terms of disease.

6. What types of functional declines are associated with senescence? What are some of the proposed hypotheses that try to explain the onset of senescence?

Answer Key

Matching I

1. a (objectives 2 & 3)
2. d (objectives 2 & 3)
3. b (objectives 2 & 3)
4. c (video lesson, introduction; objectives 2, 3, & 6)
5. f (video lesson, introduction; objectives 2 & 6)
6. e (video lesson, introduction; objectives 2 & 6)
7. g (objective 2)

Matching II

1. c (objective 2)
2. d (objective 2)
3. a (objective 2)
4. f (objective 2)
5. g (objective 3)
6. h (objectives 2 & 3)
7. b (objective 2)
8. e (objective 3)
9. i (objective 3)
10. j (objectives 2 & 3)

Completion

1. pleiotropic genes (objective 5)
2. Pleistocene; Holocene (objective 6)
3. menopause (objectives 1 & 5)
4. menarche (video lesson, introduction; objectives 1, 2, & 5)
5. fat; protein (objective 4)
6. infancy; childhood (objective 2)
7. pregnancy; transgenerational (objective 3)
8. adolescent growth spurt (objective 2)
9. evolutionary medicine (objectives 3 & 4)

Self-Test

1. d. is the correct answer. Humans are highly variable in their behavior and they have a wide array of environmental responses to environmental challenges. (objective 1)

2. d. is the correct answer. Skeletal growth rates, usually measured as length in infants or height in children and adults, are among the most common gauges of age, health, and maturity in humans. Sex differences also leave their marks on the skeleton. (objective 2)

3. d. is the correct answer. Body shape, height, and intelligence are all thought to be influenced by both genes and the environment. Albinism is a condition that an individual is born with. The expression of the condition is strictly genetic and is not influenced by the environment. (objective 2)

4. c. is the correct answer. Humans have more life cycle stages than most other animals. (objective 1)

5. c. is the correct answer. Humans are thought to have a long childhood so that a great deal of learning can take place. While human infants are born in a somewhat undeveloped state compared to other primates, much of that difference has narrowed by the end of infancy, and it is childhood that is characterized by slow growth and learning. (objective 2)

6. d. is the correct answer. The epigenome, or the instructions that determine what and how genes are expressed in cells, is influenced by lifestyle factors, especially diet and smoking. Each monozygotic twin experiences different lifestyle factors and thus, their identical genotype is expressed differently in each twin. (objective 2)

7. d. is the correct answer. The increased incidence of these medical conditions are thought to be caused by an overabundance of nutrients in the diet combined with a decreased activity level. (video lesson, segment 1; objective 5)

8. d. is the correct answer. Cortisol is secreted in response to stress. A child living in a chronically stressful situation is more vulnerable to infectious disease and may experience periods of slowed growth if the stress is prolonged. (objective 2)

9. d. is the correct answer. The highest population growth rates are currently found in developing nations. (objective 6)

10. c. is the correct answer. According to Table 17-3 in the Jurmain textbook, a tortoise has a longer maximum life span than humans. A tortoise may live to 170 years, while the maximum human life span is currently set at 120 years. (objective 5)

11. d. is the correct answer. All three systems start to decline as an individual ages (objective 5)

12. d. is the correct answer. Humans activities have included habitat destruction, contributions to global warming through carbon dioxide emissions, and use of pesticides (which has influenced the evolution of pest species). All of these actions have a strong impact on the earth. (video lesson, segments 1 & 2; objective 6)

13. a. is the correct answer. Only rickets is caused by a nutritional deficiency. Albinism and sickle-cell anemia are genetic conditions. (objective 3)

14. c. is the correct answer. Contemporary diets contain more fats and less protein, fiber, and calcium that preagricultural diets. (objective 4)

15. a. is the correct answer. Human infants and children have a longer period of dependency relative to other primates. (objective 2)

Short-Answer Questions

Your answers should include the following:

1. The long post-reproductive phase in humans is thought by some researchers to be a way for older women to contribute to the survival of their grandchildren. This is often called the "grandmother hypothesis." Another idea is that since it takes 12 to 15 years for a child to become an adult, women may be genetically programmed to live that much longer in menopause. (video lesson, introduction; objectives 1 & 5)

2. Cultural rules and practices play a major role in determining who will get pregnant, as well as when, where, how and by whom. Many cultures have dietary restrictions for women during pregnancy, which may in fact serve to limit exposure to toxins that might harm the growing fetus. Every society has rituals surrounding the birth of an infant. As bipeds, women have narrow pelves and human infants have large heads at birth. It is common for humans to have birth attendants who assist the mother throughout the delivery. Birth attendants, whether doctors, midwives, or family, also make the human birth a social event. (objective 5)

3. Humans have more life cycle stages than most other animals. Humans differ from monkeys and apes in having a post-reproductive stage. All three differ from prosimians in having a subadult stage between the juvenile and adult stages. Many mammals lack a juvenile stage and go straight from infancy into adulthood. Protozoa don't have distinct life cycle stages, while many invertebrates have only larval and adult stages. (objective 1)

4. Diets high in sugars and other refined carbohydrates along with a sedentary lifestyle can lead to obesity. Obese individuals with a poor diet and a sedentary lifestyle are far more likely to have type 2 diabetes than other individuals. Diabetes includes a malfunction of the physiological mechanism in which insulin helps break down sugars into energy. Individuals with type 2 diabetes often produce enough insulin, but the cells can't use it. As a result, sugar builds up in the bloodstream, causing damage to the heart, kidneys, and nervous system. The same diet that produces obesity contributes to type 2 diabetes. (objective 3)

5. Childhood is the period between infancy and puberty. Compared with other mammals, human childhood is long and is characterized by social dependency. It is a time when children are fed, protected and taught technological and social skills by others – family members as well as the larger community. A long period of dependency allows time for the extensive amount of learning that is required for life within a social group. Childhood can be a precarious time, depending on the availability of resources, and stresses in childhood have an impact on the growth, development and health of the child. (objective 2)

6. A "thrifty genotype" is one that allows an individual to "save" and store calories in the form of fat for use in times of food scarcity. This genotype helped people to survive time of famine, but in our current environment with a abundance of available food, this tendency to "save" calories can result in obesity. (video lesson, segment 1; objective 4)

7. Proteins, carbohydrates, lipids (fats), vitamins, and minerals are all important nutrients for proper development. This is true during gestation as well as once an infant is born, all the way through to adulthood. These nutrients must be properly balanced in order to provide a maximum benefit to an individual. (objective 3)

Application Questions

Your answers should include the following:

1. Humans are still evolving, especially in response to selective agents such as disease. As more people leave rural areas to live in urban environments, social crowding becomes a selective pressure. Those who are physiologically able to withstand social stress and/or maximize personal opportunities through social interaction are more likely to thrive in urban settings. We are also subject to a wide variety of environmental pollutants that act as selective forces. Think about the environmental and social challenges that you face in your life and then think about which responses to these challenges could possibly be rooted in your biology. (objective 6)

2. Humans have evolved a shortened, narrow pelvis with a broadened ilium as an adaptation to bipedal locomotion. (See pages 303–304 in the Jurmain textbook.) This pelvis shape leaves a birth canal opening that is relatively small compared to the size of the infant that must pass through it. At the same time, a large brain has been selected for, so infants are born with very large heads. These opposing selective forces present a challenge to human women. They must pass a large head through a narrow opening. One evolutionary compromise is that the female pelvis is generally wider than that of a male of comparable size and it is constructed so that the pelvic opening is larger. Also, human infants are born with brains that are in a relatively undeveloped state compared to other primates. In this way, the brain finishes its growth and development outside of the womb. As a result, human infants are less developed and more helpless than other primate infants, and they take a longer time to develop and grow. (objectives 1 & 2)

3. High population growth has many effects on the environment. More people means that more land is cleared for growing food and for housing. This results in habitation destruction and the degradation of environments, which, in turn, has caused the extinction of many organisms. More people also means more pollution and more carbon dioxide is released into the atmosphere. Pollutants can have a devastating effect on other organisms, and humans have made a very large contribution to global warming through the release of carbon dioxide into the atmosphere. Global warming is causing climate change and large shifts in the biodiversity of environments. These changes are happening now, as you read this. Pesticides can be powerful pollutants in an environment, killing many more organisms than just the pests that they are aimed at. Pest species also tend to evolve resistance to pesticides, causing growers to use higher and higher concentrations of pesticides that then go out into the environment, killing off other organisms. (video lesson, segment 2; objective 6)

4. The ability to grow crops and raise animals changed how people lived by providing the possibility to control production of food. Crops are stationary and take time to grow, so as people began to depend on crops instead of foraging, they became sedentary. A steady food supply allowed the population to increase without negative consequences. As populations increased, more and more land was cleared for the growing of crops and the grazing of domesticated animals. Today, modern agricultural practices in the developed world and population growth in the undeveloped world have together resulted in widespread habitat destruction and the extinction of other species.

    In a hunter-gatherer society, it is difficult to have many possessions. Food is generally not stored. Resources that cannot be consumed by one family are usually shared with others. This means that there are no large differences in "wealth" within a society. The storage of foods, such as grains, and the amassing of large herds of domesticated animals changed this social structure. Such developments meant that some individuals could amass many more resources than could others. These economic disparities had a strong impact on the social and cultural dynamics of agricultural societies. (video lesson, segment 1; objective 4)

5. The development of agriculture did not necessarily result in good diets for human populations. Monocultures do not provide the breadth of nutrients that humans need for a healthy diet, and a dependence on agriculture is also a dependence on the natural environment to provide what the crops need. It is not uncommon for agricultural societies to suffer periods of famine, when rains fail or predatory insects (such as locusts) attack.

    The preagricultural diet differs from the contemporary diet in that there was more protein, less fat, much less sodium, and much more calcium in the preagricultural diet. The amount of carbohydrates consumed was similar although contemporary diets can lack complex carbohydrates in favor of highly processed ones. Many human diseases that are related to diet result from and excess of fats and sodium and a lack of calcium in the diet. These include heart disease, obesity, diabetes, and osteoporosis. A diet that is more balanced in terms of what the body requires for efficient functioning would reduce the incidence of many of these diseases. (video lesson, segment 1; objective 4)

6. Senescence is the process of physiological decline in the systems of the body that happen toward the end of life. As we age, our cells become less effective at synthesizing protein, our immune system functioning is impaired, muscle mass is lost, bone density decreases, and the major organ system function declines. This decline in function has been explained as a result of the effects of pleiotropic genes that enhance reproductive success in youth but have detrimental effects later in life. The "telomere hypothesis" is another explanation that proposes that the telomeres at the end of chromosomes shorten every time a cell divides. This change eventually results in chromosome damage and cell death. Researchers think that this process may also contribute to senescence. Lifestyle factors also have an impact on the pace of senescence in humans. An individual who maintains a healthy lifestyle with a balanced diet, adequate exercise, and minimal exposure to environmental toxins will tend to live longer than someone who has a sedentary lifestyle, has a poor diet, smokes or drinks heavily, and is exposed to other environmental toxins. (video lesson, introduction; objectives 1 & 5)

Lesson Review

Lesson 15: Legacies of Human Evolutionary History

PLEASE NOTE: Use this matrix to guide your study and achieve the learning objectives of this lesson. It will also help you to view the video, which defines and demonstrates important concepts and principles as they relate to everyday life and actual case studies.

Learning Objective	Textbook	Student Guide	Video Lesson
1. Discuss human biocultural evolution in terms of life history theory.	pp. 483–484, 494–495	Key Terms: 13, 14, 15; Completion: 3, 4; Self-Test: 1, 4; Short-Answer: 1, 3; Application: 2, 6.	Introduction
2. Describe the general patterns of growth and development of human infants and children, including the effects of genes, environment, and hormones	pp. 484–487, 491–498	Key Terms: 1, 2, 3, 4, 5, 6, 11, 12, 14; Matching I: 1, 2, 3, 4, 5, 6, 7; Matching II: 1, 2, 3, 4, 6, 7, 10; Completion: 4, 6, 8; Self-Test: 2, 3, 5, 6, 8, 15; Short-Answer: 5; Application: 2.	Introduction
3. Discuss the effects of nutrition and nutritional stress on growth and development.	pp. 488–491	Key Terms: 7, 8, 9, 10, 11, 12; Matching I: 1, 2, 3, 4; Matching II: 5, 6, 8, 9, 10; Completion: 7, 9; Self-Test: 13; Short-Answer: 4, 7.	Introduction
4. Compare modern diet and lifestyle with preagricultural diet and lifestyle using an evolutionary perspective.	pp. 488–491, 498–504	Key Terms: 8, 18; Completion: 5, 9; Self-Test: 14; Short-Answer: 6; Application: 4, 5.	Segment 1: *Diet, Lifestyle & Consequences*

Learning Objective	Textbook	Student Guide	Video Lesson
5. Describe the general patterns of human reproductive functioning.	pp. 498–504	Key Terms: 13, 14, 15, 16; Completion: 1, 3, 4; Self-Test: 7, 10, 11; Short-Answer: 1, 2; Application: 6.	Introduction Segment 1: *Diet, Lifestyle & Consequences*
6. Discuss the impact of humans on the ecology and biodiversity of Earth.	pp. 508–517	Key Terms: 17, 19, 20; Matching I: 4, 5, 6; Completion: 2; Self-Test: 9, 12; Application: 1, 3.	Introduction Segment 1: *Diet, Lifestyle & Consequences* Segment 2: *Human Impact*

© 2012 Cengage Learning. All Rights Reserved. May not be scanned, copied or duplicated, or posted to a publicly accessible website, in whole or in part.

LESSON 16

Applied Anthropology

Checklist

For the most effective study of this lesson, complete the following activities in this sequence.

Before Viewing the Video

❑ Read the Preview, Learning Objectives, and Viewing Notes below.

❑ Review the following pages associated with the Key Terms and Concepts below: pages 10–20, 174–180, 278–281, and 508–517.

What to Watch

❑ After completing the textbook reading, watch the video for Lesson 16, *Applied Anthropology.*

After Viewing the Video

❑ Briefly note your answers to the questions listed at the end of the Viewing Notes.

❑ Review the Summary below.

❑ Review all reading assignments for this lesson, including the Viewing Notes in this lesson.

❑ Complete the Review Exercises below. Check your answers with the Answer Key and review when necessary.

❑ Use the Lesson Review matrix found at the end of this lesson to review and assess your knowledge of each Learning Objective.

Preview

A glance at the morning headlines is sometimes all it takes for a person to sense the complexity of our world. However, it is our goal that, as you have progressed through this course, you can more easily recognize the deep connection between national and world events today and how anthropological practice can influence and facilitate positive outcomes in various troubled areas of human need. The wars in Iraq and Afghanistan have been accompanied by ongoing destruction, displacement, grief, and poverty, not to mention the challenging physical and psychological injuries occurring among young soldiers fighting abroad—all of which have unanticipated long-term consequences. On the world stage, there is globalization that brings prosperity to some individuals at the same time it brings displacement and dire poverty to many others. Finally, natural disasters displace entire populations and bring mass deaths and destruction of human habitation. All of these contemporary situations are potential staging areas for applied anthropologists to implement their skills. This is not to imply that anthropology can solve all problems in all situations. Nevertheless, this course shows how the anthropological approach and perspective can be employed in many areas to help solve some of the practical problems that arise from the large-scale changes that are brought about by the circumstances enumerated above.

This lesson takes a focused look at applied anthropology, which is sometimes referred to as the fifth subfield of anthropology, and explores how applied anthropologists work to address the practical problems that groups across cultures must face when change occurs from within and without their borders. From the scene of natural disasters to the boardrooms of Wall Street, applied anthropologists work to facilitate an understanding of the interconnectedness of all peoples and to help solve the problems of daily life, especially within the context of disruption and change. Although the video for this lesson shows how applied anthropology works within all four fields of anthropology, our focus in this lesson is applied physical anthropology. There are a number of applications for physical anthropological knowledge and techniques. Using their knowledge of primate behavioral ecology, primatologists are active in efforts to conserve habitat and resources for wild primate populations and serve as advisors to organizations and governments regarding ways to protect and sustain primate species. Physical anthropologists who specialize in human growth and development provide information on the scope of human biological variability and its evolutionary bases to assist health practitioners and policy makers in addressing problems of nutrition, poverty, and health. Physical anthropologists apply their knowledge of the human skeleton and dentition to forensic situations, such as crime scenes and major disasters, by determining the age, sex, and identity of individuals based on fragmentary physical remains.

Concepts to Remember

- Lesson 1 introduced the four subfields of **anthropology**: physical, cultural, archaeology, and linguistic anthropology. Each field draws upon the methodologies and data of the others to approach the study of humankind from a holistic perspective.

- Applied anthropology uses anthropological knowledge and methods to solve practical problems, often for a specific client. Review pages 6 through 16 of the Jurmain textbook.

Learning Objectives

After you complete this lesson, you should be able to:

1. Explain the role of anthropologists in the four major fields of anthropology and how applied anthropology is embedded in each field. (pp. 10–20)

2. Discuss the contributions of applied physical anthropologists in the field of forensics. (pp. 15–17)

3. Discuss how physical anthropologists use the knowledge and techniques of their discipline to assist in crime investigations, conservation of primate species, recovery efforts following natural or human-caused disasters, and researching the spread and prevention of disease. (pp. 10–20, 174–180, 278–281, 508–517)

4. Describe the tools physical anthropologists have to assist in identifying human remains. (pp. 13–18)

At this point, review pages 10–20, 174–180, 278–281, 508–517.

Viewing Notes

The video for Lesson 16 highlights the expertise of applied anthropologists, from both academic and nonacademic settings.

In the first segment of the video, Dr. Mikel Hogan, an applied cultural anthropologist, is shown working with the staff of a large hospital. Currently, there is a critical nursing shortage in the United States. According to Dr. Hogan, the studies on the nursing crises show that work environments in U.S. hospitals have become hostile to the recruitment and retention of American nurses. Nurses are overworked because of cutbacks in personnel made to increase the profit base of hospitals, and daily work relationships between hospital personnel are strained. Experts from other countries now occupy health professions in the United States, which has deepened the culturally diverse environment within hospitals and clinics. This cultural diversity, combined with the existing hierarchical structure that exists in hospitals and clinics, increases the complexity and tension found in such workplaces. Applied cultural anthropologists, such as Dr. Hogan, who work with health professionals, can assist employers to examine the hierarchical system in hospitals, where nurses and other staff might be underappreciated by their superiors, and teach "cultural competence" to help minimize misunderstandings between staff members.

Lesson 16 also looks at an applied anthropologist's effort to help a culture maintain its traditional language. The second video segment concerns the Celtic language of Manx Gaelic, which is spoken on the Isle of Man. The Isle of Man is located in the Irish Sea, between England, Scotland, Ireland, and Wales. About half the population is Manx born, the ethnic group of the island, and the remainder is mostly British. With an influx of tourists and wealthy Scottish and English second-home owners, there is a push among some Manx to keep their heritage strong. The video points out that one way to strengthen the Manx heritage is by reviving the Manx Gaelic language, one of the Celtic languages. Jennifer Kewley-Draskau explains that the combination of Manx people departing the Isle of Man and immigrants arriving over time resulted in fewer speakers of the language by the 1960s. The people who were fluent in the Manx language were very elderly, and so the language was on the verge of extinction. Dr. Breesha Maddrell, an applied anthropologist, is currently involved in a push to reclaim Manx Gaelic. Preserving an ancient language involves many challenges, as she says in the video. Intergenerational use, with parents and grandparents teaching the sounds to their children, is key and people must be convinced that a traditional language is not a quaint part of the past but a relevant part of their culture in the present day. The singers in the video demonstrate how music is an important tool in keeping the language in people's minds, if not on the tip of their tongues.

If you are a fan of any of the *CSI* programs on television, forensic work, however glorified, is a familiar concept to you. The final video segment for Lesson 16 offers a clear definition of what forensic anthropology is and how it fits in with the investigation of crime scenes. Forensic anthropology is the application of the techniques and knowledge of physical anthropology to a medical or legal context. When a human body is found, forensic anthropologists are often asked to work with law enforcement agencies and medical examiners to analyze both the DNA and the remains themselves to establish identification of the individual and other evidence that could help solve the questions surrounding the death.

Anthropologist Amy Mundorff points out in the video that having a strong background in both the biological sciences and archaeology, such as experience with DNA analysis or with stratigraphic analysis, is important for a physical anthropologist who wants to work in forensics. The video also includes an interview with Corporal Diane Cockle, who is a crime scene investigator and a forensic anthropologist with the Royal Canadian Mounted Police (known as the Mounties). Cockle details the difference between straight archaeological excavation and forensic excavation. Being an archaeologist prepares her for the basics of analyzing a crime scene, and being trained in police work then gives her the mind-set she needs to carry out a proper crime scene analysis. Cockle discusses the high standard of proof that is required of forensic anthropologists in criminal cases. Training in the scientific method coupled with extensive knowledge of human anatomy in all its variability are two contributions that an anthropologist brings to forensic work. Cockle also explains the contributions that applied anthropologists have made in their work for the United Nations, supporting that organization's efforts to investigate and stem the incidence of genocide brought about by war. Mass graves in Rwanda, in the former republics of Yugoslavia, and in Iraq are among the examples mentioned. Applied forensic anthropologists also work in natural disaster areas, doing the work needed to identify victims of hurricanes, fires, earthquakes, and tsunamis as we have recently witnessed in various regions of the globe.

Questions to Consider

✲ Applied anthropologists bring a holistic perspective to bear on the problems that arise as a consequence of culture change. After reflecting on some of the driving forces of culture change today, what are some of the practical solutions that have been brought about through the work of applied anthropologists?

✲ Within the context of a criminal investigation involving human remains, what are the particular contributions that an anthropologist can make to the work of the team?

✲ What are the legal contexts in which forensic anthropology is practiced?

Watch the video for Lesson 16, *Applied Anthropology*.

> Segment 1: *Medical Anthropology: Nurses Helping Nurses*
> Segment 2: *Linguistic Anthropology: The Language of Man*
> Segment 3: *Forensic Anthropology: The New Detectives*

Key Terms and Concepts

Page references are keyed to *Introduction to Physical Anthropology*, 13th edition.

1. **applied anthropology**: The practical application of anthropological and archaeological theories and techniques. For example, many biological anthropologists work in the public health sector. (pp. 10, 18–20; video lesson, introduction; objective 1)

2. **medical anthropology**: A subfield of cultural anthropology that uses anthropological knowledge and methods to analyze and evaluate the social and cultural issues related to health, illness, and the practices associated with health care delivery. (pp. 18–19; video lesson, segment 1; objective 1)

3. **paleoanthropology**: The interdisciplinary approach to the study of earlier hominins— their chronology, physical structure, archaeological remains, habitats, and so on. (pp. 12–13; objective 1)

4. **molecular anthropology**: A branch of biological anthropology that uses genetic and biochemical techniques to test hypotheses about human evolution, adaptation, and variation. (pp. 14–15, 278–281; objective 1)

5. **forensic anthropology**: An applied anthropological approach dealing with legal matters. Forensic anthropologists work with coroners and others in identifying and analyzing human remains. (pp. 15–16; video lesson, segment 3; objectives 1, 2, 3, & 4)

6. **primatology**: The study of the biology and behavior of nonhuman primates (lemurs, lorises, tarsiers, monkeys, and apes). (pp. 17–18; objective 1)

7. **archaeology**: The study of human cultures through the recovery and analysis of material remains and environmental data. (p. 11; objective 1)

8. **linguistic anthropology**: The study of human languages, looking at their structure, history, and/or relation to social and cultural contexts. (p. 11; video lesson, segment 2; objective 1)

9. **Goidelic tradition:** The branch of Celtic languages and related cultures that includes Irish, Scottish, and Manx Gaelic, all of which are descended from the Old Irish language. (video lesson, segment 2; objective 1)

10. **anthropometry:** Measurement of human body parts. When osteologists practice anthropometry using bones only, the term *osteometry* is often used. (p. 13; objectives 1, 2, & 4)

11. **osteology:** The study of skeletal material. Human osteology focuses on the study of the skeletal remains from archaeological sites, skeletal anatomy, bone physiology, and growth and development. Some of the same techniques are used in paleoanthropology to study early hominins. (p. 15; objectives 1, 2, & 4)

12. **paleopathology:** The branch of osteology that studies the evidence of disease and injury in human skeletal (or, occasionally, mummified) remains from archaeological sites. (p. 15; objectives 1 & 4)

13. **primate paleontology:** The study of fossil primates, especially those that lived before the appearance of hominins. (p. 13; objective 1)

14. **genetics:** The study of gene structure and action and the patterns of inheritance of traits from parent to offspring. Genetic mechanisms are the foundation for evolutionary change. (pp. 14–15; objectives 1, 2, & 4)

Summary

Anthropology distinguishes itself from the other social sciences because of the breadth of its study of humankind through all time and in all places. As explained at the very beginning of this course, there are four subfields of anthropology: physical, or biological, the first and oldest specialty, which is the study of evolution, humans as biological organisms, and human variation; cultural anthropology, the largest subfield, which focuses on the customary patterns in human behavior, thought, and feelings; archaeology, which is the study of human cultures through the discovery of material remains; and linguistic anthropology, which is the study of the structure and history of human language in relation to social and cultural contexts. Each subfield of anthropology operates on a common body of knowledge, but looks at humankind from a particular perspective, and each subfield draws information, or data, from the others to gain the most complete picture of humanity possible. This interaction between the subfields results in a holistic perspective that tries to leave nothing out of the overall analysis of human beings.

Applied anthropology is one of the areas where the four main subfields of anthropology overlap, and the different areas of expertise are combined in both academic and nonacademic settings. All of the main subfields of anthropology participate in applied research.

A portion of the mission statement for applied anthropology, as formulated by the Society for Applied Anthropologists, states:

> Anthropologists demonstrate a particular capability in helping to solve human problems through building partnerships in research and problem solving; acknowledging the perspectives of all people involved; focusing on challenges and opportunities presented by biological variability, cultural diversity, ethnicity, gender, poverty and class; and addressing imbalances in resources, rights, and power.

This segment of the mission statement reflects the various areas of human interest where the work of applied anthropologists can be employed.

The best-known applied work in physical anthropology occurs in the field of forensic science. You already saw an example in the first video of this course, where anthropologists working as members of a forensic team described their work at the Rhode Island nightclub fire. The historical focus within physical anthropology on measuring variability in the human skeleton, and the application of that knowledge to archaeological investigations, makes physical anthropologists extremely valuable members of teams seeking to identify and interpret human remains—whether in a crime scene or in a mass catastrophe. Physical anthropologists can estimate age, height, weight, sex, and other individual features from skeletal remains, sometimes even from tiny fragments. In the video for Lesson 1, Ann Marie Mires, a forensic anthropologist with the Office of the Chief Medical Examiner in Boston, Massachusetts, explained how she determines the sex of a skeleton, by examining the pelvis and the skull. Female pelves are wider to allow for a child to pass through, while male pelves are internally narrower and tighter. Muscle attachments on the skull tend to be larger in males than in females. Once Mires develops a hypothesis based on skeletal measurements, she compares her measurements with computer databases of measurements of males and females.

More recently, forensic anthropologists are adding DNA analysis to their repertoire of techniques. In an interview, Amy Mundorff said, "It used to be the fingerprint experts and the dentists that did all the identifications. And as the science of DNA has progressed and allowed us to identify smaller and smaller fragments of bone, it's become more important for those bones to be identified. And that's where the anthropologist fits in."

The video contrasts forensic archaeology and forensic anthropology, which are complementary areas of expertise and both useful in crime investigation. Forensic archaeologists deal with human skeletal remains from archaeological investigations, while forensic anthropologists apply those techniques to modern cases. One way to view the distinction is that the forensic archaeologist might do the fieldwork—the location, excavation and recovery of the skeletal remains—while the forensic anthropologist would analyze those remains. In practice, the roles can overlap. The forensic anthropologists featured in the video for Lesson 1 who were working at the site of the Rhode Island nightclub fire explained in detail how they approached the burned building as an archaeological site. Krysta Ryzewski, a member of the Forensic Archaeology Recovery (FAR) team, said, "Our first priority was to recover human remains, biological remains and any sort of personal effects that might assist the ME (medical examiner) and the morgue in identifying the victims and repatriating the remains to the families. We set up a grid onto the site. We imposed four quadrants that encompassed the entire Station nightclub and a bit of the surrounding area as well. We treated each of those differently and proceeded investigating one at a time systematically from one corner of the quadrant to another. And we made the decisions of where to dig based on where we knew there would be human remains from the eyewitness reports and from the emergency response officials. And so when we began to dig we dug very slowly and documented each change that we came across."

The practice of forensic anthropology in a criminal or legal context means that all conclusions drawn from the evidence must meet stringent scientific criteria and rules for legal evidence. As Diane Cockle says in the video, "When you're at an archaeological site you have your notebook and you're taking notes and you might even make opinion statements in your notebook … (but) if you were at a forensic scene you can't put opinions in your notebook. You can't say, well, looking at this it looks as if the postmortem interval could be maybe a year or two years. If you change that opinion from the opinion you've written down in your notebook to one you later reach, then you might have problems in court."

Forensic anthropologists also work as members of teams summoned to identify remains from disasters or cases of genocide with mass graves. Two of the anthropologists featured in the video for Lesson 16, Diane Cockle and Amy Mundorff, have done humanitarian work in major disasters. Amy Mundorff worked in the medical examiner's office after September 11, 2001, sorting the more than 20,000 fragments of human remains to identify as many individuals as possible. Diane Cockle was a member of the Canadian team sent to Thailand at the request of the Thai government to recover and identify tsunami victims. She characterized her work as follows: "Some of the forensic anthropology that I did involved the identification of some of the smaller portions of human remains that we received. … The forensic anthropology involved measurements of long bones to determine stature, age determination, looking at the ends of ribs to see if we could extract as much information as we possibly could. And we also assisted the pathologists doing the forensic anthropology of the infants and the babies. What we tried to do was measure the femurs so we could have an estimation of age. Sometimes you can be quite accurate when you measure the length of the femur as to how old the baby was when they died."

Forensic anthropologists use and contribute expertise gained from three of the four fields of anthropology: cultural, archaeological, and physical. Identifying and repatriating human remains calls on the ability to interpret skeletal and dental remains as well as apply archaeological techniques of interpretation such as wear marks on evidence or the arrangement

When the remains of what was thought to be a missing fellow student were discovered in a nearby woods, students at a small college in northeastern Pennsylvania knew what to expect. Having watched seasons of the television shows *CSI*, *CSI: New York*, and *CSI: Miami*, they had a handle on the high-tech tools available for making positive identifications and determining the cause of death.

Or so they thought. But reality is often a far cry from television. Because the remains were skeletal, it fell to the college's forensic anthropologist and local Bloomberg police to conduct the investigation—and the tools they had at their disposal were far removed from the expensive technology that drives television investigations, relying more on logic than anything else.

All of the personal effects found at the scene—the jeans, sneakers, jacket, t-shirt, wallet, and cell phone—belonged to the missing student, leading to a tentative identification. This was confirmed by comparing dental records of the victim with teeth in the skeletal remains, a fairly low-tech but extremely accurate method.

The investigators then determined that the death was a suicide. This was based on the anthropologist's assessment that the remains showed no indication of trauma at the time of death, as well as an assessment of personal effects that had been found in the student's room and the results of interviews with friends of the missing person.

All of which took far longer than students' expectations, another divergence from fiction. The fast pace of the *CSI* shows relies on super quick insights and instant deductions from the television investigators. Plus, technology provides almost instant results on television when, in reality, such tests may take hours or days to conduct.

Finally, the answer seemed too uncomplicated for students to believe. They felt the cause of death had to be more intriguing than a simple suicide. Plus, they wanted to know, if it was a suicide, why did it take so long for the body to be found? And for that matter, why didn't the police use aerial photos, ground-penetrating radar, and other high-tech search methods they were familiar with from television and movies?

In fact, television and movie investigations—while technically feasible—boast a level of resources that are rarely available even to large law enforcement operations, much less to small-town police departments like Bloomberg's. Fortunately, while the traditional methods of the forensic anthropologist are less glitzy than those of *CSI* investigations, they still yield accurate results.

of the remains within the crime scene (taphonomy). Knowledge of cultural behavior is applied in interpreting the scene where the remains are found, as well as in the issue of repatriation of remains. Every society has specific views about death and the rituals surrounding death; an awareness of cultural concerns is something that anthropologists bring to this work.

The Jurmain textbook points out on page 18 that applied anthropology relies on the research and theories of academic anthropology and at the same time has much to contribute to those theories and techniques. Much of what physical anthropologists know can be applied to the solution of modern human problems. For instance, physical anthropologists have long been involved in the design of things to be used by humans, such as the airplane cockpits and gun turrets mentioned on page 19 of the Jurmain textbook, because of their knowledge of the human body and its range of variation. In evolutionary medicine, physical anthropologists collaborate with medical scientists working on human disease, providing an evolutionary perspective that emphasizes the biocultural and evolutionary dimensions of disease. Knowledge of primate behavioral ecology enables primatologists to help governments, agencies, and scientists design better captive settings for primates in zoos and research facilities, develop conservation plans, and fight the spread of diseases and viruses such as ebola and HIV. Far from being isolated in university laboratories and classrooms, physical anthropologists are well represented outside the university setting, in genetic and biomedical research, public health, zoos and museums, and wildlife conservation organizations. For this reason, the subdiscipline has not rigorously separated their applied work from the disciplinary research work.

The study of physical anthropology is excellent preparation for careers in medical and biological fields. In addition to the specific knowledge and expertise of the discipline, a physical anthropologist views humans and their behavior through a biocultural lens. Humans are simultaneously a product of the life forces that produced all life on Earth and unique in their ability to invent and enact cultural solutions to problems. This perspective and sensibility colors our view of human nature and leads us to a unique understanding of the extraordinary variability and flexibility that defines our species.

Review Exercises

Matching

Match each term with the appropriate definition or description.

1. ____ anthropometry
2. ____ applied anthropology
3. ____ archaeology
4. ____ forensic anthropology
5. ____ genetics
6. ____ linguistic anthropology

7. ____ medical anthropology
8. ____ molecular anthropology
9. ____ osteology
10. ____ paleoanthropology
11. ____ paleopathology
12. ____ primatology

a. The use of anthropological knowledge and methods to solve practical problems.

b. A branch of biological anthropology that uses genetic and biochemical techniques to test hypotheses about human evolution, adaptation, and variation.

c. The study of human skeletal material.

d. Applied subfield of physical anthropology that specializes in the identification of human skeletal remains for legal purposes.

e. The study of human languages, looking at their structure, history, and/or relation to social and cultural contexts.

f. The measurement of human body parts.

g. The study of living and fossil primates.

h. The branch of osteology that studies the evidence of disease and injury in human skeletal (or, occasionally, mummified) remains from archaeological sites.

i. The study of the origins and predecessors of the present human species.

j. The study of gene structure and action and the patterns of inheritance of traits from parent to offspring.

k. The study of human cultures through the recovery and analysis of material remains and environmental data.

l.   A subfield of cultural anthropology that analyzes and evaluates the social and cultural issues related to health, illness, and health care practices.

Completion

Fill each blank with the most appropriate term from the list below.

DNA	pelvis
femur	physical anthropology
forensic archaeologist	postmortem
forensic anthropologist	stratigraphy

1.   Law enforcement agencies might call upon a _____ to use skeletal remains to identify a murder victim.

2.   Measurements of the _____ can be used to tell the age of the individual.

3.   The period of time since the individual died is called the _____ interval.

4.   The archaeological tools of mapping and _____ are also of use to forensic anthropologists in investigating crime scenes.

5.   A _____ does the locating and excavation of the human remains from the field site.

6.   Applied _____ ranges from the study and identification of human skeletal remains from crime scenes to consulting with zoos and wildlife conservation organizations on conserving primate populations.

7.   At the World Trade Center following September 11, 2001, the prevalence of small bone and tooth fragments altered by the intense heat required forensic investigators to depend on _____ analysis.

8.   Measurements of the _____ can be used to tell the sex of the individual.

Self-Test

Select the best answer.

1.   Anthropology is the
   a.   study of Western culture primarily through the analysis of its folklore.
   b.   study of human culture and evolutionary aspects of human biology, including cultural anthropology, archaeology, linguistics, and physical or biological anthropology.
   c.   study of nonhuman primates through an analysis of their folklore.
   d.   study of the species *Homo sapiens* through analysis of its biological but not its cultural dimensions.
   e.   analysis of humankind from the subjective perspective of one group.

2. The applied focus of forensic anthropology has included
   a. identification of remains of missing persons.
   b. documenting human rights abuses.
   c. documentation of atrocities in Northern Iraq.
   d. investigating slavery in the United States.
   e. all of the above.

3. In the video, Diane Cockle says that a forensic anthropologist at a crime scene
   a. must be very careful to avoid writing down opinions in her field notebook.
   b. wears street clothes because other people actually touch the remains.
   c. is often the team leader because anthropologists have a holistic view.
   d. can help police increase the amount of evidence collected.
   e. does a and d only.

4. Forensic anthropology is
   a. the cross-cultural study of public speaking.
   b. the study of the human skeleton.
   c. the application of the techniques of physical anthropology applied to a medical/legal context.
   d. practiced by both cultural and physical anthropologists.
   e. practiced in most urban police departments today.

5. Physical anthropologists work in
   a. zoos.
   b. museums.
   c. biomedical research laboratories.
   d. wildlife conservation.
   e. all of the above.

6. Physical anthropologists have a biocultural perspective, meaning
   a. they view human behavior as the interaction of biological and cultural factors.
   b. they view human behavior as the product of evolution.
   c. they recognize that culture has exerted selective pressure on human biology and vice versa.
   d. they understand that the capacity for culture lies within human biology.
   e. all of the above statements are true.

7. In the video, Dr. Mikel Hogan defines medical anthropology as

    a. the applied analysis of health care costs.

    b. using anthropology to solve problems and identify issues related to health care delivery.

    c. a subdiscipline of forensic anthropology.

    d. a purely theoretical and academic discipline.

    e. the practice of medicine in non-Western cultures.

8. In the video, crime scene investigator Diane Cockle explains that she worked as a(n) _____ for 10 years before collaborating with the police force in the Canadian province of Saskatchewan on _____ investigations.

    a. molecular anthropologist; linguistic

    b. primatologist; medical

    c. paleoanthropologist; forensic

    d. archaeologist; forensic

    e. cultural anthropologist; medical

9. Forensic investigators at major disasters are concerned about

    a. identifying individuals.

    b. producing evidence for legal proceedings.

    c. handling material in a culturally sensitive manner.

    d. following proper procedures in the collection and analysis of human remains and other evidence.

    e. all of the above.

Short-Answer Questions

1. What is applied anthropology? What do applied physical anthropologists do?

2. Based on what you learned from the video for Lesson 16, what type of educational background would be most beneficial for a career in forensics?

3. Explain how primate molecular ecology is a form of applied anthropology.

4. What is anthropometry and how has it been applied to solving human problems?

Application Questions

1. What contributions can a physical anthropologist make to the investigation of a crime? To the investigation of a mass disaster?

2. How might a primatologist practice applied anthropology?

Answer Key

Matching

1. f (objectives 1, 2, & 4)
2. a (video lesson, introduction; objectives 1, 2, & 3)
3. k (objective 1)
4. d (video lesson, segment 3; objectives 1, 2, 3, & 4)
5. j (objective 3)
6. e (video lesson, segment 2; objective 1)
7. l (video lesson, segment 1; objective 1)
8. b (objective 1)
9. c (objectives 1 & 4)
10. i (objective 1)
11. h (objectives 1 & 4)
12. g (objectives 1, 3, & 4)

Completion

1. forensic anthropologist (video lesson, segment 3; objectives 1, 2, & 3)
2. femur (Figure 1-9; video lesson, segment 3; objective 4)
3. postmortem (video lesson, segment 3; objective 2)
4. stratigraphy (video lesson, segment 3; objectives 1, 3, & 4)
5. forensic archaeologist (video lesson, segment 3; objectives 1, 2, & 3)
6. physical anthropology (video lesson, segment 3; objectives 1, 2, & 3)
7. DNA (video lesson, segment 3; objective 4)
8. pelvis (course student guide, p. 417; objective 4)

Self-Test

1. b. is the correct answer. Anthropology is the holistic study of human culture through time and space. Anthropology studies all human behaviors of all human societies as well as the evolutionary aspects of human biology. (objective 1)

2. e. is the correct answer. Forensic anthropology involves the identification of human remains and has been used to identify missing persons, as well as document human rights abuses worldwide and investigate slavery in North America. (video lesson, segment 3; objectives 2 & 3)

3. e. is the correct answer. In the video, Diane Cockle points out that forensic anthropologists are involved in legal work and their field notebooks must include

only evidence, not opinion. She says that police departments are beginning to realize that using forensic anthropologists on the team can increase the amount of evidence collected, but anthropologists are still rare in police departments. (video lesson, segment 3; objective 2)

4. c. is the correct answer. The word "forensic" is Latin for "before the forum," meaning the court or legal system. In Roman times, the forum was the court. Forensic anthropology refers to the work of physical anthropologists in contexts that involve legal issues, such as the identification of human remains and the discovery of evidence concerning the circumstances of death. (video lesson, segment 3; objective 2)

5. e. is the correct answer. Physical anthropologists in zoos may conduct research on captive primate populations as well as participate in the wildlife conservation programs which are now a part of the mission of most North American zoos. In museums, physical anthropologists curate collections of human and nonhuman primate material and conduct research using the collections. Physical anthropologists are employed in biomedical research laboratories as well as in organizations such as the World Wildlife Fund where they work to save primate populations around the world. (course student guide, pp. 408, 412, 415–416; objective 3)

6. e. is the correct answer. A biocultural perspective holds that the capacity for creating and developing culture is a part of human biology. Physical anthropologists study how human biology and culture have interacted and affected each other throughout the evolution of our species, up to and including the present time. (course student guide, pp. 408, 412, 416; objective 1)

7. b. is the correct answer. Medical anthropology is an applied area within cultural anthropology that addresses issues of health care delivery, cross-culturally. Medical anthropologists work in the United States as well as around the globe, studying human behavior surrounding the delivery of health care. (video lesson, segment 1; objective 1)

8. d. is the correct answer. Forensic anthropologist Diane Cockle applies her years of experience in archaeological excavation to the crime scenes she investigates as a member of the Royal Canadian Mounted Police (also known as the Mounties). (video lesson, segment 3; objective 2)

9. e. is the correct answer. As they work on their primary task of identifying human remains, forensic anthropologists are producing evidence for the legal system while simultaneously honoring the needs and values of the community and the family of the deceased. (video lesson, segment 3; objectives 2 & 3)

Short-Answer Questions

Your answers should include the following:

1. Applied anthropology is sometimes referred to as the fifth subfield of anthropology. It is the application of anthropological principles, theories, and methods to solve the practical everyday problems. Applied cultural anthropologists may work in businesses or organizations applying the methods of anthropology to help them address and understand issues involving their organization. Applied physical anthropologists might work with police departments to solve crimes, or help a wildlife conservation

organization develop a rescue plan for an endangered primate species, or collaborate with medical professionals working on disease eradication in particular human populations. (video lesson, segment 1; objective 1)

2. According to Amy Mundorff, who was interviewed in the video for Lesson 16, it is extremely important for forensic archaeologists and anyone who is going to do excavations at crime scenes to have not only a degree in anthropology with an emphasis on physical anthropology and archaeology but also a background in biology and even chemistry to be able to carry out the DNA work that will be required. (video lesson, segment 3; objective 2)

3. Primate molecular ecology uses genetic data to investigate the evolution and ecology of wild primate populations. DNA can give us information about species boundaries, demographic history of populations, population structure and gene flow in a particular geographic location, and evolutionary relationships among populations of the same species. This information is important for physical anthropologists who are working in primate conservation. It can help primatologists develop species conservation plans, including provide evidence for assessing the health and viability of endangered species. (objectives 1 & 3)

4. Anthropometry, or the measurement of human body parts, was a very important part of the discipline of physical anthropology in its early years. In the effort to understand human variation, physical anthropologists amassed huge amounts of data on the size and dimensions of human body parts from populations around the world. This data has been used by designers and manufacturers to design workspaces, body armor, and wheelchairs. The science of ergonomics owes a great debt to physical anthropologists. Anthropometric data and insights have also been applied in the interpretation of skeletal remains from archaeological sites. (objectives 1, 2, 3, & 4)

Application Questions

Your answers should include the following:

1. Physical anthropologists know the human skeleton, its growth and its pathology. This knowledge allows them to analyze human remains from a crime scene and depending on the material, identify the age, sex, postmortem interval, and activities of living that leave marks on the skeleton. Because physical anthropologists study human population variability, they can sometimes identify features that might identify the individual as a member of a specific geographic group. If trained in archaeological techniques, they can also assist in the evaluation of the crime scene itself. For instance, marks caused by instruments, or the instruments themselves, could be analyzed for wear patterns, from which details of the crime can be inferred, just as anthropologists analyze wear patterns on tools or bones. In the case of a mass disaster, physical anthropologists are primarily engaged to identify remains—to reconstruct bones or skeletons from fragments, to identify fragments as belonging to a single individual, and to actually determine individual identity using clues such as body markings, items found with the body, or dental and other medical records, as well as the remains themselves. The long bones of the body are especially helpful in assessing age. In addition, forensic anthropologists are increasingly using both nuclear and mitochondrial DNA to identify individuals,

often following analysis of the skeletal remains themselves to narrow down the range of possibilities. (objectives 3 & 4)

2. Primatologists are specialists in behavioral ecology and know the environmental and social needs of nonhuman primate species. This knowledge is used to develop plans for captive management of nonhuman primates in zoos and laboratories, as well as plans for species conservation of wild populations. Field primatologists can evaluate a species' health in the wild—population size, impact of competitors and habitat destruction on the species, availability of resources required to maintain populations— and use this information to advise governments or conservation organizations about species in crisis. The information that primatologists have about a species behavior is also useful to biomedical scientists working on diseases for which nonhuman primates can be vectors, such as ebola and HIV. In situations such as the bushmeat crisis in Africa, primatologists have a role to play in protecting nonhuman primate populations from decimation by hunting, and by working with organizations and governmental agencies concerned about the situation they help develop solutions. Finally, the insight that primatologists have gained into the behavior of nonhuman primates and their social systems has provided social scientists with myriad ideas for new ways to look at and understand human behavior. (objectives 1 & 3)

Lesson Review

Lesson 16: Applied Anthropology

PLEASE NOTE: Use this matrix to guide your study and achieve the learning objectives of this lesson. It will also help you to view the video, which defines and demonstrates important concepts and principles as they relate to everyday life and actual case studies.

Learning Objective	Textbook	Student Guide	Video Lesson
1. Explain the role of anthropologists in the four major fields of anthropology and how applied anthropology is embedded in each field.	pp. 10–20	Key Terms: 1, 2, 3, 4, 5, 6, 7, 8, 9, 10, 11, 12, 13, 14; Matching: 1, 2, 3, 4, 6, 7, 8, 9, 10, 11, 12; Completion: 1, 4, 5, 6; Self-Test: 1, 6, 7; Short-Answer: 1, 3, 4; Application: 2.	Introduction Segment 1: *Medical Anthropology: Nurses Helping Nurses* Segment 2: *Linguistic Anthropology: The Language of Man* Segment 3: *Forensic Anthropology: The New Detectives*
2. Discuss the contributions of applied physical anthropologists in the field of forensics.	pp. 15–17	Key Terms: 5, 10, 11, 14; Matching: 1, 2, 4; Completion: 1, 3, 5, 6; Self-Test: 2, 3, 4, 8, 9; Short-Answer: 2, 4.	Introduction Segment 3: *Forensic Anthropology: The New Detectives*
3. Discuss how physical anthropologists use the knowledge and techniques of their discipline to assist in crime investigations, conservation of primate species, recovery efforts following natural or human-caused disasters, and researching the spread and prevention of disease.	pp. 10–20, 174–180, 278–281, 508–517	Key Terms: 5; Matching: 2, 4, 5, 12; Completion: 1, 4, 5, 6; Self-Test: 2, 5, 9; Short-Answer: 3, 4; Application: 1, 2.	Introduction Segment 3: *Forensic Anthropology: The New Detectives*

Learning Objective	Textbook	Student Guide	Video Lesson
4. Describe the tools physical anthropologists have to assist in identifying human remains.	pp. 13–18	Key Terms: 5, 10, 11, 12, 14; Matching: 1, 4, 9, 11, 12; Completion: 2, 4, 7, 8; Short-Answer: 4; Application: 1.	Segment 3: *Forensic* *Anthropology:* *The New* *Detectives*

CPSIA information can be obtained
at www.ICGtesting.com
Printed in the USA
FFOW021512211112
334FF